1991

SOCIAL ASPECTS OF AGING

Edited by
Ida Harper Simpson
John C. McKinney

SOCIAL ASPECTS
OF AGING

Joseph J. Spengler
Ida Harper Simpson
Kurt W. Back
John C. McKinney
Carleton S. Guptill
Alan C. Kerckhoff
Joel Smith
Herman Turk
Howard P. Myers
Kenneth J. Gergen

DUKE UNIVERSITY PRESS
Durham, North Carolina
1966

© 1966, Duke University Press

Second printing 1972

L.C.C. card no. 66-23559

I.S.B.N. 8223-0276-4

Printed in the U.S.A.

PREFACE

In the United States it is generally expected that persons who reach the age of sixty-five (with variations for specific groups and individuals) must move from a recognized and established social position into one that is relatively uncertain, undefined, and lacking in prestige. This movement involves the relinquishment of social roles and relationships typical of adulthood and the acceptance of new roles and relationships characteristic of the later years. In place of the traditional major roles of earning a living and maintaining a family, most older persons are rather abruptly faced with the task of finding and developing different roles and activities. At a time in life when stability and security are greatly desired, older persons are confronted with a period of change, uncertainty, and adaptation. Such conditions as occupational retirement, increased probability of illness and incapacity, impending death, loss of leadership positions, restriction of participation in social affairs, bereavement, loss of an independent household, economic dependency, subordination to adult offspring or institutional control, and generally decreased "life space" are among the hazards that confront the aged. In the face of these sometimes overwhelming conditions, the elderly person is forced to establish a different way of life for himself. Some individuals manage this as an achievement in the form of new and rewarding experiences; some are able to make this transition with a minimum of stress; others experience deep personal anxiety and frustration, and in some cases they fail to find and develop meaningful activities and roles in later life.

These dynamics of the life of the elderly are the focus of the research reported in this book. Our objective is to take some of the "problems" of old age and examine the ways in which variations in the life situation of the older person affect adaptation to them. Our interest is not to suggest social policy (though our research may have policy implications) but to show that these problems are experienced by older people through their social relationships and values, and that an understanding of the meaning of these problems to the aged entails our knowledge of these relationships and values. Our research will show that the personal difficulty posed by these problems is in large measure a reflection of the pre-existing social roles and values of the older person. Among the problems of old age we have selected four for study: retirement, the family, the community, and perceptual life space.

Forces underlying the institutionalization of retirement is an implicit theme of Chapter 1, in which Joseph J. Spengler shows how unemployment among older people has arisen out of the interplay of demographic changes with industrialization. This is followed by Section I, which examines retirement in more specific terms. This section (Chapters 2-7) is concerned with adaptation to retirement, viewed from the perspective of the kind of work that a man has done. It seeks to show that reactions to retirement are conditioned by social patterns which evolved around the individual's work role and yet are maintained in retirement and by the meaning which work has held for the individual.

Section II, Chapters 8-11, studies the internal structure of the family of older individuals. It examines conjugal and parental expectations held by older men and women as individuals and as couples, and shows the relation of interpersonal expectations within the family to the morale of the husband and wife.

Section III, Chapters 12-17, studies the position and the social activities of older people in a community. It shows that explicit recognition of the aged as a social group in the community is hindered by the negative attitudes toward them held by younger adults and by old people themselves. The authors show that participation in community activities by the elderly is conditioned, not by age as such, but by the same kinds of factors that affect the participation of younger people.

Section IV, Chapters 18-21, compares personal perspectives of elderly and younger adults. These chapters show a contraction of life space in the older years manifested in shorter time perspectives, pessimism, indifference, and dogmatism.

The research summarized in this book, as well as the publication of the book itself, was made possible by a Ford Foundation grant to Duke University. The grant established a five-year Program in Socioeconomic Studies of Aging at the university. Other major publications of this program include: Juanita Kreps (ed.), *Employment, Income and Retirement Problems of the Aged* (Durham: Duke University Press, 1963); Ethel Shanas and Gordon F. Streib (eds.), *Social Structure and the Family: Generational Relations* (Englewood Cliffs, N.J.: Prentice-Hall, 1965); and John C. McKinney and Frank T. de Vyver (eds.), *Aging and Social Policy* (New York: Appleton-Century-Crofts, 1966). The program benefited greatly from the service, advice, and assistance of many people. The executive committee consisted of Professors Frank T. de Vyver, Paul M. Gross, and John C. McKinney, with Professor Alan K. Manchester serving as secretary-treasurer until succeeded in that post by Miss Frances C. Thomas.

In addition to the basic support received from the Ford Foundation, the supplementary financial assistance of the Duke University Center for the Study of Aging, which is supported by grants from the National Institutes of Health of the United States Public Health Service, is gratefully acknowledged. In their capacities as director of the center and research co-ordinator of the center, respectively, Dr. Ewald W. Busse and Dr. Robert H. Dovenmuehle were very helpful advisers. All computations involved in the research reported in this volume were carried out in the Duke University Computing Laboratory, which receives partial support from the National Science Foundation.

Dr. William McGehee (Fieldcrest Mills, Inc.), Mr. Charles B. Wade (Reynolds Tobacco Co.), Mr. Guy Phillips (Jefferson Standard Life Insurance Co.), Mr. C. A. McKeel (Vicks Chemical Co.), and Mr. C. Eugene Looper (Wachovia Bank and Trust Co.) rendered invaluable advice and assistance in the planning and data collection phases of the studies reported in Sections I and II of this volume. Dr. Cyrus M. Johnson, Dr. Alfred Dean, and Mr. John C. Wooten served as field directors of these studies at various times.

A special acknowledgment is accorded Mrs. Sandra F. Mascitelli, editorial assistant for the program. Her efforts have unquestionably resulted in a more readable volume.

IDA HARPER SIMPSON

JOHN C. McKINNEY

Duke University
August 23, 1965

SOCIAL ASPECTS OF AGING

1. SOME ECONOMIC AND RELATED DETERMINANTS AFFECTING THE OLDER WORKER'S OCCUPATIONAL ROLE   *Joseph J. Spengler*   3

Section One: WORK AND RETIREMENT

2. WORK AND RETIREMENT   *Ida Harper Simpson, Kurt W. Back, John C. McKinney*   45

3. ATTRIBUTES OF WORK, INVOLVEMENT IN SOCIETY, AND SELF-EVALUATION IN RETIREMENT   *Ida Harper Simpson, Kurt W. Back, John C. McKinney*   55

4. ORIENTATIONS TOWARD WORK AND RETIREMENT, AND SELF-EVALUATION IN RETIREMENT   *Ida Harper Simpson, Kurt W. Back, John C. McKinney*   75

5. EXPOSURE TO INFORMATION ON, PREPARATION FOR, AND SELF-EVALUATION IN RETIREMENT   *Ida Harper Simpson, Kurt W. Back, John C. McKinney*   90

6. CONTINUITY OF WORK AND RETIREMENT ACTIVITIES, AND SELF-EVALUATION   *Ida Harper Simpson, Kurt W. Back, John C. McKinney*   106

7. RETIREMENT AND SELF-RATINGS   *Kurt W. Back, Carleton S. Guptill*   120

Section Two: FAMILY AND RETIREMENT

8. THE OLDER COUPLE: SOME BASIC CONSIDERATIONS   *Alan C. Kerckhoff*   133

9. NORM-VALUE CLUSTERS AND THE "STRAIN TOWARD CONSISTENCY" AMONG OLDER MARRIED COUPLES   *Alan C. Kerckhoff*   138

10. HUSBAND-WIFE EXPECTATIONS AND REACTIONS TO RETIREMENT   *Alan C. Kerckhoff*   160

11. FAMILY PATTERNS AND MORALE IN RETIREMENT
Alan C. Kerckhoff   173

Section Three: COMMUNITY AND RETIREMENT

12. CONSIDERATIONS BEARING ON A STUDY OF THE ROLE OF THE AGED IN COMMUNITY INTEGRATION *Joel Smith, Herman Turk*   195

13. THE GROUP STATUS OF THE AGED IN AN URBAN SOCIAL STRUCTURE *Joel Smith*   210

14. THE NARROWING SOCIAL WORLD OF THE AGED *Joel Smith*   226

15. AGE AND SOME BEHAVIORAL AND ATTITUDINAL ASPECTS OF URBAN COMMUNITY INTEGRATION *Joel Smith, Herman Turk*   243

16. UNDERSTANDING LOCAL POLITICAL BEHAVIOR: THE ROLE OF THE OLDER CITIZEN *Herman Turk, Joel Smith, Howard P. Myers*   254

17. URBAN COMMUNITY KNOWLEDGE FROM A NORMATIVE PERSPECTIVE *Joel Smith, Howard P. Myers, Herman Turk*   277

Section Four: AGING AND SELF ORIENTATION

18. COGNITIVE AND MOTIVATIONAL FACTORS IN AGING AND DISENGAGEMENT *Kurt W. Back, Kenneth J. Gergen*   289

19. PERSONAL ORIENTATION AND MORALE OF THE AGED *Kurt W. Back, Kenneth J. Gergen*   296

20. AGING AND THE PARADOX OF SOMATIC CONCERN *Kenneth J. Gergen, Kurt W. Back*   306

21. COGNITIVE CONSTRICTION IN AGING AND ATTITUDES TOWARD INTERNATIONAL ISSUES *Kenneth J. Gergen, Kurt W. Back*   322

INDEX   337

SOCIAL ASPECTS OF AGING

Joseph J. Spengler

1. SOME ECONOMIC AND RELATED DETERMINANTS AFFECTING THE OLDER WORKER'S OCCUPATIONAL ROLE*

The most insignificant man can be complete if he keeps within the limits of his capacities and attainments.—Goethe

While this volume focuses upon the social aspects of aging, these are not independent of other aspects (such as the economic) with some of which the present chapter deals. Indeed, the response of social variables to variations in diverse indicators of "aging" is conditioned by the state of economic variables and tends to change as these change. Similarly, changes in social variables may affect the incidence of "aging" upon the economy.

In this chapter I shall review some of the essentially economic determinants of the older worker's occupational role. What should be included in such a review and what should be excluded is subject to somewhat arbitrary determination. I have included demographic factors as well as factors which affect the retired older worker's participation in the fruits of technical progress. I have not emphasized the extent to which the older worker's occupational

* This paper is a revision of one presented at the International Gerontological Research Seminar, Markaryd, Sweden, August, 1963.

role may be affected by regnant value orientations and hence differ from society to society. Instead, I have merely indicated that international differences in value orientation may produce differences in the non-economic context within which economic and related determinants make themselves felt. I have focused my attention mainly upon societies in which active membership in the labor force is of personal and social importance to those in and even beyond their sixties.

This chapter consists of three parts. In the first I deal with the emergence of conflict between the desire of older persons to be gainfully employed and the availability of employment to them. In the second I examine the significance of the availability of such employment for the "welfare" of older people. In the third I draw attention to forces which tend to erode the older person's share in the fruits of technical progress, thereby enhancing the importance which he attaches to employment.

1. EMERGENCE OF THE PROBLEM

It is in economically advanced societies that conflict is most likely to arise between the desire of the older individual to be gainfully employed and the availability of suitable employment. This conflict flows mainly from five conditions: (1) demographic trends, (2) industrialization of the economy, (3) accelerated obsolescence of knowledge and skills, (4) social and other curbs on labor mobility and pricing, and (5) imbalance between the aggregate demand for labor and the supply of labor, given various labor-supply-price structures. It is only in advanced societies, therefore, that this conflict is of quantitative significance, even though individual older members of any society, developed or underdeveloped, may experience it. Only in advanced economies (where, as a rule, fertility is relatively low) do we find older workers forming a significant fraction of the labor force and unemployed older workers constituting a relatively large fraction of the older population.[1] Only in advanced societies may a relatively large number of older persons disengage themselves from activity and responsibility in general, or from specific types

1. E.g., see United Nations, *The Aging of Population and Its Economic and Social Implications* (ST/SOA/Series A/26 [New York, 1956]), pp. 54-58; United Nations, *Demographic Aspects of Manpower* (ST/SOA/Series A/33 [New York, 1962]), pp. 11-14, 58-62.

of activity, particularly when a society's institutions are not adapted to involving older people.

Crude activity (or labor-force participation) rates vary greatly with sex, by country, and over periods of time. For example, these rates are higher in industrialized countries, where 62.2 per cent of the males are economically active, than in semi-industrialized and agricultural countries, where the comparable percentages are 57.8 and 55.2. The corresponding percentages for females in these three sets of countries are 24.3, 21.2, and 25.4, respectively. Inter-country differences in male labor-force activity rates reflect differences in the age structure of the male populations. When these are standardized with respect to age, the male activity rates turn out to be lower in industrialized countries than elsewhere; the percentages become 60.5 in industrialized countries, 62.8 in semi-industrialized countries, and 65.1 in agricultural countries.[2] Today both crude and adjusted activity rates for males are lower than they were fifty to sixty years ago, but these rates for females are generally higher.[3] In developed countries, however, the activity rates of older women have fallen, as have those of older men, especially among those persons sixty-five and older.[4]

Demographic Trends

Demographic trends have contributed to the emergence of the conflict between the desire of older persons for employment and its availability. This conflict has been caused principally by an increase in the relative number of older persons in the population and by an augmentation in the ratio of persons of working age to the population. These trends have increased the aggregate "demand" of older persons for jobs, while at the same time they have increased the total "supply" of job seekers (and hence of substitutes for older workers) in relation to the population.

Increase in the expectation of life at later years has not contributed notably to the greater relative number of persons over sixty, even though the prolongation of life beyond sixty is intensifying the employment problem from the point of view of those beyond their early sixties. This is indirectly evident in the information

2. United Nations, *Demographic Aspects of Manpower*, pp. 6, 13-14, 62-63.
3. *Ibid.*, pp. 15, 29.
4. *Ibid.*, pp. 64-68.

Table 1. Male Survivors to Certain Exact Ages with Expectation of Life Given.

Age	Number of survivors with expectation of life at birth as given					Relative number of survivors with expectation of life at birth as given				
	50	60.4	65.8	70.2	73.9	50	60.4	65.8	70.2	73.9
60	41,120	64,008	71,880	78,710	85,330	1,000	1,000	1,000	1,000	1,000
65	33,873	56,180	63,986	70,965	78,320	824	878	889	901	918
70	25,553	46,000	53,384	60,227	68,070	621	719	742	765	798
75	16,733	33,638	40,080	46,284	53,953	407	526	557	588	632

Source: United Nations, *Methods for Population Projections by Sex and Age* (ST/SOA/Series A, Population Studies, No. 25 [New York, 1956]), pp. 76-77.

presented in Table 1. In columns 2-6 are given the number of survivors at exact ages sixty, sixty-five, seventy, and seventy-five, respectively, out of an initial 100,000 live-born males when expectation of life at birth ranges from 50 to 73.9 years.[5] In columns 7-11 the data of columns 2-6 are presented in relative terms, with the absolute number of survivors at age sixty set at one thousand for each given life expectancy. With life expectancy ranging between sixty and seventy-four, the relative number of those persons surviving at age sixty-five out of those reaching sixty does not vary greatly; given a life expectancy of 73.9, it is only about 4.6 per cent higher than for a life expectancy of 60.4, and about 11.4 per cent higher than for a life expectancy of 50. The corresponding spreads in the figures are not much wider when the relatives are based upon age sixty-five instead of upon age sixty as in Table 1; then they become 6.1 per cent and 15.2 per cent. Of course, a life expectancy of fifty is much below that found in advanced countries or even in some under-developed countries (e.g., Ceylon). It may be assumed, therefore, that in highly developed countries 82 to perhaps as many as 90 per cent of the males who reach the nominal retirement age of sixty-five will eventually attain seventy; 72 to 80 per cent or more of those who attain sixty years will eventually reach seventy.

Direct evidence points to the importance of the role played by the decline in fertility and to the insignificance of the decline in mortality. Let expectation of life at birth be held constant at levels ranging from 30 to 70.2 years; then, given a gross reproduction rate

5. The figures are taken from model life tables for males prepared by the staff of the United Nations on the basis of life tables available for a variety of nations. See United Nations, *Methods for Population Projections by Sex and Age* (ST/SOA/Series A, Population Studies, No. 25 [New York, 1956]), pp. 76-77.

(hereinafter designated GRR) of 3.0, the proportion of the population aged sixty or more years will range between 4.1 and 4.5 per cent.[6] But given a GRR of 1.5, this range becomes 11.5 to 13.1 per cent; and given a GRR of but 1.0 (which will not suffice to replace the population even under the most favorable mortality conditions), the range becomes 18.7 to 21.9 per cent, which is four and one-half to five times what it is when the GRR is 3.0. If, however, the GRR is held constant while expectation of life at birth is increased from 30 to 70.2 years, the proportion of people aged sixty and over associated with any given gross reproduction rate increases only slightly, the increase varying between 5 per cent when the GRR is 3.0 and 17 per cent when it is 1.0. The relative number of older persons is great in developed countries, therefore, because in these countries, as a rule, fertility is quite low; it is little affected by differences in the level of mortality and virtually not at all when expectation of life at birth is fifty or above.

The change in age structure just described is also accompanied by an increase in the relative number of persons of working age. Furthermore, the decrease in fertility underlying this change in age structure may release more of the average female's years of adult life for gainful employment. This trend is evident from the increase in the relative number of persons aged fifteen to fifty-nine that accompanied a decline in fertility under stable population conditions. With a GRR of between 1.0 and 1.5, the relative number of persons aged fifteen to fifty-nine (which may serve as a rough index of the persons of productive age) is about 6 per cent greater than it would be, given a GRR of 2.0; and it is about 12 to 13 per cent greater than it would be, given a GRR of 2.5. Thus, relative to the population, we have 6 to 13 per cent more job seekers than if the GRR had been 2.0-2.5 instead of 1.0-1.5. Other conditions given, we also have about 6 to 13 per cent more potential productive power per person of the population.[7] Comparable results

6. This paragraph is based upon United Nations, *Aging of Population and Its Economic and Social Implications*, pp. 26-27. On the meaning of Gross Reproduction Rate, see Mortimer Spiegelman, *Introduction to Demography* (Chicago: Society of Actuaries, 1955), pp. 168-169. There he writes: "Assume that a cohort of females is traced from birth to the end of their reproductive period and that none die meanwhile. Assume further that as they pass through their reproductive period they give birth to daughters on the basis of current age-specific fertility, counting female births only. The gross reproduction rate is the ratio of the total number of their daughters to the original number in their cohort."

7. Data based upon United Nations, *Aging of Population and Its Economic and Social Implications*, pp. 26-27.

are obtained if one uses some other age group—such as twenty to sixty-four—to reflect the "supply" of potential job seekers.[8]

While decline in mortality (as reflected in the increase in life expectancy at birth from ages forty or fifty to seventy) has diminished the relative number of persons of working age by 3 to 7 per cent, this effect has been more than offset by increases in productivity traceable to improvements in health owing to the conditions responsible for the decline in disease and mortality.[9] These improvements are particularly important in respect to the older population with whose productivity we are concerned in this chapter.

It is quite evident that decrease in fertility, together with concentration of childbearing in a small number of the average female's younger years, makes available a larger number of female participants in the labor force. Yet it is not easy to translate this increase into quantitative terms, for concomitant changes (e.g., introduction of labor-saving practices into the household economy, nursery schools, kindergartens, etc.) are often present. Activity rates, however, are roughly 50 to 100 per cent higher among single and widowed and divorced women, classified by age, than among married women.[10] Furthermore, among married women in developed countries, activity rates are greater when there are no or few children than when there are several or more.[11]

Variation in the age structure of a population may affect the employment opportunities available to older persons, since older persons are usually substitutes for younger persons. In general, under *ceteris paribus* conditions, employment opportunities for older persons vary inversely with the rate at which young persons are added to the population of working age; thus, after 1945, with young workers in short supply because of the earlier decline in fertility, labor participation of older women was high. Careful statistical analysis is essential, of course, if the effect of change in age

8. E.g., see Frank Lorimer, "Dynamics of Age Structure in a Population with Initially High Fertility and Mortality," in United Nations, *Population Bulletin*, 1 (December, 1951), 31-41.

9. See United Nations, *Aging of Population and Its Economic and Social Implications*, pp. 26-27.

10. United Nations, *Demographic Aspects of Manpower*, pp. 38-48.

11. *Ibid.*, pp. 44, 49-53. On the effects of marriage, children, etc., see C. D. Long, *The Labor Force under Changing Income and Employment* (Princeton: Princeton University Press, 1958), pp. 110-116, 121-135. See also U. S. Department of Labor, *Marital and Family Characteristics of Workers* (Special Labor Force Report No. 13, March, 1960 [Washington, 1961]), pp. 4-5 and tabular appendix; Gertrude Bancroft, *The American Labor Force* (New York: John Wiley & Sons, 1958), pp. 59-64.

structure is to be assessed, since the demand for older as for female workers is mainly a function of the aggregate demand for labor, which also tends to vary. Evidence of the importance of very high aggregate demand in improving such employment opportunities is supplied by wartime experience in the United States and postwar experience in the Soviet Union. In the United States in 1945 the employment of persons fifty-five and over was about 16 per cent above "normal" as the result of an increase in the "demand" for labor to a level about 14 per cent above "normal"—an increase occasioned mainly by the enrolment of so many adults (especially younger males) in military service and in war-connected activities.[12] After the war, in 1959, in the Soviet Union, which was deficient in number of males, there were 39 per cent more female than male workers aged fifteen to fifty-nine and 94 per cent more female than male workers aged sixty and over. Even so, it is likely that in the United States, and eventually in the Soviet Union, the age structure will become less favorable to the employment of older workers in the 1960's and 1970's than it was in the 1940's and 1950's. In the period between 1940 and 1960 the American population aged twenty to fifty-nine grew only about half as fast as the total population and about one-third as fast as those persons aged sixty to sixty-nine; in the twenty-year period between 1960 and 1980 it will grow about one-tenth faster than the total population and about three-tenths faster than those persons aged sixty to sixty-nine. Any such change in the age structure that results, however, is essentially transitory; except in times of continuing change in gross reproduction, conditions of population stability are approached and the numbers in the various age groups grow at roughly similar rates. Given approximate stability, variations in the rate of growth of the labor force as well as in the availability of employment to older persons are dominated by non-demographic conditions of the sort discussed in the next four sub-sections of this chapter.

12. U. S. Department of Labor, *Fact Book on Manpower* (Bulletin 1171, September, 1954 [Washington, 1954]), p. 15. See also C. D. Long, *The Labor Force in War and Transition: Four Countries* (NBER Occasional Paper 36 [New York: National Bureau of Economic Research, 1952]), pp. 35-37. Total military and civilian employment rose from 47.9 million in 1940 to a peak of 65.2 million in 1944 and then moved to 58.6-60.7 million in 1946-1949. See J. F. Dewhurst *et al.*, *America's Needs and Resources* (New York: Twentieth Century Fund, 1955), pp. 1065-1067; also Bancroft, *American Labor Force*, pp. 52, 131-132; and R. A. Easterlin's discussion of labor-force participation rate changes from 1930 to 1970 in *Proceedings of the American Statistical Association*, Business and Economic Statistics Section (1964), pp. 387-392.

It may be noted parenthetically that in the absence of recruits the number of persons attached to any occupation is subject to quite high rates of attrition. In a stable population based on a life expectancy of seventy and a GRR little in excess of 1.0, mortality and retirement will decrease this number initially by about 2 per cent per year, and this rate of decrease will rise with an increase in the average age of those persons still attached to the occupation in question.[13] If there is added to this rate of decline the loss caused by the transfer to other occupational groups of some of those persons (especially younger members) attached to a given occupational group, the aggregate rate of decline of a non-recruited occupational group can easily rise to and above 5 per cent per year. Accordingly, even when, because of changes in technology or tastes or income distribution, the demand for the labor services of some occupational group drops rapidly, the supply of those services can be adjusted downward rapidly unless trade-union leaders, fearful of a decline in union membership and aggregate union dues, resist the forces of attrition and intensify their struggle for a shortened work week.[14] This sort of response may or may not affect the employment opportunities of older persons significantly. Presumably it would have such an effect only if trade-union leaders and members were fortified in the belief that the aggregate demand for labor might grow slowly; a corollary effect would be the belief that early retirement should be encouraged as a general policy.

Industrialization

Employment rates among both younger and older persons are lower in the more industrialized than in the less industrialized countries. Comparative rates for males are reported in Table 2. Data on the first line in the body of the table are for twenty-one countries with less than 35 per cent of active males engaged in agriculture and related activities; on the second line, data are for thirty

13. United Nations, *Aging of Population and Its Economic and Social Implications*, p. 56; also J. J. Spengler and O. D. Duncan (eds.), *Population Theory and Policy* (Glencoe, Ill.: The Free Press, 1956), pp. 242-243.

14. This sort of response apparently is more likely to be encountered in the United States than in Europe, inasmuch as the autonomy of union officers and the ratio of paid union officers to union membership are much greater in the United States. E.g., see S. M. Lipset, "Trade Unions and Social Structure: II," *Industrial Relations,* **1** (February, 1962), 89-101. On job changes which range annually from one in twenty among upper-level white-collar workers to one in four among non-farm laborers, see R. L. Stein, "Unemployment and Job Mobility," *Monthly Labor Review,* **83** (April, 1960), 353-354.

Table 2. Activity Rates Among Males According to Age and Industrialization.

Countries according to degree of industrialization	Age				All ages standardized
	10-14	15-19	55-64	65 and over	
Industrialized	4.1	72.4	85.6	37.7	60.5
Semi-industrialized	13.2	70.3	88.9	61.0	62.8
Agricultural	23.9	78.4	91.6	70.1	65.1

Source: United Nations, *Demographic Aspects of Manpower* (ST/SOA/Series A/33 [New York, 1962]), Tables 3.2 and 3.4 on pp. 12 and 14.

countries with 35 to 59 per cent of the active males so engaged; and on the third line, the data apply to twenty-one countries with 60 per cent or more of their active males so engaged.[15] The percentages reported in column 4 reveal a significant tendency for the employment of males aged fifty-five to sixty-four to fall with an increase in industrialization. This tendency becomes very marked among males aged sixty-five or more, according to the percentages given in column 5. The activity (or labor-force participation) rates reported in column 6, which have been standardized to eliminate differences in age structure, reflect in large part this greater tendency of older persons to remain gainfully employed in less rather than in more industrialized countries. With differences in degree of industrialization, employment rates do not vary much among males aged twenty to fifty-four. While there is some difference among those aged fifteen to nineteen and marked difference among those under fifteen (see columns 2-3), these differences are not of much concern in the context of the present discussion, since there is no evidence that the employment of persons under twenty displaces workers sixty-five and over from jobs that they would otherwise fill.

It may be noted parenthetically that young people not in the labor force but who are engaged in getting a productive education are describable as at least "shadow" members of the labor force. Attendance at school will serve increasingly as the equivalent of attendance at work; this follows inasmuch as employability, especially among older workers, is increasingly becoming a function of educational attainment. It should also be noted that the term "unem-

15. The table is based on Tables 3.2 and 3.4 in United Nations, *Demographic Aspects of Manpower*, pp. 12, 14; data for individual countries are given in Tables A-2 and A-4, pp. 58-62. On international differences in Europe, see J. F. Dewhurst *et al., Europe's Needs and Resources* (New York: Twentieth Century Fund, 1961).

ployed" may be ambiguous; community surveys suggest that older persons, especially those pressured or shunted into involuntary retirement, often consider themselves unemployed even though they have long been out of the labor market.

Rates of age-specific activity among females do not vary with industrialization in quite the same manner as do corresponding rates among males. Female rates in agricultural countries, when contrasted with corresponding rates in industrial countries, are somewhat higher among females aged fifty-five to sixty-four, about twice as high among females sixty-five and over, and about four times as high among females under fifteen, but they are not greatly different among those women aged twenty-five to fifty-four. The comparative pattern among females under fifteen and over twenty-four thus resembles that among males in these age groups. Among females aged fifteen to twenty-four, however, one encounters a quite different pattern than among males: activity rates are about two-thirds higher in industrialized than in agricultural countries.[16] It is not immediately apparent whether international variation in activity rates among females produces variation in international activity rates among males (or females) aged sixty-five or over.[17] In the United States, however, the decline in the labor force participation rate of older males has been associated with increase in the labor force participation rates among both women aged twenty to twenty-four and women twenty-five to forty-four. This apparent substitution of women for older men is attributable, at least in part, to the relative lack of education among men sixty-five and older.[18]

The rough correlation of variation in employment rates among older persons with variation in degree of "industrialization" does not reveal much that is of analytical and explanatory significance; "industrialization" must be broken down into its component elements, together with their economic concomitants, and these must then be correlated with employment rates among older and younger workers. The data presented in this section, however, indicate that on simple empirical grounds it is to be expected that employment rates among both persons under twenty and persons sixty-five and

16. United Nations, *Demographic Aspects of Manpower*, pp. 21-23.
17. Some relevant data are reported in *ibid.*, pp. 6, 55-62, 77-78.
18. Long, *The Labor Force under Changing Income and Employment*, pp. 14, 179-180; see also John I. Saks, "Status in the Labor Market," *Monthly Labor Review*, **80** (January, 1957), 15-21.

over will decline in presently underdeveloped countries as these countries undergo industrialization and economic development. Industrialization implies rising average incomes, much greater educational demands than formerly, collectivistic curbs (e.g., those imposed by trade unions or the state) on the exercise of the right to work, and other changes which may affect the access of older persons to employment. Some of these are dealt with below.

Accelerated Obsolescence of Knowledge and Skills

Technological trends, together with changes in the composition of the demand for labor, are serving to produce educational, craft, and occupational obsolescence. Because of this intensification of the rate at which collective as well as individual knowledge and skill become obsolescent or fail to be sustained by current consumption patterns, the importance of periodic re-education is increasing and with it the acquisition of enough education in youth to make possible subsequent periodic re-education. Indeed, in the absence of such re-education, older members of the labor force, who in earlier and technologically less dynamic societies derived status from their role as depositories of the community's knowledge and experience, tend to lose that membership and "to become an economic and social liability for the community generally and the family in particular."[19] Of course, re-education programs can make but a limited contribution toward the employability of older persons who were unable, even in their youth, for whatever reason, to acquire much training and education; likewise, it can contribute little as a rule to the improvement of the prospects of older persons enrolled in dying or stagnant occupations. Indeed, considerable unemployment will continue to develop among older persons so long as they fail to meet the requirements of job opportunities available in modern society, even given significant downward adjustments in the wages which they ask.

Since early in this century the *relative* number of non-farm

19. United Nations, *European Seminar on Social Policy in Relation to Changing Family Needs* (Geneva, 1962), p. 11. On concentration of older workers in stagnant and dying occupations (e.g., farmers, blacksmiths, tailors, locomotive engineers, etc.), see H. L. Wilensky, "The Uneven Distribution of Leisure: The Impact of Economic Growth on 'Free Time,'" *Social Problems*, 9 (Summer, 1961), 46-47; S. L. Wolfbein, *Changing Patterns of Working Life* (Washington: U. S. Department of Labor, Manpower Administration, 1963), pp. 4-7.

white-collar workers has increased more than one-half in the United States, while the relative number of blue-collar workers has declined about one-third—even though semi-skilled workers have increased at the expense of the unskilled. The relative number engaged in agriculture has declined by about three-fourths, while that in service has changed only slightly. Turning to recent trends, one finds that between 1940 and 1960, while the labor force was growing by about 44 per cent, the number of white-collar workers was increasing about 81 per cent and that of manual workers was increasing about 45 per cent; approximately 82 per cent of this increase, however, took place from 1940 to 1950. The number of service workers grew by about 36 per cent, while the agricultural work force declined about 52 per cent. It is expected that the labor force will grow 31 per cent in the period between 1960 and 1975, and perhaps 45 per cent between 1960 and 1984. Some occupational groups will decline between 1960 and 1984, farm workers by about 30 per cent and nonfarm workers by 8 per cent. Some groups will increase commensurately with the labor force, or at a lower rate: operatives by about 23 per cent, craftsmen and foremen by about 44 per cent, and managers, proprietors, and sales workers by about 50 per cent. Some will increase faster: clerical and service workers by about two-thirds, and professional and technical personnel by more than nine-tenths. While the spread of automation and computer technology will permit economies in the use of clerical, supervisory, and middle-management personnel and thus somewhat modify expected trends, this new technology indicates that important changes are in prospect in occupational composition and in the ratio of white-collar to blue-collar workers.[20]

These compositional changes will increase over-all educational requirements, although the spread of automation will reduce skill requirements in some activities while increasing them in others. If one assumes that relative educational attainment by current occupational group is indicative of future relative educational require-

20. See Max Rutzick and Sol Swerdloff, "The Occupational Structure of U. S. Employment, 1940-60," *Monthly Labor Review*, **85** (November, 1962), 1209-1213; Carol A. Barry, "White-Collar Employment: Trends and Structure," *ibid.*, **84** (January-February, 1961), 11-18, 139-147; Howard Stambler, "Manpower Needs in 1975," *ibid.*, **88** (April, 1965), 378-383; U. S. Department of Labor, *Manpower: Challenge of the 1960's* (Washington, 1961), pp. 10-11; and U. S. Department of Labor, *A Report on Manpower Requirements, Resources, Utilization, and Training* (Washington, 1963), chaps. 3 and 7, and corresponding reports issued in 1964 and 1965.

ments by occupational group, average education will increase at least 3 per cent between 1960 and 1985. The lowest levels of education are found among workers whose numbers are growing less rapidly than the labor force (i.e., agricultural, household service, unskilled, and semi-skilled workers), while the highest levels are found among those whose numbers are increasing markedly (i.e., white-collar and skilled blue-collar workers).[21] This inference is partially corroborated by R. S. Eckaus' estimate that between 1940 and 1950 the general educational requirements of the American labor force rose about 4 per cent, while specific vocational training requirements increased about 7 per cent.[22] His estimate also throws some light upon the decline of labor force participation among older persons; it indicated that in 1950 about 78 per cent of the jobs available called for ten years or more of conventional education, whereas median years of school completed among persons forty and over ranged from 9.8 among those forty to forty-four to 8.1 among those aged seventy-five and over. In time, of course, as educational levels rise, employers may increase the educational requirements associated with particular jobs, perhaps above the level that is essential.[23]

C. D. Long found that in the United States the decline in the labor-force participation rate among males sixty-five and over was associated in part with the relatively low level of formal education attained within this group whose members had received their education some decades earlier. This decline was not associated with technological change as such, however; older workers had not been disproportionately displaced in industries in which output per unit of input had risen notably.[24] Data relating to those who are unemployed do indicate that while seniority and other provisions often

21. Department of Labor, *Report on Manpower Requirements, Resources, Utilization, and Training*, p. 11; Barry, "White-Collar Employment," pp. 144-147; Arnold Katz, "Educational Attainment of Workers, 1959," *Monthly Labor Review*, **83** (February, 1960), 121-122; Denis F. Johnston, "Educational Attainment of Workers, March, 1964," *ibid.*, **88** (May, 1965), 517-527. See also Paul Sultan and Paul Prasow, "The Skill Impact of Automation," in *Exploring the Dimensions of the Manpower Revolution* (compiled for the Subcommittee on Employment and Manpower of the Committee on Labor and Public Welfare, United States Senate [Washington, 1964]), I, 542-558.

22. Computed from "Education and Economic Growth," in S. M. Mushkin (ed.), *Economics of Higher Education* (U. S. Department of Health, Education, and Welfare, Bulletin No. 5 [Washington, 1962]), p. 121. See also Johnston, "Educational Attainment of Workers, March, 1964," pp. 526-527.

23. Mushkin, *Economics of Higher Education*, p. 121. Years of school completed are based upon the U. S. Census of 1950.

24. Long, *The Labor Force under Changing Income and Employment*, pp. 171-173, 174-180.

tend to make older workers relatively secure in their employment, these same older workers, if they happen to become unemployed, may experience difficulty in becoming re-employed.[25]

It is likely that continuation of current changes in both occupational structure and educational levels may slow down or even reverse the decline in labor-force participation rates among workers sixty-five and over. Each type of change can reinforce the other; elevation of the level of education facilitates change in occupational composition, while the latter mode of change facilitates effective use of the increasingly better-educated components of the population. Approaching universalization of secondary education—reflected in a rise from 1940 to 1962 of 40.9 to 69.3 per cent of whites aged twenty-five to twenty-nine completing secondary education and a corresponding rise from 12.1 to 41.6 per cent of non-whites aged twenty-five to twenty-nine doing the same—together with an even greater relative increase in persons completing a year or more of college, should eventually render older workers more immune to unemployment. Relatively far more persons—over 200 per cent more —will have completed at least a high school education; and of these a larger fraction than formerly will have entered occupations relatively immune to unemployment, or if subjected to unemployment, will have the capacity to enter other lines of activity.[26] Among employed persons beyond sixty the increase in level of education, together with increasing access to periodic re-education (or re-training), will also slow down the rate at which output sometimes falls with the age of the worker.[27] On-the-job training continues to play a very important role in industry, investment in this training exceeding 3 per cent of Gross National Product in the United States.[28]

25. U. S. Department of Labor, "Characteristics of Claimants under the 1961-62 TEUC Program," *Monthly Labor Review*, **85** (November, 1962), 1230-1231; "Worker Reaction to Job Displacement," *ibid.*, **88** (February, 1965), 170-172; Department of Labor, *Family Characteristics of the Long-Term Unemployed* (TEUC Report Series No. 4 [Washington, 1963]), *passim*; and Subcommittee on Economic Statistics of the Joint Economic Committee, *Unemployment: Terminology, Measurement, and Analysis* (87th Congress, 1st Session [Washington, 1961]), pp. 61-63, 78-79.

26. See Subcommittee on Economic Statistics of the Joint Economic Committee, *Higher Unemployment Rates, 1957-60: Structural Transformation or Inadequate Demand* (87th Congress, 1st Session [Washington, 1961]), pp. 66-71; also Denis F. Johnston, "Educational Attainment of Workers, March, 1962," *Monthly Labor Review*, **85** (May, 1963), 504-515, and "Educational Attainment of Workers, March, 1964."

27. This matter is discussed below.

28. T. W. Schultz, "Investment in Human Capital," *American Economic Review*, **51** (March, 1961), 9-11; also Jacob Mincer, "On-the-Job Training: Costs, Returns and Some Implications," *Journal of Political Economy*, **70** (October, 1962), Supplement, 56-59.

Social and Other Curbs on Labor Mobility and Pricing

Given adequacy of aggregate demand for labor, it pays employers to make use of additional labor so long as the value of its imputed output, translated into marginal-revenue terms, is not in excess of the *total* real differential cost of employing that labor. Assuming that employers correctly assess this value and this cost, it follows that unemployment among older workers will increase if their output is too low in relation to the total cost of employing them or if this cost is too great in relation to the value of their output. Furthermore, if artificial constraints are placed upon the power of employers to make price adjustments conducive to the employment of older workers, or if other collectivistic barriers are placed in the way of their employment, the amount of employment available to older workers will fall shorter of their "demand" for such employment than it would have fallen if the price system were flexible and artificial barriers were absent.

Output per older worker may tend to be somewhat lower than output per worker in his peak productive age. The correlation of output with age is not universal in form, however; it varies with occupation and profession and is susceptible to modification through re-education, through improvement in the health of older workers, through increasing mechanization, which decreases the physical demands of jobs, and through diminution, as workers become older, in their tendency to restrict production. A distinction needs to be made, furthermore, between the impact of age upon the capacities of persons lodged in top managerial, administrative, and entrepreneurial echelons and its impact upon the capacities of those lodged in echelons in which routine plays a greater part and the pursuit of novelty and of more favorable combinations and conjunctions plays a lesser part. For, as I have suggested elsewhere, gerontocracy can give rise to development-retarding arrangements in a dynamic society if not also in a society that is comparatively static.[29]

A great deal of work still needs to be done under appropriately defined conditions before we shall know just how productivity by occupation varies with age as such. Earnings data, unless carefully specified, are not very illuminating; they may not adequately re-

29. See J. J. Spengler, "Some Effects of Changes in the Age Composition of the Labor Force," *Southern Economic Journal*, 8 (October, 1941), 147-175.

flect productivity and they do not take account of variations in sub-occupational composition associated with age in a dynamic society.[30] Studies of job performance by age are much more revealing. Studies undertaken in the United States suggest that increase in age, if and when it does affect output adversely, is more likely to do this among plant workers where the physical demands of jobs are relatively high than among office workers where this is less true. For example, in the clothing industry the average job performance on the part of men aged fifty-five to sixty-four never fell more than 10 per cent below that for the age group thirty-five to forty-four; among women in some lines there was no decline at all. Furthermore, many workers in the fifty-five to sixty-four age group exceeded the average for the thirty-five to forty-four group.[31] Findings within the household furniture and footwear industries were essentially comparable.[32] Among office workers, output per man-hour varied little with age, the performance of many older workers exceeding the average for younger age groups. Moreover, older workers had steadier rates of output than younger workers. A larger proportion of office workers aged fifty-five to sixty-four than of other workers in this age group had performance records superior to the average for the thirty-five to forty-four age group.[33]

In many lines of activity decline in job performance as the worker moves into his sixties is deemed insufficient to warrant his retirement, even though the employer retains the right to retire workers who have attained some stipulated or conventional "retirement" age. It is in part because decline in job performance is small, as well as characteristic only of some workers, that many employers permit employees to work some years beyond age sixty-five even

30. In the United States in 1939, for example, the earnings of males employed for twelve months were at a peak in the age group thirty-five to sixty-four, 6 per cent below that peak in the age group fifty-five to fifty-nine, 12 per cent lower in the age group sixty to sixty-four, and 22 per cent lower in the age group sixty-five to seventy-four. See my "The Economic Effects of Changes in Age Composition," in Spengler and Duncan (eds.), *Population Theory and Policy*, p. 501.

31. See Jerome A. Mark, "Measurement of Job Performance and Age," *Monthly Labor Review*, **79** (December, 1956), 1410-1414. Older workers did not differ from younger ones in attendance or variation within age groups.

32. Jerome A. Mark, "Comparative Job Performance by Age," *ibid.*, **80** (December, 1957), 1467-1471. In some lines of work, job performance did not decline with age, and in others it declined very slowly; the performance of about one-third of those aged fifty-five to sixty-four exceeded the average for those aged thirty-five to forty-four.

33. R. E. Kutscher and J. F. Walker, "Comparative Job Performance of Office Workers by Age," *ibid.*, **83** (January, 1960), 39-43. See also Alan T. Welford, *Ageing and Human Skill* (London: Oxford University Press, 1958).

when this is defined as retirement age.[34] In some instances, the adverse impact of aging upon job performance may be reduced by shifting older workers out of occupations that have become unsuitable for them.[35] This process might be accelerated when inter-employer mobility is involved if pension credits and other fringe benefits were made fully portable.[36] In the event that significant decline in job performance does accompany aging, and that this decline cannot be averted through job change, re-education, etc., the continued employment of the older worker may still prove advantageous to the employer provided that he can reduce the cost of hiring this worker commensurately with the diminution in his job performance. Indeed, underlying the unwillingness of employers to continue to employ workers who have passed a certain age, or to hire older workers who newly present themselves for employment, is the fact that the cost of their employment is too high, or the belief that it is likely to become too high. For example, wage structure and wage levels for which the employer has stipulated with trade unions may be too high and too inflexible; or trade unions may oppose the use of flexible piecework or analogous arrangements which are economically feasible; or minimum wage legislation may prohibit adequate downward adjustment; or various costs of employment (e.g., underuse of equipment, fringe benefits, pension provisions) besides wages as such may push the total cost of hiring various older workers above the marginal revenue value of their output. The employment-preventing incidence of high labor costs, even when it is not immediately apparent, may be manifested indirectly (e.g., through limits upon hiring age, dislike of employers

34. See Harry L. Levin, "Involuntary Retirement Provisions," *Monthly Labor Review*, **82** (August, 1959), 855-860; also Margaret S. Gordon, "The Older Worker and Retirement Policies," *ibid.*, **83** (June, 1960), 577-585. Her findings suggest that employers may become less favorable to extension of the work life of their employees beyond the boundary fixed in pensions and contractual arrangements.

35. Margaret S. Gordon, "The Older Worker and Hiring Practices," *ibid.*, **82** (November, 1959), 1205.

36. Stein reports that workers have an added "incentive to remain with their present employers" because of fringe benefits "for which eligibility depends in part on length of employment." In particular, workers usually lose a portion of their retirement and pension credits when they change employers. In consequence, older workers are disinclined to shift from one company to another, even though because of advancing years they may be better able to perform jobs available with companies other than the one employing them. See Stein, "Unemployment and Job Mobility," pp. 350-351, 355-357; W. W. Kolodrubetz, "Vesting Provisions in Pension Plans," *Monthly Labor Review*, **82** (July, 1959), 743-756; E. K. Rowe, "Insurance and Pension Plans," *ibid.*, **80** (January, 1957), 29-36. See also Department of Labor, *A Report on Manpower Requirements, Resources, Utilization, and Training*, chap. 5.

to discriminate among employees, greater inclination to discharge high- than low-wage workers, etc.).[37]

Unemployment among older workers probably arises in greater measure from the "disappearance" of jobs than from the insistence of employers upon compulsory or involuntary retirement provisions. Often when jobs disappear as the result of mergers, plant relocation, automation, and such, too few new jobs emerge in the affected firms to permit absorption of all those who have been displaced. It is then that barriers to the employment of older workers make themselves felt, for the jobless older workers must seek employment with other employers. And other employers may be disinclined to take on older workers because of the costs (e.g., fringe benefits, pensions) involved, because the older workers' skills have declined or become obsolescent, because of difficulties supposedly attendant upon worker re-training, and because of other reasons—some of which are without foundation.[38] If, as often happens, trade-union leaders propose early retirement as a solution, even though it is not a solution desired by the workers affected, pressure upon employers and others to facilitate the re-employment of displaced workers is reduced.[39] It is perhaps because pressures upon employers and trade-union leaders are inadequate to lead to employment-generating accommodation that governmental intervention is increasing.[40]

Such governmental intervention, however, may not prove very effective. Quite fundamental among the causes of the non-employment of older workers may be the inertia of corporate and trade-union bureaucracies, each of which may find it easier to acquiesce

37. E.g., see Gordon, "The Older Worker and Hiring Practices," and "The Older Worker and Retirement Policies"; Saks, "Status in the Labor Market"; Juanita Kreps, "A Case Study of Variables in Retirement Policy," *Monthly Labor Review*, **84** (June, 1961), 587-591.

38. E.g., see works cited in notes 25, 35, and 37 above. See also *Unemployment: Terminology, Measurement, and Analysis*, pp. 61-63, 78-79, 94; *Impact of Automation on Employment*, report of hearings held March 8-25, 1961, by the Subcommittee on Unemployment and the Impact of Automation of the Committee on Education and Labor in the U. S. House of Representatives, 87th Congress, 1st Session (Washington, 1961), esp. pp. 219, 248-249, 384, 426, and 625-627.

39. For evidence of American trade-union attitudes, see *Impact of Automation on Employment*, esp. pp. 116, 428; *Hours of Work*, hearings before the Select Subcommittee on Labor of the Committee on Education and Labor of the U. S. House of Representatives on H.R. 355, H.R. 3102, H.R. 3320, and H.R. 1680, Parts I and II (Washington, 1963, 1964), *passim*.

40. E.g., see Anna-Stina Ericson, "The Employment of Older Workers Abroad," *Monthly Labor Review*, **83** (March, 1960), 270-274. This is a summary of the December, 1956, report by the Manpower Committee of the Organization for European Economic Co-operation and of more recent reports. Governments are particularly concerned in Europe, as in the United States, to dissipate unfounded prejudice against the employment of older workers and to facilitate their employment.

in the premature retirement or non-employment of older persons than to devise flexible arrangements permitting their employment. In smaller or paternalistic enterprises not yet in the vise of bureaucratic control and not yet confronted by a bureaucratic type of trade union, rational solutions may be achieved even though there often is less room for maneuver in a small firm than in a large one. The bureaucrat as well as the monopolist inclines to a life of tranquillity. It is questionable, therefore, if intervention on the part of a government bureaucracy can overcome the inertia of private bureaucracies.

Automation or accelerated technological change need not always affect the situation of older workers adversely, particularly when employment levels are relatively high and when there is considerable inter-industry and interoccupational mobility.[41] While automation may increase boredom on the job, it often reduces the physical demands of jobs and thereby diminishes the likelihood that job performance will decline with age.[42] At present, when automation changes the qualifications or increases the educational qualifications associated with job performance, younger rather than older workers may be transferred to jobs consequent upon automation, assuming that employers doubt the capacity of older workers to master these jobs and are able to employ them in other capacities.[43] However, as the level of education of older workers rises and as vocational training is improved and becomes more routine, it can be expected that more workers will be able to shift to these new jobs as well as to jobs somewhat similar to those which they had filled in the past.[44]

Imbalance Between Aggregate Demand and Aggregate Supply

Of the various kinds of unemployment to which older workers are subject, the most important are attributable to structural trans-

41. See Stein, "Unemployment and Job Mobility"; *Automation and Technological Change*, a Report of the Subcommittee on Economic Stabilization to the Joint Committee on the Economic Report, 84th Congress, 1st Session (Washington, 1955); *Higher Unemployment Rates, 1957-1960*, pp. 67-71.

42. E.g., see R. W. Riche, "Impact of Automation in the Pulp and Paper Industry, 1947-60," *Monthly Labor Review*, **85** (October, 1962), 1114-1119.

43. See Edgar Weinberge, "Experience with the Introduction of Office Automation," *ibid.*, **83** (April, 1960), 376-380.

44. On various aspects of the transferability of skills, see Sidney A. Fine, "A Reexamination of 'Transferability' of Skills," *ibid.*, **80** (July-August, 1957), 803-810, 938-948. Eckaus estimates that about half the jobs in existence in the United States in 1950 could be learned in six months or less. See Mushkin, *Economics of Higher Education*, p. 121.

formation and to inadequacy of aggregate demand. The former type of unemployment is associated with defective training, restraints upon competition, and acceleration of the rate of technological change. It is largely concentrated at any given time in particular population groups or industries. Supposedly, it is especially prevalent among blue-collar workers, many of whom, because of age limits on hiring new workers and because of the mobility-reducing impact of fringe benefits, are disinclined to seek jobs in other occupations, industries, and geographic areas. Unemployment attributable to inadequacy of aggregate demand arises when the aggregate demand for goods and services grows less rapidly than their supply would grow under full employment. Given either kind of unemployment, many displaced older workers are likely to suffer because they find it difficult, under the circumstances surrounding the employment of older workers, to secure new jobs. Even so, the situation of the older worker would be worse under unemployment associated with structural transformation, both because his share of this type of unemployment would tend to be greater and because, having become unemployed, he would find it more difficult than younger workers of comparable skill to find jobs in other locations or occupations. It is to be expected, of course, that even should the bulk of existing unemployment be traceable to inadequacy of demand, some of it would be associated with structural transformation. Yet it will always be much easier to reduce or eliminate the latter type of unemployment if over-all demand is high and barriers to the employment of older workers are not being accentuated by inadequacy of aggregate demand.

While both types of unemployment may emerge, it is highly probable that inadequacy of aggregate demand tends to be responsible directly or indirectly for a considerable part of the somewhat persisting unemployment experienced in a country, particularly in periods when industrial capacity can be increased rapidly. In any given instance, however, whether one or the other type is predominant is a matter not of conjecture but of empirical fact. In the United States, for example, unemployment in 1957-1960 has been attributed largely to inadequacy of demand, although barriers to the mobility of labor and capital were found to accentuate persistence of unemployment. In this period, and just before and since, unemployment has been unevenly distributed by occupational and social categories. With several recently emerging exceptions (teen-agers, workers with little education), this unevenness has not in-creased; nor in particular has the relative position of older workers still in the labor force worsened. (Here we ignore the impact of somewhat involuntary premature retirement.) In sum, unemploy-ment is structural and a concomitant of a too slowly rising aggregate demand for labor; both are factors which require correction if em-ployment opportunities are to be improved for older workers and pressure toward early retirement is to be reduced.[45]

It may be noted parenthetically that efforts to reduce unem-ployment could hurt the older population more than they could benefit it. Price stability preserves the purchasing power of older persons with relatively fixed incomes, but it tends to be associated with an over-all unemployment rate of around 5 to 6 per cent (say, 5.5 per cent). Reducing unemployment to 3 per cent may entail an annual price rise of 4.5 per cent per year and yet not bring about a much higher employment rate among older persons. But it would rapidly erode the purchasing power of the incomes of most older people.[46] Indeed, so great is the income-eroding effect of in-flation and so small the comparable cost of relieving unemployable breadwinners—perhaps $800 million—that their outright support is preferable.[47]

In view of what has been said, it is essential that unemployment rates, always a political football, be put into proper perspective and that relief of need associated with unemployment be achieved as economically as possible. Several characteristics of unemployment require to be noted. Initially, however, when considering unemploy-ment rates among older workers, we must distinguish between those who have been pushed out of the labor force by premature retire-

45. See R. A. Gordon, "Has Structural Unemployment Worsened?" *Industrial Re-lations*, **3** (May, 1964), 53-77; *Higher Unemployment Rates, 1957-1960*, chaps. 5 and 7. See also Juanita Kreps (ed.), *Employment, Income, and Retirement Problems of the Aged* (Durham: Duke University Press, 1963), chap. 4; *Employment and Un-employment*, hearings before the Subcommittee on Economic Statistics of the Joint Committee, Congress of the United States, 87th Congress, 1st Session, Pursuant to Section 5 (a) of Public Law 304, 79th Congress (Washington, 1962), pp. 312-398. Considerable information is given in the manpower report for 1963-1965, cited in n. 20 above.

46. Paul A. Samuelson ar 1 Robert M. Solow, "Analytical Aspects of Anti-inflation Policy," *American Ec nomic Review*, **50** (May, 1960), 177-194, esp. 191-193. This paper is included and ccmmented on in *Employment and Unemployment*, pp. 357 ff.

47. See "Unemployment and Monetary Policy," *Cleveland Trust Company Business Bulletin*, **45** (April 25, 1964), 1 ff. (The article is unsigned.)

ment arrangements, etc., and are not counted as unemployed, and those who remain in the labor force even if unemployed. When only the members of the labor force are considered, three facts stand out.[48] First, most reported unemployment is transitory, often amounting only to labor turnover and usually lasting no more than fourteen weeks. Thus, in February, 1963, to February, 1965, with unemployment in the 5 to 6 per cent range, about three-fourths of all unemployed had been out of work less than fifteen weeks, and only 10 to 13 per cent had been unemployed twenty-seven or more weeks. Second, while unemployment rates in excess of fourteen weeks are close to average among members of the labor force aged forty-five and over, those in this age group who were unemployed fifteen or more weeks and twenty-seven or more weeks made up only about 10 and 5 per cent, respectively, of all unemployed in February, 1964. Third, while male breadwinners unemployed fifteen or more weeks formed about 16 to 17 per cent of all the unemployed, and those unemployed twenty-seven or more weeks made up about 7 per cent, many in the latter group may have been unemployable for reasons only partly connected with age. The contribution of the aged to persisting reported unemployment, therefore, is quite limited, even though age may be a deterrent to securing employment and an important correlate of pressure upon individuals to withdraw prematurely from the labor force. Furthermore, monetary measures intended to reduce employment among older people are not to the advantage of the older population, even given insufficiency of demand. A flexible wage structure, better information concerning job opportunities, re-training programs, and facilitation of labor mobility provide a better and non-inflationary set of alternatives.[49]

Researchers concerned with estimating future prospects take it for granted that the rate of employment among older males will continue to fall as it has in the recent past. It is estimated that in Western Europe by 1970 the percentage of males sixty-five and over

48. Data are from *ibid.*, and U. S. Department of Labor, *Monthly Report on the Labor Force* (February, 1964).

49. Gerald G. Somers finds that while manpower re-training programs have considerable potential, it is far from being realized. See "Retraining the Unemployed: A Preliminary Survey," reprinted from hearings before the Subcommittee on Employment and Manpower of the Committee on Labor and Public Welfare, United States Senate, 88th Congress, 1st Session, June 7, 1963 (Washington, 1963). See also U. S. Department of Labor, *A Report on Manpower Requirements* (Washington, 1965), pp. 125-140.

in the labor force—37.6 in 1955—will be down to 30.2, with every country sharing in the decline. Female activity rates are expected to remain unchanged among those aged sixty-five and over but to increase about one-tenth among those aged twenty to sixty-four. Thus, older male labor will have been replaced in part by younger female labor.[50] According to projections of trends in labor-force participation rates in the United States from 1960 to 1975, the rate may decline slightly for males aged sixty to sixty-four and appreciably (i.e., from 45.8 per cent in 1960 to 34.5 per cent in 1975) for males aged sixty-five to sixty-nine as well as for all males sixty-five and over (i.e., from 36 per cent in 1960 to 25.4 per cent by 1975). These trends may persist, some believe, even after 1975. Meanwhile, it is expected that activity rates will continue to rise among women below sixty but no longer markedly among those aged sixty to sixty-nine. In the United States as in Europe, therefore, the relative importance of females in the total labor force will increase, with female labor perhaps partly replacing older male labor.[51] Should the relative importance of white-collar workers continue to increase while that of blue-collar workers declines, employment among older males may not decline as much as current forecasts suggest, even though female employment continues to rise.

2. EMPLOYMENT VERSUS LEISURE

In the first section of this chapter I have dealt with conditions that affect the access of older job-seekers to employment. In this section I shall deal with the impact of the desire for discretionary time or leisure upon the rate of employment of older workers. I do not, however, give much attention to the older person's temporal pattern of disengagement, although this pattern reflects the order in which he is inclined to withdraw from employment and other types of activity. My argument is focused mainly upon two issues: (a) the extent to which work and leisure are complements rather than substitutes; and (b) the extent to which the welfare of the worker can be augmented through changes in the temporal distribution of the amount of leisure that falls to his lot in the course

50. Dewhurst et al., Europe's Needs and Resources, pp. 65-69, 930-932.
51. Sophia Cooper, "Interim Revised Projections of U. S. Labor Force, 1965-75," Monthly Labor Review, 85 (October, 1962), 1089-1099. Also see Cooper and Denis F. Johnston, "Labor Force Projections for 1970-80," ibid., 88 (February, 1965), 129-140.

of his potentially productive lifetime. While my discussion will be confined to the essentially economic aspects of these issues, account needs to be taken of the heterogeneity of the labor force (a heterogeneity that is more significant in an urban-industrial society than in a less developed society) and of variation in the individual's socioeconomic participation, engagement, obligations, etc., as he moves through the life cycle.[52] These obligations, demands, range of engagement, etc., affect the response of the individual to external constraints and stimuli of the sort discussed in the first section, and they may condition his adjustment to decline in absolute or relative income as described in the third section. Unfortunately, our information is limited. We know that the holding of more than one job varies somewhat with age, being relatively low among workers over sixty-four, for example, but our explanations remain incomplete. It may be assumed that the response of an individual's pattern of engagement in work and other activities to change in age is conditioned by both his internalized self and his perceived environment of externalized alternatives. Yet these conditions, the impact of which we understand only imperfectly, are changing and in ways not wholly predictable. Thus, much of what is inferred remains conjectural.

Major Economic Changes

There have taken place in the present century a number of changes that may affect the interrelation of work and leisure, and these changes are likely to continue. Output and income per worker have long been rising, although not as fast as output per man-hour, since the number of hours worked per week has fallen. In Western Europe output per capita rose about 1.5 per cent per year between 1870 and 1913, around 0.5 per cent per year between 1913 and 1940, and close to 3 per cent in the 1950's. In the United States per capita income rose nearly 1.75 per cent per year between the early 1880's and 1914, around 1.35 per cent between 1914 and 1940, and

52. See Wilensky, "Uneven Distribution of Leisure," and his "Life Cycle, Work Situation, and Participation in Formal Associations," in R. W. Kleemeier (ed.), *Aging and Leisure* (New York: Oxford University Press, 1961), chap. 8; and his "Work, Careers, and Social Integration," *International Social Science Journal*, 12 (Fall, 1960), 543-560. Demographic and other aspects of the life cycle are treated by Paul C. Glick in *American Families* (New York: John Wiley & Sons, 1957), chaps. 3-5. See also Irving Rosow, "Old Age: One Moral Dilemma of an Affluent Society," *The Gerontologist*, 2 (December, 1962), 182-191. On the social role of time, see W. E. Moore, *Man, Time, and Society* (New York: John Wiley & Sons, 1963), *passim*.

since 1950 per capita disposable income has increased about 1.75 per cent annually.[53] Should these rates of growth persist, or move upward somewhat, most workers may believe they can afford more leisure than at present. Indeed, one may infer from the decline in hours worked that the demand for leisure rises with income. In the United States the average number of hours worked per week declined from sixty-four in 1880 to fifty in 1920, and from forty-six in 1930 to around forty in the 1950's. In Europe the corresponding average fell from about sixty-nine in 1890 to sixty in 1910 and to about forty-five in the 1950's.[54]

During the past half-century man's work-life expectancy has increased, but not as much as his life expectancy. In 1900 in the United States a man of twenty had a life expectancy of 42.2 years and a work-life expectancy of 39.4; by 1960 these expectancies had become 49.6 and 42.6, respectively. More than a decade ago it was conjectured that by the year 2000 the corresponding figures might approximate 53.8 and 45.1, but since the 1950's working life expectancy at age twenty has declined, as it also has at age sixty. The period of retirement, 2.8 years in 1900 and 7.0 in 1960, would then have become 8.7 in 2000. The number of years of expected work-life per year of expected retirement would have fallen from 14.1 in 1900 and 6.1 in 1960 to below 5.2 in 2000.[55] The temporal trend present in these data is reflected in corresponding data relating to countries in different stages of development, as summarized in Table 3.[56] The number of years of work-life per year of retirement declines with industrialization, even though it varies somewhat from one industrialized country to another.[57] Accordingly, while the ratio of adults to persons under fifteen or twenty and over seventy is

53. See Dewhurst et al., Europe's Needs and Resources, pp. 109-116; U. S. Bureau of the Census, Historical Statistics of the United States (Washington, 1960), p. 139; also Annual Report of the Council of Economic Advisers (Washington: U. S. Government Printing Office, 1964), p. 227.

54. See Dewhurst et al., Europe's Needs and Resources, pp. 84-87, and America's Needs and Resources, p. 40; W. S. and E. S. Woytinsky, World Population and Production (New York: Twentieth Century Fund, 1953), p. 367; Long, The Labor Force under Changing Income and Employment, pp. 5-7, 270-274. See also Wilensky, "Uneven Distribution of Leisure," pp. 32-36.

55. Stuart Garfinkle, "Changes in Working Life of Men, 1900 to 2000," in Spengler and Duncan (eds.), Population Theory and Policy, p. 106; Seymour L. Wolfbein, Changing Patterns of Working Life (Washington: U. S. Department of Labor Manpower Administration, 1963), p. 12.

56. The data in Table 3 are taken from United Nations, Demographic Aspects of Manpower, p. 20.

57. Ibid., pp. 71-72. The number ranges from about 6.4 in Switzerland to below 4.0 in a number of countries.

Table 3. Average Life and Work-Life Expectancy at Age Fifteen for Men by Degree of Industrialization.

Countries according to degree of industrialization	Expectation of life in years at age fifteen			
	Life expectancy	Work-life expectancy	In retirement	Work-life retirement
Industrialized	54.5	45.3	9.2	4.9
Semi-industrialized	49.5	43.1	6.4	6.7
Agricultural	46.1	41.5	4.6	9.0

Source: United Nations, *Demographic Aspects of Manpower*, p. 20.

higher in developed countries, part of this advantage in respect to potential productivity per capita is lost through early retirement as well as through shortening of the work week.

Even though improvement in output per capita and in life expectancy has increased the relative importance of leisure in advanced countries, different categories of a population respond differently to such improvement, and this improvement itself is accompanied by changes in the relative importance of the differentially responding categories composing the population. For example, H. L. Wilensky finds long hours characteristic of the work week of bureaucratic intellectuals and professionals (e.g., types of professors, firm lawyers), the middle bureaucracy (e.g., managers, officials, etc.), high-income blue-collar workers (e.g., skilled craftsmen, foremen, etc.), independent professionals (e.g., solo lawyers), non-professional entrepreneurs (e.g., small proprietors), and agriculturalists. He finds short hours characteristic of engineers, semi-professional employees, clerical and sales personnel, craftsmen, operatives, service personnel, and non-farm laborers. He estimates that in 1950, 20.5 and 63.1 per cent, respectively, of the American labor force were in the non-agricultural long-hours and short-hours groups; that by 1970 these percentages will have become 26.9 and 67.2; and that meanwhile the agricultural labor force will have fallen from 15.2 per cent in 1950 to 5.9 per cent in 1970. While these crude data suggest that with the exhaustion of the decline in the relative size of the agricultural labor force the relative importance of long-hours groups will at least persist and may even rise, it is still possible that the short-hours groups will increase in relative importance if occupational constraints are relaxed and work schedules are permitted to reflect workers' tastes for leisure more fully than at present.[58] While these estimates are based on studies of the American labor force, they probably are applicable to highly industrialized countries elsewhere, for inquiry reveals "an extremely high level of agreement, going far beyond chance expectancy, as to the relative prestige of a wide range of specific occupations, despite the variety of sociocultural settings in which they are found."[59] Perhaps this similarity extends to the pattern of response to the potential availability of leisure.

The Work-Leisure Relationship

Economists treat leisure as a "superior" good, subject to substitution and income effects as well as to changes in taste. Hence, under *ceteris paribus* assumptions, an individual with a certain income will purchase more leisure at a relatively low price than at a relatively high price, and with the price of leisure given, he will purchase more when his income is high than when it is low. Statements of this sort are of but limited helpfulness, however. With other conditions given, it is true that an individual will work more hours per week, month, or year if the price of his labor (i.e., his wage or salary rate) is high than if it is low. But it is also true that an increase in wages or salary amounts to an increase in income, and that with other conditions given, an increase (decrease) in such income will be accompanied by an increase (decrease) in the consumption of leisure, that is, by a decrease (increase) in the number of hours of work offered. We do not know, however, whether the substitution effect of work for leisure consequent upon a wage (salary) increase will be wholly or only partially swamped by the income effect consequent upon this same wage (salary) increase. Nor do we know if the change in circumstances which brought about the change in rate of pay, and hence in income, produced any change in taste for leisure. In the past, of course, the concomitance of the decline in number of hours worked with increases in wages, though not universal, has suggested that the substitution effect was swamped by the income effect, or that changes in

58. Wilensky, "Uneven Distribution of Leisure," pp. 37-45; "Work, Careers, and Social Integration," pp. 18-20; and "Life Cycle, Work Situation," pp. 234-235.
59. Alex Inkeles and Peter H. Rossi, "National Comparisons of Occupational Prestige," *American Journal of Sociology,* **61** (January, 1946), 339.

income and tastes together more than offset the substitution effect.[60] Therefore, we might expect the demand for leisure to rise among both old and young workers as income rises, with retirement age falling as a result. It is essential to remember, however, that only when "leisure time and hours of work in the market in fact constitute an exhaustive dichotomy" may we analyze the supply of labor to the market "by way of the theory of demand for leisure time viewed as a consumption good."[61] On the other hand, this condition may not be present even as the condition of unchanging tastes may not be present.

The work-leisure relationship may be dominated by non-economic considerations or it may be quite sensitive to economic considerations. In either instance individuals will choose between work and leisure, although this choice will be subject to collectivistic constraints at any given time. Presumably, if these conditions adversely affect the welfare of many adults, the constraints are likely to be modified. But should only older persons be affected adversely, as by compulsory retirement provisions, there will be much less pressure for modification of the constraints in effect.

If the work-leisure relationship is affected very little by economic considerations, it may, supposedly, assume one of three forms. (1) A very strong orientation to work may motivate an individual to devote most of his time to work and little to leisure. This strong work commitment flows from the gratification which particular kinds of work yield and the prestige and status which such work confers; it could be somewhat reinforced by the requirements of an expensive style of living and by the absence of perceived moral substitutes for work. (2) A worker's physical and/or mental capacity to enjoy leisure may be contingent upon his remaining strongly committed to work. If an older worker with a strong work commitment is denied opportunity to express it, his "welfare," however defined, is substantially reduced. He is a victim of compulsory withdrawal from work, or of enforced leisure which is a discommodity, even as voluntarily chosen leisure is a superior commodity. His situation is a

60. E.g., see Long, *The Labor Force under Changing Income and Employment*, chaps. 4-8 and summary, pp. 5-12. See also Wilensky's reference ("Uneven Distribution of Leisure," p. 32) to the unpublished dissertation of T. A. Finegan which reports a significant negative correlation between hours actually worked and earnings, and in the main confirms the earlier findings of Paul H. Douglas.

61. See Jacob Mincer, "Labor Force Participation of Married Women: A Study of Labor Supply," in National Bureau of Economic Research, *Aspects of Labor Economics* (Princeton: Princeton University Press, 1962), p. 65.

counterpart to that of any bureaucratized member of the labor force who is compelled to work longer hours than he would work if free. (3) It is possible, however: (a) that some individuals with strong work commitments may also be quite capable of finding functional equivalents for work and its correlates, and hence, having retired, prove able to find satisfaction in retirement; and (b) that some individuals with relatively weak work commitments may not be very capable of finding functional equivalents for work and its correlates (including reduction in income), and hence may not prove able to derive much satisfaction from retirement. The three forms here identified probably are too simple; for a variety of elements—internal and external to workers—conditions response to retirement and within limits these may be variously combined. Much further inquiry is needed before we shall have identified all these elements and their modes of combination.[62] Sustained longitudinal and cross-sectional studies are required, and these will take a decade or more to complete.

When work yields little gratification and contributes little to the worker's status and social prestige, his work commitment will be weak. His supply of effort will be dominated by economic consideration, by the income to be had from work, and by the intensity of his demand for goods and services. For him leisure is a superior good and one to be increasingly enjoyed as his income rises, though within limits and subject to the condition that consumption of leisure entails consumption of complements to leisure which may be expensive and are normally to be gained through the exchange of work for the requisite purchasing power. An older worker's welfare is therefore reduced if he is denied the employment which is essential to supply him with the complements requisite to the enjoyment of leisure.

In the future it is likely that as average income rises the consumption of leisure will rise among those members of the labor force whose work commitment is weak and whose division of time between work and leisure is dominated by economic considerations. Yet this tendency may be restrained in several ways. There is a strong tendency for consumption to increase as permanent income increases, and what the worker looks upon as the permanent com-

62. E.g., see Jacob Tuckman and Irving Lorge, *Retirement and the Industrial Worker* (New York: Columbia University, Teachers College, Bureau of Publications, 1953).

ponent of his rising current income is likely to be a very large fraction of this current income if it increases steadily.[63] Tastes, too, may change in ways that elevate the propensity to consume. Furthermore, as has been suggested, few people enjoy leisure as such; they require along with leisure various complementary goods and services which may be expensive and which may increase in cost through time. Finally, in proportion as leisure is substituted for paid work, the household is required to supply goods and services which might otherwise have been bought with the proceeds of paid work. Unpaid household work, though not directly subject to taxation as is paid work, is unlikely to be nearly so efficient as paid work, or even to provide many of the goods and services which are desired in ordinary consumption or as complements essential to the effective use of leisure.

The direct and indirect cost of enforced leisure to older persons will be high even if the tendencies just reviewed are not powerful. By enforced leisure I mean compulsory retirement before seventy, for example, with the result that the older person's income is materially reduced. In 1949, for instance, median income among white males with a high school education or better and aged sixty-five to seventy-four was 30 to 35 per cent below that of persons aged fifty-five to sixty-four; the spread was much greater among persons who had not completed high school. In 1963, median income among family heads sixty-five and over was 42 to 49 per cent below that of those aged fifty-five to sixty-four with comparable education.[64] It is doubtful that many older persons can readily adjust to this drop in income; they lack the liquid assets on which to draw and they cannot, without suffering distress, cut their aspirations and customary consumption commensurately with their reduction in receipts.

Premature retirement reduces retirement income by reducing the amount of savings accumulated and augmenting the number of years of life the diminished amount of savings must support.

---

63. Milton Friedman finds consumption is closely associated with income that is not considered transitory. See his *A Theory of the Consumption Function* (Princeton: Princeton University Press, 1957), pp. 222 ff., summarizing the argument. See also Franco Modigliani and Richard Brumberg, "Utility Analysis and the Consumption Function: An Interpretation of Cross-Section Data," in K. K. Kurihara (ed.), *Post-Keynesian Economics* (New Brunswick, N. J.: Rutgers University Press, 1954), chap. 15.

64. Herman P. Miller, *Income of the American People* (New York: John Wiley & Sons, 1955), p. 67. U. S. Bureau of the Census, *Consumer Income* (Series P-60, No. 43, September 29, 1964), Table 8, p. 26.

Suppose a white male works w years and lives in retirement r years. Then, if he would maintain his average consumption during retire-

ment, he would have to defer spending $\dfrac{r}{w}$ of his earnings should he earn no interest on the "saved" portion. Given 1963 mortality and retirement at sixty, he would work forty years and live in retirement about sixteen years, or about two-sevenths of his lifetime after the age of twenty; but were he not to retire until age seventy, these figures would become about ten and one-sixth, respectively. In the former case he would have to save about two-fifths of his income, but in the latter only about one-seventh. Interest is not zero, however. So let us suppose he saves 10 per cent of his income each year and earns 4 per cent per year interest on it. Then, given the same income pattern in each case, he would accumulate about six-tenths more savings to support him for about ten years instead of sixteen years. He therefore would be over twice as well off. Since a worker's annual income increases 1 to 2 per cent per year, his post-retirement income almost certainly will be much below his pre-retirement income, particularly if he retires prematurely.

When discussing the welfare of older workers, it is essential as a rule to define it in a comprehensive sense indicative of the state of an individual such that when he prefers A to B, A embodies more "welfare" than B. When we so define welfare we may identify at least two alternative ways of maintaining it. The superior and only practical alternative is to permit the older person to remain in the labor force as long as he prefers, up to seventy, for instance. Then he will be able to enjoy a post-retirement income that may be one-third or more in excess of what it would have been had he retired at sixty-five, and he will experience all the non-economic advantages of being employed. An inferior alternative is possible, namely, to allow a person more leisure in his younger years and in compensation somewhat less in his older years. For example, let us abstract from the possibility of death and suppose that an individual will attain at least the age of seventy. If he worked from age twenty until age sixty-five and averaged 1,920 hours per year, he would work 86,400 hours in the course of his active lifetime. If these hours were spread over the fifty years between age twenty and age seventy, he would average only 1,728 hours per year, with the reduction from 1,920 hours permitting either a shorter work week, or fewer weeks of work per year, or longer vacations. This alternative, though it may make for a preferable distribution of work over time under conditions of certainty, holds little appeal to a rational person, even though under the given conditions a distribution over fifty years may be preferable for many persons to one over forty-five years when the hour total is fixed for life. Too much uncertainty is involved. A person could never count upon getting the work in his older years that he supposed he was stipulating for when young, and he would not be free of the possibility of premature death, disability, etc. The arrangement itself, even were it possible to administer (which is doubtful), implies that there is only so much work to go round and that the level of employment cannot be raised to a level at which most able older persons may work about as much as they wish. Even if the fund of work were fixed, men would doubt this fixity and would expect to do better and to prefer a bird in hand. Moreover, what I called the superior alternative is in keeping with welfare-maximizing policy and can be approximated, given a flexible wage structure and policies suited to generate fairly full employment. Indeed, only if older workers are relatively free of constraint and of pressure to retire prematurely will they be able to distribute their time optimally between work and leisure. For then they can work many hours over many years or fewer hours over many years, particularly if the latter arrangement should gradually take the form of a work year of forty or forty-five weeks of forty or more hours per week.

3. EQUITY AND EMPLOYMENT

In the previous section it was noted that current consumption on the part of older persons (as of the population generally) largely depends, as Milton Friedman has shown, on past incomes or longer-run income status. Therefore, it is not easy for older persons to adjust their actual consumption downward when current income falls notably below that enjoyed in the past. As long as they can reduce their rate of saving, their consumption need not be reduced; nor need their adjustment to a decline in current income entail much "distress" as long as they are able to draw on savings in addition to the savings component of the receipts flowing to them under pension or other annuity-like contracts. It is when the flow of receipts from dissaving and current income falls short of the requirements of customary consumption that older persons experience hardship, and this hardship is intensified when unusual expenditures (e.g., for medical purposes) raise outlays upon annual "consumption" above customary levels.

As was suggested in the preceding section, the older person's requirement of employment may be associated with the extent to which he is exposed to hardship because his annual consumption requirements exceed his annual receipts from dissaving and current income. This exposure depends significantly upon whether or not the purchasing power of his annual monetary receipts is secure against the erosion of inflation, and upon whether or not older persons share "equitably" in the fruits of technical progress or at least fully enough to offset the unusual or non-customary expenditures associated with advancing years. If prices are stable and if older workers receive enough receipts analogous to "impermanent" or transitory income to offset transitory or non-recurring expenditures, their need of employment will be decidedly less, at least on purely economic grounds, than when these conditions are not present. Under these circumstances older persons may be said to enjoy equity.

Prices are not sufficiently stable, as a rule, to preserve the value of money. It is true that the rates at which money depreciates are generally higher in countries in which the relative number of older persons is small and agriculture remains relatively important. Thus, between 1951 and 1961 the annual rate at which the value of money declined exceeded 10 per cent in a number of underdeveloped countries though it was quite low (under 2 per cent) in many others. It is also true that the rate of decline ranged between 1 per cent and about 4 per cent in many developed countries in which the relative number of older persons is large and that this rate of decline remained comparably high in 1956-1961.[65] Inflation therefore constitutes a continuing threat to the real value of the current receipts of older persons, for a considerable proportion of these receipts is drawn from sources whose nominal money value remains unchanged or increases very little as prices rise.

Inflation must be prevented, or its depreciating impact upon the

65. Rates are reported for forty-four countries in the *Monthly Economic Letter* of the First National City Bank of New York, August, 1962, p. 95; also U. S. Bureau of the Census, *Consumer Income* (Series P-60, No. 43, June, 1965), p. 71.

real value of money must be offset, if older persons are to enjoy
income equity and not be under increasing pressure to seek employment. Presumably, major emphasis needs to be placed upon the
prevention of inflation. For while there is no consistent relationship
between inflation and investment, together with rate of economic
growth,[66] by no means is there assurance that rising prices will
cause the emergence of surpluses and eventually of increased capacity with which to offset the losses (or forced saving) initially imposed upon older persons. Accordingly, if there is inflation and its
effects are not offset, the older person's "demand" for employment
and the income yielded thereby will increase.

As has been suggested, older persons are probably more likely
than younger persons to be exposed to irregular expenditures which
elevate their annual expenditures appreciably above a customary
level. Even if the exposure of older persons to this sort of "unantici-
pated" expenditure is not much greater than the corresponding
exposure of younger persons, their ability to cope with the task of
meeting both their regular and their transitory needs is inferior to
that of younger persons. For one thing, their ability to borrow
against future earning power is less, since this power will be declining and increasingly subject to the likelihood of marked diminution. The main recourse of many older persons so situated will be
to seek employment or additional employment; otherwise their customary level of consumption will tend to be reduced.

There exists at least one factor that can offset such exposure to
irregular expenditure. That is the right to share in the fruits of
technical progress. The income associated with this right, though
not really impermanent income, may be treated as such in respect
to older persons and thus may be made analogous to irregular expenditure. Therefore, if this right is materialized, older persons will
be much better able to meet irregular expenditures associated with
aging and will be less exposed to hardship and under less pressure
to seek employment.

For purposes of the present discussion we shall simply hypothesize a rate of technical progress. Let us suppose that annual income
rises about 2 per cent per year, half of which may be traced to

66. E.g., see Dewhurst *et al.*, *Europe's Needs and Resources*, pp. 458-468; *Economic
Survey of Asia and the Far East, 1961* (Bangkok: United Nations, 1962), pp. 41-42;
Erik Lundberg, "Inflation and Stability—An International Comparison," *Skandina-
viska Banken Quarterly Review*, **44** (1963), 105-114.

investment in physical and personal capital and half to the accumu-
lation and application of income-increasing knowledge. This assumption is in keeping with estimates of experience during the past
forty or fifty years in various countries. Indeed, the contribution of
this knowledge may be even greater than is implied by the assumption of a 1 per cent increase per year in average income.

Participation of older persons in the fruits of technical progress
presupposes the solution of two problems. First, their claim must
be established to what may be labeled a *social credit for the aged*.
Here we can do no more than indicate the rationale on which such
a claim might be based. One may argue that the increasing store
of income-increasing knowledge is mainly a social product paid for
in a largely collectivistic manner and resembling urban land rent—
the appropriation of which by and for the community was favored
by Henry George and his followers. Insofar as this argument is
acceptable, the community may be assumed to have a share in the
fruits of technical progress, which can be used to supplement fixed
incomes of the aged who do not share in these fruits. The magnitude of the shares of individual aged persons may be associated in
some acceptable fashion with the contribution each such individual
has made to the national product or income in the past. Thus, the
supplement to the individual's income may be made part of the
prevailing system of rewards and incentives. For example, the supplement might be proportioned to the whole of a person's non-
property income or to some fraction of that income.

It is not easy to accomplish this sort of proportioning. There
would be no problem, of course, if the prices of finished goods fell
in proportion as technical progress reduced input per unit of output.
Then everyone would share in the fruits of technical progress in
rough proportion to his income, the size of which would rise as he
rose in the occupational hierarchy or otherwise benefited from scar-
city, and the purchasing power of which would rise with the downward movement of prices. Even in the absence of inflation, however,
the level of prices does not tend to move downward as a result of
technical progress, although the prices of many individual items do
decline. Instead, the level remains fairly stable and individuals share
in technical progress principally through receipt of increases in
money income made possible by such progress. But under these
circumstances only some and not all income receivers tend to ex-

perience increases in money income; these people include recipients
of wages, profits, rents, royalties, and the like, but not the recipients
of interest and dissavings under pension and other contractual arrangements which assure individuals a fixed flow of nominal receipts. Older persons predominate among those for whom all or
most of their receipts are fixed under pension and similar contractual arrangements. Therefore, they do not share very fully in
the fruits of technical progress. For example, suppose that an older
person retires on a pension at the age of sixty-five, and that he
survives to age seventy-five, even though the probability of his doing
so is less than unity. Then, if his over-all average income rises 2
per cent per year while his annual receipts remain unchanged in
amount, the ratio of his income to the national average will be
about 18 per cent lower by the time he is seventy-five than it was
when he retired a decade earlier.

This increasing disparity between the income of a retired person
and average income for all persons may be interpreted in two ways.
If one supposes that the propensity to consume is a function of the
ratio of one's income to that of one's neighbors, or to the communal
average, a person retiring at age sixty-five under the conditions assumed would be increasingly dissatisfied if his rising propensity to
consume could not be satisfied through a progressive reduction in
his rate of saving or through an increase in his rate of dissaving.
Indeed, if at age sixty-five he had anticipated this outcome, he would
have been less inclined to retire. However, one may suppose that
an older person's current consumption is determined predominantly by what has been customary for him. In this event, a person
retiring at age sixty-five would not experience much increase in
his propensity to consume as the incomes and consumption rates
of his younger neighbors rose relative to his own; if he had planned
well and his anticipated receipts were adequate at retirement, he
would be able to meet his requirements nicely out of his planned
retirement income, assuming that prices remained stable. He therefore would be more willing to retire at age sixty-five, given some
specified income, than he would, given this same income but in
addition the belief that his requirements would rise as his neighbors' incomes rose relative to his own. In short, if our older person
supposed that his customary level of consumption would not rise
much after he retired, his inclination to continue at work would

turn largely upon what he expected his irregular expenditures to be and upon his estimate of his capacity to meet these expenditures.

Given either hypothesis, the disposition of an older person to continue to work beyond the age of sixty-five, for instance, would depend *ceteris paribus* upon whether he expected to share in the fruits of technical progress. The *ceteris paribus* qualification is introduced principally to allow for the fact that other conditions besides level of income (among them occupational attributes and other factors discussed earlier) might prompt an older person to work beyond age sixty-five. It is not our concern here to devise arrangements whereby older workers may be enabled to share more fully in the fruits of technical progress than they do today. This objective might be realized in considerable measure, however, if after a worker had retired (say, at age sixty-five) the state were increasingly to supplement—though not beyond certain stipulated limits—that part of his income which was drawn from fixed-income instruments or under pension arrangements. Thus, the state might contribute enough out of income tax revenue to increase the retired worker's receipts under fixed income arrangements by 1 per cent per year, for instance, with the proviso that this increase apply only on receipts not in excess of some limit (e.g., $10,000). If such action were taken, the demand of older persons for employment beyond a nominal retirement age of sixty-five would be lower than at present, insofar as dearth of income is a determinant of demand for employment.[67]

4. SUMMARY

The significance attached to an occupational role by older workers depends partly upon non-economic circumstances (among them non-economic aspects of the specific occupations engaging older workers), and partly upon economic circumstances. This chapter has dealt with the latter.

In the first section it was shown that it is in advanced industrial countries rather than in underdeveloped ones that older workers and older job-seekers are relatively numerous. This condition is asso-

67. The case for a "social credit" for the aged is developed more fully by Juanita Kreps and the author in Kreps (ed.), *Employment, Income, and Retirement Problems of the Aged*, chap. 7.

ciated largely with the lower rate of fertility characteristic of advanced peoples and in part with the nature of the employments found in advanced economies; it also reflects the relatively great collectivization of control over access to employment found in these economies. In some measure, accelerated technological progress is responsible for the current plight of older workers with limited education, in that it has sometimes made their knowledge and skill obsolescent and difficult of modernization. It is to be expected, however, that as older workers in their younger days attain higher educational levels, and hence as their capacity for subsequent re-education increases, older workers will prove much more capable of keeping abreast of changing job requirements; with greater education they will be much more able than now to retain employment, or lacking it to find new employment. Furthermore, changes in the occupational composition of the labor force associated with technological progress and higher educational levels may somewhat increase the relative amount of employment that is comparatively immune to forces making for unemployment, especially among older workers. It is essential, however, that collectivistic practices which make for the uneconomic use or the non-use of resources, among them older workers, be eliminated. It is essential also that the aggregate demand for labor be sustained at a high level, since otherwise whatever pressure exists against the employment of older workers tends to be intensified. It is essential, finally, that policy decisions within industry or under governmental auspices be made in keeping with the requirements of the future and not solely in the light of today's problems, many of which are transitory. In civil as well as in military affairs great harm is done by preparing for yesterday's instead of tomorrow's confrontations.

In the second section it was shown that the relationships obtaining between income, employment, and leisure are more complicated, as a rule, than simpler economic models suggest. It was implied also that much more research on the nature and determination of these relationships is needed. Frequently, work and leisure are complements rather than substitutes, with the degree of complementarity affected by occupational, social, and other circumstances, some of which are predominantly economic and some of which are essentially non-economic in character. Accordingly, while rising income will increase the amount of leisure that a representative employee prefers to "purchase" in the course of his lifetime, in many instances it will not induce him to concentrate this demand into his lifetime after sixty or even after sixty-five. As a rule, he will prefer to distribute this demand throughout his active lifetime, e.g., from age twenty to age seventy, and consume his augmented leisure in the form of longer vacations and/or shorter workdays or work weeks or work years. In short, for every adult member of society at any given time, there is a temporally optimal distribution of leisure and a temporally optimal distribution of work extending over his lifetime; but the pattern of this optimum may change as he passes through life and modifies his estimate of the future in the light of his previous experience and fortune. This somewhat variable optimal distribution of work and leisure is most likely to be realized if each member of society is essentially free, under a flexible wage and price system, to distribute his time between "work" and "leisure" as he sees fit in the light of his conspectus of alternatives, which may become more or less conducive to an increase in his "demand" for leisure. If he is not entirely free, and his "welfare" is reduced accordingly, it still will be reduced less in many and perhaps most instances if he is not denied employment in his older years.

In the third section it was shown that the older individual's "demand" for employment will be affected by the extent to which the purchasing power of his "savings" is diminished by uncompensated inflation. It also was shown that this "demand" will be influenced by the extent to which he is permitted to participate in the fruits of technical progress through the institution of what I have called a *social credit for the aged* or through some functionally equivalent arrangement. Even given such a credit, together with protection against inflation, older persons will suffer marked diminution in income if they are condemned to premature retirement by trade-union leaders and industrial and governmental bureaucrats. So-called early voluntary retirement also may be found unattractive because of the resultant reduction in income. Continuation in the labor force probably is the alternative really preferred by most workers, particularly since it can be facilitated by periodic re-training and establishment of a sufficiently flexible wage and price structure.

Section One

WORK AND RETIREMENT

Ida Harper Simpson
Kurt W. Back
John C. McKinney

2. WORK AND RETIREMENT*

Work is among the most important avenues for integrating an
individual into society. His identity, style of life, and participation
patterns are conditioned by his work. This importance of work in
placing an individual (and his family) in the social structure underlies the assumption that retirement undercuts the major social supports of an individual by removing him from the world of work
in which the supports are rooted.[1] Research on older people chal-
lenges this assumption with evidence, showing that the social and
psychological trauma occasioned by retirement is not as radical as
the assumption supposes. For instance, Gordon F. Streib has shown
that non-work aspects of the older individual's situation, including
poor health and low socioeconomic status, depress the morale of
the older person as much as retirement.[2] Despite such evidence the
assumption persists.

We know that patterns of adaptation which a man evolves
while working depend heavily on the *kind* of work he does,[3] not

* We appreciate the contribution of Carlton Guptill in processing the data for
chapters 2 through 6, and the helpful suggestions made by Richard L. Simpson for
analyzing and writing up the findings.

1. See for example, Talcott Parsons, *Essays in Sociological Theory Pure and Applied*
(Glencoe, Ill.: The Free Press, 1949), pp. 230-231; Ernest W. Burgess, "Preface,"
The Journal of Social Issues, **14** (1958), 1. (This issue is entitled "Adjustment in
Retirement.")

2. "Morale of the Retired," *Social Problems*, **3** (1955-1956), 270-276. A similar
conclusion to that of Streib's is drawn by Williams from a review of research on
the changing status, roles, and relationships of older people. He concluded that
retirement in and of itself does not necessarily involve a traumatic shift in social
position, but that its effects should be viewed in the context of the older person's
health, economic security, and social life space. See Richard H. Williams, "Changing
Status, Roles, and Relationships," in Clark Tibbitts (ed.), *Handbook of Social
Gerontology: Societal Aspects of Aging* (Chicago: University of Chicago Press, 1960),
p. 294.

3. For example, see Joel E. Gerstl, "Leisure, Taste and Occupational Milieu,"
Social Problems, **9** (Summer, 1961), 56-68; Seymour Martin Lipset, Martin Trow,

merely upon the fact that he is working. Since the supposed trauma of retirement occurs because of the loss of social supports built up through one's work, and since the nature and extent of these supports differ according to the kind of work in which one is engaged, it seems reasonable that the effect of retirement on behavior depends heavily upon the kind of work from which a man retires. This section will attempt to study the effect of a man's previous work role on his behavior in retirement.[4] Only in Chapter 7 will we be directly concerned with the influence of retirement on older individuals. The other four chapters in the section will instead focus upon aspects of the work role and the relation of these to patterns of retirement behavior, thus providing indirect evidence of the impact of retirement upon the older person's later years.

In attempting to see if the kind of work done by a man affects his retirement, we have proceeded from two basic assumptions: work means different things to different workers, and it can provide one of the strongest structural supports for integrating an individual into society. Perhaps the best predictor of the meaning of work and the extent of structural support which work provides is occupational status. It is our most basic variable in studying the relation of work to retirement; we will use it both as an explanatory and as a control variable. We have grouped occupational status into three levels: upper-white-collar workers; a middle level consisting of lower-white-collar workers and upper-blue-collar workers; and semi-skilled workers. This classification seems consistent with our basic assumptions and with the kind of occupational structure most readily available for study. In many ways these three levels represent fairly distinct strata; to the extent that they do, factors that predict the retirement behavior of one stratum may not predict the same behavior for another stratum. This is to be expected in view of what we know about the effect of work within each level.

Upper-white-collar work, performed by executives, professionals, and governmental officials, provides the highest job satisfaction.[5]

and James S. Coleman, *Union Democracy* (Garden City, N.Y.: Doubleday Anchor Books, 1962), pp. 77-159.

4. To our knowledge little research has been done on this question. Exceptions include Eugene A. Friedmann and Robert J. Havighurst, *The Meaning of Work and Retirement* (Chicago: University of Chicago Press, 1954); and Ernest W. Burgess, Leonard G. Corey, Peter C. Pineo, and Richard T. Thornbury, "Occupational Differences in Attitudes toward Aging and Retirement," *Journal of Gerontology*, **13** (April, 1958), 203-206.

5. Friedmann and Havighurst, *Meaning of Work and Retirement*; Robert Blauner,

This satisfaction depends partially on the recognition which the high prestige of upper-white-collar work bestows, but it is also affected by other factors, including work autonomy and occupational culture.[6] Prestigious occupations involve the performance of highly skilled tasks and carry much responsibility.[7] Execution of these job requirements necessitates work autonomy, which thus seems to be a built-in characteristic of prestigious work. A prestigious occupation also tends to evolve an occupational culture. The culture specifies norms to direct behavior on and off the job, thus providing a strong structural encouragement for participating in society.

Workers in the middle stratum include clerks, salesmen, skilled workers, and foremen; they vary considerably in their degree of job satisfaction and the extent to which they share occupational norms with other workers in the same occupation.[8] This variability seems to result mainly from diversity of work histories and conditions of employment. Work histories may be orderly or they may be chaotic,[9] lacking the pattern of systematic advancement that is characteristic of upper-white-collar workers. The turnover of personnel within an occupation undercuts the development of occupational norms, and those norms that do exist are unlikely to be internalized by the unstable worker. Workers are often employed in line organizations fitted neatly into authority systems. They may be further controlled by technologically built-in features of work.[10] Lacking the work autonomy of upper-white-collar workers, middle-status workers have less chance to decide how to carry out their jobs through interaction with others in their occupation. This limited job autonomy hampers the development of occupational norms transcending the

"Occupational Differences in Work Satisfaction," in Walter Galenson and Seymour Martin Lipset (eds.), Labor and Trade Unionism: An Interdisciplinary Reader (New York: John Wiley & Sons, 1960), pp. 339-360; Nancy C. Morse and Robert S. Weiss, "The Function and Meaning of Work and the Job," American Sociological Review, 20 (April, 1955), 191-198.

6. Blauner, "Occupational Differences in Work Satisfaction."

7. Pitirim A. Sorokin, Social Mobility (New York: Harper & Bros., 1927), pp. 100-101; Kingsley Davis and Wilbert E. Moore, "Some Principles of Stratification," American Sociological Review, 10 (June, 1945), 242-249; Richard L. Simpson and Ida Harper Simpson, "Correlates and Estimation of Occupational Prestige," American Journal of Sociology, 66 (September, 1960), 135-140.

8. Morse and Weiss, "Function and Meaning of Work and Job"; Blauner, "Occupational Differences in Work Satisfaction."

9. Harold L. Wilensky, "Orderly Careers and Social Participation," American Sociological Review, 26 (August, 1961), 521-539.

10. For a discussion of the effect of autonomy on various aspects of work satisfaction, see Blauner's "Occupational Differences in Work Satisfaction," and his Alienation and Freedom: The Factory Worker and His Industry (Chicago: University of Chicago Press, 1964).

employing organization.[11] Their work, however, does bestow some recognition along with providing other rewards which, together with work skills and existing work norms, may provide job satisfaction and encourage participation in the community.

Job satisfaction of semi-skilled workers is low and limited mainly to economic considerations.[12] The limited development of their skills and their low work autonomy, especially of those employed in bureaucratic settings, render difficult the evolvement of occupational norms. Norms related to the work situation do evolve, but rarely are they oriented to the occupation itself. Since their work limits self-involvement in it, it means little to them, apart from the living, the routine, and the sociability which any job might provide. Moreover, since it accords little social recognition, it does not lead community organizations to seek out the worker for participation.

As noted earlier, some gerontological literature has tended to view retirement as the removal of the main structural support for meaningful and purposeful participation in society.[13] This assumption seems unjustified in many cases in view of the fact that work does not provide the same meaning or social support to all workers. Furthermore, it seems questionable to assume that retirement necessarily removes all the social supports associated with work. Although a retiree loses his work position, this loss does not necessarily entail loss of all relationships which the work position has supported. When any major structural change occurs, norms grow up around the change, and these norms tend to evolve out of existing patterns of relationships. Institutionalization of retirement would thus seem to sanction continued participation and perhaps extension of participation in pre-retirement activities. Therefore, in studying retirement we should examine the reaction to loss of the work position within a context of the social relationships and activities of the individual.

For example, upper-white-collar workers tend to be more committed than others to their work; yet they also tend to be the most highly involved in the organizational and institutional structures of

11. Exceptions are found among craftsmen in industries whose labor force is organized on a craft rather than a bureaucratic basis. For a comparison of differences in traditional and bureaucratically organized industries, see Arthur L. Stinchcombe, "Bureaucratic and Craft Administration of Production: A Comparative Study," *Administrative Science Quarterly*, 4 (1959), 168-187.

12. Morse and Weiss, "Function and Meaning of Work and Job."

13. See Parsons, *Essays in Sociological Theory*, and Burgess, "Preface" to "Adjustment in Retirement."

their communities. Thus, we would expect them to miss their work more than other workers. But their higher involvement which is likely to continue in retirement may substitute for loss of their work positions. On the other hand, semi-skilled workers find little meaning in their work beyond economic considerations. But since their social involvement in the community at large is narrow and limited mainly to their work role, they might react to loss of work more strongly than their low evaluation of their work would suggest. Moreover, if economic concerns have been a guiding force in their lives, and if their retirement income is not adequate for their needs, these economic worries may heighten their sense of loss.

The feeling of uselessness which retirement supposedly produces by removing an individual from the world of work with its productive and worthwhile activities may also depend on the kind of work the individual did. If an individual's work was in a field undergoing rapid change in technical knowledge and skills, younger workers more schooled in current techniques and knowledge may have displaced him some time before retirement. The pattern of promoting executives "upstairs," labeling older college professors as thirty years behind, or transferring lower-white-collar or blue-collar workers to makeshift jobs in order to replace them with machines means that a worker may lose his usefulness, influence, and authority before he retires. If an older worker has experienced loss of status in his work group, he is likely to look upon retirement differently than will the older worker whose influence is high among his fellow workers.

With these considerations in mind, we will attempt to examine how various factors related to the work position influence reactions to retirement. In this examination we shall focus our attention on the evaluation the retiree makes of himself in retirement. This evaluation is presumably the result of the various influences we have been discussing. Our study will be divided as follows: In Chapter 3 we will examine the effects of occupational status, social involvement in retirement, and loss of pre-retirement involvement on self-evaluation. In Chapter 4 we will examine several explanations of pre-retirement attitude toward retirement and then observe the relation of this attitude to self-evaluation in retirement. Chapter 5 will try to explain differences among workers in exposure to information on retirement and then observe the effect of exposure on self-evaluation in retirement. In Chapter 6 we will examine factors associated with the continuation of style of work activities in retirement and the effect of this continuity on self-evaluation in retirement. Chapter 7 will examine the effect of retirement on the self-rating of older individuals.

Data for the study come from questionnaires and interviews administered to 304 retired workers and to 161 workers within five years of retirement in the Piedmont area of North Carolina and Virginia in 1960 and 1961. The main criterion in selecting the sample was to obtain occupations of widely varying status. Subjects were obtained from lists of retired workers and workers within five years of retirement provided by a tobacco, a textile, and a chemical factory, an insurance company, three universities, and from local membership lists of the American Bar Association, the American Medical Association, and executive directors of a local Young Men's Christian Association. All subjects were white males and long-time residents of the area. The interview was divided into two parts, administered on separate days. During the first part of the interview a questionnaire was left with the subject, who was instructed in filling it out; it was picked up during the second part of the interview. The interview contained mainly unstructured questions and the questionnaire structured ones. Virtually all subjects co-operated, but data were incomplete for some. Some failed to complete the ques-

Table 1. Percentage of Different Kinds of Occupations Included in Prestige Strata of the Retired and Pre-Retired Samples.

Occupations	Retired	Pre-Retired	Total
Upper-white-collar (N)	(78)	(84)	(162)
College professors	53.8	69.0	61.7
Executives	28.2	20.2	24.1
Physicians	11.5	—	5.6
Lawyers	6.4	10.7	8.6
Middle stratum (N)	(123)	(38)	(161)
Clerical and sales	26.0	18.4	24.2
Foremen	30.9	55.3	36.6
Skilled	43.1	26.3	39.1
Semi-skilled (N)	(105)	(39)	(144)
Textile workers	82.9	82.1	82.6
Tobacco workers	13.3	17.9	14.6
Chemical workers	3.8	—	2.8
Total	(306)	(161)	(467)

tionnaire or failed to follow instructions in completing it. Circumstances including illness and death made it impossible to administer the second part of the interview to a few subjects. For these reasons the sample size will vary with the topics investigated.

Table 1 presents the occupational distribution of retired and pre-retired workers within the three status levels. (There are no unskilled workers in the sample, since it was restricted to white persons, and most unskilled jobs in the South are held by Negroes.) Only within the middle level do we have much variability in kinds of occupations; the upper-white-collar level is overweighted with college professors and the semi-skilled level with textile workers. Of the middle level, all except six retired workers and all except eight of the pre-retired workers were employed by the textile or tobacco factory. All subjects included in the middle level and semi-skilled level were employees of bureaucratically organized industries; the upper-white-collar level includes free professionals—doctors and lawyers—although the bulk were employees of bureaucratic organizations. Given the biases of our sample we will be unable to generalize our findings, although we do feel that they will be suggestive of the influences stemming from work on behavior in retirement.

The number of years the retirees had been retired ranged from less than a year to eighteen years, with a median of four years. The occupational status groupings differed only slightly in the median number of years retired: semi-skilled workers averaged 5.11 years, upper-white-collar workers 4.21 years, and middle-status workers 3.53 years.

The age of the retirees ranged from fifty-five to ninety-one, with a median age of sixty-nine. Age differences among the occupational groups were small: upper-white-collar retirees were the oldest with a median age of 71.18; the other two levels had virtually the same median age (69.14 for the middle stratum and 69.60 for the semi-skilled). The same age pattern was found among pre-retirees: upper-white-collar workers had a median age of 63.16, the middle stratum averaged 62.06, and the semi-skilled averaged 62.42. (The age of pre-retirees ranged from fifty-nine to seventy-two, and their median age was sixty-two.) The age differences among the occupational groupings reflect differences in their retirement age. The median age at which upper-white-collar workers retired was 67.25, the middle stratum 65.22, and the semi-skilled 64.19.

Self-evaluation in retirement is our main dependent variable. Two measures of it are used, a scale of job deprivation and a general morale measure. The job deprivation scale is adapted from one used by Wayne E. Thompson, which he calls satisfaction with retirement.[14] It is a Guttman-type scale with four attitude statements dichotomously scored, and it has a reproducibility coefficient of .97. The statements, arranged in order from little to much job deprivation, include:

> I often miss being with other people at work. (Strongly agree, agree)
> I often miss the feeling of doing a good job. (Strongly agree, agree)
> I often wish I could go back to work. (Strongly agree, agree)
> I often worry about not having a job. (Strongly agree, agree)

Scale scores ranged from zero through four. Scores zero through two, which fell below or at the median, were grouped together as low job deprivation; scores three and four, which were above the median, were grouped together as high job deprivation.

The general morale measure, which is also a Guttman-type scale, was developed by Bernard Kutner and associates.[15] We used only five of their seven attitude statements, which we scored dichotomously. The statements which we used, arranged in order from low to high morale, include:

> On the whole, I am very well satisfied with my way of life today. (Strongly agree, agree)
> As I get older, things seem to get better than I thought would be the case. (Strongly agree, agree)
> I often feel that there is no point in living. (Strongly disagree)
> Things just keep getting worse and worse for me as I get older. (Strongly disagree)
> All in all, I find a great deal of unhappiness in life today. (Strongly disagree)

This morale scale has a reproducibility coefficient of .94. Scale scores were divided around the median; scores zero through two,

14. For a discussion of this scale, see "Pre-retirement Anticipation and Adjustment in Retirement," *The Journal of Social Issues*, **14** (1958), 37. Whereas the scale as used by Thompson asked questions, we restated the questions in the form of attitude statements with which the respondent might agree or disagree.

15. For a discussion of this morale scale, see Kutner, David Fanshel, Alice M. Togo, and Thomas S. Langner, *Five Hundred over Sixty: A Community Survey on Aging* (New York: Russell Sage Foundation, 1956), pp. 48-49. The scale as used by them included seven items, but we eliminated two.

falling at or below the median, are called low morale; scores three through five, falling above the median, are called high morale.

Our two measures of self-evaluation focus upon two different feelings. The job deprivation scale is concerned with the feeling of missing one's work, whereas the morale scale pertains to a feeling of worthwhileness. It is more general in meaning than the job deprivation measure and is thus likely to be subject to more influences. In Chapters 18 and 19 Kurt Back and Kenneth Gergen discuss different meanings of morale, one of which is based on David Riesman's definition of the autonomous older person.[16] The morale scale appears to rely upon the kind of personal characteristics associated with the autonomous person—a broad life space coupled with a high activity level.

Table 2. Percentage of Retirees with Low Job Deprivation by Occupational Prestige and Morale.

	Percentage with low job deprivation	
	Low morale	High morale
Upper-white-collar retirees	87.5 (16)	66.7 (39)
Middle-status retirees	58.8 (51)	72.2 (54)
Semi-skilled retirees	31.3 (48)	57.6 (33)

The scales are correlated, but they relate differently within the occupational levels. Table 2, which presents the percentage of retirees with low job deprivation, cross-classified by morale and occupational status, shows that within the middle and semi-skilled levels retirees with high morale were more likely than those with low morale to feel little job deprivation. But within the upper-white-collar stratum, retirees with high morale missed their work more than those with low morale. We interpret the differing relations of the two measures of self-evaluation within the occupational levels as indicating that the scales tap different, though related, feelings and that the influences on each are likely to vary by occupational level.[17]

16. "Some Clinical and Cultural Aspects of the Aging Process," in his *Individualism Reconsidered* (Garden City, N.Y.: Doubleday Anchor Books, 1955), pp. 164-173.
17. Chapters 18 and 19 will review the literature and will show from survey data the relation of aging to morale. Conceivably the findings on self-evaluation which we will report in chapters 3 through 6 might be affected by age, since the occupational levels do vary by age, even though slightly. However, correlational analysis showed only small relationships between age and our measures of self-

In Chapters 3 through 6, where we use the two measures to study the effects of aspects of the work role on self-evaluation in retirement, we shall find the job deprivation measure related more consistently to work-connected factors—our independent variables—than did the morale measure. This lesser relation of the morale measure to the independent variables probably means that many other influences, such as health, family situation, and other personal factors, help in upholding a sense of personal worth, as much as or more than factors associated with one's previous work. Since our findings on job deprivation add up to a more coherent pattern than those on morale, we are more confident of their meaning and have therefore relied more heavily upon the measure of job deprivation in our presentation than upon the morale measure of self-evaluation.

Chapter 7 uses still another measure of self-evaluation. Unlike the job deprivation and the morale scales, which measure personal feelings by asking the respondent to react to statements by agreeing or disagreeing with them, the measure of self-evaluation in Chapter 7 is a description which the respondent gave of himself. The description was obtained through a semantic differential method of ascertaining the meaning of the word "myself" to the respondent. The self-description scales showed inconsistent and low correlations with both the job deprivation scale and the morale scale (see Chapter 7, Table 1). More details on the correlation of these measures are given in Chapter 7.

In our presentation we have not attempted to relate systematically these measures of self-evaluation. The correlational patterns, coupled with a scrutiny of the content of the measures, suggest that their interrelations are complex. We felt that to try to clarify and explain these interrelations would divert our attention from our main objective in these chapters, namely, to see if aspects of one's work affect evaluative behavior in retirement. Different meanings of morale are studied, however, in Chapters 18 and 19. Other variables and their measures will be discussed in the chapters as they are used.

---

evaluation, the Kutner and job deprivation scales. The correlation coefficients for the total retired sample and for each occupational level are as follows:

	Kutner scale	Job deprivation scale
Upper-white-collar	—.01	.16
Middle stratum	.31	.28
Semi-skilled	.11	.03
All retirees	.18	.16

Ida Harper Simpson

Kurt W. Back

John C. McKinney

3. ATTRIBUTES OF WORK, INVOLVEMENT IN SOCIETY, AND SELF-EVALUATION IN RETIREMENT

Some gerontological literature sees retirement as undercutting the social supports provided by work. One dimension of this disruption is reduced social involvement.[1] The presumed ill effects of reduced involvement have been dwelt upon in the literature, but to our knowledge there has been no systematic attempt to relate reduction of involvement or level of post-retirement involvement to the pre-retirement anchorages which work provided. This chapter will deal with the question.

Research has shown that supports of pre-retirement involvement associated with work include the status of one's occupation and the orderliness of his work history. Upper-white-collar workers are highly involved in society, controlling its major organizational and institutional structures, while those at the bottom of the status scale —unskilled and semi-skilled workers—participate little in the organizational structure. The middle-status group—lower-white-collar and upper-blue-collar workers—are intermediate in social involvement.[2] This relation of occupational status to social involvement holds whether involvement is measured by membership in or attendance

1. See, for example, Ernest W. Burgess, "Preface," *Journal of Social Issues*, **14** (1958), 1 (issue on "Adjustment in Retirement"); Talcott Parsons, "Age and Sex in the Social Structure of the United States," *American Sociological Review*, **7** (October, 1942), 604-616.

2. See, for example, August B. Hollingshead, *Elmtown's Youth* (New York: John Wiley & Sons, 1949), pp. 85-120.

of meetings of voluntary associations,[3] number and type of social organizations participated in,[4] voting behavior,[5] or reading habits.[6] The middle stratum is characterized by much more variability in involvement than the upper or the lower stratum. Harold L. Wilensky accounts for this intra-stratum variability by orderliness of work history. Workers whose work histories have followed an orderly pattern of advancement in rewards and responsibility are more involved in society than those whose work histories lack an orderly pattern.[7] Wilensky sees an orderly work history for these middle-status workers as approximating a career. He defines a career as "a succession of related jobs, arranged in a hierarchy of prestige, through which persons move in an ordered (more-or-less predictable) sequence."[8] Orderliness of job movement is among the most important features of the career. It may prevail in either horizontal or vertical job changes, so long as the change represents a stable, predictable progression. Of two foremen in a textile shop, the one who was promoted to the position from machine operator has experienced an orderly job change, but the other, who previously operated a small farm, has made a disorderly move. Work histories in the lower occupational stratum are typically disorderly,[9] while those of upper-white-collar workers are typically orderly.

Among the reasons why workers with careers are involved in society more than those with sequences of unrelated jobs are normative patterns external and internal to the career. A worker whose

3. See, for example, Mirra Komarovsky, "The Voluntary Associations of Urban Dwellers," *American Sociological Review*, **11** (December, 1946), 689-698; Leonard Reissman, "Class, Leisure and Social Participation," *ibid.*, **19** (February, 1954), 76-84; John M. Foskett, "Social Structure and Social Participation," *ibid.*, **20** (August, 1955), 431-438.

4. Participation of the working class is restricted largely to their neighborhoods and families, whereas the upper-white-collar workers participate in community-wide and society-wide organizations. See, for example, Genevieve Knupfer, "Portrait of the Underdog," *Public Opinion Quarterly*, **11** (Spring, 1947), 103-114; Robert and Helen Lynd, *Middletown* (New York: Harcourt, Brace & Co., 1929), pp. 272-312.

5. See, for example, Paul F. Lazarsfeld, Bernard Berelson, and Hazel Gaudet, *The People's Choice* (New York: Duell, Sloan & Pearce, 1944), pp. 40-51; Seymour M. Lipset, Paul F. Lazarsfeld, Allen H. Barton, and Juan Linz, "The Psychology of Voting: An Analysis of Political Behavior," in Gardner Lindzey (ed.), *Handbook of Social Psychology* (Cambridge, Mass.: Addison-Wesley, 1956), II, 1126-1135.

6. W. Lloyd Warner and Paul S. Lunt, *The Social Life of a Modern Community* (New Haven: Yale University Press, 1941), pp. 378-421.

7. "Orderly Careers and Social Participation: The Impact of Work History on Social Integration in the Middle Mass," *American Sociological Review*, **26** (August, 1961), 521-539.

8. *Ibid.* A similar definition of career is given by Everett C. Hughes in *Men and Their Work* (Glencoe, Ill.: The Free Press, 1958), p. 63.

9. See, for example, Lloyd G. Reynolds and Joseph Shister, *Job Horizons: A Study of Job Satisfactions and Labor Mobility* (New York: Harper & Bros., 1949), pp. 65-70.

work history is characterized by orderly advancement in responsibility and rewards is accorded recognition and respect in his community; he is said to be successful. He tends to identify and to be identified by his occupation. His occupational success advertises his proven worth.[10] Voluntary associations often solicit, and almost always welcome, membership from the occupationally successful. Furthermore, most occupations in which workers have or may evolve a career[11] include norms favoring involvement in society. Exactly which organizations the occupational culture favors may vary with the kind of work tasks, work setting, and clients of the occupation,[12] but interest in society is nonetheless nurtured by norms. Workers with orderly work histories are more likely to internalize occupational norms favoring societal involvement than are those with disorderly job histories. The latter are more likely to work in occupations with poorly developed occupational cultures or in ones which lack norms stressing societal involvement; they spend less time in a given occupation, and while in it they are less frequently rewarded by advancement.

The difference in the social involvement of middle-status workers with orderly and disorderly work histories reported by Wilensky suggests that the former more than the latter resemble upper-white-collar workers in participation.[13] The extent and kind of their involvement is nonetheless likely to differ from that of upper-white-collar workers. Their work histories, although successful relative to those of others within their stratum, lack the prestige of upper-

10. Hughes, *Men and Their Work*, p. 64.

11. Occupations, as well as the institutional structure in which one works, differ in the opportunities offered for evolving a career. Occupations or jobs which carry little responsibility, little authority, and limited skill appear to provide few opportunities for evolving a career.

12. Joel E. Gerstl found that dentists, advertising executives, and college professors, all of whom are of roughly the same prestige, tended to belong to different kinds of voluntary associations. See "Leisure,' Taste and Occupational Milieu," *Social Problems*, 9 (Summer, 1961), 63-65. Wilensky interprets the findings of Gerstl in terms of the kind of clients served by the three occupations. Dentists, in addition to membership in professional associations, tended to participate across and down in organizations, such as fraternal orders, local churches, and neighborhood associations, where they might meet potential patients. Advertising men tended to participate across and up in such organizations as country clubs and community-wide civic organizations, where they kept in touch with clients. College professors, who have neither clients nor customers, tended to avoid non-professional contacts. Wilensky also relates work tasks and work setting to work commitment, and these in turn to patterns of leisure. See "Life Cycle, Work Situation, and Participation in Formal Associations," in Robert W. Kleemeier (ed.), *Aging and Leisure* (New York: Oxford University Press, 1961), pp. 232-234.

13. Since Wilensky reports only differences in social involvement of workers with orderly and disorderly work histories, we are unable to compare their rates of involvement with those of upper-white-collar workers reported by other studies.

white-collar careers. Voluntary associations which encourage their participation are likely to differ in number and kind from those which solicit the participation of upper-white-collar workers. The kinds of interests which the norms of their occupations nurture are also likely to differ. Orderliness of work history affects involvement, but prestige of one's work also affects it.

In this chapter we will be concerned with variations in social involvement among retired workers. The objective of the first section is to see if prestige and orderliness of pre-retirement jobs affect post-retirement involvement. Wilensky hypothesizes that where occupation is central to identity and the career curve permits aspirations of mobility to run high, participation in voluntary associations continues well into a person's fifties and sixties.[14] Research has shown that differences in social participation between the social classes are not affected by age or retirement.[15] Individuals with orderly work histories and high occupational status evidently internalize expectations of involvement, and these expectations, though cultivated while still employed, persist in retirement. High occupational status and orderliness support involvement and reduce the amount of loss of involvement which accompanies retirement.

A study of changes in participation of different age groups, cross-classified by social classes, in four rural communities was conducted by Philip Taietz and Olaf F. Larson. They found that the sharpest drop in participation between different age groups occurred within the lower socioeconomic level; the least change took place within the highest socioeconomic level; and the middle level was intermediate in change.[16] The authors do not show the effect of retirement on participation within the different social classes, although they do find that retired individuals participate less in occupationally oriented organizations than do employed individuals. Their findings thus appear to support our hypothesis that loss of involvement associated with retirement is inversely related to socioeconomic level.

14. Wilensky, "Life Cycle, Work Situation, and Participation in Formal Associations," p. 235.
15. For a discussion of this research, see Wilma Donahue, Harold L. Orbach, and Otto Pollak, "Retirement: The Emerging Pattern," in Clark Tibbitts (ed.), *Handbook of Social Gerontology: Societal Aspects of Aging* (Chicago: University of Chicago Press, 1960), p. 384.
16. The points at which the sharpest decline in participation was observed were between the ages of forty-five to sixty-four for the lower and higher socioeconomic levels and between the ages of sixty-five to seventy-four and age seventy-five and over for the middle-status level. See "Social Participation and Old Age," *Rural Sociology*, **21** (September-December, 1956), 229-238.

Specifically, we will test the following hypotheses: (1) Occupational status is related to post-retirement involvement; the higher the status, the greater the involvement. (2) Orderliness is related to post-retirement involvement; the more orderly the work history, the greater the post-retirement involvement. (3) Not only is post-retirement involvement higher among the prestigious and orderly; it is less reduced from the same individuals' pre-retirement involvement. Thus, those who have disorderly work histories and have lacked in prestige enter retirement less involved, lose more of the involvement which they do have, and have much lower involvement during retirement. (4) The effects of occupational status and orderliness on involvement are separate and cumulative, so that of two people on the same occupational level the more orderly one has more involvement and less loss; of two people, both of whom are orderly or disorderly, the one with higher status has more involvement and less loss.

The gerontological literature which assumes that retirement reduces the involvement of an individual in society also sees this undercutting of social supports as adversely affecting the individual's self-conception.[17] Studies have shown that self-conception varies with prestige of work, both among working and retired individuals.[18] This is to be expected, since high prestige bestows recognition, and an individual with such recognition has reflected from society more favorable attributes in terms of which he may view himself. Since orderliness of work history provides a degree of success and a relatively stable situation for internalizing norms of involvement, we further expect individuals with orderly work histories to evaluate themselves in retirement more favorably than those with disorderly work histories. In the second section of this chapter we seek to ascertain the effects of occupational status and orderliness of work history on self-evaluation in retirement. We predict: (1) Occupational status is related to self-evaluation; the higher the status of the pre-retirement job, the more favorable the self-evaluation of the retiree. (2) Orderliness of work history is re-

17. Burgess, "Preface" to "Adjustment in Retirement." See, for example, Bernard S. Phillips, "A Role Theory Approach to Adjustment in Old Age," *American Sociological Review*, **22** (April, 1957), 212-217.

18. For a comparison of the morale of employed and retired workers of different socioeconomic status, see Bernard D. Kutner, David Fanshel, Alice M. Togo, and Thomas S. Langner, *Five Hundred over Sixty: A Community Survey on Aging* (New York: Russell Sage Foundation, 1956), pp. 73-74.

lated to self-evaluation in retirement; the more orderly the work history, the more favorable the self-evaluation. (3) The effects of status and orderliness on self-evaluation are separate and cumulative, so that among individuals of the same status level the ones with more orderly work histories will give a more favorable self-evaluation; and of individuals similar in having orderly or disorderly work histories, the ones with higher status will give the more favorable self-evaluation.

Assuming that the above hypotheses are borne out by the data, we do not know whether favorable self-evaluations are supported by occupational status and work histories per se or simply by social involvement or some other correlates of status and orderliness. Some gerontological studies have shown that among older persons personal adjustment (happiness) is correlated with social participation.[19] But, as Wilensky observes, it may well be that "there is a self-selection of the sane, the adjusted, the healthy and happy into clubs." Furthermore, he argues that the available studies do not permit an assessment of the effects of ties with intimates relative to the effect of ties to voluntary associations. "Whether club membership in the absence of lively informal relations can provide much ego support for those who need it remains to be shown."[20] On the other hand, other studies suggest that *level* of involvement is not as important for self-evaluation as are *changes* in involvement. Zena Smith Blau has found that individuals who thought of themselves as old (an unfavorable self-evaluation) were more likely than those who thought of themselves as young or middle-aged to have experienced considerable change in their recent past.[21] Her findings suggest that constancy of involvement, more than level of involvement, supports a favorable self-evaluation, assuming, of course, that there is some involvement. Caution must be exercised, however, in drawing this hypothesis from the findings of Blau; the changes in involvement with which she is concerned pertain to intimate, personal relations. Her data do not show whether loss of involvement in secondary relations affects self-evaluation in the same way or to the same extent as do changes in personal status, such as death of a spouse.

19. For a summary of these studies, see Arnold M. Rose, "The Impact of Aging on Voluntary Associations," in Tibbitts (ed.), *Handbook of Social Gerontology*, pp. 684-686.
20. "Life Cycle, Work Situation, and Participation in Formal Organizations," p. 236.
21. "Changes in Status and Age Identification," *American Sociological Review*, **21** (April, 1956), 198-203.

In the third section of the chapter we will try to ascertain the effects of different levels of involvement and of loss of involvement on self-evaluation to see if these two variables account for the effects associated with occupational status. Specifically, we will study the following hypotheses: (1) Among workers matched in status and orderliness, a high level of involvement is associated with favorable self-evaluation in retirement. (2) Among workers matched in status and orderliness, retention of involvement is associated with favorable self-evaluation. (3) Among workers matched in level of involvement, status and orderliness are not systematically associated with self-evaluation. (4) Among workers matched with respect to loss of involvement, status and orderliness are not systematically associated with self-evaluation. To see if involvement and changes in involvement affect self-evaluation separately from orderliness of work histories, we ought to control orderliness of work history while examining the effects of involvement and its loss. However, we will not be able to control level and loss of involvement simultaneously because of the smallness of our sample, though we will use a simultaneous control to observe the effects of status.

PROCEDURES

Wilensky's classification of orderliness was used to code work histories. The classification includes those who have changed jobs with an orderly horizontal progression, orderly vertical progression, borderline orderly vertical progression, disorderly horizontal movement, disorderly vertical movement, and those who have held only one job.[22] These categories were combined to form two classes, orderly and disorderly, with "only one job" and "borderline orderly" being grouped with the orderly. All except three upper-white-collar workers had orderly work histories; the semi-skilled workers, except twelve who had only one job, had disorderly work histories. Since there were so few deviant cases among the upper-white-collar and semi-skilled workers, the three upper-white-collar retirees with disorderly work histories and the twelve semi-skilled retirees who had held only one job were eliminated from the sample for this study. Substantial diversity of work history patterns was found only

22. "Orderly Careers and Social Participation," p. 525. See pp. 52-53 above for a discussion of measures of self-evaluation.

in the middle stratum, where sixty-nine retirees had orderly work histories and forty-eight had disorderly work histories.

The studies we have mentioned in the discussion of involvement deal with different aspects of social participation. Dimensions of participation studied by Wilensky are the most inclusive, covering secondary attachments, primary and informal relations, and institutional spheres.[23] We constructed an index of involvement composed of three measures: the number of different kinds of interests, the number of friends, and the number of non-church organizational memberships. Whereas Wilensky's dimensions of participation measure various aspects of ties to the larger communal society, because of the nature of our sample we have included in our index only one relation to the larger society. Our blue-collar sample is made up of tobacco and textile workers. Voluntary associations are rare in textile communities, though a strong informal community exists.[24] The textile factories were partially unionized, but only a minority of our sample had been members. Although we have no systematic evidence, our impressions from interviewing suggest that the communities of tobacco workers also do not emphasize voluntary associations, and the plant was not unionized. In marked contrast to the blue-collar workers are the upper-white-collar workers, most of whom are college professors, who tended to be cosmopolitan in outlook and to belong to organizations rooted in the larger society. Since we wanted to study the effect of status on involvement, to include mainly dimensions of ties to the larger community would bias the index against the kinds of involvements which our blue-collar sample would have had an opportunity to develop. Thus, the decision was made to include in the index the number of different kinds of interests and the number of friends, along with membership in voluntary associations; our thinking was that the blue-collar sample might have had as great a structural opportunity as the higher status workers to have a fairly wide range of interests and friends.

Using the three measures, a total involvement score was computed for each worker. A value of one was given for each kind of interest, for each friend seen often, and for each organization to which a person belonged. If an individual saw no friends often or

23. *Ibid.*, pp. 526-529.
24. Robert Blauner, *Alienation and Freedom: The Factory Worker and His Industry* (Chicago: University of Chicago Press, 1964), p. 79.

belonged to no organizations, but had one kind of interest, he received a score of one; if he belonged to two organizations, but saw no friends frequently or had no interest, he received a score of two, and so forth. Scores ranged from zero through thirteen; scores of five and over, which fall at and above the median, were grouped together as high involvement, and scores below five were grouped together as low involvement.

Change in pre-retirement involvement is measured by a scale in which values were assigned for dropping out of organizations, changing friends, and losing interests. If no change had occurred in these patterns since retirement, a score of zero was given. If membership in organizations was dropped, a positive score of one was given for each organization dropped. If an individual had lost friends, regardless of number, a positive score of two was given; if he had added new friends, he received a negative score of two. If interests had been lost since retiring, a positive score of one was given for each kind of interest lost; a negative score was given for each kind of interest added since retiring. We did not have reliable information on the number of pre-retirement friends lost, and thus we were unable to score this category in the same way as the others. A score of zero means no change in involvement; a negative score means that the individual is more involved while retired than while working; and a positive score means loss of pre-retirement involvement. For the total sample, scores ranged from minus five to plus seven. Individuals with scores from plus one through plus seven are defined as losers, having lost involvement in retirement; those with scores of zero or negative scores are defined as non-losers. (Only sixteen individuals had minus scores indicating more involvement after than before retirement.)

STATUS AND ORDERLINESS OF WORK HISTORY, AND LEVEL AND LOSS OF INVOLVEMENT

Our first hypothesis predicts that involvement in retirement varies directly with the status of pre-retirement jobs. Table 1, which presents the percentage of each status group highly involved, supports the hypothesis. Upper-white-collar retirees were most likely to be highly involved, semi-skilled retirees were the least likely,

Table 1. Percentage with High Involvement and Percentage with Loss of Involvement by Status and Work History.

Status and work history	High involvement[a]	Loss of involvement[b]
Upper-white-collar	85.5 (69)	61.4 (70)
Middle-status	55.8 (120)	40.0 (115)
Orderly work history	62.3 (69)	36.8 (68)
Disorderly work history	47.1 (51)	44.7 (47)
Semi-skilled	37.2 (94)	50.6 (89)

[a]High involvement refers to scores of 5 or more.   Scores range from $+1$ through 13.
[b]Loss of involvement refers to scores of $+1$ or more.   Scores range from -5 through $+7$.

and middle-status retirees were intermediate. We also predicted that orderliness of work history would be related to involvement: the more orderly the work history, the higher the post-retirement involvement. Examination of the middle stratum, the only one for which we have disparate work histories, shows that retirees who had orderly work histories were more involved than those with the same status but with disorderly work histories. Thus, status and orderliness have separate effects on involvement in the manner predicted.[25]

In addition to occupational status and orderliness of work history being related to level of involvement, we also predicted that loss of pre-retirement involvement would vary inversely with occupational status and orderliness of work history: the higher the status of the occupation, the less pre-retirement involvement lost; and the more orderly the work history, the less loss. Table 1 also gives the percentage of retirees, classified by status and orderliness of work

25. The contribution of each of the three items in the index to the total involvement score was essentially the same for each stratum, with one exception. Interests contributed the most to the total score of each stratum. For upper-white-collar workers 41.3 per cent of the total score was contributed by interests, for orderly middle-status retirees 48.1 per cent, for disorderly middle-status retirees 47.1 per cent, and for semi-skilled retirees 51.0 per cent. Number of friends seen frequently was second in contributing to the total score of middle-status and semi-skilled retirees, but it was third for upper-white-collar retirees. For upper-white-collar retirees it contributed 23.4 per cent of their total score, 32.7 per cent of the total score of middle-status retirees with disorderly work histories, and 36.4 per cent of the score of semi-skilled retirees. The number of organizations to which a person belonged contributed 35.3 per cent of the total score of upper-white-collar retirees, 19.1 per cent of middle-status retirees with orderly work histories, 16.9 per cent of middle-status retirees with disorderly work histories, and 12.8 per cent of the semi-skilled retirees.

history, who lost pre-retirement involvement—but it fails to support our hypothesis. Upper-white-collar retirees had experienced the greatest loss of pre-retirement involvement, the middle-status retirees the least, and semi-skilled retirees were intermediate in loss of pre-retirement involvement. These findings might mean that a larger percentage of upper-white-collar retirees had experienced a loss, but the extent of their loss was less than among retirees of lower status. The mean loss for each category of retirees, however, shows the same pattern as that obtained when they are classified simply as losers or non-losers. (On a seven-point scale, upper-white-collar workers had a mean loss of 1.51, middle-status workers .83, and semi-skilled workers 1.04.)

Although prestige of work is not inversely related to loss of pre-retirement involvement as predicted, orderliness of work history does appear to be associated with less loss (see Table 1). Among middle-status retirees, those whose work histories had been orderly were less likely to have lost pre-retirement involvement than those with disorderly work histories. Since the difference in the two work-history groupings is small, and since we have only one stratum within which to examine the effect of orderliness on loss of pre-retirement involvement, caution is warranted in accepting the hypothesis that orderliness of work history lessens loss of pre-retirement involvement.

Perhaps the failure of occupational status to relate consistently to loss of pre-retirement involvement reflects differences in the appropriateness of patterns of pre-retirement involvement to the retirement situation. The finding by Taietz and Larson that retired individuals tended to participate less in work-oriented organizations[26] suggests that patterns geared specifically to the work situation were the most likely to be given up, since their meaning and function are lost outside the institutional setting of work. For example, a semi-skilled worker might give up union membership since the union is seen mainly as a protective device while working; or participation in the chamber of commerce might be dropped by a retired executive; or an interest in fishing might be given up if fishing had been an activity engaged in solely because it was an expectation of a work group. Since the work situation of upper-white-collar workers includes normative pressures for extensive involvement,

26. "Social Participation and Old Age."

Table 2. Percentage with Little Job Deprivation and Percentage with High Morale by Status and Work History.

Status and work history	Little job deprivation[a]	High morale[b]
Upper-white-collar	75.5 (53)	68.3 (60)
Middle-status	63.4 (112)	52.3 (107)
Orderly work history	73.4 (64)	59.7 (62)
Disorderly work history	50.0 (48)	42.2 (45)
Semi-skilled	40.5 (79)	42.7 (75)

[a]Low job deprivation is defined as scores 0 through 2.   Scores range from 0 through 4.
[b]High general morale is defined as scores 3 through 5.   Scores range from 0 through 5.

perhaps upper-white-collar workers lost more of their pre-retirement involvement because a larger proportion of it had been work-connected. Of the three items used in the index, interests would be the least influenced by the work situation. This interpretation of the greater loss of pre-retirement involvement by upper white-collar retirees than by semi-skilled and middle-status retirees is supported by the data: they lost fewer interests but more organizational memberships than middle-status and semi-skilled retirees; however, the three strata differed little in loss of friends.[27] Upper-white-collar retirees tended to have lost slightly more work-related friends than did retirees from lower status jobs (70.0 per cent vs. 67.6 per cent among middle-status workers and 66.7 per cent among semi-skilled retirees). Most of the organizations the upper-white-collar retirees had dropped out of were work-related (61.8 per cent). While they lost fewer interests, a larger percentage of these losses were work-related than among middle-status and semi-skilled retirees (50.0 per cent vs. 9.7 per cent among middle-status retirees and 34.6 per cent among semi-skilled retirees). Essentially, the same pattern of loss exists for semi-skilled as for middle-status retirees. However, more of the semi-skilled experienced loss of involvement; and of the involvement lost, a larger percentage was work-related.

In summary, we have found that level of involvement in retire-

27. Among upper-white-collar workers, 16.4 per cent lost interests compared to 27.8 per cent of the middle-status retirees and 29.5 per cent of the semi-skilled retirees. The tabulations for loss of friends were 32.8 per cent of upper-white-collar retirees, 29.6 per cent of the middle-status retirees, and 35.2 per cent of semi-skilled retirees. Organizational memberships were lost by 37.7 per cent of the upper-white-collar retirees, 5.2 per cent of the middle-status retirees, and 10.2 per cent of semi-skilled retirees.

ment is related to occupational status and orderliness of work history. But status is not inversely related to loss of pre-retirement involvement as we predicted, though orderliness of work history is. Upper-white-collar workers lost more pre-retirement involvement than those lower in status, and we have attempted to explain their greater loss as a result of a larger proportion of their pre-retirement involvement being work-connected.

OCCUPATIONAL STATUS, ORDERLINESS OF WORK HISTORY, AND SELF-EVALUATION IN RETIREMENT

Our second objective in this chapter is to see if occupational status and orderliness of work history are associated with favorable self-evaluation in retirement. We have argued that prestigious and orderly work histories bestow recognition and approval. If an individual's work history has been prestigious and orderly, this success supports favorable self-evaluation in retirement. Table 2 presents the percentage of retirees, classified by occupational status and orderliness of work history, who felt little job deprivation and who had high general morale (our measures of favorable self-evaluation). It shows that prestige is related to both measures. Upper-white-collar workers were most likely to feel little job deprivation, semi-skilled workers least likely, and middle-status workers were intermediate. Essentially the same pattern exists for high morale: upper-white-collar retirees were the most likely to have high morale, semi-skilled retirees the least likely, and middle-status retirees were intermediate. Orderliness of work history also appears to support favorable self-evaluation; a larger percentage of retirees with orderly work histories felt little job deprivation than of those with disorderly work histories; and a larger percentage of retirees with orderly work histories had high general morale than of those with disorderly work histories.

Whether prestige and orderliness of work history separately promote high general morale is questionable. Semi-skilled retirees were as likely to have high general morale as middle-status retirees with disorderly work histories. Similarly, the percentage who felt little job deprivation is virtually the same among orderly middle-status retirees as among upper-white-collar retirees.

INVOLVEMENT, CHANGES IN INVOLVEMENT, AND SELF-EVALUATION IN RETIREMENT

Our third set of hypotheses predicts that the relation of occupational status and orderliness of work history to self-evaluation results from the differentials in involvement associated with prestige and orderliness. We have found that status and orderliness are associated with involvement and that orderliness is inversely associated with loss of involvement, though status is not. We have also found that favorable self-evaluation varies directly with status and orderliness of work history. This section of the chapter seeks to ascertain whether the relation of status and orderliness to self-evaluation holds when level of involvement and loss of involvement are controlled. This hypothesis may indicate whether the relations are rooted in status and orderliness apart from level and stability of involvement. (Loss of involvement may be inversely related to self-evaluation, despite the fact that we did not find it related to prestige; therefore it seemed advisable to control this variable.)

Table 3 presents the percentage of retirees who felt little job deprivation, cross-classified by level of involvement, loss of involvement, and occupational status. In support of the hypothesis, level of involvement shows a fairly consistent inverse relationship to job deprivation. Among middle-status and semi-skilled retirees (for whom there are sufficient cases to make the comparison), whether

Table 3. Percentage of Retirees with Low Job Deprivation by Level of Involvement, Constancy of Involvement, and Occupational Status.

	Percentage with low job deprivation	
Occupational status and level of involvement	Involvement unchanged	Involvement lost
Upper-white-collar		
High involvement	68.8 (16)	76.9 (26)
Low involvement	———	———
Middle-status		
High involvement	72.5 (40)	72.2 (18)
Low involvement	57.7 (26)	52.4 (21)
Semi-skilled		
High involvement	57.1 (14)	33.3 (12)
Low involvement	27.3 (22)	50.0 (26)

there had been a loss of pre-retirement involvement or not, those with high involvement felt less job deprivation than those with low involvement, with one exception. The relation is reversed among semi-skilled retirees who had lost pre-retirement involvement. On the other hand, the data in Table 3 show no consistent relation of loss of pre-retirement involvement to job deprivation. Out of five comparisons, only in two did we find any differences in the direction we hypothesized.

Table 3 shows also that with level and loss of involvement controlled, the relation of status to job deprivation remains when comparing middle-status and semi-skilled retirees—contrary to our third and fourth hypotheses—though in one of the four comparisons the difference is slight. Here, as in Table 2 on the relation of status to job deprivation, little difference exists in the feeling of job deprivation between middle-status and upper-white-collar retirees. (Of the two comparisons, one difference is in the hypothesized direction, the other is reversed, and both differences are small.)

Because our small sample does not permit the necessary cross-tabulations, we were unable to control simultaneously level and loss of involvement in testing the hypothesis that these variables explain the relation of orderliness to self-evaluation. We applied one control at a time and found that high involvement sharply reduces job deprivation among retirees with disorderly work histories, though it has little effect on those with orderly work histories. (Among middle-status retirees with orderly work histories, 69.6 per cent of those with low involvement felt little job deprivation; this compared with 75.0 per cent of those with high involvement. But among the retirees with disorderly work histories, 38.5 per cent with low involvement felt little job deprivation, compared with 66.7 per cent with high involvement.)

Loss of involvement, however, shows no consistent relation to job deprivation, despite the fact that it is related to orderliness; orderliness, however, is related to job deprivation. Among retirees with orderly work histories, 73.2 per cent of the non-losers and 72.7 per cent of the losers felt little job deprivation. Among those with disorderly work histories, 56.0 per cent of the non-losers and 50.0 per cent of the losers felt little job deprivation. The relation of orderliness of job deprivation remains, however, if involvement is low; high involvement reduces the effect.

These data suggest that whatever effects the level of involvement has on feelings of job deprivation, these feelings operate mainly *within* a prestige level, and more so within the middle-status than the semi-skilled retirees. The relation of occupational status to job deprivation does not appear to have resulted from level of involvement, since controlling the level of involvement does not materially alter the pattern of status group differences in the feeling of job deprivation. However, the relation of orderliness to job deprivation does appear to have been influenced by involvement, since high involvement reduces the differences in the work-history groups.

The relation of level of involvement to job deprivation among semi-skilled workers is inconsistent. Furthermore, semi-skilled retirees were much more likely than retirees with higher status to miss their work, despite their having been less committed to it and its having had less intrinsic appeal to them.[28] Thus, the sources of the feeling of job deprivation among semi-skilled retirees appear to differ from those underlying job deprivation among middle-status retirees. Wayne E. Thompson and Gordon F. Streib found that financial need was associated with job deprivation.[29] Our findings, coupled with the findings of Thompson and Streib, suggest that a crucial factor affecting job deprivation among semi-skilled retirees may be financial deprivation, while social involvement seems to be the cause among middle-status retirees whose financial situation tends to be better. To test this explanation, income deprivation in retirement is defined as a retirement income less than 50 per cent of one's pre-retirement income. Table 4, which presents the percentage of retired persons who felt little job deprivation, cross-classified by level of involvement, status, and deprivation of retirement income, shows again that involvement affects middle-status and semi-skilled retirees differently. Among semi-skilled retirees, level of involvement shows no effect on job deprivation with income controlled; but income deprivation consistently enhances job deprivation. However, among middle-status workers, if retirement income was less than 50 per cent of the income enjoyed

28. See pp. 84-89 below for data on the relation of work commitment to job deprivation.
29. "Situational Determinants: Health and Economic Deprivation in Retirement," *Journal of Social Issues,* **14** (1958), 25-37. We also find that income deprivation affects job deprivation for semi-skilled retirees; see p. 71.

Table 4. Percentage of Retirees with Low Job Deprivation by Income Deprivation,[a] Level of Involvement, and Occupational Status.

Occupational status and involvement	Percentage with low job deprivation	
	Deprived financially	Not deprived financially
Upper-white-collar		
High involvement	——	72.2 (18)
Low involvement	——	——
Middle-status		
High involvement	61.9 (21)	76.3 (38)
Low involvement	35.7 (28)	80.0 (20)
Semi-skilled		
High involvement	31.3 (16)	50.0 (8)
Low involvement	36.1 (36)	45.5 (11)

[a]Income deprivation is defined as the retiree's current income expressed as a percentage of his pre-retirement income. If the figure is less than 50 per cent, the person is called deprived; if it is 50 per cent or more, not deprived. We were unable to get information on the income of large numbers of upper-white-collar retirees.

while working, high involvement lessened job deprivation while not completely removing the effect of reduction in income. On the other hand, little income reduction in retirement removes the effect of involvement on job deprivation among the middle-status retirees. The relation of status to job deprivation seen above tended to hold. (In two of five comparisons the prestige differences are reversed, though small; these are the same groups in which status showed little effect in Table 3.)

In summary, reduction in income appears to be a more important influence than level of involvement on job deprivation among semi-skilled retirees. But involvement appears as influential as income in reducing job deprivation among middle-status workers. (Of course, their incomes are likely to be higher than the incomes of semi-skilled retirees.)

Our other measure of self-evaluation—morale—appears unrelated to level or loss of involvement. Table 5 shows no consistent relation in any of the status groups between morale and either level or loss of involvement. The status differences found when level of involvement and loss of involvement are uncontrolled generally continue to exist, though they are reduced in one comparison and removed in another.

Similarly, when orderliness of work history is controlled, neither

Table 5. Percentage of Retirees with High Morale by Constancy of Involvement, Level of Involvement, and Occupational Status.

Occupational status and level of involvement	Percentage with high morale	
	Involvement unchanged	Involvement lost
Upper-white-collar		
High involvement	72.2 (18)	71.0 (31)
Low involvement		
Middle-status		
High involvement	57.5 (40)	44.4 (18)
Low involvement	50.0 (24)	60.0 (20)
Semi-skilled		
High involvement	53.3 (15)	54.6 (11)
Low involvement	38.1 (21)	43.5 (23)

level of involvement nor loss of involvement shows a consistent relation to morale. Among workers with orderly work histories, those with low involvement had higher morale than those with high involvement (68.2 per cent vs. 53.9 per cent). A different story obtained among those with disorderly work histories where high involvement was associated with high morale (50.0 per cent), while retirees with low involvement displayed lower morale (37.5 per cent). Among those with orderly work histories who had lost involvement, 63.6 per cent had high morale compared with 57.5 per cent of the non-losers. But among workers with disorderly work histories, the non-losers had higher morale than the losers (50.0 per cent vs. 41.2 per cent). On the other hand, the relation of orderliness to morale tended to hold when level and loss of involvement were controlled, though the differences were negligible if there was high involvement (53.9 per cent vs. 50.0 per cent) and if involvement was unchanged (57.5 per cent vs. 50.0 per cent).

Thus, the relation of status and orderliness to self-evaluation, as measured by feelings of job deprivation and general morale, does not appear to be explained by differences in level or loss of involvement associated with status or orderliness.

CONCLUSION

Much of the gerontological literature has implied that retirement reduces involvement in society by removing the strong structural support for involvement which work provides.[30] Yet studies have shown sizable variations in participation among older as among younger people. Thus, we hypothesized that the variables of occupational status and orderliness of work history, which are correlated with participation in earlier stages of the life cycle, help to explain variations in involvement among retired workers. We further wanted to know whether self-evaluation in retirement, as during work, is associated with status and orderliness, and whether such an association holds when level and loss of pre-retirement involvement are controlled.

We have found that status and orderliness are positively related to high involvement in retirement, and that orderliness of work history—though not status—reduces the likelihood that pre-retirement involvement will be lost. We further found that status and orderliness are inversely related to feelings of job deprivation and directly related to morale, and that these relations tend to persist when level and loss of involvement are controlled. Loss of pre-retirement involvement, as we have measured it, is not related to self-evaluation. However, level of involvement does lessen feelings of job deprivation within the middle stratum, though not within the semi-skilled stratum. (We did not have sufficient variability within the upper-white-collar stratum to make the analysis.)

Juxtaposing our findings with those of Thompson and Streib, we formulated and found support for the hypothesis that sources of job deprivation differ by strata. Within the semi-skilled stratum they involve a sharp drop in income, but among middle-status retirees involvement is as important as a high ratio of post-retirement to pre-retirement income in lessening job deprivation.

Our findings thus suggest that the influence of work is not completely lost with retirement but that many patterns of social involvement supported by work persist, reflecting the same effect of occupational status and orderliness of work history evidenced in earlier life stages by other studies. This is not to imply that retirement does not affect the life patterns of an individual; it does, and we found more loss of pre-retirement involvement by upper-white-collar retirees than by other status groups because less of their pre-retirement involvement could be meaningfully maintained outside

30. Besides withdrawal of structural support, there may be voluntary withdrawal from society. See Elaine Cumming and William E. Henry, *Growing Old* (New York: Basic Books, 1961). This aspect will be discussed in chapters 18 and 19 below.

the work setting. (How loss of work setting affects job deprivation in retirement will be examined in Chapter 6.) It does appear, however, that retirement did not destroy the supports of occupational status and orderliness of work history in maintaining involvement and favorable self-evaluations in retirement. Yet our data indicate that, regardless of status, if these social involvements have not been built up before retirement, they are unlikely to be established in retirement. Similarly, those individuals whose work had not provided these supports—semi-skilled and disorderly middle-status retirees—had less involvement and less favorable self-evaluations in retirement. It is not retirement per se which is responsible for their lack of self-anchorage, but their work histories which had not allowed them to develop ties with society. Support from other sources is needed if these individuals are to enjoy favorable self-evaluations. Our data indicated that one such support is financial aid.

The most general conclusion we draw from our findings is that any study of retirement should take into account status of the occupation from which an individual retires. The influence of occupational status appears as pervasive in retirement as before retirement. In studying the influence of specific aspects of work or work-connected social patterns on retirement, each stratum should be studied separately. In fact, a given variable may explain a given retirement behavior in one stratum but not in others. In the chapters on work and retirement which follow, occupational status will therefore be controlled. Our findings suggest that orderliness of work history should also be controlled, but our small sample size does not permit the necessary cross-tabulations within the middle stratum whose respondents vary in this respect.

Ida Harper Simpson

Kurt W. Back

John C. McKinney

4. ORIENTATION TOWARD WORK AND RETIREMENT, AND SELF-EVALUATION IN RETIREMENT

Wayne E. Thompson has shown that the adjustment of persons to retirement is foreshadowed by the orientations they hold toward retirement while they are still at work.[1] Several interpretations have been advanced to explain how individuals feel about retirement. These include the idea that orientations toward retirement reflect orientations toward work, that they reflect achievement of ambitions, and that they are influenced by retirement income.[2] The first two explanations view orientations toward retirement as a derivative of one's attitude toward work. In the first case, if one is committed to his work he will be unfavorably disposed toward retirement; in the second case, if personal ambitions have not been achieved through work, one will wish to continue working rather than retire in order to try to achieve his ambitions. The third explanation—that retirement income influences orientations toward retirement—specifies a condition of the retirement situation, rather than a condition of the work situation, as underlying one's attitude toward retirement.

Effects of work orientations on subsequent attitudes toward retirement were found by Eugene A. Friedmann and Robert J. Havighurst

1. "Pre-Retirement Anticipation and Adjustment in Retirement," *Journal of Social Issues,* **14** (1958), 35-45.
2. For a discussion and a review of pertinent literature on these explanations, see Margaret S. Gordon, "Work and Patterns of Retirement," in Robert W. Kleemeier (ed.), *Aging and Leisure* (New York: Oxford University Press, 1961), pp. 28-31.

in their study of the meaning of work and retirement in different
occupations.[3] They found that workers who assigned instrinsic value
and meaning to their occupations preferred to continue working
rather than retire more than those who worked for extrinsic benefits. They qualify their explanation with the condition of an "adequate" retirement income for those whose job satisfactions were
extrinsic. Since commitment to work and attribution of intrinsic
value to it vary directly with occupational status,[4] we would expect
an increasingly favorable orientation to retirement as occupational
status decreases. Such a relation, however, has not been supported by
some research. In studying workers in an oil company, Ernest W.
Burgess and associates found that manual workers had slightly less
favorable attitudes toward retirement than workers with higher
status.[5]

The explanation that orientations toward retirement grow out
of the achievement (or lack of achievement) of one's ambitions is
suggested by the research of Edrita G. Fried.[6] She claims that the
unsuccessful person tenaciously rejects retirement in order to try
to fulfil aspirations. She does not explicitly claim that the successful
accept retirement; instead, she says "those who are convinced of
their value both as individuals and as older persons experience their
task as completed and find retirement more easily acceptable."[7]

The explanation that orientations toward retirement are influenced by retirement income is suggested by data of Wayne E.
Thompson and Gordon F. Streib. As we have indicated above,
Friedmann and Havighurst cite it as a condition for their explanation. Thompson and Streib do not concern themselves with influences on pre-retirement attitude toward retirement; however, in

3. *The Meaning of Work and Retirement* (Chicago: University of Chicago Press,
1954), pp. 170-186.

4. Robert Blauner, "Occupational Differences in Work Satisfactions," in Walter
Galenson and Seymour Martin Lipset (eds.), *Labor and Trade Unionism: An Inter-
disciplinary Reader* (New York: John Wiley & Sons, 1960), pp. 339-360; Nancy C.
Morse and Robert S. Weiss, "The Function and Meaning of Work and the Job,"
American Sociological Review, **29** (April, 1955), 191-198.

5. Burgess, Leonard G. Corey, Peter C. Pineo, and Richard T. Thornbury, "Occupational Difference in Attitudes toward Aging and Retirement," *Journal of Gerontology,* **13** (April, 1958), 203-206. For a summary of much literature bearing on
the hypothesis, see Wilma Donahue, Harold L. Orbach, and Otto Pollak, "Retirement: The Emerging Social Pattern," in Clark Tibbitts (ed.), *Handbook of Social
Gerontology: Societal Aspects of Aging* (Chicago: University of Chicago Press, 1960),
pp. 375-386.

6. "Attitudes of the Older Population Groups Toward Activity and Inactivity,"
Journal of Gerontology, **4** (February, 1949), 141-151.

7. *Ibid.,* p. 148.

examining the simultaneous influence of pre-retirement attitude and economic deprivation in retirement upon satisfaction with retirement, they present data which show a positive relation between favorable pre-retirement attitude toward retirement and lack of economic deprivation.[8] Jacob Tuckman and Irving Lorge found many older workers who were favorably disposed toward retirement but unable to retire because of limited finances.[9]

The first explanation, based on work commitment, would suggest a negative relation between occupational status and favorable retirement orientation, as we have noted above. The second and third explanations, based respectively on achievement of ambitions and on income, would suggest the opposite relation of occupational status to retirement orientation. If each explanation proves to have some validity, the relation of occupational level to retirement orientation may be complex, and the effects of the variables involved in the three explanations may not be the same among workers in all occupational levels. Therefore, we shall examine influences on occupational orientation within separate occupational levels.

The explanations above imply that these factors which influence workers' orientations also have direct effects on retirement behavior.[10] Of the retired workers whom they studied, Friedmann and Havighurst found that those who had attributed intrinsic meaning to their work were more dissatisfied in retirement than those whose work satisfaction had been extrinsic.[11] In addition, the effect of orientations toward retirement upon retirement behavior may differ according to the factors influencing the orientation. After examining explanations of orientations toward retirement, we will see if the source of the orientation makes any difference in its effect upon self-evaluation in retirement. (Self-evaluation will be measured by a job deprivation scale and a general morale scale discussed above, pages 52-53.)

8. "Situational Determinants: Health and Economic Deprivation in Retirement," *Journal of Social Issues*, **14** (1958), 25-34. In Table 8 they give marginals for their sample who are willing to retire and who are reluctant to retire, classified by economic deprivation. Of a total of 325 who were not deprived, 69.5 per cent were willing to retire; but of a total of 152 who were deprived, only 48 per cent were willing to retire.

9. *Retirement and the Industrial Worker* (New York: Columbia University, Teachers College, Bureau of Publications, 1953).

10. In "Pre-Retirement Anticipation and Adjustment in Retirement," Thompson found that pre-retirement attitude toward retirement and preconception of retirement separately influenced adjustment in retirement.

11. *Meaning of Work and Retirement*.

MEASURES OF VARIABLES

Orientations toward retirement are determined from an interview question which asked whether the worker looked forward to retirement or not.[12] Saying that they had looked forward to retirement were 49.4 per cent of the upper-white-collar retirees, 67.5 per cent of the retirees of the middle stratum, and 56.2 per cent of the semi-skilled retirees. Among the pre-retired, 50.0 per cent of the upper-white-collar workers looked forward to retirement, along with 86.8 per cent of the middle stratum and 69.2 per cent of the semi-skilled. Middle-status workers were thus the most likely to look forward to retirement and upper-white-collar workers the least likely.

Orientations toward work are determined by two measures. One is a Guttman-type scale, which measures work commitment. It consists of five items dichotomously scored and has a reproducibility coefficient of .91.[13] The scale scores ranged from zero through five and were grouped into high and low categories: low scores, zero through two, falling at or below the median; and high scores, three through five, above the median. Among retirees, 65.1 per cent of the upper-white-collar workers had been highly committed to their work, together with 35.7 per cent of the middle stratum and 24.7 per cent of the semi-skilled. Among the pre-retirees, 57.6 per cent of the upper-white-collar segment were highly committed, as were 40.6 per cent of the middle level and 29.4 per cent of the semi-skilled.[14]

The other measure of orientations toward work is based on a

12. Retired workers were asked to think back to the time before they retired. They were then asked, "Did you look forward to retirement or not? And why?"

13. The items for the scale were constructed by Richard L. Simpson. Arranged in order from low to high intrinsic work value, the five items are:

Even if I had had an entirely different job, I would have liked to do the same kind of work I used to do sometimes, just for fun. (strongly agree, agree)

If I had inherited a million dollars, I would still have wanted to keep on doing the work I did. (strongly agree, agree)

I wouldn't have taken a better paying job if it had meant I would have had to do work different from what I did. (strongly agree, agree)

Nobody would have done the kind of work I did, if he didn't have to. (strongly disagree)

Toward the end of the day, it often seemed as if quitting time would never come. (strongly disagree)

The questions were stated in the present tense for pre-retired workers.

14. The pattern we find on the relation of work commitment to occupational prestige corresponds to that found by Morse and Weiss, "Function and Meaning of Work and Job."

question which listed different descriptions of work and asked the retiree to think back to the time he had been working and indicate which of the descriptions he considered the most important in determining how satisfied he had been with his work. The descriptions were grouped into two categories, ones involving intrinsic aspects of work and ones involving extrinsic aspects.[15] For retirees, intrinsic aspects of their job were the most satisfying for 77.4 per cent of the upper-white-collar workers, 45.1 per cent of the middle stratum, and 31.0 per cent of the semi-skilled; and for pre-retirees, 74.4 per cent of the upper-white-collar, 48.6 per cent of the middle stratum, and 41.7 per cent of the semi-skilled. Essentially the same pattern is obtained when work orientations are described in terms of a scale of work commitment and when the individual lists the most important aspect of his job satisfaction. Most upper-white-collar workers were highly committed to their work and found satisfaction in it, but less than one-half of the middle-status workers, and still fewer semi-skilled workers, derived such meaning from their work.

ORIENTATION TOWARD WORK AND RETIREMENT

Three explanations of orientations toward retirement will be examined in the following few pages. The first is that they express one's orientation toward work: if one is committed to his work, he will not be favorably disposed toward retirement. Table 1 presents the percentage of retired and pre-retired workers, cross-classi-

15. Pre-retirees were asked the same question, but it was stated in the present tense. Descriptions classified as intrinsic include:

My job involved interesting kinds of tasks.
My job gave me a chance to do the things I am best at.
In my job I worked mainly with people rather than things.
In my job I was able to experiment with doing things in new ways.
My job left me fairly free of supervision, let me be independent.
The work I did in my job involved figuring things out much of the time.
My work day involved mainly familiar things.
In my job I worked mainly with things.
The work I did in my job involved doing new things quite frequently.

Descriptions classified as extrinsic include:

My job was highly regarded by others.
My job carried good pay.
My job left me a good deal of time to spend with my family.
My job was stable and secure.
My fellow workers liked me.
My job provided for regular advancements.
My family approved highly of the work I did.

Table 1. Percentage of Retired and Pre-Retired Workers Who Looked Forward to Retirement by Occupational Status and Work Commitment.

Occupational status and work commitment	Percentage who looked forward to retirement	
	Retirees	Pre-Retirees
Upper-white-collar level		
High commitment	42.9 (35)	44.2 (43)
Low commitment	75.0 (16)	61.5 (26)
Middle-status level		
High commitment	64.9 (37)	84.6 (13)
Low commitment	75.4 (65)	89.5 (19)
Semi-skilled level		
High commitment	65.2 (23)	80.0 (10)
Low commitment	51.6 (64)	70.8 (24)

fied by status level and commitment to work, who said they looked forward to retirement. As the explanation would predict, an inverse relationship is evident among retired and pre-retired upper-white-collar and retired middle-status workers, although the difference is small in the latter case. Among the semi-skilled, both working and retired, a positive relation exists. And among the pre-retired middle-status workers the two are unrelated.

The second measure of work orientations, which is based on the main source of satisfaction with one's job, fails also to show

Table 2. Percentage of Retired and Pre-Retired Workers Who Looked Forward to Retirement by Occupational Status and Source of Job Satisfaction.

Occupational status and source of job satisfaction	Percentage who looked forward to retirement	
	Retirees	Pre-Retirees
Upper-white-collar		
Intrinsic satisfaction	52.1 (48)	48.3 (58)
Extrinsic satisfaction	70.0 (10)	83.3 (12)
Middle-status		
Intrinsic satisfaction	69.6 (46)	82.4 (17)
Extrinsic satisfaction	69.6 (56)	94.4 (18)
Semi-skilled		
Intrinsic satisfaction	53.9 (26)	73.3 (15)
Extrinsic satisfaction	58.6 (58)	71.4 (21)

a systematic relationship between work orientations and orientations toward retirement (see Table 2). The predicted inverse relation obtains among retired and pre-retired upper-white-collar workers, but the two are unrelated among middle-status and semi-skilled retired and pre-retired workers. Given the lack of consistent patterns among the middle and semi-skilled levels for the two measures, it appears that source of work satisfaction has little bearing on orientations toward retirement, other than among upper-white-collar workers.

It may be that among semi-skilled and middle-status workers financial worries or some other limiting conditions obscure the relation of work commitment to orientations toward retirement, as Friedmann and Havighurst cautioned. Because of small cell frequencies we will not be able to control income or other external impingements to see if the relation has been obscured. Nevertheless, as we shall see in Table 4, retirement income is related to anticipation of retirement among the semi-skilled retirees but has little influence on the orientations of middle-status retirees.

The second explanation of orientations toward retirement views them as arising out of achievement of ambitions: individuals who have not achieved ambitions will have looked with disfavor upon retirement, whereas those who have achieved ambitions will have looked favorably upon retirement.[16] Table 3 presents the percentage of retired and pre-retired workers, cross-classified by status level and achievement, who looked forward to retirement; it shows that the predicted relation obtains only among retired and pre-retired upper-white-collar workers. Among the other groupings, achievement fails to show an effect on orientations toward retirement. (The differences are in the expected direction, though small in one case and negligible in the other two.) Thus again it appears that the influence of orientations toward work upon attitudes toward retirement is largely restricted to the upper occupational stratum.

The third explanation involves retirement income. This is measured in terms of percentage of income deprivation, rather than

16. Respondents were asked, "In looking back over your life as a worker, would you say you have been able to achieve the things from life you wanted?" They indicated their response by choosing from among five response categories: I have been able to achieve most of the things, some of the things, a few of the things, none of the things, and I did not want anything from life. Those who said they had been able to achieve most things were classified in the high achievement category and the others in the low achievement category.

Table 3. Percentage of Retired and Pre-Retired Workers Who Looked
Forward to Retirement by Occupational Status and Achievement
of Ambition.

Occupational status and achievement of ambition	Percentage who looked forward to retirement	
	Retirees	Pre-Retirees
Upper-white-collar		
High achievement	53.6 (56)	56.1 (57)
Low achievement	35.0 (20)	31.8 (22)
Middle-status		
High achievement	68.1 (72)	90.0 (20)
Low achievement	66.7 (51)	83.3 (18)
Semi-skilled		
High achievement	60.0 (50)	73.3 (15)
Low achievement	51.9 (54)	66.7 (24)

Table 4. Percentage of Retired Workers Who Looked Forward to Retirement by Occupational Status and Income Deprivation in Retirement.[a]

Occupational status	Percentage who had looked forward to retirement	
	Not deprived financially	Deprived financially
Upper-white-collar	55.6 (27)	——
Middle-status	72.1 (61)	68.4 (57)
Semi-skilled	66.7 (24)	51.4 (70)

[a]Income deprivation is defined as the retiree's current income expressed as a percentage of his pre-retirement income. If the figure is less than 50 per cent, the person is called
deprived; if it is 50 per cent or more, not deprived. We were unable to get information
on the income of large numbers of upper-white-collar retirees.

amount of income, and is based on the ratio of post-retirement income to pre-retirement income. (We assume workers knew what
their retirement income would be before retiring.) Thompson and
Streib have shown that within a short time after retirement retirees
tended to work out some adjustment to a reduction in income.[17]
Seemingly, a measure of percentage of income deprivation would give
a more reliable picture of the stresses occasioned by reduced income
than one based solely on amount of income. One possible exception
involves lowest income workers, who are concentrated among the
semi-skilled. Workers were defined as "deprived" if their retirement

17. Thompson and Streib, "Situational Determinants."

income was less than 50 per cent of their pre-retirement income. Table 4 presents the percentage of retired workers who had looked forward to retirement, cross-classified by status level and income deprivation in retirement. Only among semi-skilled retirees is deprivation of income related to orientations toward retirement. It may be that a sharp drop in income was expected by workers of higher prestige, yet it failed to influence their orientations since their retirement income would be adequate to meet needs despite anticipated accommodations to a loss of income. But among semi-skilled workers a reduction of 50 per cent or more in income during retirement may make the meeting of even minimal needs difficult or impossible.

We have examined three explanations of pre-retirement orientations toward retirement, but we have failed to find systematic support within all prestige groupings for any of them. A summary of findings is given in Table 5. Among upper-white-collar workers, orientations toward retirement appear to have been influenced more by orientations toward work than by income loss. Each of the three measures of work orientations—work commitment, source of work satisfaction, and achievement of ambitions, which for them were mainly occupational achievements—showed that those who held work-centered orientations were less likely to have looked forward to retirement than those who did not. However, many who held work-centered orientations also looked forward to retirement, indicating that other influences were present and that orientations to-

Table 5. Summary of Findings on Influences upon Pre-Retirement Orientation to Retirement Within Occupational Groups.

Independent variable	Table number	Upper-white-collar		Middle-stratum		Semi-skilled	
		Retired	Pre-Retired	Retired	Pre-Retired	Retired	Pre-Retired
Work commitment	1	+	+	+	o	−	−
Source of job satisfaction	2	+	+	o	o	o	o
Achievement of ambitions	3	+	+	o	o	o	o
Income deprivation	4	*		+		+	

Note: + signifies positive relation; − signifies a negative relation; the symbol o means the findings were not related; and * means there were not enough cases to analyze.

ward retirement are not a simple reaction to orientations toward work.

Among semi-skilled workers, financial considerations appear to have influenced orientations; those whose incomes were markedly lower in retirement than while employed tended not to have looked forward to retirement. Undoubtedly they were worried about finances. The finding that semi-skilled workers with high work commitment were more likely to have looked forward to retirement than the uncommitted may be related to the findings on income deprivation. Since high work commitment is relatively infrequent among semi-skilled workers, those with high work commitment are likely to have been long-time employees of their companies who through seniority enjoyed higher wages and thus built up bigger pensions and social security benefits.

Among middle-status workers, none of the explanations we have examined accounts for much of the variability within the grouping. These workers more than any others looked forward to retirement; yet they were the most variable in their orientations toward work and in reduction of income in retirement. This variability suggests that the orientations of middle-status workers may be more affected by idiosyncratic, personal factors than by work-related or income factors. While they are intermediate in both respects, they resembled the semi-skilled workers in lack of work commitment and the upper-white-collar workers in lack of income loss. Without the work commitment that makes the upper-white-collar group reluctant to retire or the financial worries that make the semi-skilled segment fear retirement, they are more favorably disposed to retirement than either of these groups.

ORIENTATIONS TOWARD WORK AND RETIREMENT AND SELF-EVALUATION IN RETIREMENT

As indicated above, in a study of pre-retirement anticipation Thompson found that pre-retirement attitude (what we are calling orientations) affects adjustment in retirement, as measured by length of time necessary to get used to retirement, difficulty in keeping busy, and dissatisfaction with retirement.[18] Here we shall see if pre-retirement orientations toward retirement affect self-evaluation in

18. Thompson, "Pre-Retirement Anticipation and Adjustment in Retirement."

Table 6. Orientation Toward Retirement and Self-Evaluation in Retirement.

Occupational status and orientation toward retirement	Percentage with low job deprivation	Percentage with high morale
Upper-white-collar		
Favorable orientation	84.9 (33)	68.6 (35)
Unfavorable orientation	54.6 (22)	70.4 (27)
Middle-status		
Favorable orientation	72.8 (81)	54.0 (76)
Unfavorable orientation	38.7 (31)	48.4 (31)
Semi-skilled		
Favorable orientation	56.9 (51)	48.9 (47)
Unfavorable orientation	21.1 (38)	34.2 (38)

retirement as indexed by job-deprivation and general morale. Our measure of job deprivation is essentially the same as Thompson's measure of dissatisfaction with retirement. The analysis for this section is limited to retirees.

Table 6 presents the percentage of retirees with low job deprivation and with high morale, cross-classified by status level and orientations toward retirement. It shows, as Thompson found, that job deprivation is inversely related to pre-retirement orientations toward retirement. But it does not show a consistent relation between pre-retirement orientations and morale in retirement. A positive relation between pre-retirement orientations toward retirement and current morale is evident among semi-skilled retirees, but among upper-white-collar workers and middle-status workers the two appear unrelated. As noted in an earlier chapter, the morale scale focuses on feelings of worthwhileness. The relation of orientations toward retirement to morale among semi-skilled retirees may mean that those who already had had higher morale before they retired had tended to look forward to retirement, rather than that these anticipatory orientations had bolstered morale once retirement occurred.

Let us now see if the influences on the orientations toward retirement—separate from the orientations themselves—affect self-evaluation. As we have seen, factors influencing orientations differ by occupational status, and for each influencing factor many exceptions occur. Since orientations are not systematically related to morale, our examination will be limited to job deprivation. Table

Table 7. Percentage of Retirees Who Felt Little Job Deprivation by Occupational Status, Pre-Retirement Orientation Toward Retirement, and Work Commitment.

	Percentage who felt little job deprivation	
Occupational status and work commitment	Favorable orientation toward retirement	Unfavorable orientation toward retirement
Upper-white-collar		
High commitment	80.0 (15)	47.1 (17)
Low commitment	91.7 (12)	——
Middle-status		
High commitment	66.7 (24)	46.2 (13)
Low commitment	79.6 (49)	33.3 (15)
Semi-skilled		
High commitment	66.7 (15)	——
Low commitment	53.1 (32)	27.6 (29)

7 presents the percentage of retirees who felt little job deprivation, cross-classified by orientation toward retirement, occupational status, and work commitment. It shows that work commitment is not related in the manner expected when orientations are controlled. If orientation toward retirement had been favorable, upper-white-collar and middle-status retirees with low work commitment more

Table 8. Percentage of Retirees Who Felt Little Job Deprivation by Occupational Status, Pre-Retirement Orientation Toward Retirement, and Source of Job Satisfaction.

	Percentage who felt little job deprivation	
Occupational status and source of job satisfaction	Favorable orientation toward retirement	Unfavorable orientation toward retirement
Upper-white-collar		
Intrinsic satisfaction	82.6 (23)	47.1 (17)
Extrinsic satisfaction	——	——
Middle-status		
Intrinsic satisfaction	71.9 (32)	57.1 (14)
Extrinsic satisfaction	81.6 (38)	20.0 (15)
Semi-skilled		
Intrinsic satisfaction	66.7 (12)	30.0 (10)
Extrinsic satisfaction	46.9 (32)	18.2 (22)

than those with high work commitment felt little job deprivation. Among semi-skilled retirees, the relation is reversed. But if orientation toward retirement had been unfavorable, those with high work commitment were less likely than those with low work commitment to feel little job deprivation. Essentially the same relations exist for source of job satisfaction (see Table 8). If orientation toward retirement had been favorable, those whose work satisfaction had been extrinsic felt slightly less job deprivation than those whose work satisfaction had been intrinsic. However, if orientation toward retirement had been unfavorable, those whose work satisfactions had been intrinsic were considerably more likely than those whose work satisfactions had been extrinsic to feel little job deprivation. These reversals probably mean that those workers who had not looked forward to retirement, yet who had not been committed to their work or whose work satisfaction had been extrinsic, missed their work in retirement for financial and/or sociable reasons. Actual income deprivation in retirement is related to job deprivation, although we do not know if workers included in these reversed relations experienced income deprivation as we have measured it.

The other influences on orientations—achievement of ambitions and income deprivation—are related to job deprivation in the expected manner when orientation toward retirement is controlled.

Table 9. Percentage of Retirees Who Felt Little Job Deprivation by Occupational Status, Pre-Retirement Orientation Toward Retirement, and Achievement of Ambitions.

	Percentage who felt little job deprivation	
Occupational status and achievement of ambitions	Favorable orientation toward retirement	Unfavorable orientation toward retirement
Upper-white-collar		
High achievement	81.5 (27)	53.3 (15)
Low achievement	——	——
Middle-status		
High achievement	81.3 (48)	45.0 (20)
Low achievement	60.6 (33)	27.3 (11)
Semi-skilled		
High achievement	66.7 (27)	29.4 (17)
Low achievement	45.8 (24)	14.3 (21)

Table 10. Percentage of Retirees Who Felt Little Job Deprivation by Occupational Status, Pre-Retirement Orientation Toward Retirement, and Income Deprivation in Retirement.

Occupational status and income deprivation	Percentage who felt little job deprivation	
	Favorable orientation toward retirement	Unfavorable orientation toward retirement
Upper-white-collar		
Not deprived	78.6 (14)	——
Deprived	——	——
Middle-status		
Not deprived	86.4 (44)	50.0 (14)
Deprived	56.8 (37)	21.4 (14)
Semi-skilled		
Not deprived	64.3 (14)	——
Deprived	53.3 (30)	17.2 (29)

Retirees who had achieved most of their ambitions were likely to feel less job deprivation than those who had not (see Table 9). Retirees whose retirement incomes were at least 50 per cent of their work incomes were likely to feel less job deprivation than those with lower retirement incomes (see Table 10). A summary of the above findings on the relation of different influences to job depriva-

Table 11. Summary of Findings on Influences Upon Job Deprivation in Retirement Cross-Classified by Orientation Toward Retirement for Each Occupational Group.[a]

Independent variable	Table number	Middle-status		Semi-skilled	
		Favorable	Unfavorable	Favorable	Unfavorable
Work commitment	6	+	–	–	b
Source of job satisfaction	7	+	–	–	–
Achievement of ambitions	8	+	+	+	+
Income deprivation	9	+	+	+	b

[a]Upper-white-collar retirees were omitted from this summary because they agreed so much on measures for each variable that no breakdown was possible (See Tables 6-9). (Orientation toward retirement consistently predicts job deprivation when each of the above influences is controlled.)
[b]An insufficient number of cases to analyze.

tion, cross-classified by occupational status and orientation to retirement, is presented in Table 11. These findings should be viewed with caution, since we do not have sufficient cases to make all the necessary comparisons. (The comparisons that cannot be made are different, depending on which variable is being controlled.)

The finding in Table 5 that orientation to retirement predicts job deprivation is consistently supported when each of the influences discussed above is controlled. (Compare the second and third columns in Tables 7-10.) In fact, the differences between the groupings based on orientation toward retirement are larger than between the groupings based on any one influence. These findings suggest that many factors may enter into the shaping of an orientation toward retirement. In turn, the orientation is more important in feelings of job deprivation than any one influencing factor.

SUMMARY

This chapter has examined explanations of pre-retirement orientations toward retirement. It has found that orientations toward work were the main influence on pre-retirement orientations to retirement among upper-white-collar workers, that income deprivation in retirement was the main influence on semi-skilled workers, and that none of the explanations accounted for much variability within the middle stratum. Despite differences in influences on pre-retirement orientations in different prestige groupings, we found, as did Thompson, that pre-retirement orientation consistently predicted feelings of job deprivation in retirement, although it did not predict morale. We further found that achievement of ambitions and income deprivation were related to job deprivation when pre-retirement orientations were controlled. However, work commitment and source of work satisfaction were related in the manner expected only if orientation toward retirement was favorable. No influence on pre-retirement orientation toward retirement appeared to affect job deprivation as much as the orientation itself, which probably reflects the many influences which shape an orientation.

Ida Harper Simpson
Kurt W. Back
John C. McKinney

5. EXPOSURE TO INFORMATION ON, PREPARATION FOR, AND SELF-EVALUATION IN RETIREMENT

In contrast to other phases of the life cycle, retirement lacks institutionalized roles. It is characterized by much role uncertainty, with the individual depending on his own resources to find substitutes for his work role. A way for the individual to reduce this role uncertainty might be through gathering information on retirement in order to learn what to expect.[1] This chapter will be concerned with factors associated with exposure to information on retirement, the effects of exposure on preparation for retirement, and on self-evaluation in retirement.

Orientations toward roles and events influence acquisition of information on them. For example, studies of exposure to political information have shown that voters committed to a party are more

1. In a study of the influence of vocational counseling upon choice of first job, Richard L. Simpson found that workers who move into lower-white-collar jobs from upper-blue-collar families were more likely than workers in any other status group to report vocational counseling to have had an important influence on their decisions to enter their first job. He reasoned that since the bridge from the blue-collar stratum to the white-collar level is the most difficult status barrier to cross, these individuals who came from blue-collar parental backgrounds were likely to have had fewer intimate models or contacts for discussing their occupational choices. This being so, vocational counselors were readier sources for discussing occupational aspirations. This finding appears significant for us in that these individuals who moved into white-collar occupations were initiating a new life pattern about which they had limited information and no set guides for behavior. See "Occupational Careers and Mobility," in F. Stuart Chapin, Jr. and Shirley F. Weiss (eds.), *Urban Growth Dynamics* (New York: John Wiley & Sons, 1962), pp. 405-408.

informed politically than non-committed ones.[2] Studies ot exposure
to expert information among farmers have shown that those who
regard their farms as businesses tend to obtain more expert information on farming and to use such information more than traditional
farmers do. This difference is partially due to their greater contact
with agricultural specialists, but it is also affected by their rational
orientation toward farming which predisposes them to look ahead
and to seek information in formulating and carrying out their
plans.[3] A parallel which might be drawn from these studies is that
a favorable orientation toward retirement encourages the seeking of
information on retirement, but a non-favorable orientation blocks
the seeking of such advice. Our first hypothesis is that orientation
toward retirement affects exposure to information on retirement:
workers who look forward to retirement will have higher exposure
to information on retirement than workers who do not look forward to retirement. (Occupational prestige will be controlled in
observing the relation of orientation of retirement to exposure to
information, since, as noted in the previous chapter, orientation toward retirement is associated with occupational prestige.)

In addition to orientation toward retirement, social pressures
toward seeking advice on retirement may exist within a worker's
social stratum. The presence of such pressures makes it more likely
that a worker will seek advice. Zena Smith Blau accounted for racial
and class differences in exposure to expert information on child-
rearing on the basis of normative pressures;[4] Richard L. Simpson
and Ida Harper Simpson[5] interpret differences they find in advice-
seeking of workers considering white-collar and blue-collar jobs on
the basis of norms associated with job-seeking situations.

Several factors suggest that within the middle stratum pressures
toward the seeking of advice are more likely to occur than within
the upper-white-collar or the semi-skilled stratum. One factor
is that counseling services on retirement inside and outside of industry appear to be addressed more to middle-status and lower-blue-

2. See, for example, Gerhart H. Saenger, "Social Status and Political Behavior,"
American Journal of Sociology, **51** (September, 1945), 103-113.

3. See, for example, F. E. Emery and O. A. Oeser, *Information, Decision, and
Action* (Melbourne: Melbourne University Press, 1958), pp. 17-53; James West, *Plain-
ville, U.S.A.* (New York: Columbia University Press, 1945), pp. 221-225.

4. "Exposure to Child-rearing Experts: A Structural Interpretation of Class-Color
Differences," *American Journal of Sociology*, **69** (May, 1964), 596-608.

5. "Social Origins, Occupational Advice, Occupational Values, and Work Careers,"
Social Forces, **40** (March, 1962), 264-271.

collar workers than to upper-white-collar workers.[6] Upper-white-collar workers who manage work organizations have been responsible for formulating and executing retirement policies. They have instituted retirement and played the leading roles in disseminating information about it, but they have directed little of this information to their own kind.

Furthermore, if orientation toward retirement is associated with exposure to information on retirement, middle-status workers are likely to have the highest exposure. We found in the previous chapter that they are much more likely to look forward to retirement than semi-skilled workers, who in turn are more likely to look forward to retirement than upper-white-collar workers. Despite the fact that semi-skilled workers are more likely than upper-white-collar workers to look forward to retirement, advice-seeking is likely to be less prevalent among them because semi-skilled workers participate less in the larger society. People in this stratum tend neither to question the inevitability of a pattern or event, such as retirement, nor to understand much about it. They raise few questions, mainly because being more apart from society at large[7] they have never developed the practice of exploring or trying to cope with future events. They tend to accept happenings but fail to develop expectations regarding an involvement in them. Their limited literacy probably furthers their withdrawal.

The greater autonomy of upper-white-collar workers in defining their schedules of work may lessen their uncertainty about retirement and their need to seek advice about it. One concern of retirement is the question of how to use the time one previously spent working. When work is defined only in general terms, giving the worker an opportunity to exercise discretion in deciding the routine of his activities, he is likely to habituate himself to evolving his own daily routine. When a man with such a work situation retires, he is likely to continue the habit and organize a routine to substitute for work activities. However, if a worker's activities are defined in detail by others, he is likely to come to expect a daily set of activities to be established for him. In retirement a worker is freed from organiza-

6. Perrin Stryker, "How to Retire Executives," in Editors of Fortune (eds.), *The Executive Life* (Garden City, N.Y.: Doubleday, 1956), pp. 198-199, 206-207.

7. For a discussion of social withdrawal of lower-status individuals, see Genevieve Knupfer, "Portrait of the Underdog," *Public Opinion Quarterly*, 11 (Spring, 1947), 103-114.

tional constraints. Now he may order his day as he pleases; but if he has had little experience in establishing a daily schedule, he may face problems in deciding what to do with his time. Thus, we assume that evolving roles in retirement will be less problematic for upper-white-collar workers than for those of lower status; for this reason upper-white-collar workers will feel somewhat less need to seek advice on retirement.

Organizational constraints on the work of middle-status workers tend to be less controlling than those on semi-skilled workers; yet these workers, like the semi-skilled, are not wholly free to pace their day. Therefore, any difference in these two groups' success in evolving retirement roles is probably not due to differences in organizational constraints. What does appear important is that middle-status workers are more socially involved than semi-skilled workers, as we noted in Chapter 3. They are also more literate. Yet their social involvement, compared with that of upper-white-collar workers, is less socially structured by participation in associations. Having social involvements that are fairly extensive but not firmly fixed in associations would seem to render perception of roles in retirement problematic. This lack of formal, structural participation, coupled with their expectation of continued social involvement, sensitizes the middle-status workers to a need to seek information on retirement. It is not that they have less knowledge of retirement than the semi-skilled worker or that they ultimately desire more knowledge than the white-collar worker; rather the *gap* between what they want to know and what they do know is greater.

Thus, we hypothesize that the seeking of advice on retirement will be most widespread among middle-status workers and least widespread among semi-skilled workers, and that upper-white-collar workers will be intermediate in this pursuit.

If uncertainty of retirement is lessened through exposure to information on retirement, as we have argued, then exposure to information should be manifested in planning for retirement. Wayne E. Thompson found that pre-retirement anticipation and preconception of retirement separately facilitated adjustment in retirement. However, he did not find that planning for retirement aided adjustment in retirement, although his data do show that planning is related to pre-retirement anticipation and to preconception of retirement.[8] Since planning may involve unrealistic expectations, perhaps realization of retirement plans would be a better measure of whether or not exposure results in clearer expectations of retirement. We predict that workers with high exposure to information on retirement are more likely to plan for retirement than workers with low exposure; of those who plan, ones with high exposure are more likely to realize their plans than ones with low exposure. Finally, if expectations of retirement are shaped through exposure to information on retirement, workers who have had wide exposure before retirement should have role expectations of retirement which will support more favorable self-evaluation in retirement. Thus, we predict that workers with high exposure to information will have more favorable self-evaluations in retirement than will workers with low exposure.

ORIENTATION TOWARD RETIREMENT, OCCUPA-TIONAL PRESTIGE, AND EXPOSURE TO INFORMATION

We have hypothesized that both orientation toward retirement and occupational status are associated with exposure to information on retirement. Exposure to information on retirement was ascertained by two sets of questions. First, we asked about the number of different kinds of people with whom retirement had been discussed.[9] Second, we asked workers if they read articles or listened to radio or television programs about retirement. Table 1 gives the median number of different kinds of people with whom retirement had

8. "Pre-Retirement Anticipation and Adjustment in Retirement," *Journal of Social Issues*, **14** (1958), 39. Table 1 gives marginals for the sample who had plans for retirement and those who did not have plans, classified by preconception of retirement and pre-retirement attitude. Relating planning to preconception of retirement and pre-retirement attitude, we obtained the following distribution:

Percentage Who Planned for Retirement

	Favorable attitude	Unfavorable attitude
Had an idea of what retirement would be like	52.6 (380)	31.5 (257)
Did not have an idea of what retirement would be like	41.9 (124)	21.8 (156)

9. Conversations with family members were excluded from the tally of number of kinds of people with whom discussions were held, such as company officials, social security personnel, fellow workers, and retired people. Retirees were asked specifically to report only discussions they had had previous to their retirement. The mass media questions also asked about exposure previous to retirement.

Table 1. Median Number of Different Kinds of People with Whom Retirement was Discussed by Orientation Toward Retirement, Occupational Status, and Retirement Status.

Occupational status and orientation toward retirement	Retired	Pre-Retired
	Median	Median
Upper-white-collar level	1.11 (77)	1.03 (82)
Looked forward to retirement	1.38 (38)	1.29 (41)
Did not look forward to retirement	.96 (39)	.81 (41)
Middle-status	2.02 (122)	1.86 (38)
Looked forward to retirement	2.33 (83)	2.05 (33)
Did not look forward to retirement	1.63 (39)	.33 (5)
Semi-skilled level	1.18 (105)	.48 (39)
Looked forward to retirement	1.35 (59)	.57 (27)
Did not look forward to retirement	.98 (46)	.35 (12)

been discussed by retired and pre-retired workers, cross-classified by occupational status and orientation toward retirement. It shows that both orientation toward retirement and occupational status are positively related to exposure, as predicted. Within each status grouping, those who had looked forward to retirement had discussed it with a larger number of different kinds of people. The difference in the exposure to this type of information that was attributable to orientation was greatest in the middle-status level.

We hypothesized a rank ordering of prestige groupings in exposure to information. As we predicted, middle-status workers had the highest exposure. But among the retired sample, semi-skilled workers had discussed retirement with slightly more kinds of people than upper-white-collar workers, which was contrary to our hypothesis. Among the pre-retired sample, upper-white-collar workers had talked to more different types of people than had semi-skilled workers, which was as we predicted.

Table 2 gives the percentage of retired and pre-retired workers, cross-classified by occupational status and orientation toward retirement, who had discussed retirement with retired people, company officials, fellow employees, and social security personnel. It shows that a larger percentage of middle-status workers had discussed retirement with each of the four types of people. In contrast, the discussions of upper-white-collar workers were concentrated. The retired upper-white-collar workers had talked mainly with company

Table 2. Percentage Who Discussed Retirement with Retired People, Fellow Employees, Company Officials, and Social Security Personnel by Occupational Status, Orientation Toward Retirement, and Retirement Status.

Retirement status, occupational status, and orientation toward retirement	N	Percentage who discussed with:			
		Retired people	Fellow employees	Company officials	Social Security personnel
Retirees					
Upper-white-collar	77	15.6	32.5	57.1	15.6
Looked forward to retirement	38	21.1	36.8	60.5	23.7
Did not look forward to retirement	39	10.3	28.2	53.9	7.7
Middle-status	123	34.1	40.7	74.0	44.7
Looked forward to retirement	83	42.2	43.4	75.9	51.8
Did not look forward to retirement	40	17.5	35.0	70.0	30.0
Semi-skilled	105	21.9	27.6	58.1	26.7
Looked forward to retirement	59	25.4	35.6	61.0	33.9
Did not look forward to retirement	46	17.4	17.4	54.4	17.4
Pre-Retirees					
Upper-white-collar	82	29.3	51.2	35.4	8.5
Looked forward to retirement	41	39.0	56.1	34.2	9.8
Did not look forward to retirement	41	19.5	46.3	36.6	7.3
Middle-status	38	55.3	57.9	44.7	5.3
Looked forward to retirement	33	60.6	60.6	51.5	6.1
Did not look forward to retirement	5	—	—	—	—
Semi-skilled	39	23.1	35.9	23.1	0.0
Looked forward to retirement	27	25.9	33.3	29.6	0.0
Did not look forward to retirement	12	16.7	41.7	8.3	0.0

officials, and the pre-retired mainly with fellow employees. The discussions of retired semi-skilled workers were more diversified than those of upper-white-collar workers, but they were more concentrated than the discussions of middle-status workers. Discussions with company officials and social security personnel were mainly concerned with technical matters, whereas the discussions with fellow employees and retired people covered all aspects of retire-

Table 3. Percentage Who Learned Through News Media About Retirement by Retirement Status, Occupational Status, and Orientation Toward Retirement.

Retirement status, occupational status, and orientation toward retirement	N	Percentage who read about retirement	Percentage who listened to or watched programs on retirement
Retirees			
Upper-white-collar	77	58.4	23.4
Looked forward to retirement	38	63.2	23.7
Did not look forward to retirement	39	53.9	23.1
Middle-status	123	68.3	40.7
Looked forward to retirement	83	72.3	48.2
Did not look forward to retirement	40	60.0	25.0
Semi-skilled	105	50.5	39.0
Looked forward to retirement	59	50.9	47.5
Did not look forward to retirement	46	50.0	28.3
Pre-Retirees			
Upper-white-collar	82	68.3	24.4
Looked forward to retirement	41	70.7	24.4
Did not look forward to retirement	41	65.9	24.4
Middle-status	38	60.5	28.9
Looked forward to retirement	33	63.6	33.3
Did not look forward to retirement	5	—	—
Semi-skilled	39	30.8	28.2
Looked forward to retirement	27	37.0	29.6
Did not look forward to retirement	12	16.7	25.0

ment. Thus, it appears that middle-status workers, more than others, seek varied information on retirement.

Exposure to information on retirement through mass media does not show as consistent a pattern as the one evidenced in personal discussions (see Table 3). Orientation toward retirement is positively associated with reading articles about retirement for each status and retirement grouping, other than retired semi-skilled workers, among whom it is unrelated. It is positively associated with listening to radio and television programs among all groupings except retired and pre-retired upper-white-collar workers, among whom it is unrelated. Among retired workers, middle-status ones rank first in reading articles on retirement, followed by the upper-white-collar and the semi-skilled, in that order. However, among the pre-retired workers slightly more upper-white-collar than middle-status workers had read about retirement. Fewer workers had listened to programs than had read about retirement. Middle-status and semi-skilled workers showed about the same tendency to have listened to such programs; upper-white-collar workers were less likely to have listened. The lack of a consistent pattern in the relation of media exposure to orientation or occupational status suggests that the mass media are not an important avenue through which information on retirement is obtained.[10] This failure may reflect the kinds of information which are given as well as the impersonal nature of the media, or it may be that little information on retirement is carried by the available mass media.

In summary, favorable orientation toward retirement appears to encourage the gathering of information on retirement, especially through personal discussions. The worker from the middle stratum is the most likely to seek information on retirement. Furthermore, orientation toward retirement seems to add more to the likelihood of exposure in the middle stratum than in the others. Yet judging from responses of the retired sample, as retirement nears, even those middle-status workers who have not looked forward to retirement are more likely to seek information than ones from other strata.

EXPOSURE TO INFORMATION ON RETIREMENT AND PLANNING FOR RETIREMENT

We have seen that exposure to information on retirement is associated with the anticipation of retirement and with occupational status. We argue that the high exposure of middle-status workers stems partially from their uncertain expectations about retirement. If exposure is a function of uncertainty, we expect workers with high exposure to use the information to plan for retirement. In addition, since planning involves the rational manipulation of al-

10. Elihu Katz and Paul F. Lazarsfeld, in *Personal Influence* (Glencoe, Ill.: The Free Press, 1955), pp. 175-186, found personal contacts more effective than the mass media in influencing consumer behavior. We do not have findings on the effectiveness of information in evolving expectations of retirement on the basis of sources of information. But since we found, as had Katz and Lazarsfeld, that personal contacts are relied upon more heavily than the mass media, in all likelihood the information obtained from personal discussions actually contributed more to expectations of retirement than that obtained through the mass media.

ternatives, it is likely to be more prevalent among upper-white-collar workers, whose work involves such manipulation, than among workers of lower status, regardless of the degree of certainty about expectations of retirement. Therefore, the effect of exposure on planning is likely to be more marked among middle-level and semi-skilled workers than among upper-white-collar workers.

Since the mass media do not appear to be as important a source of information as personal discussions, we will base our measure of exposure on the number of different kinds of people with whom the worker about to retire had discussed retirement. Since exposure varied notably by occupational status, high versus low exposure is defined separately for each occupational grouping. Upper-white-collar and semi-skilled workers are said to have had low exposure if they had talked to no one or only one kind of person about retirement (the median number and below). They are considered to have had high exposure if they had talked to two or more different kinds of people (above the median). Middle-status workers are classed as having had low exposure if they had talked to two or fewer kinds of people (the median number and below), and high exposure if they had talked to three or more kinds of people (above the median).

Table 4 presents the percentage of retired and pre-retired workers who planned for retirement, cross-classified by exposure to information on retirement and occupational status. High exposure appears to have had a favorable influence on planning among retired

Table 4. Percentage Who Planned for Retirement by Occupational Status, Exposure to Information on Retirement, and Retirement Status.

Occupational status and exposure	Percentage who planned	
	Retirees	Pre-Retirees
Upper-white-collar		
High exposure	73.3 (30)	52.9 (34)
Low exposure	70.2 (47)	42.9 (49)
Middle-status		
High exposure	68.8 (48)	83.3 (12)
Low exposure	39.2 (74)	23.1 (26)
Semi-skilled		
High exposure	42.1 (38)	22.2 (9)
Low exposure	11.6 (69)	6.7 (30)

Table 5. Workers Who Planned for Retirement and Realized These Plans by Occupational Status and Exposure to Information on Retirement.

Occupational status and exposure	Percentage who realized plans
Upper-white-collar	
High exposure	77.3 (22)
Low exposure	69.7 (33)
Middle-status	
High exposure	78.1 (32)
Low exposure	69.0 (29)
Semi-skilled	
High exposure	73.3 (15)
Low exposure	37.5 (8)

and pre-retired middle-status and semi-skilled workers, but it had no influence on retired upper-white-collar workers and little on the pre-retired ones. However, planning is more likely to have been engaged in by upper-white-collar workers than by ones of lower status: almost three-fourths of the retired upper-white-collar workers had planned for retirement, compared with one-half the middle-level workers and slightly less than one-fourth of the semi-skilled. Among pre-retired workers, not quite one-half of upper-white-collar workers had planned for their retirement. This compared with slightly less than one-half of the middle-status level and about one-tenth of the semi-skilled. The marked tendency of middle-status and semi-skilled workers with high exposure, in contrast to those with low exposure, to plan for retirement suggests that these workers seek advice in order to structure their expectations of retirement, whereas acquisition of information by upper-white-collar workers appears less important in their retirement planning.[11]

If exposure to information helps a person learn what to expect in retirement, then the seeking of advice should be associated with successful realization of retirement plans. Table 5 presents the percentage of retired workers whose pre-retirement plans were realized, cross-classified by occupational status and exposure to information. It shows a slight relationship between having high exposure and

11. The greater tendency of upper-white-collar people to plan is indicated in areas such as the spacing of children. See, for instance, Clyde V. Kiser and P. K. Whelpton, "Social and Psychological Factors Affecting Fertility: IX. Fertility Planning and Fertility Rates by Socio-Economic Status," *Milbank Memorial Fund Quarterly*, **27** (April, 1949), 188-244, esp. 210-244.

carrying out retirement plans among upper-white-collar and middle-status retirees and a considerable relation among semi-skilled retirees. Plans were more often realized in the two top prestige groupings, but exposure to information made more difference in realization of plans among semi-skilled workers. Information which the semi-skilled received through exposure appears to have made possible realistic planning for retirement activities.

We have seen that orientation toward retirement is related to exposure, and, as we have noted, data presented by Thompson show that orientation toward retirement and planning for retirement are related. This question thus arises: Does the relation between exposure and planning among middle-status and semi-skilled workers result from the association between orientation and exposure? Table 6, which presents the percentage of retired workers who planned

Table 6. Percentage of Retired Workers Who Planned for Retirement by Occupational Status, Orientation Toward Retirement, and Exposure to Information on Retirement.

Occupational status and orientation toward retirement	Percentage who planned	
	High exposure	Low exposure
Upper-white-collar		
Looked forward to retirement	88.9 (18)	70.0 (20)
Did not look forward to retirement	50.0 (12)	70.4 (27)
Middle-status		
Looked forward to retirement	71.8 (39)	43.2 (44)
Did not look forward to retirement	55.6 (9)	33.3 (30)
Semi-skilled		
Looked forward to retirement	42.3 (26)	12.1 (33)
Did not look forward to retirement	41.7 (12)	11.8 (34)

for retirement, cross-classified by occupational prestige, orientation toward retirement, and exposure to information on retirement, suggests that the relation is not spurious. Within the middle-status and semi-skilled groupings, exposure is consistently related to planning when orientation is controlled. The data suggest, in fact, that exposure aided planning more than did orientation toward retirement. When exposure is controlled, orientation toward retirement does not appear to influence planning among semi-skilled workers,

Table 7. Percentage of Retirees with Low Job Deprivation and with High Morale by Occupational Status and Exposure to Information on Retirement.

Occupational status and exposure	Percentage with low job deprivation	Percentage with high morale
Upper-white-collar		
High exposure	80.0 (25)	73.1 (26)
Low exposure	66.7 (30)	66.7 (36)
Middle-status		
High exposure	74.5 (47)	52.2 (46)
Low exposure	55.4 (65)	52.5 (61)
Semi-skilled		
High exposure	47.1 (34)	53.1 (32)
Low exposure	38.2 (55)	35.9 (53)

and its apparent influence is sharply reduced among middle-status workers. But exposure shows a notable salutary effect.[12]

EXPOSURE TO INFORMATION AND SELF-EVALUATION IN RETIREMENT

We have argued that retirement is characterized by institutional uncertainty, that expectations of retirement may be evolved through exposure to information, and that these expectations can support a favorable self-evaluation in retirement. Self-evaluation is measured by a scale on job deprivation and a scale on morale, which are discussed in Chapter 2. Table 7 presents the percentage of retired workers who felt little job deprivation, cross-classified by occupational status and exposure to information on retirement. It shows that workers with high exposure to information were less likely to feel job deprivation than ones with low exposure, although the differences are small among semi-skilled retirees.

Also in Table 7 is presented the percentage of retirees with high morale, cross-classified by occupational status and exposure. Exposure is positively related to morale only among semi-skilled retirees;

12. Similarly, orientation does not affect realization of retirement plans. Of workers with plans for retirement who realized those plans, there were 73.3 per cent of those on the upper-white-collar level who favorably anticipated retirement and 72.0 per cent of those with unfavorable orientations; 73.9 per cent of the middle stratum with favorable orientations and 73.3 per cent with unfavorable orientations; and 64.3 per cent of the semi-skilled who looked forward to retirement and 55.6 per cent who did not look forward to retirement.

among the other two groupings it appears to have had no effect on morale. Whether exposure actually contributed to the morale of retired semi-skilled workers we cannot say; it may be that those who had high morale in retirement also had had high morale prior to their retirement and that this higher morale had contributed to their seeking advice on retirement.

In Chapter 4 we saw that orientation toward retirement helped to offset feelings of job deprivation. Since orientation encourages the seeking of advice on retirement, the possibility arises that the salutary effect of exposure in lessening job deprivation might be only apparent; the effect very likely was contributed by orientation toward retirement. Table 8 shows that both orientation and exposure aided in lessening job deprivation. However, orientation toward retirement appears more important in lessening job deprivation: within each prestige level, differences between the orientation groupings with exposure controlled are considerably greater than the differences between the exposure groupings with orientation controlled. The differences between the exposure groupings are greatest within the middle stratum. Evidently exposure aids in evolving expectations of retirement, but orientations influence acceptance of retirement.

Data given in Chapter 4 and in Table 7 made it seem that orientations were unrelated to morale. Table 8, however, reveals

Table 8. Percentage of Retirees with Low Job Deprivation and with High Morale by Occupational Status, Exposure to Information on Retirement, and Orientation Toward Retirement.

Occupational status and exposure	Looked forward to retirement		Did not look forward to retirement	
	Low job deprivation	High morale	Low job deprivation	High morale
Upper-white-collar				
High exposure	93.8 (16)	68.8 (16)	55.6 (9)	80.0 (10)
Low exposure	76.5 (17)	68.4 (19)	53.9 (13)	64.7 (17)
Middle-status				
High exposure	79.5 (39)	50.0 (38)	50.0 (8)	62.5 (8)
Low exposure	66.7 (42)	57.9 (38)	34.8 (23)	43.5 (23)
Semi-skilled				
High exposure	63.6 (22)	57.1 (21)	16.7 (12)	45.5 (11)
Low exposure	51.7 (29)	42.3 (26)	23.1 (26)	29.6 (27)

that orientations and exposure are each related to morale when the other is controlled. Among the people who had looked forward to retirement, exposure seems to have made a substantial difference in subsequent morale; among those who had not looked forward to it, exposure aided morale only within the semi-skilled group. The most interesting group here includes the respondents who had not looked forward to retirement but in spite of this had sought out information about retirement. These people, a minority in each group, apparently had experienced some conflict because of their fear of retirement, but nevertheless they had been willing to prepare themselves for it. When they retired they had made some emotional investment in this new status; this may have led to higher scores in the morale scale.

This joint consideration of anticipation of retirement and exposure to communication helps us to understand that there is some lack of relation of these to morale, especially in the two upper socioeconomic groups. The semi-skilled apparently have so little information about retiring that they are helped by exposure to information no matter what their previous attitude toward retirement. For the other groups, unfavorable anticipation may be offset by pre-retirement activities, especially information-seeking, so that morale in retirement is high. This latter combination, although somewhat rare, attenuates the first-order relationship of each of the variables to morale.

The above findings appear to support a portion of the theses of this chapter. We have argued that retirement is characterized by uncertainty and that through exposure to information on retirement uncertainty may be lessened. But we also have said that the extent of uncertainty varies by occupational status and consequently so does exposure to information on retirement. On the basis of their position in the occupational and community structures, middle-status workers are assumed to have felt the most uncertain about retirement; among the members of this group, advice-seeking had been the most prevalent and the most varied, as we expected. Advice-seeking among retired upper-white-collar workers had been no more prevalent and even more restricted in scope than among retired semi-skilled workers. Their lesser tendency to seek advice suggests that retirement occasions less uncertainty for upper-white-collar workers than for workers of lower status.[13]

Direct evidence on this question is needed. Our contention that exposure to information on retirement lessens uncertainty about retirement appears supported by the finding that exposure is associated with planning for retirement among middle-status and semi-skilled workers, and that it influences the realization of retirement plans among semi-skilled retirees. However, we did not find that exposure to information consistently reduces job deprivation, as we had hypothesized. It does lessen job deprivation among middle-status workers when orientation toward retirement is controlled, but it lessens job deprivation for upper-white-collar and semi-skilled workers only if orientation toward retirement is favorable. (In no group does it increase job deprivation.) If expectations of retirement are formulated on the basis of information obtained through exposure, then clarity of expectations supports acceptance of retirement, as measured by low job deprivation, if coupled with a favorable view of retirement. A favorable orientation toward retirement appears to facilitate anticipatory socialization to retirement. Such an orientation encourages exposure to information, and when this occurs job deprivation is likely to be markedly offset.

13. One might argue that the lesser tendency of upper-white-collar workers to seek advice on retirement results from greater self-confidence. They are likely to be more confident since, as we have seen, they are likely to have higher morale. But does not a feeling of confidence help to guard against uncertainty? Being more confident would aid in ordering roles in retirement.

Ida Harper Simpson
Kurt W. Back
John C. McKinney

6. CONTINUITY OF WORK AND RETIREMENT ACTIVITIES, AND SELF-EVALUATION

We have seen in Chapter 3 that retirement does not necessarily lead to a marked severance of pre-retirement social involvements other than those directly connected with the work position itself. In this chapter we will investigate whether the style of activities associated with a work status is maintained in retirement. We begin with the assumption that work and retirement need not be an entirely discontinuous status sequence. Just as aspects of early roles are carried into later situations in other transitional phases of the life cycle, behavioral patterns associated with the work role might be applied in non-work situations, including post-retirement activities. Behavioral patterns which are carried over into retirement may either bridge the status transition, or if their enactment fails to coincide with the newly assumed status, they may create problems for the individual.[1] Their carry-over might either impede or facilitate acceptance of retirement.

Although in some respects retirement resembles other transitional phases of the life cycle, it is not completely analogous. Other transitional phases involve an increase in the number of one's statuses by the introduction of the individual into institutional areas in which he has not previously participated. But retirement signifies a decrease in the number of one's statuses. Moreover, for earlier

1. Ruth Benedict has argued that the status transition from adolescent to young adult male creates problems stemming from the incongruity of behavioral patterns of the two statuses. See "Continuities and Discontinuities in Cultural Conditioning," *Psychiatry*, **2** (May, 1939), 161-167.

transitions, cultural expectations guide the expansion of one's life space through such prescriptions as mandatory school attendance and the validation of adult male status through gainful employment. But no firmly set social patterns guide the status shift occasioned by retirement. Given the conditions of his life situation, the individual retiree is left to decide the institutional area or areas in which he will invest himself. Shifts in activities are bound to occur with retirement, but the style of activities may be maintained. Thus, the activities of work and retirement may not always be discontinuous.

One attribute of work roles which seems pertinent to the linkage of pre-retirement work activities to post-retirement activities is the type of skills exercised in work. In the application of skills, action is performed upon, or in relation to, some aspect or aspects of the environment. Skills then may be classified in terms of the principal type of object that is manipulated in work. Objects of work situations include symbols, people, and things.[2] Studies of occupational identity have shown that work attitudes include orientations associated with work skills and the objects to which they are applied.[3] Orientations pertaining to objects of work are likely to be more prevalent in occupations with developed cultures. But even in occupations with little cultural elaboration, including poorly developed techniques, it seems reasonable to assume that through years of manipulation of a kind of object, individuals will have inculcated a subjective set toward it. For instance, a person who works with things is more likely to prefer physical to symbolic activities.

The first objective of this chapter is to ascertain whether the activities of retirees center around the same type of object manipulated in their work. Since the type of object manipulated in work bears at least a rough relation to occupational status—the lower-class occupations being concerned mainly with things and the higher ranking occupations being concerned mainly with people and symbols[4]—status of occupation will be controlled. The relationship be-

2. For a discussion of types of objects manipulated in work situations, see Theodore Caplow, *The Sociology of Work* (Minneapolis: University of Minnesota Press, 1954), p. 52; Nancy C. Morse and Robert S. Weiss, "The Function and Meaning of Work and the Job," *American Sociological Review,* **20** (April, 1955), 191-198; C. Wright Mills, *White Collar* (New York: Oxford University Press, 1951), p. 65.

3. For a discussion of the influence on occupational attitude of the object manipulated in work, see Everett C. Hughes, *Men and Their Work* (Glencoe, Ill.: The Free Press, 1958), pp. 35-36.

4. Morse and Weiss, "Function and Meaning of Work and Job."

tween object manipulated and status is not perfect, however, and it seems likely that through their work people will learn different preferences for activities based on whether they manipulate things, people, or symbols, regardless of the status of their occupations.

In the second section of this chapter we will try to find out whether attitudes toward pre-retirement work affect continuity of work and retirement activities. Individuals who were highly committed to their work would seem more likely to carry over orientations associated with it than those who were not highly committed. On the other hand, through years of object manipulation even an uncommitted individual may have developed an attitudinal set toward the style of activities associated with work skills. However, this attitudinal set may not be as central among his interests as it would be for the individual highly committed to his pre-retirement work. Thus, a lack of work commitment need not preclude continuity of work and retirement activities, but commitment should make it more likely.

Differences in continuity of work and retirement activities may be largely a function of the length of time since leaving the labor force. Retirees who have been out of the labor force for several years may have lessened their interest in activities whose style is similar to that of their work, increased their interest in other areas, or sharply reduced their over-all rate of activity; in any of these cases they would show less continuity than the recently retired. If such is the case, continuity should be viewed as a temporary adaptive mechanism to lessen the status shift from work to retirement.

In the third section of this chapter we will examine the effect of continuity on the retiree's self-evaluation. Retirees who pursue activities involving the same style as that of their work are defined as experiencing less discontinuity in the status shift from work to retirement than retirees who pursue activities involving styles which differ from that of their work. It is often assumed that the less discontinuity experienced in moving from one phase of the life cycle to another, the less personal stress is engendered; hence, the more favorable are self-evaluations.[5] As we have indicated above, many of the earlier transitions in the life cycle, especially ones immediate-

5. For example, Ruth Benedict, "Continuities and Discontinuities in Cultural Conditioning" assumes that continuity of cultural expectations promotes favorable self-evaluations.

ly preceding retirement, focus upon the individual in the world of work. The transition from work to retirement, however, moves the individual from the world of work to a poorly defined status having less social acclaim. Continuity in style of work and retirement activities may thus impede rather than promote acceptance of the status shift, discontent being manifested in feelings of job deprivation.

CONTINUITY IN STYLE OF WORK AND RETIREMENT ACTIVITIES

Continuity in style of work and retirement activities was inferred from classification of the main object manipulated in work activities and the object around which most retirement activities centered. The job which the retiree considered the main one of his work history, which in almost all cases was in the same occupation as the job held at the time of retirement,[6] was classified according to its principal object of manipulation—symbols, people, or things. Each job was checked with the *Dictionary of Occupational Titles*; the type of object mentioned most often in the job description was used as the basis of the classification. Working independently of each other, three coders classified all jobs with 90 per cent agreement.[7]

Jobs of the seventy-eight upper-white-collar retirees included thirty-eight which involved manipulation of symbols, thirty-nine the manipulation of people, and one the manipulation of things. (The one upper-white-collar retiree whose job involved things was eliminated from the sample for this chapter.) Of 122 middle-status jobs, 18 per cent were classified as manipulating symbols, 55.7 per cent as manipulating things, and 26.2 per cent as manipulating people. Clerical jobs constituted most of those in which symbols were manipulated; skilled work such as that of an electrician made up most of the jobs which dealt with things; and foremen and a few salesmen represented the jobs whose activities were oriented

6. A few semi-skilled workers had been transferred to new jobs shortly before retiring; however, the object manipulated in these jobs was the same.

7. The job of college professor, which makes up 53.8 per cent of the jobs of upper-white-collar retirees in our sample, involves as its object of manipulation both symbols and people. To reduce this ambiguity, the decision was made to classify all college professors who taught mainly undergraduates as manipulating people and those who taught mainly graduate students or spent much of their time in research as manipulating symbols.

Table 1. Percentage of Activities of Retirees Oriented Around Symbols, People, and Things by Occupational Status and Object Manipulated in Work.

Occupational status and work object	Percentage of activities oriented around:			Total activities
	Symbols	People	Things	
Upper-white-collar retirees				
Symbol manipulators	43.8	25.4	30.8	146
People manipulators	36.6	36.1	27.3	183
Middle-status retirees				
Symbol manipulators	28.6	24.7	46.8	77
Thing manipulators	20.7	22.9	56.4	188
People manipulators	21.1	44.0	34.9	109
Semi-skilled retirees				
Thing manipulators	18.7	27.3	54.0	278

toward people. All semi-skilled jobs involved the manipulation of things.

To ascertain the main style of activity patterns in retirement, each retiree was asked to think of the previous day, and if there was nothing unusual about it, to tell what he did. (If the day was unusual, he was asked to take a typical day.) To facilitate recall, the day was split into five periods[8]—the morning, around noon, afternoon, around supper time (dinner), and night. The activities of each were classified on the basis of the objects around which they were oriented. Activities which did not involve active participation on the part of the retiree were excluded—for instance, watching television, listening to the radio or records.

Table 1 classifies retirees by the status levels and objects manipulated in their jobs and shows the percentage in each category whose retirement activities emphasized symbols, people, and things. The retirement activities of each category tended to emphasize the same object as that manipulated in work as often or more often than they emphasized either of the other two objects. There is one exception to this pattern: symbol manipulators in the middle stratum. Some 46.8 per cent of their activities involved the manipulation of things, but only 28.6 per cent were oriented toward symbols. However, their activities emphasized symbols more than did those of the other

8. For a discussion of splitting the day or some time-unit into intervals, see Sebastian De Grazia, "The Uses of Time," in Robert W. Kleemeier (ed.), *Aging and Leisure* (New York: Oxford University Press, 1961), pp. 126-130.

two categories within the middle stratum. These patterns of retirement activities indicate that the style of work activities tended to remain dominant in retirement.

Further differences in patterns of retirement activities associated with the different objects manipulated in work are also shown in Table 1. Within both the upper-white-collar group and the middle stratum, the activities of retirees whose work had involved dealing with people were the most diversified, suggesting that variety in activities is valued among those who manipulated people. Activities of the other two categories clustered more heavily around one object. The most heavily concentrated were those activities of retirees whose work had involved performing physical tasks; slightly over half of them were centered around the manipulation of things. In fact, activities of retirees of the middle stratum whose work had been largely physical in nature resembled the activities of the semi-skilled retirees, all of whom had manipulated things in their work, more than they resembled those of other retirees within their own stratum. This similarity in the activities of retirees who manipulated things, though differing in prestige, suggests that not only is the style of work activities carried over into retirement, but manipulation of things restricts the development of interests centered around other types of objects much more than does the manipulation of symbols and people.

Further evidence of differences in activities being associated with

Table 2. Mean Number of Different Activities Engaged in During a Typical Day and Mean Number of Settings of Activities by Object Manipulated in Work and by Occupational Status.

Object of work and occupational status	Number of retirees	Mean	
		Activities	Settings of activities
Upper-white-collar			
Symbol manipulators	38	3.84	1.95
People manipulators	39	4.69	2.18
Middle-status			
Symbol manipulators	22	3.50	1.50
Thing manipulators	68	2.76	1.71
People manipulators	32	3.41	1.97
Semi-skilled			
Thing manipulators	105	2.65	1.66

the object manipulated in work is shown in Table 2, which gives the mean number of different activities participated in during a typical day and the mean number of social settings where the activities occurred. Among upper-white-collar workers, retirees whose work had involved people participated on the average in almost one more activity a day than retirees whose work had involved symbols. Within the middle stratum, those who had worked with symbols averaged slightly more activities than those who had worked with people; but both averaged about two-thirds of an activity more than those who had worked with things. Middle-status retirees who had worked with things averaged only slightly more activities than the semi-skilled, who had also been manipulators of things. The object manipulated in work showed considerably less influence on the number of different social settings of activities. The most striking pattern indicated is that retirees who had worked with people averaged the highest number of settings within both the upper-white-collar and the middle stratum. This suggests that to engage in activities involving people requires more varied social settings than participation in activities involving things or symbols. The lack of any marked differences in number of social settings probably reflects a restricted range of settings available for activities of retirees.

In summary, these data suggest that through work stylistic preferences for activities are developed and that these preferences guide the participation of retirees.

FACTORS ASSOCIATED WITH CONTINUITY IN STYLE OF WORK AND RETIREMENT ACTIVITIES

We have seen that a tendency exists for activities of retirees to emphasize the type of object manipulated in their work more than other types. But as is evident in the distribution, many activities do not reflect the style of work. We have suggested that differences in continuity between the style of work and retirement activities may be associated with commitment to pre-retirement work and with length of time since retiring.

The style of retirement activities is defined as continuous with work activities if the retiree engages in activities which emphasize the same objects as manipulated in work during two or more of the five periods of a typical day. The style is called discontinuous if the main object associated with work is the focus of activities in fewer than two periods of the day. This method seemed preferable to other measures of continuity, such as the proportion of one's total activities involving the object associated with his work, because it automatically controlled the duration of activity. A measure based on sheer number of activities would equate brief, unimportant activities with those consuming large parts of the day. (Those with a pattern of inactivity, who spent much of the day in napping, viewing television, and other pursuits which we did not define as "activities," were for this reason unlikely to engage in activities involving the main object of their work during two or more periods of the day.) Continuity for semi-skilled and skilled workers is largely a measure of activeness, for the bulk of their activities are oriented around things. This is not the case, however, with other retirees. For them discontinuous styles are based as much upon dealing with an object different from that used in work as upon low activity levels. As Table 1 has shown, retirees who manipulated things tended to have the lowest activity level.

Retirees who had worked with different objects differed notably in the number of activities participated in as well as in the types of objects used in these activities. It is conceivable that these differences might result in our measure of continuity favoring retirees with a particular work object. Among upper-white-collar workers, 11 per cent more of retirees whose work had involved symbols than of those whose work had involved people engaged in continuous activities (57.9 per cent vs. 46.2 per cent). But the object manipulated in work is unrelated to continuity among middle-status retirees: 40.9 per cent who had worked with symbols engaged in continuous activities, as did 46.9 per cent of those who had worked with people and 41.2 per cent of those who had worked with things. Of the semi-skilled retirees, 45.3 per cent are classed as engaging in retirement activities continuous with work. These differences do not appear sufficient to indicate a bias of the measure in favor of either of the objects of work.

Data on the relation of work commitment to continuity in style of work and retirement activities are given in Table 3. (For a discussion of the scale used to measure work commitment, see

Table 3. Percentage of Retirees of Different Occupational Levels with Continuous Styles of Work and Retirement Activities by Work Commitment and by Length of Time of Retirement.

Commitment to work and length of time of retirement	Percentage with continuous style		
	Upper-white-collar retirees	Middle-status retirees	Semi-skilled retirees
Commitment to work			
High commitment	68.8 (32)	36.1 (36)	57.1 (21)
Low commitment	37.5 (16)	48.4 (62)	45.3 (64)
Length of time of retirement			
Less than four years	61.5 (26)	41.4 (58)	54.8 (31)
Four or more years	50.0 (30)	42.3 (51)	40.0 (55)

page 78 above.) The table shows that commitment to work is associated with continuity among upper-white-collar and semi-skilled workers, but the pattern is reversed for the middle stratum. This finding, together with the findings in Chapter 4 on the relation of meaning of work to orientation toward retirement, suggests that work commitment means different things within different occupational strata. The meaning for each stratum most likely reflects the work culture of that stratum. If so, work commitment for upper-white-collar workers signifies the internalization of occupationally oriented norms. The highly committed worker has a self-conception built around his work role. This self-view appears to be upheld in retirement, and in fact it is publicly recognized for the upper-white-collar retirees who are identified in retirement by their work positions—retired physicians, lawyers, executives, and college professors. This self-view and its public recognition seem to foster continuity in style of work and retirement activities.

The occupational culture of middle-status workers is less developed. Their work norms pertain to specific job tasks and work situations, and rarely are they built into over-all work-related roles as among upper-white-collar workers. In retirement the committed, middle-status individual is likely to look for opportunities to duplicate the specifics he found rewarding at work, but suitable situations for this may not be available. Thus, he either turns to other types of activities or becomes inactive.

The relation of work commitment to continuity among semi-skilled retirees appears to be imposed by lack of alternatives for activities different in style from those of their work. Table 1 shows that semi-skilled retirees engaged mainly in activities oriented around things. Since the education of such retirees is limited, and avenues for broad social participation are closed to them because of their low social standing, they have no alternatives to the style of their work. Those we studied who had been committed to their work tended to be the most active in retirement, and those who had not been committed tended to be inactive.

We also speculated that length of time since retiring might affect continuity in style of work and retirement activities. The number of years the retirees had been retired ranged from less than a year to eighteen years, with a median of four. Table 3 gives the percentage of continuous activities for retirees of different status levels, classified by length of time retired. It shows a tendency for continuity to decline with length of retirement among upper-white-collar and semi-skilled, but no effect is indicated in the middle stratum. Despite the fact that continuity of work and retirement activities among the long-time retired upper-white-collar and semi-skilled individuals was less prevalent than among those recently retired, much continuity among the long-time retirees prevailed. One-half of long-time upper-white-collar retirees and forty per cent of the long-time semi-skilled retirees engaged in retirement activities resembling their work activities. These sizeable proportions suggest that continuity in style of activities should be viewed as a more than temporary adaptation to the event of retirement. The reduction in continuity for an individual may have resulted from a lessening of physical vigor, poor health, lessening of interest in activities similar to those of work, or from other reasons.

CONTINUOUS ACTIVITY STYLES AND SELF-EVALUATION IN RETIREMENT

It is conceivable that continuity in the style of activities of work and retirement may either promote favorable self-evaluation in retirement by bridging the status shift from work to retirement, or it may impede acceptance of retirement by supporting orientations inseparable from work so that meaningful substitutes for work are not found. Two measures of self-evaluation are used, a Guttman-

Table 4. Percentage of Retirees with Low Job Deprivation and with High Morale by Continuity in Style of Work and Retirement Activities and by Occupational Status.

Occupational status and continuity of style	Low job deprivation	High morale
Upper-white-collar		
Continuous style	58.1 (31)	74.2 (31)
Discontinuous style	88.0 (25)	58.6 (29)
Middle stratum		
Continuous style	80.4 (46)	58.7 (46)
Discontinuous style	51.6 (62)	47.3 (57)
Semi-skilled		
Continuous style	33.3 (39)	44.5 (36)
Discontinuous style	51.1 (47)	41.4 (46)

type scale which measures job deprivation (the feeling of missing one's work), and a scale which measures general morale. These scales are discussed on pages 52 and 53 above. Table 4 examines the effect of continuity in activity styles on the self-evaluation of retirees of different strata. According to the first measure of self-evaluation (job deprivation), upper-white-collar and semi-skilled retirees with discontinuous styles tended to feel less job deprivation than did those with continuous styles. Continuing the style of work activities in retirement appears to hamper acceptance of retirement. However, continuity in style of work and retirement activities is inversely related to job deprivation among retirees of the middle stratum. Those with continuous styles missed their work less than did those with discontinuous styles.

As we have seen in Table 2, commitment to pre-retirement work is inversely related to continuity in style of work and retirement activities among middle-status retirees. But the two are directly related among upper-white-collar and semi-skilled retirees. Thus, within the middle stratum the relation of continuity to job deprivation might be spurious. Rather than resulting from continuity in style, the relation could possibly stem from the fact that retirees with continuous styles tended to have had little commitment to their pre-retirement jobs; low commitment might be associated with low job deprivation. (We found in Chapter 4 that when orientation toward retirement is controlled, work commitment and job deprivation are related within the middle stratum.)

Table 5. Percentage of Retirees with Low Job Deprivation by Occupational Status, Continuity in Style of Work and Retirement Activities, and by Commitment to Work.

Occupational status and continuity in style	Percentage with low job deprivation	
	Low commitment	High commitment
Upper-white-collar		
Continuous	—— (6)	50.0 (22)
Discontinuous	80.0 (10)	90.0 (10)
Middle-status		
Continuous	83.3 (30)	76.9 (13)
Discontinuous	59.4 (32)	47.8 (23)
Semi-skilled		
Continuous	26.9 (26)	50.0 (12)
Discontinuous	52.9 (34)	44.4 (9)

To see if such is the case, we controlled commitment to pre-retirement job while observing the effect of continuity on job deprivation. The results are shown in Table 5. Although the totals for some cells are small, the distribution suggests that the relation is not spurious within the middle stratum. Among retirees with continuous styles, commitment to pre-retirement jobs had little effect on feelings of job deprivation. But among retirees with discontinuous styles, those who had had low commitment to their pre-retirement jobs tended to miss their work somewhat less than those whose commitment had been higher. Thus, it appears that continuity affects the occupational strata differently. It offsets feelings of job deprivation among the middle-status retirees but aggravates such feelings among upper-white-collar and semi-skilled retirees. This latter fact appears to be a manifestation of differences in social evaluation of work. For an upper-white-collar individual, work involves more than the isolated acts of work. For him the acts are imbedded in an institutional context which involves the function of the acts and the goal toward which the acts are oriented. In working he relies heavily on general bodies of knowledge. The generality of his work skills facilitates using them in settings other than that of work, but this ease of invoking them may only indicate the lack of an institutional context in his work. In contrast, a retired electrician (middle-status individual) might derive as much satisfaction and social esteem within his neighborhood by the electrical maintenance of his house as he did at work before retirement. Upper-white-collar retirees may continue the basic form of their work activities, but these activities lack social meaning outside the institutional context of work. Continuing the style of work in retirement may only remind them of their lost social function.

Semi-skilled individuals whose retirement activities are continuous with those of their work tended to be fairly active. That they also tended to miss their work may stem from the lack of opportunities for sociability which they enjoyed on the job, as well as from financial worries. This may help to account for many of the home-oriented activities in which they engage, such as gardening and house repairs.

Table 3 also presents data on the relation of continuity in style of work and retirement activities to general morale among retirees of different strata. Among those in the upper-white-collar and middle strata, continuity is associated with high morale, but the two are unrelated among semi-skilled retirees. Continuing the style of activities of one's work presumably bolsters a feeling of worth-whileness and satisfaction, on which the morale scale focuses.

CONCLUSION

Through years of working with a particular type of object, stylistic preferences for activities involving that object are inculcated. These are carried into retirement and help to structure retirement activities. Among upper-white-collar retirees whose occupations included developed cultures, the style preferences appear work-related. Retirees who had been highly committed to their work, more than those who had not, were likely to engage in retirement activities involving the same style as that of their work. However, among middle-status retirees, work commitment was unrelated to continuity. We interpret this as resulting from the lack of occupational norms with which the work style might have been imbued. In contrast to earlier stages of the life cycle, continuity between work and retirement does not automatically lessen the difficulties of accepting the new status. When the work role forms a part of one's self-conception, and when the style which is carried over into retirement cannot be divorced from the institutional context of the work role, continuity increases job deprivation. But when work is viewed as a series of isolated acts and its style is carried over into retirement, acceptance of retirement is facilitated; this holds if the retiree enjoys fairly high social involvement (as do middle-status retirees) and if financial worries are not too pressing.

Kurt W. Back

Carleton S. Guptill

7. RETIREMENT AND SELF-RATINGS

The principal means of self-identification for the adult male in today's Western society is derived from his work activity. His organization of time, his style of life, and many of his social associations depend on his work situation. Age, sex, and occupation are the principal means of identifying a person in private and public listings. Other possible means of self-identification such as lineage, residence, or community position are less important.

It is not surprising, therefore, that the loss of the work role due to retirement is considered one of the major crises in the process of aging. The foregoing chapters, however, have shown that many aspects of the life of the aged are less dependent on retirement than on the previous work role, and that many activities and attitudes carry over into retirement. This contrast is surprising and may be worth some further consideration. The parts of the interview on which this conclusion was based were questions about specific activities, or feelings about specific attitudes, to which the respondent was supposed to give his reaction. Similarly, corroborating evidence from other studies is based on questions of this kind; there is little evidence from survey interviews of traumatic changes during retirement. Nevertheless, much of the literature of gerontology speaks of the shock of retirement, especially among those retirees who were very much involved with the work role—in general, professionals or businessmen. A closer look, however, shows that the evidence here is mainly impressionistic and clinical and does not come from a consideration of objective circumstances and endorsement of attitude statements. We have here two lines of evidence which may describe two aspects of the condition of the aged. On the one hand, we find that in many respects very little of the life pattern is changed during retirement and that the aging person will adjust to his retirement role in the same way as he did to his work role. On the other hand, we have the expressed complaints of the aged to members of the health professions, who form a receptive audience. Ethel Shanas[1] has noted that these groups perpetrate what she has called the myth of the aged; that is, the aged person sets a standard for himself which he can no longer reach, or perhaps never has reached, and he may thus give the impression of unhappiness.

METHOD

The technique of obtaining self-ratings was adapted from the semantic differential method of ascertaining meanings of concepts which was developed by Charles E. Osgood, G. J. Suci, and P. H. Tannenbaum.[2] The word *myself* was presented to respondents, who were asked to describe it by using seven descriptive scales defined by polar adjectives. The polarity for each scale was separated by seven spaces, and the respondent was instructed to indicate the space on each scale which corresponded to what the word *myself* meant to him. The scales included:

free to do things	not free to do things
useless	useful
look to the future	look to the past
ineffective	effective
satisfied with life	dissatisfied with life
respected	disregarded
busy	inactive

Interrelations of the scales showed two sets of three scales highly related and one scale which did not correlate significantly with any of the others. These interrelations we interpret as representing different dimensions of the self. They include (1) an involvement dimension represented by the scales "useful—useless," "effective—ineffective," and "busy—inactive"; intercorrelation coefficient of these scales is .40 for our retired sample and .27 for our pre-retired

1. "The Unmarried Old Person in the United States: Living Arrangements and Care in Illness, Myth and Fact," paper prepared for the International Gerontological Research Seminar, Markaryd, Sweden, August, 1963.
2. *The Measurement of Meaning* (Urbana, Ill.: University of Illinois Press, 1957).

sample; (2) an optimism component composed of the scales "look
to the future—look to the past," "satisfied with life—dissatisfied with
life," and "respected—disregarded"; the average intercorrelation
coefficient for these scales is .44 for our retired sample and .59 for
our pre-retired one; and (3) an autonomy dimension represented by
the scale "free to do things—not free to do things."

The average score for each dimension was used to make the three
scores comparable. Parametric measures (means, correlations, and
analysis of variance) are used, although some of the assumptions
for these measures could not be fully met, especially because of
the skewed distributions of the ratings and ambiguities of meanings
of the distances between rating points. The main analyses were repeated using median and non-parametric tests, yielding essentially
the same results. Thus, we feel confident in using these more powerful methods which also are frequently used by Osgood and others
in work with the semantic differential.

RESULTS

The first question to be considered is the relation of the self-
ratings to the measures derived from interview questions. Table 1

Table 1. Correlations of Self-Concept Dimensions with General Morale
Scale and Job Deprivation Scale for Retirement Status and Occupational Status.

Retirement status and self-concept dimensions	General morale			Job deprivation		
	Upper-white-collar	Middle-status	Semi-skilled	Upper-white-collar	Middle-status	Semi-skilled
Pre-Retirees						
Involvement	.33*	.51*	.03	—	—	—
Optimism	.44*	.46*	.18	—	—	—
Autonomy	.21	.08	.23	—	—	—
N	67	31	33	—	—	—
Retirees						
Involvement	.19	.26*	.19	.03	−.38*	.03
Optimism	.12	.15	.48*	−.01	−.18	−.17
Autonomy	.11	.31*	.25	−.003	−.24*	−.10
N	60	105	84	55	109	88

*$p < .05$.

shows the correlations of the three self-rating dimensions with the two morale measures which we have been using, general morale and job deprivation. Among the retirees the correlations are quite low, but they reach statistical significance in the middle stratum. Autonomy rating correlates positively with morale and negatively with job deprivation; the largest correlation is found in this group between involvement and job deprivation—the less a retiree misses his job, the higher he rates his involvement.

For the pre-retirees, only the general morale scale is available. The relations here are quite substantial for upper-white-collar and middle-status groups. For men who are still working, general morale and self-ratings of optimism and activity are highly related. It is only later, after retirement, that self-ratings become almost completely distinct from other morale measures. This development can explain some of the contradictions about the morale of the aged and effects of retirement. With this distinction in mind we can now investigate the conditions of different self-ratings.

Table 2 shows the self-ratings along the three dimensions for our sample, divided into retirement and occupational groups. Looking at the over-all absolute values, we see that the men in our sample have rated themselves on the positive side of the scale. This result is not surprising in view of the fact that our sample was basically composed of healthy, ambulatory, independent men who lived at

Table 2. Mean Values on Self-Concept Dimensions for Retirement Status and Occupational Status.[a]

Self-concept dimensions and retirement status	Occupational status			Significance		
	Upper-white-collar	Middle-status	Semi-skilled	Occupational status	Retirement status	Interaction
Involvement						
Pre-Retirees	5.95	6.00	5.76	$F=3.21$	$F=24.09$	n.s.
Retirees	5.54	5.37	5.03	$p<.05$	$p<.001$	n.s.
Optimism						
Pre-Retirees	5.60	6.08	6.01	$F=5.61$	n.s.	n.s.
Retirees	5.59	5.99	5.89	$p<.01$	n.s.	n.s.
Autonomy						
Pre-Retirees	5.22	5.86	5.84	n.s.	n.s.	n.s.
Retirees	5.83	5.96	5.56	n.s.	n.s.	n.s.

[a]The possible scores range from 1 (most negative) to 7 (most positive).

home and had no obvious reasons for feeling despondent, other than the fact of retirement or approaching retirement. Some other wide and significant variations did occur; and these, of course, are the focus of our attention. We must keep in mind, however, that any differences are only relative and that concerning the sample as a whole we find a general feeling of well-being.

The most striking difference is shown in the involvement factor. Here there is a definite decline in rating between retirees and pre-retirees, and also a consistent decline in the two groups lower on the socioeconomic ladder. Retirees do not feel as useful, effective, and busy as pre-retirees; in fact, there is no overlap in the means of these rating scales. The highest retiree group, the upper-white-collar workers, is still considerably lower than the lowest pre-retiree group of the semi-skilled workers. The influence of socioeconomic status is less definite. Among the retirees it is quite consistent, semi-skilled workers being lower than middle-status workers, and these in turn lower than the upper-white-collar workers. However, among pre-retirees, there is hardly any difference between the two upper groups. In fact, upper-white-collar workers are a little lower in their involvement ratings.

In the other two dimensions we find little effect of retirement. Optimism does vary by socioeconomic status, but not consistently, and the middle occupational group is the highest. Looking at this factor more closely, we see that the upper-white-collar workers show little difference between retirees and pre-retirees, while the other two occupational groups do vary in the expected direction. Among the three scales which make up these factors—looking to the future, satisfied with life, and respected—it is the last one, respected, which shows this relationship most strongly. There is a possible explanation for this in the fact that our upper-white-collar group consists primarily of college professors. In these days of rapidly changing technology and ideas, the older college professor usually has a position of less respect on the university campus because his ideas and methods are frequently thought of as outdated. Also, as Theodore Caplow and Reece J. McGee[3] have pointed out, he is much less mobile than younger professors and must remain in his present location whether he likes it or not. Whether this speculation is correct or not, it shows a possibility that some groups are rating themselves

3. *The Academic Marketplace* (New York: Science Editions, 1961), pp. 86, 224.

lower because of the higher standards which they set for themselves. This factor may account for the difference with scales made up from direct questions.

Table 2 has shown that retirement status primarily affects involvement but not optimism or autonomy. A loss of the work role brings a decline of other morale factors. In fact, we have seen a hint that release from the tension of the work role may compensate for the loss of the role itself. As we have found in Table 1, we see again that for the older person and the retiree, activity is not necessary for the good life. We shall now investigate two further questions. Is it the loss of the work role or some other factor which leads to this decrease in involvement? Secondly, are there activities which the retiree can undertake which may compensate for the loss of the work role?

The most important physical factor which might account for the differences between retirees and pre-retirees is the factor of aging itself. However, because of the high correlation between retirement status and age, it is impossible for us to control the retiree and pre-retiree groups by actual chronological age. We must, therefore, leave open the question of the degree to which the differences are due to chronological age and to retirement. However, we can investigate another physical condition, the influence of health. The questionnaire included a question on self-rating of health: "How do you rate your health at present: good, fair, not so good, or bad?" Those who rated themselves as good were put in the good health group and the other ones in the poor health group. Table 3 shows the result of this analysis. We find that health in itself is an important factor in involvement, as could be expected. However, even when controlling for health, there is still a significant difference between retirees and pre-retirees. The significant interaction between health and retirement status shows that the difference between retirees and pre-retirees is mainly carried by the people in poor health. Among the people in good health, the difference is much smaller and even reversed in the case of the semi-skilled worker. The semi-skilled worker can be considered to be least involved in his work, and he does not feel less involved if he keeps his health and loses his work role. However, in all occupational groups, loss of work role is found to cause a decrease in involvement if activity is curtailed because of ill health. The same phenomenon is shown by

Table 3. Mean Values on Self-Concept Dimensions for Retirement Status, Occupational Status, and Health.[a]

Self-concept dimensions and retirement status	Upper-white-collar		Middle-status		Semi-skilled		Significant F values
	Good health	Poor health	Good health	Poor health	Good health	Poor health	
Involvement							Retirement status: $F=15.38$, $p<.001$. Health rating: $F=5.78$, $p<.05$. Interaction of retirement and health: $F=7.08$, $p<.01$.
Pre-Retirees	5.94	6.01	6.10	5.87	5.61	5.87	
Retirees	5.62	5.41	5.88	4.97	5.66	4.85	
Optimism							Occupational prestige: $F=6.10$, $p<.01$.
Pre-Retirees	5.60	5.58	6.22	5.90	6.09	5.96	
Retirees	5.65	5.43	6.25	5.83	6.05	5.87	
Autonomy							None significant.
Pre-Retirees	5.31	4.75	5.85	5.87	5.73	5.91	
Retirees	5.80	5.93	6.27	5.73	5.95	5.54	

[a]The possible scores range from 1 (most negative) to 7 (most positive).

the fact that Table 3 does not exhibit consistent and significant differences according to occupational status. Among those in good health, the upper-white-collar workers score lower than the middle-status group. Only among the respondents in poor health is the rank order preserved, although the difference between the two lower groups is negligible. We see here, again, that the vigorous upper-white-collar workers, the professionals, may have a higher standard of involvement than the other groups and feel more deprived on this score. In the optimism dimension we find the difference between occupational groups preserved and even made stronger in the case of the healthy retirees. Thus, although health is important in the self-ratings, it cannot account for the differences we have found between retirees and pre-retirees.

As the loss of the work role becomes so important for self-ratings of involvement, the question arises as to whether there is anything which can compensate for activities which occurred at work. In previous chapters we have used several measures to account for different retirement patterns, all of which could have compensatory features for the loss of the work role. These included number of friends and organizations, the involvement index, and number of interests. These four variables were tested as controls in the distribution of self-ratings. Number of friends and organizations did not have any significant effects on the ratings. The involvement index showed significant effects on the dimension which we have called involvement, but it did not affect the other relationships. Number of interests had the strongest effect on the ratings of semantic differential. This is shown in Table 4. Number of interests also had a definite relation both to the self-ratings of involvement and to optimism. This is the only time we have found a significant relationship on the latter dimension for any variable except occupational prestige. The more interests the individual has, the more optimistic he is about his life; the more the individual is involved in many interests, the less chance he has to feel pessimistic. We also find an interaction between interests and retirement status on the involvement factor. Number of interests leads to a higher self-rating primarily among the retired respondents. Among the pre-retirees we find much smaller differences, and there is even a slight difference in the reverse direction in the two upper-occupational groups. It seems reasonable that the number of interests becomes important

Table 4. Mean Values on Self-Concept Dimensions for Retirement Status, Occupational Status and Number of Interests.*

Self-concept dimensions and retirement status	Upper-white-collar		Middle-status		Semi-skilled		Significant F values
	0 to 2 interests	3 or more interests	0 to 2 interests	3 or more interests	0 to 2 interests	3 or more interests	
Involvement							Retirement status: $F=23.64$, $p<.001$. Number of interests: $F=10.84$, $p<.001$. Interaction of retirement and interests: $F=5.07$, $p<.05$.
Pre-Retirees	5.96	5.95	6.05	6.01	5.60	6.04	
Retirees	5.18	5.75	5.00	5.81	4.82	5.47	
Optimism							Number of interests: $F=6.42$, $p<.05$. Occupational prestige: $F=8.46$, $p<.001$.
Pre-Retirees	5.40	5.69	6.06	6.14	5.96	6.11	
Retirees	5.19	5.84	5.94	6.13	5.76	6.17	
Autonomy							None significant.
Pre-Retirees	5.30	5.18	6.26	5.33	5.87	5.79	
Retirees	5.38	6.09	5.78	6.15	5.63	5.42	

*The possible scores range from 1 (most negative) to 7 (most positive).

only when the work role is lost. Especially among the two upper socioeconomic groups who are more interested in their work, outside interests have little effect on the involvement of the person who is still working. There is some possibility of compensation for the retiree in other interests which he might have. However, even controlling for number of interests, the retirees feel much less involved than pre-retirees. Interests cannot fully make up for the loss of the work role.

CONCLUSIONS

In this chapter we have looked at some of the dimensions of the self-concept of retired and pre-retired men. The overriding point of interest has been that retirement leads to a feeling of loss of involvement for the males in this study. Without the job around which their life had been built for some forty or fifty years, these retired men were unable to avoid feeling less useful, less effective, and less busy than the men who were still employed. Different conditions of life in retirement did little to alter these feelings.

Our findings indicate that if the retiree were healthy, had had a middle- or upper-stratum occupation, and was highly involved, especially in personal interests, he would feel less of a loss in the activity dimensions. Yet even these retirees did not successfully plug the gap left by the loss of their job; they felt less active than the pre-retirees. This self-rating of loss contrasts with the objective determination of actual attitudes and activities, and seems to depend on comparison with an ideal standard. This difference may account for several discrepancies found in the literature concerning factors in the morale of the aged. Impressionistic and clinical studies based mainly on complaints of the aged show a great loss of morale due to retirement itself. On the other hand, studies based on survey analyses indicate that this loss is mainly a function of the general life style of the retiree, and only incidentally is it a result of the retirement process.

Section Two

FAMILY AND RETIREMENT

Alan C. Kerckhoff

8. THE OLDER COUPLE: SOME BASIC CONSIDERATIONS

Although the general literature on old age is growing in both quantity and quality, there has been very little increase during the past decade in literature on the family life of older persons. Many studies which have been primarily concerned with other issues have provided some additional knowledge of the family patterns of older people, but very little research has been focused specifically on this topic. This statement applies particularly to family patterns in the retirement period. There are three major issues which have received some attention, however, and which deserve mention here.

One issue which has been widely discussed recently might be termed the degree of nucleation of the American family. Following the emphasis in the earlier work of Talcott Parsons and others[1] on the separation of the generations in our society, several studies have led to the counterposition that our family system is not nearly as nucleated as had been indicated, and that the older person has continuing contact with and support from his children.[2] These studies have indicated that most older persons live relatively close to one or more of their children, see their children as often as they wish, and can depend on their children for assistance when it is needed.

The position taken here with respect to this body of literature

1. "Age and Sex in the Social Structure of the United States," *American Sociological Review*, **7** (October, 1942), 604-616; "The Kinship System of the Contemporary United States," *American Anthropologist*, **45** (January-March, 1943), 22-38; and Robin M. Williams, Jr., *American Society* (New York: Alfred A. Knopf, 1954), chap. 4.

2. A review of this literature is presented in Marvin B. Sussman and Lee Burchinal, "Kin Family Networks: Unheralded Structure in Current Conceptualizations of Family Functioning," *Marriage and Family Living*, **24** (November, 1962), 320-332.

is that it has too often led to an exercise in polemics which emphasized polar positions on the subject and has thus perhaps overlooked
some very important points of investigation. The crucial issue here
does not seem to be whether we do or do not have a fully nucleated
family system. It is not only obvious from these studies that there
is some continuing relationship between the generations; it is also
apparent that the nature of this relationship varies considerably
among American families. One important question that requires
more careful examination, therefore, is the question of the significance of variations in the quality and intensity of the intergenerational relationships—for both the older and younger generations. This
basic question underlies both Chapters 9 and 11 of this book.

A second issue that has been dealt with to some extent is the
kinds of changes in family roles that occur with advancing age.
Bernard S. Phillips[3] has suggested such an approach to the general
aging process. With respect to the intergenerational relationship, it
has been suggested that the older couple tends to occupy an increasingly dependent position vis-à-vis their children and that there is
thus a kind of role reversal which occurs between parent and child.
Reuben Hill[4] has provided some of the best evidence on this subject with respect to the flow of economic assistance between the
generations. Alteration of conjugal roles with advancing age has
also been noted, although for the most part the variable seen as
responsible for these changes has been the husband's retirement
rather than age as such.[5]

The difficulty with work in this area of inquiry is that it is often
impossible to know if the characteristics of the family life of older
people is the result of *changes* which have occurred in their roles,
or if the differences noted between their family life and that of
younger persons are due to the changed conditions within which
families function. It is not possible to say that the family patterns
of the older generation were once like those of the younger generation but have changed as they became older, nor is it possible to
predict with much confidence that the patterns of the younger gen-

3. "Role Theory Approach to Adjustment in Old Age," *American Sociological Review*, **22** (April, 1957), 212-217.
4. "Decision Making and the Family Life Cycle," in Ethel Shanas and Gordon F. Streib (eds.), *Social Structure and the Family: Generational Relations* (Englewood Cliffs, N.J.: Prentice-Hall, 1965).
5. Aaron Lipman, "Role Conceptions and Morale of Couples in Retirement," *Journal of Gerontology*, **16** (July, 1961), 267-271.

eration will change so as to be more nearly like those of their parents as they (the children) grow older. This is not a fault of the research that has been carried out, however, so much as it is a result of the difficulty of conducting longitudinal studies of families and the fact of general social change in our society.

A third relevant area of inquiry where some progress has been made is the analysis of the relationship between the family patterns of older persons and the impact of specific events in their lives. The most clearly relevant event in the present case is the retirement of the husband. Here we find that the work of Aaron Lipman[6] is relevant, as is the work of Gordon F. Streib and his associates.[7] There are two possible perspectives in this area of inquiry, one which takes the family pattern as an independent variable and one which takes it as a dependent variable. One may raise the question of what impact the fact of retirement has on family patterns, both conjugal and intergenerational. This has been the implicit or explicit perspective of most of the literature that is relevant here. On the other hand, one may also ask what implications various family patterns have for the retiree, his spouse, his children, etc. In this way one may raise questions about the kind of family pattern which is most "favorable" in retirement, given some objective definition of favorableness. Both of these perspectives are valuable in furthering our knowledge of the family life of older persons. It is the latter perspective, however, that is taken in the present analysis.

The three chapters which follow contribute in several ways to the body of literature just discussed. In Chapter 9 the discussion of the first issue is furthered by posing the question of the relationship between normative definitions of family patterns, on the one hand, and one's attitude toward the value of change and toward the geographical and social mobility of one's children, on the other. Given this analysis and an indication of the distribution of these norms and values in the social structure, we are in a better position to discuss the significance of *degrees* of nucleation of family systems in our society. Chapter 9 also provides an analysis of the effects of the degree of agreement of husbands and wives on such norms and values.

Chapter 10 views the retirement process in a simulated longitudinal manner by examining the responses of some couples before

6. *Ibid.*
7. "Family Patterns in Retirement," *Journal of Social Issues,* **14** (1958), 46-60.

retirement, others soon after retirement, and still others well after retirement. It calls attention to differences between husbands' and wives' expectations and reactions to retirement and to varying patterns of differences according to the man's occupation and the point in the retirement process at which the data were collected. To the extent that it points to husband-wife differences and to alterations through time, it contributes to our knowledge of conjugal role relationships and specifies some potential sources of strain in that relationship. To the extent that these differences vary by the occupational level of the husband, it suggests that such sources of strain vary in distribution according to socioeconomic level.

Chapter 11 is most directly relevant to the third issue discussed above. Using family patterns as independent variables, it examines the relationship between a number of family dimensions and the level of morale expressed by retired men and their wives. By holding the variable of retirement constant (using only retired couples), it provides evidence with respect to the kinds of family patterns which are most predictive of high morale in retirement.

The subjects from whom the data were collected were obtained in the same manner and at the same time as those used in the previous section on "Work and Retirement." The men's names were all obtained from lists of retired workers and workers within five years of retirement provided by a tobacco, a textile, and a chemical factory, an insurance company, three universities, and from local membership lists of the American Bar Association, the American Medical Association, and a list of executive directors of the Young Men's Christian Association. Only those men who were living with their wives at the time of the interviews were included in the sample used here. All were white, and all were living in the Piedmont region of North Carolina and Virginia at the time of the interviews.

Contacts were made with 337 couples during 1960 and 1961. An attempt was made to interview both husband and wife simultaneously by using two interviewers in a team. Because of the length of the interview, two visits were required. A total of 264 pairs of completed interviews were obtained, 174 from couples in which the man had already retired, ninety from couples in which the man was within five years of retirement. Although almost half of the sample loss was due to refusals, a larger proportion was due to the unavailability of either or both of the subjects, either for the entire interview or for the second half of the interview. In most cases, either poor health or vacation travel was the reason for a subject's unavailability.

Since the discussions presented in the following three chapters deal at least in part with questions of intergenerational relations and of the process of retirement, not all of the subjects interviewed are included in the analysis in each chapter. There were 201 couples who had at least one child who was married or at least twenty-five years of age. Only these are considered relevant to discussions of intergenerational relationships. Of these, 135 were retired and sixty-six were pre-retired couples. The subsample of 201 is used in Chapter 9 where our interest is in the older couple irrespective of the occupational status of the husband; the subsample of 135 retired couples is used in Chapter 11 where level of morale in retirement is the central interest.

In Chapter 10 our interest is in the expectations of retirement and reactions to it expressed by older couples. Because we were unsure of the effect of the variation in age at retirement on the responses given, we used only retired couples of which the man had retired after the age of sixty but before the age of seventy. There were 108 such cases. These, together with the ninety pre-retired couples (in which all of the men were between sixty and sixty-nine), therefore, were the subjects for the analysis in Chapter 10.

Alan C. Kerckhoff

9. NORM-VALUE CLUSTERS AND THE "STRAIN TOWARD CONSISTENCY" AMONG OLDER MARRIED COUPLES*

The basic theme of this chapter is that there is a discernible "strain toward consistency" in the norm and value orientations taken by older married couples, and that this is predictable from a systemic view of our society and the older person's position in it. In addition, we will examine the expectation that such a clustering of norm and value orientations should reflect both the general social situation of the older person and the fact that he (or she) is married to a particular spouse who accepts a particular set of norms and values. The discussion will be presented in three parts. The first will outline the logic for expecting a clustering of the set of norms and values, as well as the data available and relevant to this expectation. The second will pose the question of the relevance of husbands' and wives' norms and values for each other and will attempt to show the importance of viewing these individual orientations from a dyadic perspective. The third will discuss the degree to which the norm-value clusters are associated with couples occupying different positions in the larger social system.

* I am indebted to Cyrus M. Johnson for assistance in the development of some of the measures and for his contribution to the basic logic of the analysis in this chapter. The importance of this earlier work is reflected in his unpublished doctoral dissertation, "Family Structure and Occupational Success Orientation" (Duke University, 1963), and in a joint publication of which he is first author: Johnson and Alan C. Kerckhoff, "Family Norms, Social Position, and the Value of Change," *Social Forces*, **43** (December, 1964), 149-156. I am also indebted to Adam Clarke Davis for his careful attention to the many problems of data processing in this and the two following chapters.

As noted in the previous chapter, the data came from interviews with older white couples living in the Piedmont region of North Carolina and Virginia.[1] In all cases the husband had either retired or was within five years of the normal retirement age of the organization for which he worked at the time of the interviews. The subjects were chosen so as to maximize the occupational distribution of the husbands, and they are thus not to be considered as a representative sample of any particular population.

Since the present interest is in normative and value statements which are relevant, at least in part, to the parent-child relationship in old age, the data to be presented here are limited to those from subjects for whom such statements have personal relevance. Not all of the subjects had children, and some of those who did had only relatively young children. Therefore, only those couples who had at least one child who was married or was at least twenty-five years of age were included in the present analysis. There were 201 such couples.

RELATIONSHIPS AMONG NORM-VALUE POSITIONS

The general perspective of this section of the chapter is systemic in the sense that it assumes there is a "strain toward consistency" in the orientations that persons have toward various elements of their life space. More specifically, it examines variations in family norms relevant to both intergenerational and conjugal relationships, as well as variations in values central to our industrial society, in order to discern the degree to which these several orientations are consistent one with the other. The expectation is that the strain toward consistency discernible at the level of the individual's normative and value orientations should be associated with the interinstitutional relationships found in our society. This perspective is reflected in the following statement by Robin M. Williams, Jr.:

The members of the society may not and usually do not think of separate religious, familial, economic, or political activities—they simply carry out their daily activities, that we, as outside observers, see as a

1. Some of the data have been published elsewhere, although in a rather different form. See Johnson and Kerckhoff, "Family Norms, Social Position, and the Value of Change"; Kerckhoff, "Nuclear and Extended Family Relationships: A Normative and Behavioral Analysis," in Ethel Shanas and Gordon F. Streib (eds.), *Social Structure and the Family: Generational Relations* (Englewoods Cliffs, N.J.: Prentice-Hall, 1965).

web of behavior controlled by norms that we call institutional. In the course of a lifetime, any particular individual will participate in all of these non-nucleated institutions; for the most part there are no specialized personnel to maintain specific institutional subsystems. To the degree that this is the situation, *interinstitutional* relations are largely synonymous with *intrapersonality* adjustments; the integration of institutions is the integration of personalities.[2]

Following the logic expressed in this statement, we would expect that an individual's normative definitions of "proper" parent-child and husband-wife relationships would be associated with each other and would have some relation to his position on issues relevant to the economic-technological aspects of our social system. In defining the specifics of our expectations, we were guided, in part, by the work of Talcott Parsons. Two propositions derivable from his writings are central. The first is that a nucleated family system with attenuated relationships between the adult and his parents is most consistent with the occupational-technological aspects of our social system. The second is that a nucleated intergenerational system is most clearly associated with what may be called a "joint conjugal role relationship," and an extended intergenerational system is most clearly associated with a "segregated conjugal role relationship." The first of these propositions is well known and clearly stated by Parsons and others in many writings.[3] It will, therefore, not be discussed in detail here. The second proposition, however, is less well known and is derived from both Parsons' work and the work of others. It thus requires some clarification.

Parsons' analysis of the nucleated family system in our society includes a discussion of the structure of both the intergenerational relationship and the conjugal pattern within each of the nucleated units. According to his analysis of this nucleated system, which he sees as characteristic of our society, attenuation of intergenerational ties is associated with intensification of the conjugal tie. Although

2. *American Society* (New York: Alfred A. Knopf, 1954), p. 488. In this passage, Williams is describing an ideal type of simple undifferentiated society, and he explicitly makes the point that in a society such as ours this type of intrapersonality adjustment of interinstitutional relations is much *less* noteworthy because of the high degree of specialization of social structures related to various cultural institutions. Although I would agree with such a comparative statement, the present analysis is predicated on the claim that the intrapersonality strain toward consistency is still an important factor in our contemporary society. Taking Williams' full discussion of this issue into account, I feel that the position taken here is consistent with his, although some differences in degree of emphasis undoubtedly exist.

3. Perhaps the earliest and one of the clearest presentations of this position is found in Talcott Parsons, "The Kinship System of the Contemporary United States," *American Anthropologist*, **45** (January-March, 1943), 22-38.

most of his discussion has focused on the conjugal relationship of the younger couple, a similar expectation with respect to the older couple seems in order. Viewing it as a whole, and contrasting it with other possible family systems, the nucleated system appears to be characterized by both minimal intergenerational ties *and* intense conjugal ties. For instance, Parsons has stated that:

[In] comparison with other kinship systems, [the individual in our system is] drastically segregated from his family of orientation, both from his parents—and their forbears—and from his siblings. His first kinship loyalty is unequivocally to his spouse and then to their children if and when they are born. Moreover, his family of procreation, by virtue of a common household, income, and community status, becomes a solidary unit in the sense in which the segregation of the interests of individuals is relatively meaningless, whereas the segregation of these interests of ego from those of the family of orientation tends relatively to minimize solidarity with the latter.[4]

The opposite situation may be expected in an extended intergenerational family system—which Parsons contrasts with the nucleated American system. Given salient outside points of familial reference (outside the conjugal unit, that is), it is reasonable to expect that in an extended family system the conjugal relationship would be considerably less intense and functionally less important in the lives of the conjugal pair. A number of studies, especially in England, give support to the expectation that a more attenuated relationship will be found between husband and wife when a continuing close relationship is found between one of the parents (in the English case it is the mother) and the adult children.[5] We will follow Elizabeth Bott in referring to the closer, less differentiated husband-wife relationship associated with nucleated systems as a "joint conjugal role relationship," and to the more separate relationship associated with extended systems as a "segregated conjugal role relationship."[6]

4. *Ibid.*, p. 30.
5. This is especially true of the English working-class family. See John M. Mogey, *Family and Neighbourhood* (London: Oxford University Press, 1956); Michael Young and Peter Willmott, *Family and Kinship in East London* (London: Routledge & Kegan Paul, 1957).
6. In "Urban Families: Conjugal Roles and Social Networks," *Human Relations*, **9** (1956), 340, she defines these terms as follows: "A joint conjugal role-relationship is one in which the husband and his wife carry out many activities together, with a minimum of task differentiation and separation of interests; in such cases husband and wife not only plan the affairs of the family together, but also exchange many household tasks and spend much of their leisure together. A segregated conjugal role-relationship is one in which husband and wife have a clear differentiation of tasks and a considerable number of separate interests and activities; in such cases,

We have, therefore, defined a basis for expecting a connection between the character of the conjugal relationship and the parent-child relationship. Both of these are also expected to be associated with predictable types of orientation to the economic-technological aspects of our society. Not only should a nucleated intergenerational normative definition be associated with a joint conjugal normative definition, but both of these should be associated with an acceptance of the values of our technological system. In contrast, an extended intergenerational normative definition should be associated with both a segregated conjugal normative definition and with less acceptance of these technological values.

Measures

Since the concern here is with normative and value orientations rather than the actual structure of the relationships involved,[7] each measure is available for each subject, and husband and wife may not be found at the same position on the several measures. There are four central measures: "normative family type" (parent-child relationship), "task sharing" (conjugal relationship), "acceptance of change" (technological value), and "perceived conflict" (conflict between family values and the social and spatial mobility of children). Each of these will be discussed briefly.

The "normative family type" classification was made according to two measures. Following Eugene Litwak, we differentiated between three family types: the extended, the modified extended, and the nucleated.[8] The extended type includes persons who think that when children grow up they should live close to their parents *and* who think there should be considerable mutual aid and affection between the generations. The modified extended type includes persons who do not expect propinquity but who do expect considerable

husband and wife have a clearly defined division of labor into male and female tasks; they expect to have different leisure pursuits; the husband has his friends outside the home and the wife has hers." It will be clear that the operational definition used in this study is more restricted than this comprehensive definition. The measure used is seen as a crude index of the kind of differentiation she describes.

7. The study from which these data came also included data relevant to the actual structure of the relationship between parents and child and between spouses. Some of those data are reported in Chapter XI of this volume as well as in Kerckhoff, "Nuclear and Extended Family Relationships."

8. "Occupational Mobility and Extended Family Cohesion," *American Sociological Review*, **25** (February, 1960), 9-21; and "Geographic Mobility and Extended Family Cohesion," *ibid.*, **25** (June, 1960), 385-394. Here again the operational definition used in this study is more limited than the definition Litwak gives to these three types, but the measures used are central to his definition.

mutual aid and affection. Finally, the nucleated type includes persons who expect neither propinquity nor very much mutual aid and affection.

The norm of propinquity was measured by asking the subjects if they agreed with the statement: "Married children should live close to their parents." The measure of degree of expected mutual aid and affection was a Likert scale made up of the following items:

Children should take care of their parents, in whatever way necessary, when they are sick.
The older couple should take care of their children, in whatever way necessary, when they are sick.
The children should give their parents financial help.
The older couple should give their children financial help.
If children live nearby after they grow up, they should visit their parents at least once a week.
If children live nearby after they grow up, their parents should visit them at least once a week.
Children who live at a distance should write to their parents at least once a week.
Parents should write to their children who live at a distance at least once a week.
The children should feel responsible for their parents.
The older couple should feel responsible for their children.

Those subjects who agreed with seven or more of these items *and* who agreed with the propinquity item were classified as having extended family norms. Those who had equally high mutual aid and affection scores but did *not* agree with the propinquity item were classified as having modified extended norms. Those who agreed with fewer than seven of these items and who did not agree with the propinquity item were classified as having nucleated family norms. There were two husbands and six wives who agreed with the propinquity item but who had low mutual aid and affection scores. Since they did not fit into the typology, and since there were too few cases to warrant the creation of a new type, they were dropped from the analysis.

A Likert scale called "task sharing" was used as an indication of the individual's place on the joint-segregated continuum. This scale, which deals with the definition of the "proper" activities of husbands and wives, consists of the following items:

Yard work is the man's job, and his wife should not be expected to help with it.
Unless it is absolutely necessary for the family support, a wife should not work.

A man should simply "stay out of the way" as far as housework is concerned.

There are certain family tasks which are "women's work" and other tasks which are "men's work," and it is best to keep them separate.

Although fathers are concerned with their children's welfare, the raising of children is really the mother's job.

When the children need to be punished or scolded, the father should do it.

When it comes to money matters, what the man says should be the rule.

A woman's place is in the home, not on a job.

This scale was scored so that a high score indicates an acceptance of task sharing by husbands and wives, and a low score indicates a preference for task segregation and specialization.

The best measure available for both husbands and wives which dealt with a value central to the economic-technological aspects of our way of life was a measure of the "acceptance of change." This value has been recognized by many as one of the most important in the American value system[9] and is perhaps most clearly relevant to the economic aspects of our society. The measure used is a Likert scale constructed from the following items:

If I could have my way, I would keep things the same rather than having them change all the time.

When you come right down to it, the old ways are the best.

Sometimes I feel all the changes that go on are too much for me.

What was good enough for our fathers is good enough for me.

I have never felt I was too old to take up new ways.

I am somewhat leery if I try something new.

The fourth measure used lies conceptually somewhere between the measure of intergenerational norms and the measure of acceptance of change. It deals with the degree of conflict the older person sees between geographic and social mobility of one's children on the one hand and family cohesion on the other. We have called this measure an index of "perceived conflict." It consists of the following items which form a Likert scale:

In choosing their life work, it is most important that children consider getting ahead in life no matter how far from home this may take them.

Children who move far away are not being fair to their parents.

9. See, for instance, Lee Coleman, "What is American: A Study of Alleged American Traits," *Social Forces*, **19** (May, 1941), 496; Williams, *American Society*, p. 433; Arnold W. Green, *Sociology* (New York: McGraw-Hill, 1960), p. 303.

When children move far away, family ties become broken.
When children move away they get different ideas and lose re-
    spect for their parents.
Children who move up in the world tend to neglect their
    parents.
Getting ahead in the world can be a bad thing if it keeps your
    family from being close.

In one form or another, all of these items ask: "Can adult children be mobile without disrupting a satisfying parent-child relationship?" In this, they deal with the strain between institutional
requirements as felt by individuals in our society. One would expect,
if our previous logic is accepted, that those who espouse extended
family norms, who prefer a segregated conjugal role relationship,
and who reject the value of change, should also report the greatest
degree of conflict as measured by this scale.

Findings

Three of the four measures just described are clearly ordinal
scales on which scores represent positions along a continuum. The
fourth measure, the "normative family type," can also be viewed
as a scale, although it was designed originally as a typology based
on two dimensions. Given the fact that the extended type is defined
in terms of two kinds of expectations of relationships with children
(propinquity and mutual aid and affection), the modified extended
type in terms of only one of these expectations (mutual aid and
affection), and the nucleated type in terms of no such expectations,
the typology is also a Guttman scale with three scale types. In the
analysis that follows it was used in this way, scores of zero, one, and
two being assigned to the extended, modified extended, and nucleated types, respectively.[10]

If our general perspective is correct, we would expect the four
variables described above to be related to each other. To test the
adequacy of this expectation, we have computed the zero-order
product-moment correlation coefficients of each variable with every
other one for husbands and wives separately. The results of this
analysis are presented in Table 1. (The full matrix, which repeats
each coefficient, is presented to make later comparisons more con-

10. In all of this analysis I am taking some liberties in that correlation and
regression analysis is being used on ordinal data, but the degree of distortion of
the relationships involved is not likely to be very great.

Table 1. Correlations Among Norm-Value Measures for Husbands and Wives Separately.

	Family type	Acceptance of change	Task sharing	Perceived conflict
Husbands				
Family type	——	.200	.281	.227
Acceptance of change	.200	——	.223	.340
Task sharing	.281	.223	——	.241
Perceived conflict	.227	.340	.241	——
Wives				
Family type	——	.129	.242	.225
Acceptance of change	.129	——	.257	.265
Task sharing	.242	.257	——	.010
Perceived conflict	.225	.265	.010	——

Note: In this and all other tables in this chapter, the signs of the coefficients have been adjusted so that a positive sign indicates a relationship in the expected direction and a negative sign indicates a reversal. The full four-by-four matrix is presented here, even though it requires reporting each coefficient twice, to make comparison with later tables, especially Table 3, easier.

venient.) There are several notable outcomes. First, although all of the relationships are in the expected direction and all but one of the twelve coefficients are statistically significant at the .05 level or better, none of the relationships is extremely strong. Most of the coefficients are on the order of .25. Second, the pattern of correlations is more significant for the husbands' measures than for the wives'. The only coefficient which fails to reach a statistically significant level and the only other coefficient below .20 are both between pairs of measures for the wives. Third, there is no one variable which is more clearly or less clearly associated with the others. The variation in the size of the coefficients is very slight, and in those two cases where the coefficients are the lowest, completely different variables are involved.

In general, we have found support for our contention that there is a "strain toward consistency" in individuals' positions on norm and value measures relevant to four different issues. Although the relationships are not strong, they all point to the kind of consistency predicted. To speak of "consistency" in this context, however, requires a systemic view of the life space of the individual, such that he cannot completely segregate the several issues from each other. This is the same kind of systemic consistency referred to by Parsons, Litwak, and others, when they state that one type of family system is consistent with a highly specialized industrial society. However, in this case we are examining the degree to which this social system consistency is also reflected in the analysis of intrapersonal orientations relevant to the various aspects of the social system. In Robin Williams' words, we are examining the degree to which "the integration of institutions is [or is reflected in] the integration of personalities."

We turn now to a second issue: To what extent is there evidence of a "strain toward consistency" within the conjugal dyad?

CONSISTENCY WITHIN THE CONJUGAL DYAD

The previous section approached the problem of a strain toward consistency as if the individuals involved were unrelated and tended to orient themselves to the several segments of their life space independently of each other. It seems unlikely that this is in fact the process involved. Given the fact that these individuals are husband-wife pairs who have, on the average, been living together for a generation or more, it seems likely that the kind of adjustment each has made to the various points of reference salient in the scales used here has been influenced by their relationship with each other. One of the scales, of course, is a measure of the normative definition each has of his relationship with the other, and we would expect some agreement on that. But all of the measures refer to elements in their lives which they have experienced together and which must have been reflected in their patterns of interaction with each other.

If this reasoning is accepted, one would predict that the husbands' scores on these four scales should be positively associated

Table 2. Correlations of the Husbands' Norm-Value Measures with Those of the Wives.

	Husbands			
Wives	Family type	Acceptance of change	Task sharing	Perceived conflict
Family type	.141	.237	.269	.286
Acceptance of change	.172	.207	.130	.122
Task sharing	.229	.195	.327	.162
Perceived conflict	−.001	.098	.121	.204

Note: A positive coefficient indicates a relationship in keeping with the expectations of agreement between spouses and inter-scale consistency.

with the wives' scores. To test this prediction, the husbands' scores on each scale were correlated with the wives' scores. So that a more complete picture of the pattern of relationships might be presented, however, *each* of the husbands' scores was correlated with *each* of the wives' scores. This set of correlations is presented in Table 2.

As expected, there is a positive relationship between the husband's score on each of these scales and the wife's score on the same scale. These coefficients are on the upper left to lower right diagonal in the table. Not surprisingly, also, the highest coefficient of the four is found with the measure relevant to the conjugal relationship itself, "task sharing." Somewhat more surprising is the fact that the lowest of these four coefficients is found between the husband's and wife's "normative family types." Although this level may in part be due to the fact that this scale has only three points and is thus a very crude measure, the weak relationship between the two scores is puzzling.

With respect to the other relationships, all but two reach an acceptable level (.05 or better) of statistical significance, but the size of the coefficients is not large in most cases. It is interesting to note, however, that the most consistently sizable relationships are found between the wife's "normative family type" and the other three measures for husbands. Also, the only other coefficient to exceed .20 (except those on the diagonal) is between the husband's "normative family type" and the wife's "task sharing." The salience of this measure of "normative family type" will also be noted in the analysis which follows.

If we are going to deal with the question of patterns of consistency within the conjugal dyad, however, it is not sufficient to note that husbands and wives in general agree on the measures used beyond the level of chance association. We are concerned with the question of the *effect* of this relationship between the scores of husbands and wives. Is it true that the *combination* of scores in the dyad on a given measure "makes a difference" for the position of each member of the dyad on the *other* measures? In raising this question, we are suggesting that there is an *interpersonal* as well as an *intrapersonal* strain toward consistency operating in this situation. If one's position on measure "A" is logically related to his own position on measure "B," *and* if there is a pattern of mutual influence within the conjugal dyad, any disagreement between husband and wife on "A" should have some influence on the *relationship* between the "A" and "B" measures for both of them. It should tend to decrease this relationship. Conversely, if the husband and wife agree on one measure, this should increase the tendency for both of them to exhibit the expected (intrapersonal) association between that measure and the others.

To provide an indication of the importance of the spouse's norm-value orientations, we used multiple correlation and multiple regression analysis. In each case, the multiple correlation coefficient and the multiple regression equation were computed for the prediction of one individual's score on a particular measure from the score made by that individual *and* the score made by his spouse on another measure. For instance, we computed the regression equation for predicting the husband's "acceptance of change" score from both the husband's "task-sharing" score *and* his wife's "task-sharing" score. This procedure also gave us the multiple correlation coefficient for this multiple relationship. There were twenty-four such relationships, one for each variable (for husbands and wives separately) predicted from the husband and wife scores on each of the other three variables—four variables for two persons from three pairs of predictors for each.

Table 3 presents the set of multiple correlation coefficients produced in this way. A comparison may be made between these coefficients and those presented in Table 1. It will be noted that there are two coefficients here for every one in Table 1; the addition of

Table 3. Multiple Correlations Between Norm-Value Measures and Pairs of Husband-Wife Measures.

| Dependent variables | Independent variables for husband and wife | | | |
	Family type	Acceptance of change	Task sharing	Perceived conflict
Husbands				
Family type	——	.250	.319	.229
Acceptance of change	.297	——	.258	.339
Task sharing	.358	.238	——	.249
Perceived conflict	.347	.348	.265	——
Wives				
Family type	——	.220	.320	.311
Acceptance of change	.206	——	.266	.276
Task sharing	.311	.294	——	.121
Perceived conflict	.223	.271	.112	——

a spouse variable may be made to either of the original pair of variables correlated, thus producing two multiple correlations for every zero-order correlation. The full (redundant) matrix is presented in Table 1 to make comparison easier. There are sizable increases in some of these coefficients when compared with their counterparts in Table 1, and in some other cases there is no discernible change associated with the addition of the second variable. Perhaps most notable is the fact that the greatest increases are in relationships involving "normative family type" as either an independent or dependent variable. Of the twelve relationships involving this measure, nine are at least .05 greater than the comparable zero-order coefficient.

A better means of coping with the issue at hand, however, is to examine the structure of the regression equation for these relationships. Since we are concerned with the question of the significance of the spouse's score on one measure for the individual's score on another measure, we are really asking whether the spouse's score contributes anything to our understanding of the individual's score on the dependent variable. We thus analyzed the Beta coefficients of the multiple regression equation with two questions in mind: Do both of the independent variables contribute to the multiple regression equation in the same way; do the two Beta coefficients have the same sign? If they do, do either or both contribute to our prediction of the dependent variable at an acceptable level of significance?

The results of this analysis are presented in Table 4. For each relationship, the Beta coefficient for each independent variable is presented along with the level of significance of the contribution made by that variable. If the contribution is in the expected direction (in keeping with our definition of "consistency") and is a significant contribution, the number of asterisks following it represents the level of significance. If the contribution is in the expected direction but does not reach the .05 level of significance, no asterisk or sign is recorded. If the contribution is in the direction opposite to that expected, a minus sign appears before the coefficient.

The contribution of the individual's own independent variable is in the expected direction in twenty-two of the twenty-four cases, and the contribution of the spouse's independent variable is also in the expected direction in twenty-two cases. The individual's own

Table 4. Beta Coefficients for Variables Contributing to Multiple Regression Equations.

Dependent variables	Independent variables							
	Family type		Acceptance of change		Task sharing		Perceived conflict	
	Husband	Wife	Husband	Wife	Husband	Wife	Husband	Wife
Husband's								
Family type	——	——	.147*	.175*	.236**	.150*	.233**	−.048
Acceptance of change	.183**	.207**	——	——	.180*	.134	.331***	.035
Task sharing	.240***	.230***	.206**	.084	——	——	.214**	.090
Perceived conflict	.198**	.262***	.333***	.053	.220**	.097	——	——
Wife's								
Family type	——	——	.188*	.081	.220**	.170*	.214**	.186*
Acceptance of change	.156*	.116	——	——	.064	.240**	.068	.256**
Task sharing	.197**	.213**	.149*	.224**	——	——	.123	−.016
Perceived conflict	−.019	.224**	.071	.247**	.116	−.023	——	——

$*p < .05.$
$**p < .01.$
$***p < .001.$

Note: If there is a minus sign preceding a variable, the direction of the contribution of that variable to the multiple regression equation is the opposite of that predicted. If there is no asterisk or minus sign, there is a non-significant contribution in the direction predicted.

contribution reaches an acceptable level of significance in twenty of the cases, while the spouse's contribution reaches this level in eleven of the cases. Thus, although the contribution of the individual's own score is certainly more consistent and obvious, the spouse's contribution is very noteworthy.

Perhaps most noteworthy of all is the distribution of those relationships to which the spouse's score makes a significant contribution. If those relationships in which the "normative family type" is involved as either independent or dependent variable are differentiated from all other relationships, a striking difference is seen. In all twelve cases in which the "normative family type" is involved, either the individual's own *or* his spouse's score makes a significant contribution. In eleven of the twelve cases the individual's own score makes a significant contribution, and in ten of the twelve cases the spouse's score makes a significant contribution. In contrast, of the other twelve relationships, there are two in which neither the individual's own nor the spouse's score makes a significant contribution. And, although the individual's own scores make a significant contribution in the other ten, the spouse's scores make a significant contribution in only *one* of the twelve cases.[11]

These data seem to justify two conclusions. First, the strain toward consistency we have referred to evidently involves both an intrapersonal and interpersonal pattern of relationships. Second, the focal point of this interpersonal pattern is the "normative family type," the interpersonal relationships involving the other variables being much less significant. The centrality of this measure will be used as the basis of the analysis in the next section, in which we examine the distribution of the norm-value clusters with which we have been concerned here.

DISTRIBUTION OF NORM-VALUE CLUSTERS

Earlier in the introductory discussion, we noted that if we found the clusters of norm and value scores predictable from a systemic view of these variables, we would also expect to find these clusters concentrated in segments of the population definable in terms of social position. That is, it would be expected that the view of the elements of one's life space reflected in different scores on these measures would be (at least in part) a function of the position one occupied in the social system. One kind of definition of one's position in that system is his socioeconomic status. We thus wish to determine if there are indeed differences among our subjects on socioeconomic variables which parallel their differences on the norm-value measures previously analyzed.

The degree of centrality of the "normative family type" measure in the previous findings makes it possible to simplify this analysis. Given the previous findings, it is reasonable to state that the greatest degree of norm-value clustering on all measures should be found in those cases in which the husband and wife agree on their normative definition of the parent-child relationship. We have thus separated out those cases in which agreement is found. There are seventeen

11. These findings, of course, are in part a reflection of the data reported in the previous tables. The fact that the husband's family type does not contribute to the prediction of the wife's perceived conflict score is a reflection of the fact that these two scores are not correlated (see Table 2), and the same is true for the failure of the wife's perceived conflict to contribute to the prediction of the wife's task-sharing score (see Table 1).

Table 5. Mean Norm-Value Scores of Couples Having the Same Normative Family Type.

	Couples agreeing on:		
	Extended family type (N=17)	Modified extended family type (N=59)	Nucleated family type (N=17)
Husband's			
Mean acceptance of change[a]	11.82	9.57	6.67
Mean task sharing	12.06	17.64	21.53
Mean perceived conflict	14.38	11.31	8.33
Wife's			
Mean acceptance of change[a]	11.80	9.45	9.31
Mean task sharing	16.50	18.16	24.81
Mean perceived conflict	10.27	9.91	8.14

[a]The scoring of the acceptance of change scale was such that a low score indicated a high degree of acceptance. Thus, as we move from left to right in the table, the scores indicate an increasing acceptance.

cases in which both husband and wife accept an extended family definition, fifty-nine cases in which both accept a modified extended definition, and seventeen cases in which both accept a nucleated definition. This is almost exactly half of those couples for whom we have complete "normative family type" information.

To insure that our use of the "normative family types" as the basis of the analysis is well-founded, we computed the mean scores on the other six measures for these three sets of couples. The results of this computation are presented in Table 5. It will be noted that all six of the measures vary systematically as we move from the extended, to the modified extended, to the nucleated types. Because of the scoring methods used with these scales, the direction of variation is not the same for all scales, but in every case the direction is as expected. Those couples who agree on an extended normative definition of parent-child relationships are made up of husbands *and* wives whose average scores indicate the most rejection of change as a value, the greatest approval of a conjugal segregation of tasks, and the greatest awareness of a conflict between children's mobility and family values. Conversely, those couples who agree on a nucleated definition of parent-child relationships are made up of husbands and wives who exhibit the strongest acceptance of change as a value, the clearest acceptance of a conjugal sharing of tasks, and the least indication of an awareness of conflict between children's

Table 6. Social Characteristics of Couples Having the Same Normative Family Type.

	Couples agreeing on:		
	Extended family type ($N=17$)	Modified extended family type ($N=59$)	Nucleated family type ($N=17$)[a]
Characteristics (in percentages)			
White collar	11.8	31.0	82.4
Husbands high school graduates	11.8	35.6	82.4
Wives high school graduates	35.3	35.6	76.5
Husbands "comfortable" financially	31.3	60.0	88.2
Wives "comfortable" financially	46.7	57.4	82.4
Average number of children	4.0	3.6	2.4
Characteristics (in percentages)			
Husbands belonging to an organization	23.5	37.7	75.0
Husbands from a farm	47.1	46.6	23.5
Wives from a farm	47.1	37.3	11.8
Husbands living within 50 miles when in teens	82.4	65.5	5.9
Wives living within 50 miles when in teens	64.7	61.0	00.0
Husbands reporting "very close" family	75.0	64.2	75.0
Wives reporting "very close" family	87.5	87.7	100.0

[a]In some cases, data on these questions were not available, and the indexes were computed on smaller frequencies. In only two cases did this reduce the frequency by more than 10 per cent.

mobility and family values. The couples who share a modified extended definition of parent-child relationships have average scores between these two extremes on all six measures.

Given this added evidence of a clustering of the measures we have been discussing, we turn to the question of the relationship between these three clusters and the socioeconomic position of the three sets of couples. To make this comparison, we used several indexes of socioeconomic positions. The results of this analysis are presented in the upper part of Table 6. By whatever measure is used, there are clear differences in the socioeconomic levels of these three groups. As we move from extended to modified extended to nucleated, we find that an increasing proportion of the men hold or used to hold white-collar positions, both husbands and wives have higher levels of education, and both husbands and wives are more likely to say that they are financially "comfortable" or "well-to-do." Clearly, those couples who agree on an extended normative definition of parent-child relationships are from lower socioeco-

nomic levels than those who agree on a modified extended definition, and the latter are from lower levels than those who agree on
a nucleated definition.[12]

The rest of Table 6 presents other characteristics of these three
groups of older parents. In keeping with their differences in socioeconomic level, the extended family type couples have the most
children on the average, and the men are least likely to belong to
any organizations. In much the same way, it is not surprising to
find that those agreeing on an extended family normative definition
are most likely during their adolescence to have lived on a farm
close by to where they lived at the time of the interview.

Finally, we also examined the responses to a question concerning the parents' perception of the cohesiveness of their families. It
might have been expected that those espousing a nucleated normative position did so because their relations with their children were
strained and they could "expect" nothing other than a nucleated
relationship. They would therefore be expected to say that they
and their children did *not* form a very close family group. On the
other hand, one might have argued that those who espoused an
extended normative position would be most likely to have their
norms violated by their children's behavior. Therefore, *they* would
be less likely to say that they had a very close family group. Either
both of these arguments are valid or neither of them is, because
the proportions reporting a very close family group are very similar
for all three normative types. Not surprisingly, the wives are more
likely than the husbands to give this response in all three groups,
but all three groups are very similar.

Before leaving our examination of Table 6 it is worth noting
that for almost all of those indexes showing a variation in response
by normative type the difference between the modified extended
and the nucleated types is strikingly greater than the difference
between the extended and the modified extended types. The nucleated normative type couples are *much* more likely to be white-
collar, to be highly educated, to have fewer children, to have
husbands belonging to organizations, and to have been reared farther

12. In both Tables 5 and 6, the intertype differences are more striking than
in similar tables in which the types are defined in terms of just the husband's or
just the wife's normative definitions alone. Thus, *couples* in which there is normative consensus with regard to family norms are more distinguishable on social characteristics than are *individuals* (husbands or wives) whose normative definitions
differ.

away and in towns or cities rather than on farms. The *only* index which fails to fit this striking pattern is the proportion of the husbands saying they are "comfortable" or "well-to-do" financially. Here, there is an almost perfect sequence from extended, to modified extended, to nucleated. The wives' responses to this same question, however, fit the dominant pattern. Evidently the nucleated normative type couples are a more definite type than either of the other two.

SUMMARY AND CONCLUSION

A body of data measuring the norm and value orientations of older couples was examined from a systemic perspective, which led to an expectation of a "strain toward consistency" among the various measures. This strain toward consistency was predicated on the assumption that the several facets of the subjects' life space dealt with in the measures were related to each other within the larger social system; it was also expected that there would be a tendency for the positions taken on the various measures to reflect this interrelationship. In this sense, an intrapersonal strain toward consistency was expected, based on the structure of the society within which these subjects lived. It was further expected that there would be evidence of the effects of one person's norm-value positions on those of his spouse. Thus, in addition to the intrapersonal strain toward consistency, we also expected an interpersonal strain toward consistency.

Using measures of parent-child norms, normative definitions of husband-wife division of labor, the degree of acceptance of the value of change, and the degree to which a conflict was seen between children's mobility and family values, these expectations were supported by the data. Although the magnitude of the individual statistical relationships was not great and no "errorless" pattern was found, there was considerable evidence of a clustering of these measures in the manner expected, both for individuals and for the couples as units. Three relatively clear norm-value clusters were found, based largely on the respondents' normative definitions of the parent-child relationship. In what might be called the extended family cluster, both husband and wife expected both propinquity and considerable mutual aid and affection in relation to their children, and a segregation of tasks between husband and wife; they did not accept the value of change; and they saw considerable conflict between mobility of children and family values. At the other extreme was the nucleated family cluster in which both husband and wife rejected propinquity and any considerable mutual aid and affection as norms with respect to their children; they most clearly accepted the norm of task sharing within the conjugal dyad; they most fully accepted the value of change; and they saw little conflict between the mobility of children and family values. A third cluster, which might be called a modified extended family cluster, was one in which both husband and wife rejected the norm of propinquity but accepted the norm of considerable mutual aid and affection in relation to their children, and in which the scores of both the husband and wife on all other measures were intermediate between those of the other two clusters.

Finally, those couples who most clearly represented these three norm-value clusters were found to be clearly differentiated on a number of measures of social position. Those who represented the extended family cluster were most likely to have a husband who had (or used to have) a blue-collar job, to have relatively low levels of education, to have lived on a farm, to have lived their earlier lives nearby, and to have larger families. In contrast, those who represented the nucleated family cluster were most likely to be white-collar, to have had high levels of education, to have lived in towns or cities in their youth, to have been geographically mobile, and to have relatively small families. Again the modified extended family couples were intermediate on all of these measures, although they tended to be more like the extended family couples than like the nucleated family couples.

The present analysis supports the position of Talcott Parsons and others who have noted that a nucleated family system is "consistent" with the economic-technological aspects of our way of life, and that a nucleated parent-child relationship is "consistent" with a joint conjugal role relationship. The general conclusion we can make is that there is a tendency for the norms and values espoused by individuals to "hang together" in a way that agrees with this definition of "consistency." Not only is an acceptance of a central value in our technology associated with an acceptance of both a nucleated parent-child relationship and a joint conjugal relationship, but the rejection of any one of these positions tends to be associated with the rejection of the others. In addition, we have noted the tendency for these relationships to be most salient in those cases where husband and wife agreed on any one of the norms or values, but especially in those cases where they agreed on the normative definition of the parent-child relationship.

The fact that the level of acceptance of those norms and values which are defined as characteristic of our way of life varies according to the social position of the couple also suggests that some older couples are more "in tune" with our way of life than others. It is noteworthy that, according to these data, those most "in tune" are those who have attributes which are defined as most valuable within that system: a high level of education, a "better" job, an urban background, high levels of social participation, and a "comfortable" financial situation.

This observation also raises further questions about the more general implications of these findings. If we assume that the general direction of change in our society is toward greater affluence, higher levels of education, an upgrading of job characteristics, greater urbanization, and high levels of spatial mobility, we would be led to expect greater emphasis on what has here been termed a nucleated intergenerational and a joint conjugal relationship. Since such patterns of change would be expected to be most apparent in the younger generation, there would be some tendency for the younger generation to deviate from their parents in the direction of greater espousal of nucleated family norms. The "strain toward consistency" noted here at the intrapersonal and interspousal levels presumably also operates at the intergenerational level, although the effectiveness of the influence between the generations might be expected to be less noteworthy than at the levels analyzed here. If the pattern of change is as suggested here, however, those older couples espousing the nucleated family norm-value cluster have a higher probability of sharing normative definitions with their children than do those espousing the extended family norm-value cluster.

This would lead us to expect that older persons espousing the extended family norm-value cluster would be less satisfied with their experiences vis-à-vis their children than would other older people.

It is noted elsewhere[13] that when the actual experiences of the couples discussed here are compared with their normative definitions, there is considerable evidence of deviation between norms and behaviors. This is true for both the conjugal relationship and the intergenerational relationship. In that analysis it was noted that those older couples in which the man had (or had had) a relatively high occupational position were likely to experience more mutual aid and affection than called for by the nucleated normative position they generally espouse. On the other hand, those couples in which the man had a lower-level occupational position are likely to experience less mutual aid and affection than called for by the extended normative position they generally espouse. Thus, although there is considerable difference between norms and behaviors in both cases, the higher occupation couples experience more intergenerational affection and aid than they require, and the lower occupation couples experience less.

All of this is based on data collected from the older couples themselves, however. The adequacy of the conceptualization suggested here cannot be determined with any confidence until relevant data are simultaneously collected from both older couples and their mature children. The several reports of the data from the present study all point to the expectation that such a study would demonstrate a greater emphasis on extended family norms for the older couples and a greater incidence of unsatisfactory intergenerational relationships in those cases in which the older couple does espouse extended family norms. With respect to our concern for a "strain toward consistency" in this chapter, we are led to expect a greater intergenerational "consistency" where the older couple accepts nucleated family norms, and a greater intergenerational "strain" where the older couple does not. Although it does not explicitly test this proposition, the analysis in Chapter 11 is consistent with this expectation.

13. Kerckhoff, "Nuclear and Extended Family Relationships."

Alan C. Kerckhoff

10. HUSBAND-WIFE EXPECTATIONS AND REACTIONS TO RETIREMENT*

The literature on retirement has been concentrated almost exclusively on the reactions of the male retiree to the experience of leaving his work and entering a more leisurely, economically deprived, and less fruitful period of life.[1] Those previous studies which have been concerned with the family have usually focused on the parent-child relationship or on only very limited aspects of the husband-wife relationship; with rare exceptions, they have not collected data from and about members of the family other than the retiree himself.[2]

As noted in the previous chapter, the present study used the conjugal pair as the sampling unit, and independent interviews were held with both husband and wife. In this and the next chapter we will examine some of the data from these interviews which bear on the general process of retirement as it is experienced by the older couple. In the present chapter we will focus directly on the expectations of retirement and reactions to it with the primary concern of comparing husband's and wife's responses.

* This chapter is a revised version of an article by the same title published in the *Journal of Gerontology*, **19** (October, 1964), 510-516.

1. For a review of this literature, see Wilma Donahue, Harold L. Orbach, and Otto Pollak, "Retirement: The Emerging Social Pattern," in Clark Tibbitts (ed.), *Handbook of Social Gerontology: Societal Aspects of Aging* (Chicago: University of Chicago Press, 1960), pp. 330-407.

2. Most of this literature is reviewed in Gordon F. Streib and Wayne E. Thompson, "The Older Person in a Family Context," in *ibid.*, pp. 447-488. A recent study not reviewed in the above which does include data from husbands and wives is Aaron Lipman, "Role Conceptions and Morale of Couples in Retirement," *Journal of Gerontology*, **16** (July, 1961), 267-271.

Two general expectations guided the analysis. First, it seemed reasonable that the event of retirement would be more significant to the husband than to the wife, whatever over-all implications it might have for her. Second, knowledge of the work orientations of men in different kinds of occupations led us to expect that the husbands might have different expectations of (and presumably different reactions to) retirement, depending on their occupational level. For instance, the greater involvement in the intrinsic reward of work in upper-level occupations would probably lead such men to resist retirement. Those in lower occupations presumably would also prefer not to retire, but this would more frequently be due to financial reasons rather than work commitment. Thus, we expected men in middle-level occupations (i.e., those who were relatively comfortable financially but who were less committed to their work than men of professional positions) to be most favorably disposed toward retirement.

In order to have as homogeneous a sample as possible and still to permit important dimensions to vary, the data to be reported here are limited to those retirees who retired after the age of sixty but before the age of seventy. There were 108 such cases. Their ages at the time of the interview ranged from sixty-one to eighty. Some 50 per cent of them were in the sixty-six to seventy age range and 31 per cent were between seventy-one and seventy-five. All of the ninety pre-retirees were between sixty and sixty-nine; only six were over sixty-five.

The questions which elicited the data to be discussed here were scattered throughout the extensive interview. Those issues to be dealt with here are the following: Did the man and his wife look forward to retirement favorably? Would they prefer for him to retire earlier or later than the usual age for one in his company or organization? Have they made definite plans for retirement? Are they satisfied with their ability to undertake the kinds of interesting activities they enjoy? Do they expect to be able to do more (or fewer) of these things after the husband retires? After retirement, do they report that they are able to do more (or fewer) of these things? Although the interview explored the *kinds* of "interesting things" they could or could not do, the present report will be concerned only with the couples' sense of deprivation or satisfaction with their activity level.

FINDINGS

The data will be discussed with a longitudinal perspective in mind. This is not to suggest that the pre-retired couples' responses may be taken in any simple sense as representing the responses retired couples "would have given" before they retired. Nor is it to say that the responses of the retired couples may be seen as representing those the pre-retirees will give after retirement. There are too many obvious reasons for discounting this simple interpretation. However, since the occupational distributions of the two groups were roughly comparable, and the work settings from which the men were sampled were the same, it seems reasonable and potentially fruitful to make some comparisons between the groups.

Husbands and Wives

Because of the rather complicated kinds of comparisons which become relevant to the issues being examined here, it may be well

Table 1. Item Responses of Pre-Retiree Husbands and Wives (in Percentages).

Item	Husbands $(N=90)$	Wives $(N=90)$
Do you look forward to your (your husband's) retirement?		
(a) Yes	66	66
(b) No	27	20
(c) Indifferent or mixed feelings	7	14
Would you like (him) to retire earlier or later than the usual age?		
(a) Earlier	26	16
(b) Later	30	26
(c) Normal time or indifferent	44	59
Do you have any definite plans for when you (your husband) retire(s)?		
(a) Yes	29	16
(b) No	71	84
Would you like to do more of the things you are interested in than you do now?		
(a) Yes	78	60
(b) No	22	40
Do you think you will be able to do more or fewer things you are interested in after (his) retirement?		
(a) More	61	47
(b) Fewer	15	7
(c) Same	24	46

Table 2. Item Responses of Retiree Husbands and Wives by Length of Time Retired (in percentages).

Item	Total ($N=108$)		Retired less than five years ($N=56$)		Retired five years or more ($N=52$)	
	Husbands	Wives	Husbands	Wives	Husbands	Wives
Did you look forward to your (husband's) retirement?						
(a) Yes	64	61	74	72	53	49
(b) No	31	23	21	28	47	31
(c) Indifferent or mixed feelings	5	16	5	—	—	20
Would you have liked (for him) to retire earlier or later than you (he) did?						
(a) Earlier	11	13	9	18	14	8
(b) Later	42	24	35	18	50	30
(c) Normal time or indifferent	47	63	56	64	36	62
Did you have any definite plans for when you (your husband) retired?						
(a) Yes	28	18	33	15	22	22
(b) No	72	82	67	85	78	78
Have you been able to do more or fewer of the things you are interested in since you have (he has) retired?						
(a) More	52	30	57	28	46	34
(b) Fewer	27	20	24	23	32	18
(c) Same	21	50	19	49	22	48
Would you like to do more of the things you are interested in than you do now?						
(a) Yes	51	53	45	50	58	57
(b) No	49	47	55	50	42	43

simply to summarize what seems to be the pattern found in the comparison of husbands and wives rather than to present a detailed item-by-item discussion of the specific response percentages. First, the over-all patterns in the pre-retired (Table 1) and retired samples (Table 2) will be examined.

Although the majority of men and women claimed to look (or have looked) forward to retirement, few of them made any definite plans for the event, nor did many of them say they would prefer retirement to be earlier than the usual age. Before retirement, the husbands were more dissatisfied than their wives with their ability to do things in which they were interested. They also expected more often than their wives that after retirement they would be able to engage in more of these interesting activities. The retired men did report that they were able to do more of these things since retirement. The wives, on the other hand, were less dissatisfied before retirement, they expected less change after retirement, and they were less likely than their husbands to have experienced any change since retirement. Thus, the husbands seemed to look forward to retirement more than their wives did, and in many cases they actually seemed to experience the improvement they anticipated.

The long-term patterns for husbands and wives are even more divergent when the retired couples are divided into those who have been retired only a short time (less than five years) and those who have been retired five years or more. These data are presented in the last four columns of Table 2. There was a general tendency for long-term retiree couples to respond more negatively than recently retired couples, but this was somewhat more pronounced for the husbands than for the wives. Short-term retiree husbands and wives were more likely than long-term ones to say they looked forward to retirement. Long-term retiree husbands were much more likely than any other group to say they wished retirement had occurred later. They were also more likely than any other group to say they could do fewer of the things they were interested in since retirement. On the other hand, short-term retiree husbands were more likely than any other group to say they could do more since retirement, and least likely to say they wished they could do more. In all these cases, the pattern for wives was more stable than for husbands. Fewer notable differences were found between short-term and long-term retiree wives.

Viewed from a long-term perspective, then, the general pattern among husbands and wives seems to be for the wife to be much less deeply involved than her husband in both expectations of and reactions to retirement. Her responses to comparable questions before, soon after, and well after retirement were rather constant. The husband, on the other hand, tended to have high expectations of retirement. The experience soon after retirement evidently met these expectations and an expression of satisfaction was common. But as time went on he became less satisfied, and his responses, if anything, became more negative than his wife's. These patterns are consistent with the emphasis given to the male role in our society. Although just prior to retirement the husband may be weary of this role and evidently enjoys the escape from it for a while, he does not remain content very long without a job. This type of interpretation, of course, goes beyond the content of these data, but it seems reasonable in light of the rest of the literature on retirement.

Occupational Groups

Some of the general patterns noted above, however, vary among different occupational groups. The subjects were divided into three groups according to the current or pre-retirement occupation of the husband: (1) professional and managerial, (2) white-collar and skilled craftsmen, and (3) semi-skilled, unskilled, and service workers. Most of the latter were semi-skilled, because in the organizations from which our subjects came, unskilled and service jobs are

Table 3. Item Responses of Pre-Retiree Husbands and Wives by Occupational Level (in percentages).

Item[a]	Upper[b] occupations (N=29)		Middle[b] occupations (N=26)		Lower[b] occupations (N=30)	
	Husbands	Wives	Husbands	Wives	Husbands	Wives
Look forward to retirement?						
(a) Yes	45	41	77	81	73	77
(b) No	41	28	19	12	23	20
(c) Indifferent or mixed feelings	14	31	4	8	3	3
Like to retire earlier or later?						
(a) Earlier	24	14	35	23	20	13
(b) Later	35	48	31	15	30	17
(c) Normal time or indifferent	41	38	35	62	50	70
Have you any definite plans?						
(a) Yes	48	17	27	27	13	3
(b) No	52	83	73	73	87	97
Like to do more things you are interested in?						
(a) Yes	79	52	88	54	70	77
(b) No	21	48	12	46	30	23
Will you be able to do more or fewer things after retirement?						
(a) More	52	38	81	58	50	47
(b) Fewer	21	10	—	4	23	3
(c) Same	28	52	19	39	27	50

[a]These are short forms of the items. The full items are listed in Tables 1 and 2.
[b]These occupational groups are as follows: upper are professional and managerial; middle are white-collar and skilled craftsmen; lower are semi-skilled, unskilled, and service workers.

Table 4. Item Responses of Retiree Husbands and Wives by Occupational Level (in percentages).

Item[a]	Upper[b] occupations ($N=25$)		Middle[b] occupations ($N=46$)		Lower[b] occupations ($N=37$)	
	Husbands	Wives	Husbands	Wives	Husbands	Wives
Look forward to retirement?						
(a) Yes	58	56	78	64	51	59
(b) No	38	36	20	16	49	24
(c) Indifferent or mixed feelings	4	8	2	20	—	17
Liked to retire earlier or later?						
(a) Earlier	9	16	13	17	12	5
(b) Later	29	20	37	25	57	26
(c) Normal time or indifferent	63	64	50	58	31	69
Had any definite plans?						
(a) Yes	43	36	22	9	24	17
(b) No	57	64	78	91	76	83
Able to do more or fewer things since retirement?						
(a) More	71	40	48	27	44	24
(b) Fewer	21	28	30	20	28	15
(c) Same	8	32	22	53	28	61
Like to do more things you are interested in?						
(a) Yes	23	60	48	47	74	60
(b) No	77	40	52	53	26	40

[a]These are short forms of the items. The full items are listed in Tables 1 and 2.
[b]These occupational groups are as follows: upper are professional and managerial; middle are white-collar and skilled craftsmen; lower are semi-skilled, unskilled, and service workers.

usually held by Negroes. For simplicity, these will be referred to as upper-, middle-, and lower-occupational groups. A brief description of the pattern in each group may be derived from a review of the data in Tables 3 and 4. Five pre-retired cases were omitted from Table 3 because inadequate occupational information made classification impossible.

Before retirement, husbands and wives in the upper-occupational groups were by a wide margin the least likely to say they looked forward to retirement. They were also most likely to want the husband to retire later. This is especially true for the wives. In spite of this, the husbands were most likely and the wives second most likely to say they had definite plans for retirement. The pre-retiree husbands in this group were about average in their desire to do more of the things in which they were interested, and they did not expect more often than other pre-retirees that they would be able to do more after retirement. However, the retirees in this group were the most likely to say they could do more after retirement, and they were less likely than other husbands to say they could do fewer of these things. The same general pattern held for the retiree wives. Upper-occupational group wives did not express any outstanding desire to do more interesting things before retirement, and they did not anticipate that retirement would make such activities more possible. But they reported more often than other wives that they could do more of these things after retirement. The major deviation here is that the wives more frequently reported that they could do *fewer* things after retirement than would be anticipated from the responses of the pre-retiree wives. Thus, the wives' post-retirement report was a mixed one, although it was generally favorable.

Middle-occupational couples (both husbands and wives) were most likely to say they looked forward to retirement. They were both also more likely than others to want the husband to retire early, and they more frequently than others expected to be able to do more of the things they were interested in after retirement. Perhaps even more impressive is the fact that *none* of the husbands in this group expected to be able to do fewer of these things, whereas more than one-fifth of both upper- and lower-occupational husbands had that expectation. On the other hand, husbands in this group were less likely than those in the upper-occupational group to have plans for retirement, although middle-level husbands and wives were both much more likely to have plans than were their counterparts in the lower-occupational group. After retirement, middle-occupational husbands and wives reported that they were able to engage in more interesting activities about as frequently as lower-level couples and less frequently than upper-level couples. Thus, the great expectations of the husbands were not fully realized, and the wives' retirement experience was no more favorable than that of the upper-occupational wives.

The lower group is clearly different from either of the other two. One receives the general impression from them of indifference mixed with dissatisfaction prior to retirement. They were almost as likely as the middle-occupational couples to say they looked forward to retirement, but they were least likely of any of the groups to have any plans for retirement. They also expressed a desire for early *or* late retirement less often than others. Frequently they were indifferent or content with the normal pattern of retirement. Their responses regarding the desire to do more of the things in which they were interested were the reverse of the general pattern. Instead of the pre-retiree husbands saying more frequently than their wives that they wanted to do more, there was no difference between husbands and wives. This deviation was mainly due to the fact that many more of the wives in this group than in the other groups said they would like to do more. In the lower-occupational groups after retirement, however, we found that the husbands were more likely than their wives to say they would like to do more of these things. This different pattern came about because of both the increase in satisfaction between pre-retirement and retirement on the part of the wives in the lower group and a failure to exhibit an increase in satisfaction on the part of the husbands. Both of these are opposite to the general pattern noted in Tables 1 and 2 and exhibited by the upper-occupational couples in Tables 3 and 4. The middle-occupational couples fell between the other two groups in this respect. We also found that both husbands and wives in the lower-retiree group were most likely to report that they would have preferred for the husband to have retired later than the usual time. The difference was particularly striking for the husbands. More than half of the lower-occupational husbands said they would have preferred a later retirement, compared with about one-third of the husbands in the other two groups. Since this difference was not found in the pre-retiree responses, we may surmise that the experience of retirement was such as to influence these lower-occupational couples negatively.

Although the patterns are not completely clear in this analysis of the different occupational levels, we seem to find the following themes running through the three segments of our sample: (1) Upper-level husbands and wives do not welcome retirement, but they are likely to plan for it. Their experience in retirement is comparatively favorable, and their reactions to the experience are generally rather positive. (2) Middle-level husbands and wives do welcome retirement and expect it to be a rather pleasant experience. They also seem to have relatively good experience in retirement, although not as good as the upper-level couples, and they respond fairly positively. (3) Lower-level husbands and wives are much more passive in anticipation of retirement and have few plans and no outstanding expectations. They evidently do not experience retirement as a particularly pleasant change in their lives, and they tend to be much more negative than the others in their reactions to it.

DISCUSSION

Granted the definite limitations of the sample and the kinds of data presented here, patterns have emerged which make further investigation and clarification promising. The husband-wife comparisons suggest that the conjugal relationship will undergo different kinds and degrees of strain at various points in the retirement process. The deep involvement and concern in the fact of retirement on the part of the husband, if it is accompanied by a much lower concern on the part of the wife, will make *family* planning for retirement difficult at best. The difference in concern may indeed be the basis for the impressively low proportion of our couples who had made any plans for retirement. The husband's great expectations of retirement, if followed by less than complete satisfaction and ultimately by a negative response to the whole experience, also present an adaptation problem to both the husband and wife, however "uninvolved" she may feel herself to be.

The occupational differences noted above not only suggest that retirement is viewed rather differently by couples depending on their position in the stratification system; they also imply that the kinds of strain in the conjugal system are likely to be found in differing proportions in the various strata.

Other data from the same subjects are also consistent with this interpretation. For instance, the distribution of what has been called conjugal "role tension" is noteworthy.[3] Basically, this is a measure of the degree of favorableness of each spouse's perception of the personality of the other spouse. These two perceptions may be viewed separately or combined into a couple score. For the present samples, the outcome is the same whichever is done. The upper- and middle-level couples' scores are very similar and are very much more favorable than those of the lower-level couples. The latter, then, exhibit considerably more role tension.

3. This measure is taken from Bernard Farber, "An Index of Marital Integration," *Sociometry*, 20 (June, 1957), 117-134. It is discussed in greater detail in the next chapter.

Another finding which points in the same direction is concerned
with the participation of the husband in normal household tasks.[4]
Data were collected on both actual behavior and the husband's and
wife's normative evaluations of such behavior. We found that lower-
level husbands and wives normatively rejected participation of the
husband in normal household tasks more frequently than either of
the other two groups. In spite of this, however, lower-level husbands
actually participated in such tasks about as often as other husbands.
The fact that they did this in the face of norms which preclude
such behavior was undoubtedly one of the reasons for the conjugal
role tension noted above. It seems very likely that this behavior
also indicates a degree of situational constraint on the husband to
help his wife (which they may both resent) and/or a lack of other
interesting and suitable alternative activities. This may very well
be a basis for so many lower-level retired husbands saying they wish
they could have retired later than they did.

The interpretation of the findings has been stated in terms of
the dynamics of conjugal relations and the degree of investment
of self the man makes in his job. It is possible to question this
interpretation on at least two grounds. We may ask, for instance,
whether it is the length of time retired that is responsible for the
pattern found in Tables 1 and 2, or is the pattern simply a function of age? Also, we may ask whether the pattern in Tables 3 and 4
is a function of differences in values and attitudes of persons variously situated in the occupational structure, or are these findings
simply a reflection of the fact that persons who retire from lower-
level occupations are at an economic disadvantage and therefore
more negative about their retirement experiences than those with
higher incomes? Some of our other data bear on these two issues.

Although there was a relationship between the age of the man
and the length of time he had been retired, the variation in the
age at retirement made this relationship less than perfect. Thus,
when we substitute age for length of time retired in Table 2, we
get very different results; this supports our contention that length
of time retired is a significant variable independent of age. For
instance, when the men were divided into those who were seventy

4. The data on this issue are reported in Alan C. Kerckhoff, "Nuclear and
Extended Family Relationships: A Normative and Behavioral Analysis," in Ethel
Shanas and Gordon F. Streib (eds.), *Social Structure and the Family: Generational
Relations* (Englewood Cliffs, N.J.: Prentice-Hall, 1965).

or younger and those who were over seventy, no differences between them were found with respect to the percentage who said they looked forward to retirement (66 per cent vs. 63 per cent) or who said they would like to do more of the things in which they were interested (53 per cent vs. 50 per cent). On both of these items there were notable differences between those who have been retired less than five years and those who have been retired more than five years. Therefore, we cannot explain the findings in Table 2 on the basis of differences in age.

The other question cannot be dealt with so easily. There is a relationship between occupation and retirement income, and the relationship between retirement income and the responses to our questions is approximately the same as that reported in Table 4. Therefore, there is no way in which we may demonstrate the greater adequacy of our interpretation over a purely economic interpretation. An economic interpretation of such findings is far from simple, however. Differentials in income exist throughout the lives of men in different occupational strata. If there is merely a continuation of these differentials into retirement, we might not expect to find attitudinal differences among the men as a result. Given varying changes in income with retirement, however, there would probably be variations in attitude as well. It would also be necessary to establish some level of income as a minimum below which a "decent way of living" becomes impossible. Thus, the evaluation of the relative merits of an interpretation based on occupational values and commitment and one based on income would require considerably more and different kinds of data than those available for this study.

SUMMARY AND CONCLUSIONS

Using data from a sample of older couples, responses to questions regarding expectations and reactions to retirement have been analyzed with a view to comparing the responses of husbands and wives at three points in the retirement process (before, soon after, and well after retirement) and according to the occupational level of the husband. Pre-retired husbands looked forward to retirement with greater expectations, and retired husbands generally exhibited a greater sense of improvement and satisfaction in retirement than did their wives. However, men who were retired less than five years showed the greatest satisfaction; those retired longer than five years responded more negatively. The wives indicated much less involvement in the retirement process and less response (positive or negative) to the experience.

When couples were grouped according to the occupation (or pre-retirement occupation) of the husband, upper-level (professional and managerial) couples did not welcome retirement, but their experience was comparatively favorable and their reactions to the experience were generally rather positive. Middle-level (white-collar and skilled) couples welcomed retirement, and they seemed to have relatively good experiences in retirement, but they did not respond to it as favorably as did upper-level couples. Lower-level (semi-skilled, unskilled, and service) couples were much more passive in anticipation of retirement; they did not find the experience pleasant, and they tended to respond much more negatively than did the others.

These data have been interpreted in part as suggesting that a greater strain in the conjugal relationship might be experienced during retirement by couples in the lower socioeconomic level, and other data from the same subjects are described which support this interpretation. We have also suggested in the previous chapter that because of their greater support for the extended family norm-value cluster, couples in the lower occupational levels may be expected to have more "counter-norm" experiences in their relationships with their children. In both of these chapters, therefore, there has been the suggestion that various family dimensions are related to the level of morale of the older couple during retirement. This relationship is considered more directly in the next chapter.

Alan C. Kerckhoff

11. FAMILY PATTERNS AND MORALE IN RETIREMENT

The two preceding chapters have suggested that variations in family normative or behavioral patterns may have an effect on the level of morale of the older couple in retirement. We focus on this issue more directly in the present chapter. Since in the study reported here the conjugal pair was used as the sample unit and independent interviews were held with both husband and wife, it will be possible to raise questions about the relationship between family patterns and morale in retirement for both the retired man and his wife.

The general hypothesis underlying all of this analysis is that the family context of both members of the older couple should make a difference in their level of morale. Although there is little consistency in the theoretical underpinnings of discussions of morale in old age, most studies of the changed activities and interpersonal relationships associated with aging at least imply that the loss of social involvement is demoralizing.[1] In the context of the present analysis, this would lead to the expectation that high morale would be associated with high levels of familial involvement. At the level of the conjugal relationship, this should mean that those couples who have the most in common, who do more together, and who "get along well" together should have high morale. With respect to the parent-child relationship, this would seem to indicate that

1. See "Successful Aging," and "Relations with Family and Society" in Richard H. Williams, Clark Tibbitts, and Wilma Donahue (eds.), *Processes of Aging* (New York: Atherton Press, 1963); Elaine Cumming and William E. Henry, *Growing Old* (New York: Basic Books, 1961), pp. 12-23.

older parents who have the closest ties to their children and who most highly value these ties should have high morale.

On the other hand, there are indications in the literature on aging which would point to somewhat different expectations. The general position of "disengagement theory" would lead one to expect that older people prefer to withdraw from intense interpersonal relationships.[2] Although there is some doubt as to how much and at what point in the life cycle this general proposition applies to family relationships, to the extent that it does apply to them, the expectation that morale will be positively related to familial involvement is called into question.

This positive association between familial involvement and morale may also be questioned on other grounds, at least to the extent that it involves parent-child relationships. There is considerable evidence that the relationships between the generations are rather limited in the United States, at least when compared with an idealized version of familism.[3] It was suggested in Chapter 9 that if this is so, an older person who attempts to maintain a high level of involvement with his adult children is very likely to find this difficult; as a result, he may be expected to have low morale. Also, it might be argued that in this society a highly functional relationship between an older married parent and his adult children, since it is atypical, may be an indication of some difficulties in general social adjustment on the part of the members of either or both generations.[4] In such cases, the intergenerational relationship, although it meets the needs of one or both generations, may be the source (or the reflection) of difficulties which would lead to low morale.

Finally, it might be reasoned that the relationship between family involvement and morale should vary with the socioeconomic level of the family in question. Some of the findings in Chapter 9 indicate, for instance, that those from higher socioeconomic levels are more likely to accept a nucleated intergenerational relationship than are those from a lower level. It seems reasonable, also, to ex-

2. Cumming and Henry, *Growing Old*, esp. pp. 51-67.

3. Eugene Litwak, "Occupational Mobility and Extended Family Cohesion," *American Sociological Review*, **25** (February, 1960), 9-21; Ruth Albrecht, "Relationships of Older Parents with their Children," *Marriage and Family Living*, **16** (January, 1954), 32-35.

4. Edrita G. Fried and Karl Stern, "The Situation of the Aged Within the Family," *American Journal of Orthopsychiatry*, **18** (January, 1948), 31-54.

pect that those from lower socioeconomic levels would be more in need of assistance of various types from their children. Although we have taken a different position in the previous chapters, one might reason from this that intergenerational familial involvement will be associated with high morale for older persons at a low socioeconomic level but that this would be less so for those of higher status.

Since rather different patterns of association can be predicted from the several discussions just noted, it will not be possible for us to state a set of hypotheses neatly derived from a consistent theoretical position. An attempt will be made, however, to examine these several kinds of predictions to the extent that the data at hand permit. First, the associations between morale and various characteristics of the conjugal relationship of the older couple will be examined. This will be followed by an analysis of the associations between morale and various aspects of the intergenerational relationship. Finally, the data will be examined for indications of the importance of the socioeconomic level of the family involved.

The subjects are a more restricted subsample of the same subjects used for the analysis in Chapter 9. They are the 135 couples in which the husband had already retired. All of these couples are white, and husband and wife were living together at the time of the interviews. All of them lived in the Piedmont region of North Carolina and Virginia, mostly in small cities and towns. And all had at least one child who was either married or was at least twenty-five years of age.

MEASURES OF MORALE

Three measures of morale were used in the analysis. Two of these (one for husbands and one for wives) were measures derived from the morale scale of Bernard Kutner.[5] They contained the following items which formed a Guttman scale:

I often feel that there is just no point in living.
As I get older, things seem to get better than I thought would be the case.
On the whole, I am very well satisfied with my way of life today.

5. Kutner, David Fanshel, Alice M. Togo, and Thomas S. Langner, *Five Hundred over Sixty: A Community Survey on Aging* (New York: Russell Sage Foundation, 1956), chap. 3 and appendix 4.

> Things just keep getting worse and worse for me as I get older.
> I am the kind of person who plans ahead the things I will do in
> the weeks ahead.

Scores on this scale will be referred to as measures of "husband's morale" and "wife's morale."

The third measure used was appropriate for men only, and the items were not used with the wives. This scale will be referred to as a measure of "adjustment to retirement." It consists of the following items which form a Guttman scale:

> As far as I am concerned, retirement is the best time in a man's
> life.
> Generally speaking, retirement is bad for a person.
> I am happier now than when I was working.
> I liked the idea of retiring, even before I retired.
> I feel useless now that I am retired.
> Even if my income stayed the same as when I worked, I would
> still dislike retirement.

The association of each of these three measures with the several measures of family characteristics will be reported. In each case, the mean morale score will be reported for categories of subjects defined according to the kinds of family characteristics they reported. When referring to all three scales, the single term "morale" will be used. If one or more of the specific scales is to be singled out, it will be referred to by name: "husband's morale," "wife's morale," or "husband's adjustment to retirement."

THE CONJUGAL RELATIONSHIP

Three aspects of the conjugal relationship were examined with respect to their association with the level of morale of the husband and wife. These were "value consensus," "role tension," and "husband's participation." Each of these measures will be described, followed by a discussion of their relationship to morale.

The first two measures were derived from the work of Bernard Farber,[6] who suggested that marital integration depends on both a sharing of goals and an agreement on the means of their attainment. He offered a measure of value consensus as an index of the former and a measure of what he called "role tension" as an index of the

6. "An Index of Marital Integration," *Sociometry*, **20** (January, 1957), 117-134.

latter. Farber gave ten value statements. Each respondent was asked to rank them with respect to their importance "in judging the success of families." The ranks given by the husband and wife were then compared by means of the Spearman rank-correlation coefficient. This was what was done in the present study, except that only seven of Farber's value statements were used. This reduction was the result of the pretest which indicated that many of the older persons with whom we were dealing had difficulty carrying out this task with so many items. As will be indicated by the relatively low frequencies of cases using this measure, difficulty was experienced by some of the subjects with only seven items. The seven items they were asked to rank were as follows, the measure of "value consensus" being the rank-order correlation coefficient for the husband's and wife's rankings.

> *A place in the community.* The ability of a family to give its members a respected place in the community and to make them good citizens (not criminals or undesirable people).
> *Companionship.* The family members feeling comfortable with each other and being able to get along together.
> *Satisfaction in affection shown.* Satisfaction of family members with the amount of affection shown and of the husband and wife in their sex life.
> *Economic security.* Being sure that the family will be able to keep up or improve its standard of living.
> *Emotional security.* Feeling that the members of the family really need each other emotionally and trust each other fully.
> *Moral and religious unity.* Trying to live a family life according to religious and moral principles and teaching.
> *Everyday interest.* Interesting day-to-day activities having to do with house and family which keep family life from being boring.

"Role tension" in the Farber formulation was measured by means of a set of personality characteristics which the subject was asked to use in evaluating his own and his spouse's personalities. The subject was asked to state whether he (or his spouse) was "very much," "considerably," "somewhat," "a little," or "not at all" like the personality traits listed. Although a larger list was used, only the replies for what could be called "negative" personality traits were scored. The resulting total scores thus indicated the degree to which the subject attributed negative traits to himself and his spouse. In Farber's original work, "role tension" was measured by summing the total of these negative traits attributed by both spouses to themselves and to each other—a summing of four scores. In the present discussion, "role tension" is measured by summing only the total of these negative traits which the spouses attribute to each other—a summing of two scores. This change is based on the difficulty in justifying the inclusion of self-ratings in this measure. It seemed reasonable to say that if there were tension in the conjugal role relationship, it would be expressed by attributing negative personality traits to the *other* person; but it did not seem justifiable to expect such tension to be expressed in the attribution of negative traits to one's self. The ten negative traits used were: dominating or bossy, moody, gets angry easily, jealous, stubborn, feelings easily hurt, self-centered, nervous or irritable, easily depressed, and easily excited.

In addition to these two measures of marital integration, we also developed a measure of participation in household activities on the part of the husband. The expected importance of this variable was based on the assumption that with retirement the man would be around the house more and would thus potentially interact with his wife in "her realm" more frequently than before retirement. It was expected that the man who shared the usual wifely activities would not only help his wife but would also thereby develop a regular round of activities which would contribute a pattern and meaning to his own daily life. The index used was based on the response given to items which asked "who does" the following tasks in the family: washes and dries the dishes; pays the monthly bills; sweeps and scrubs the floors; does the grocery shopping; makes the beds on weekends; dusts the furniture; does minor household repairs; hangs out the clothes to dry; sets the table. For each item the possible responses were: wife always; wife usually; usually done together; sometimes one, sometimes the other; husband usually; husband always. A score of zero was given if the wife always did it; a score of five was given if the husband always did it; and the intermediate responses were scored accordingly. The final index was an average of the scores on the individual items.

Using these three measures of the conjugal relationship as independent variables, it is now possible to examine their association with the three dependent variables—the measures of morale. In each case, the couples were divided into high and low groups on the independent variable, and the mean scores on the dependent vari-

Table 1. Mean Morale Scores of Husbands and Wives by Dimensions of the Conjugal Relationship.

	N	Husband's morale	Wife's morale	Husband's adjustment to retirement
Low value consensus	55	2.65	2.18	2.40
High value consensus	50	2.50	2.11	2.27
High role tension	67	2.26	2.33	2.27
Low role tension	66	2.61	2.12	2.48
Low husband participation	64	2.39	2.04	2.27
High husband participation	71	2.49	2.42	2.41

Note: Variations in the total frequencies indicated here and in later tables for the various comparisons result from a lack of data for some subjects. These variations are seldom much greater than 10 per cent of the frequencies listed, however.

ables for these groups were computed. The results of this analysis are shown in Table 1. If we approach these data with the expectation that marital integration and the husband's participation in household tasks should be associated with high morale, the data are rather disappointing. In none of the three tests is high value consensus related to high morale. In fact, all three of the differences are in the wrong direction. With respect to role tension, the differences are in the right direction and of a notable magnitude for "husband's morale" and "husband's adjustment to retirement," but there is a reversal of the direction of the difference for "wife's morale." The only independent variable providing consistently supporting results is husband's participation, and here the size of the difference is notable only with respect to "wife's morale."

Generally, then, there is support for the hypothesis calling for high morale to be associated with "favorable" conjugal relationships in only five out of nine tests, and the differences are relatively small except in two cases. In the first of these two cases, the husband's participation in household tasks is more clearly related to his wife's morale than to his own. In the second, role tension is more clearly related to low morale for the husbands than for the wives, the morale scores of the latter reflecting an opposite trend. It is possible to interpret these findings as indicating a greater sensitivity to interpersonal relationships in the conjugal unit on the part of the husband and a greater concern with the practical activities of daily living on the part of the wife. If such an interpretation is accepted, it would indicate a kind of role reversal from the presumed model husband-wife relationship in our society which calls for the husband to emphasize an instrumental orientation and the wife to have more of an expressive orientation. The limited value of these data and the questions we must raise later in the paper about the adequacy of one of the variables prevent us from leaning too heavily on this interpretation, but it is undoubtedly worthy of further study.

THE INTERGENERATIONAL RELATIONSHIP

Our analysis of the association between characteristics of the parent-child relationship and morale is based on two types of measures of the intergenerational relationship. In each of these types, there are two measures used. The first two are measures of propinquity of the child(ren) of the older couple and of the degree of mutual support given between the generations. The other two are measures of the normative expectations of the older couple with respect to propinquity and mutual support.

Real difficulties were involved in the development of a measure of propinquity. There seemed to be three kinds of possible measures. We could classify the subjects according to the distance from the parental home of the closest child, or we could do so according to the distance of the most distant child, or we could attempt to arrive at some kind of average distance for the children. None of these was completely satisfactory. In a family with three children, one might be living next door, one in western Tennessee, and one in California. To classify this family on the three bases noted would lead to very different results in the three classifications, and none of them would very adequately represent the true situation. The measure of average distance from the parental home was finally chosen as a reasonable, if not ideal, index of propinquity. Each child's distance was classified according to a set of categories ranging from "in parent's home" to "more than 1,000 miles away," and the average of these categories was used as the family propinquity measure.[7]

7. Some further understanding of the meaning of this measure may be gained from the knowledge that about 80 per cent of the couples studied had at least one child living within a fifteen-mile radius of their home. Thus, there was a very high degree of propinquity in the sample if the "closest child" measure was used. The "average distance" measure thus tends to "correct" for those cases in which there are more distant children in addition to the one(s) close to home.

Our measure of "mutual support" was based on the answers given to the following items:

Have any of your children helped out when either of you were sick?

Have any of your children given advice on business or money matters?

Have you helped your children in any way when someone was sick in their family?

Have you given any of your children advice on business or money matters?

Have any of your children ever offered you financial assistance?

How willing would you say your children are to make sacrifices for you?

In each case, if there had not been a need for the particular type of assistance (such as in the illness of the parents), a score of one was given; if the need had been present and had been met, a score of two was given; if a need had been present and had not been met, a score of zero was given.[8]

On the basis of these two measures it was also possible to divide the cases into a typology which corresponds to some of the intergenerational family types discussed in the literature on the American family. Those who are high on both the mutual support and the propinquity indexes (who have exchanged aid and who have children living relatively close) may be referred to as the "extended family type." Those who have children living relatively far away but who have high mutual support scores may be referred to as the "modified extended family type." Those with distant children and little mutual support will be called the "nucleated family type." And those with children living relatively close but with low mutual support scores will be called the "individuated family type."[9]

8. Here again the problems of measurement are apparent. This system was considered superior, however, to the alternative of having a positive score only in those cases in which a need had been present and met. When these items were constructed, it was hoped that a symmetrical index could be devised. However, it was not possible (for reasons of maintaining rapport) to ask the parent how willing he was "to make sacrifices" for his children. Also, the question regarding the parents' offering the children financial assistance was included, but it was evidently frequently misunderstood as referring to any time during the children's lives, and almost all the subjects said they had offered such assistance. Finally, although the questions were asked of both husband and wife, the husband's responses were arbitrarily chosen for the index, the two sets of responses being very similar.

9. The "modified extended type" was based on the discussion of Litwak, "Occupational Mobility and Extended Family Cohesion." The term "individuated" is borrowed from Elizabeth Bott, although the use is somewhat different from hers. She defines the individuated family as one "separated off, differentiated out as a distinct, and to some extent, autonomous group"; see "Urban Families: Conjugal Roles and Social Networks," *Human Relations*, **9** (1956), 325. Such a definition could very well

Also available were similar measures which dealt with the normative expectations of the parents with respect to parent-child relationships. The development of these measures is described in Chapter 9. The norm of propinquity was measured by the response to the single item: "Married children should live close to their parents." The normative expectation of continuing intergenerational aid was measured by a Likert scale (called mutual aid and affection) made up of ten agree—disagree items. These two normative measures may also be combined into a typology, but only three types are formed in this way since very few subjects accepted the norm of propinquity but rejected the norm of mutual aid and affection. Therefore, there is no normative type comparable to the behavioral individuated family type. It is possible to classify most of the subjects into the extended, modified extended, or nucleated normative types, however.

The association between these various independent measures and the measures of morale are presented in Table 2. It will be noted that propinquity is not related to either of the husband's morale measures to any appreciable degree, but high propinquity is related to *low* morale for the wives. There is a notable relationship between degree of mutual support and morale for both husbands *and* wives, but this is in the direction of high morale being associated with *low* levels of mutual support. Using the normative measures, there is a consistent association between low expectations of the parent-child relationship and high morale. Husbands and wives who reject the norm of propinquity have higher morale than those who accept this norm. Similarly, husbands and wives who expect high levels of mutual aid and affection have lower morale than those who expect low levels. Thus, all of the measures of familism at both the behavioral or normative levels tend to be *negatively* associated with morale.

Given this analysis of the single measures, it is not surprising to find that the nucleated family type is associated with high morale. The highest average morale scores of any behavioral family type are found in that category of couples who have relatively distant

be seen as covering both the "nucleated" and the "individuated" types in the present study. The combination of geographical proximity and minimal mutual assistance, however, is seen as involving greater individuation than such minimal assistance combined with greater distance. There is increased opportunity for interaction when distances are reduced, and failure to provide assistance under those conditions amounts to active rejection of mutuality.

Table 2. Mean Morale Scores of Husbands and Wives by Dimensions of the Parent-Child Relationship.

	N	Husband's morale	Wife's morale	Husband's adjustment to retirement
High propinquity of children	71	2.41	2.05	2.36
Low propinquity of children	51	2.53	2.54	2.37
High mutual support	57	2.41	2.14	2.23
Low mutual support	73	2.51	2.32	2.48
Parent accepts propinquity norm[a]		2.18 (45)	2.15 (26)	2.02 (43)
Parent rejects propinquity norm[a]		2.53 (85)	2.30 (85)	2.53 (83)
Parent expects high mutual aid[a]		2.27 (100)	2.22 (93)	2.26 (96)
Parent expects low mutual aid[a]		2.87 (30)	2.50 (18)	2.67 (30)
Extended behavioral type	34	2.62	2.10	2.50
Modified extended behavorial type	23	2.09	2.21	1.82
Individuated behavorial type	36	2.22	2.00	2.24
Nucleated behavioral type	37	2.81	2.69	2.75
Extended normative type[a]		2.18 (45)	2.08 (26)	2.02 (43)
Modified extended normative type[a]		2.35 (55)	2.22 (66)	2.45 (53)
Nucleated normative type[a]		2.87 (30)	2.33 (18)	2.67 (30)

[a]In the cases where normative measures are used for the independent variables, the mean scores reported are for the categories defined in terms of *that person's* norm. For instance, the mean scores in the third set in the first column are the mean morale scores of *husbands* who accept or reject the norm of propinquity. The scores in that same set in column two are based on the morale scores of *wives* who accept or reject the norm of propinquity. Thus, the frequencies can vary from column to column in these sets and are reported in parentheses following the mean scores.

children *and* who have a relatively limited mutual support relationship with these children. Similarly, the highest morale scores of any normative family type are found for couples who expect neither propinquity nor much mutual aid and affection in relation to their adult children. High morale is thus associated with both actual and expected independence between the generations.

TWO OTHER NOTABLE PATTERNS

The findings reported thus far raised some further questions about the kinds of family characteristics associated with high morale in retirement. Before turning to the question anticipated in the introductory discussion with regard to the importance of socioeconomic level in the interpretation of the basic findings, we will note some of these other questions and the data related to them.

Table 3. Mean Morale Scores of Husbands and Wives, by Level of
Mutual Support and Mutual Aid and Affection Norms.

	Husband's morale	Wife's morale	Husband's adjustment to retirement
High mutual aid norm–high support	2.27 (47)	2.22 (33)	2.25 (47)
High mutual aid norm–low support	2.29 (49)	2.24 (55)	2.35 (46)
Low mutual aid norm–high support	2.88 (8)	2.00 (9)	2.00 (8)
Low mutual aid norm–low support	2.90 (21)	3.00 (9)	2.86 (21)

Note: As in Table 2, the normative measure used in each column was the one based on
those persons' (husbands' or wives') responses. Thus, the frequencies in columns
one and three are different from those in column two.

We have found that high morale is associated with low expectations of the parent-child relationship. We have also found that high
levels of mutual support are associated with *low* levels of morale.
These findings raise the question of whether it is somehow a relationship between expectations and the actual level of mutual support that leads to the second finding. That is, is it simply that low
levels of mutual support are found associated with low expectations,
thus making it the low expectations rather than the low level of
support which is associated with high morale? In order to clarify
this situation, we combined categories to produce four groups based
on high and low expectations of mutual aid and affection, and high
and low levels of actual mutual support. As indicated in Table 3,
for all three measures of morale the highest mean score is found in
the low-low group, although the difference between the low-high
and low-low groups for "husband's morale" is negligible. It is rather
clear that even when (in fact, especially when) expectations are
low, the highest level of morale is found in those cases in which
the level of mutual support is also low.

The fact that the level of the husband's participation in household activities is associated with high morale, together with the fact
that the independence of the older couple from their children is
associated with high morale, suggests that high morale is found in
those conjugal units which have worked out a viable internal organization independent of other familial involvements. If this is the
case, we would expect the highest levels of morale to be found
among couples having *both* high levels of husband's participation
and low levels of mutual support with respect to their children.
The analysis relevant to this expectation is reported in Table 4. The

Table 4. Mean Morale Scores of Husbands and Wives, by Husband's Participation and Mutual Support.

	Husband's morale	Wife's morale	Husband's attitude to retirement
Low participation–high mutual support	2.46 (22)	1.88 (17)	2.14 (21)
Low participation–low mutual support	2.44 (39)	2.12 (37)	2.36 (36)
High participation–high mutual support	2.37 (35)	2.30 (27)	2.29 (35)
High participation–low mutual support	2.59 (34)	2.54 (33)	2.61 (33)

Note: Classification of cases with respect to the normative measure is as in Tables 2 and 3.

data correspond with the expectation for all three dependent variables. In two of the three ("wife's morale" and "husband's adjustment to retirement"), the order of the means is quite clear: the lowest levels of morale occurring in the low participation–high mutual support category, and the highest levels of morale occurring in the high participation–low mutual support category. The magnitude of the differences and the order of the means is not so clear with respect to the "husband's morale" score, although here also the highest mean score is found in the high participation–low mutual support category.

SOCIOECONOMIC VARIATIONS

It was suggested in the introductory statement of this chapter that the socioeconomic position of the older couple might well be an important condition influencing the relationship between our independent and dependent variables. It was noted there, for instance, that the normative definitions of both the conjugal and the intergenerational relationships are different at the upper and lower levels of the stratification system and that the kinds of mutual support likely at these different levels would be different. In order to evaluate the importance of socioeconomic position for the associations just discussed, these associations were re-examined holding socioeconomic position constant. Two measures of socioeconomic position were used: the pre-retirement occupational position of the husband and the current family income of the retired couple. In

Table 5. Distribution of Dependent and Independent Variables, by Socioeconomic Level.

	White collar (N=48)	Blue collar (N=87)	High income (N=56)	Low income (N=73)
Mean husband's morale	2.98	2.15	2.87	2.15
Mean wife's morale	2.36	2.17	2.50	2.00
Mean husband's adjustment to retirement	2.50	2.27	2.50	2.25
		(in percentages)		
High husband's participation	50.0	54.0	51.8	53.4
Low role tension	71.7	38.8	61.1	43.7
High value consensus	50.0	47.8	46.9	47.3
Low propinquity (far away)	53.3	41.2	50.0	40.0
Low mutual support	51.1	58.8	63.0	47.1
Husbands rejecting propinquity norm	70.2	62.7	74.5	59.4
Wives rejecting propinquity norm	91.7	67.1	88.9	65.7
Husbands low mutual aid expectations	27.7	20.5	30.9	14.5
Wives low mutual aid expectations	33.3	5.1	27.8	6.0

Note: In some cases the mean scores or percentages were computed on smaller frequencies than those noted in the column headings due to incomplete data. This was most notable in the case of value consensus where complete data were available on only 109 of the 135 cases.

each case, the sample was divided into two groups. With respect to occupation, the line was drawn so as to combine professionals, managers, clerical workers, and sales personnel into one group, and craftsmen, operatives, service personnel, and laborers in a second group. For simplicity, these will be referred to as white-collar and blue-collar groups.[10] With respect to retirement income, the sample was divided into those having a monthly income of less than $350 and those having a monthly income of $350 or more.[11] These will be referred to as low-income and high-income groups.

Before discussing the relationships between family patterns and morale using these controls, it is worth noting the distribution of the independent and dependent variables among the groups defined by these control variables. The basic information is presented in Table 5. Perhaps most noteworthy is the fact that the morale scores of white-collar and high-income oldsters are consistently higher than their blue-collar and low-income counterparts. This is most striking

10. There were very few laborers in this sample since all subjects were white; most laborers were Negroes in the industries supplying the names of our subjects.

11. In a few cases, the husband had refused to supply us with this information, but some information was available from the company. Although it was found that in general the company's information understated the actual total retirement income, it was possible in these few cases to place the couple into one of the two income groups with little danger of serious error. There were six cases which could not be classified by either means.

with respect to "husband's morale," but it is found with the other two measures as well.

With respect to the independent variables, there is a tendency for white-collar and high-income couples to exhibit those characteristics associated with nucleated intergenerational relationships. They have more distant children with whom they have experienced little mutual support, and they espouse norms which call for relatively loose intergenerational relations. The only exception to this picture is the smaller proportion of white-collar than blue-collar couples in the "low mutual support" category. There are fewer differences with respect to the conjugal measures. There is no appreciable difference between the pairs of socioeconomic categories in the degree of value consensus or the amount of husband's participation in household tasks. However, there is much more evidence of role tension in the lower-income and blue-collar groups.

Comparisons between the husbands' and wives' normative definitions of intergenerational relations are also worthy of note. In all cases, the husbands support the norm of propinquity between the generations more than do the wives. The differences between the spouses in this regard are particularly notable for white-collar and high-income couples. On the other hand, the blue-collar and low-income wives are more likely than their husbands to support the norm of mutual aid and affection between the generations, no notable differences being found on this measure between husbands and wives in the white-collar or high-income groups.[12]

We turn now to the effects of the use of these controls on the relationships discussed earlier. Since the presentation of all of the relevant tables would consume an undue amount of space, only a general discussion of the findings will be offered. This analysis was limited to those previous findings involving single independent variables; the use of the control variables on the data reported in Tables 3 and 4, for instance, led to such small cell frequencies that the means based on them were highly unreliable and of little value.

In brief summary fashion, it may be said that the earlier analysis has shown that high morale is associated with high levels of husband's participation, low levels of mutual support between the gen-

12. No significance may be attributed to the absolute size of the proportions here since the measure in question is a multiple-item scale, and the division into "high" and "low" scores was determined arbitrarily. Since the same division point was used for husbands and wives, however, the relative size of these proportions is noteworthy.

erations, a rejection of the norm of children's propinquity, and a rejection of the norm of high mutual aid and affection between the generations. In addition, low levels of role tension are associated with high morale for husbands, and low levels of children's propinquity are associated with high morale for wives.

These findings involve fifteen pairs[13] of mean morale scores which differ in the directions stated above. If we apply each of our control measures to the re-analysis of these fifteen differences, we produce four pairs of means for each of them: one pair for blue-collar, white-collar, low-income, and high-income subjects, respectively. Thus, there are sixty pairs of means, with the direction of the differences between them being predicted by the original findings. If the use of the controls makes no difference whatsoever for the original associations, all sixty of these differences should be in the direction predicted. In point of fact, forty-eight of the sixty are in the predicted direction. Of the twelve which are not in the predicted direction, two involve means based on frequencies of less than five cases, two involve tied mean scores, and three involve reversed differences of .08 or less. There are thus only five reversals from the predicted direction which are sufficiently large and sufficiently reliable to be worthy of discussion.

Two of these five reversals occur in the associations between role tension and the husbands' morale. It will be recalled that low role tension was associated with high morale for husbands, but not for wives. There was, in fact, a reversed relationship for the wives, high "wife's morale" being associated with *high* role tension. The initial reaction to this was simply to say that the basic hypothesis was not supported for wives but was supported for husbands. When the controls are applied, however, we find that the white-collar husbands exhibit the same general reversed pattern that the wives exhibited in the original analysis. This reversal occurs on both measures of husband's morale. We also find (although these data are not part of the retest of the original findings) that for wives the reversal is strongest of all for the white-collar group, the differences between the mean morale scores of blue-collar and low-income wives being only .08 and .14, respectively. Thus, the *only* place there is

13. The fifteen are: three each using husband's participation, mutual support, the propinquity norm, and the norm of mutual aid and affection as independent variables; the two husbands' morale scores using role tension as an independent variable; and the wives' morale scores using children's propinquity as an independent variable.

any sizable difference (more than .10) in the direction of *low* role tension being associated with *high* morale is for blue-collar and low-income husbands. All four of the differences (two pairs of measures each for blue-collar and low-income groups of husbands) in these cases are sizable, ranging from .26 to .47.

If we follow a logic which assumes that the husband is more threatened, dependent, and therefore sensitive to the quality of the conjugal relationship than is the wife at this point in the family life cycle, and if we assume that the blue-collar, low-income husband is more restricted in his life space than is the white-collar, high-income husband, then the greater association between role tension and morale for the lower-level husbands appears to be reasonable. However, how do we explain the *reversed* relationship found in the other cases? How can it be that *high* role tension is associated with *high* morale for white-collar and high-income husbands and wives? Although it is clearly a *post hoc* explanation, it may be that those persons who are more secure in their interpersonal relationship (and who thus have high morale) are able to analyze the personality of the other person more objectively and to attribute *some* negative characteristics to that other person without at the same time reflecting a serious strain in the relationship.

Whatever the evaluation of these findings, however, the analysis of the data using the controls of occupation and income have cast some doubt on the original findings relevant to role tension. It may be that the findings reflect a genuine difference between husbands and wives and between upper- and lower-level couples in their response to actual levels of role tension. On the other hand, these data may simply reflect differences in response tendencies of persons differentially situated in the stratification system. It is not possible, however, to judge the relative adequacy of these two explanations with the data at hand.

Two of the other reversals from the original findings occur in the associations between morale and the level of mutual support between the generations. For the high-income group, there is an association between high mutual support and *high* scores on both "husband's morale" and "wife's morale," although high mutual support is associated with *low* "adjustment to retirement" for the husband.[14] This is a peculiar finding, partly because it does not occur

14. In this case the difference between the means is .49, which is very sizable.

with respect to the white-collar—blue-collar comparison, and partly because it is not consistent for the three dependent variables. One might hazard a guess that mutual support is more threatening and thus more likely to be related to low morale for low-income than for high-income persons, but there is little to support this argument besides the two reversals already reported. Thus, although the size of the cell frequencies are adequate (ranging from thirteen to thirty-five) and the differences between the means are noteworthy (.18 and .23 for the men and women, respectively), no very satisfactory clarification can be offered.

The fifth and last reversal of note occurred in the association between accepting the norm of children's propinquity and the level of the "husband's adjustment to retirement." For the white-collar group, rejection of this norm is associated with *low* "adjustment to retirement," whereas it is related to *high* levels on all morale measures for all other groups. Thus, although the findings using the control variables are generally in keeping with the original finding (and this is most clearly true for the men), there is this one sizable reversal (a difference of .30) which remains unexplained.

In general, the use of the control variables of occupational position and retirement income have done little to alter the original pattern of findings.[15] The vast majority of the associations, using the controls, are clearly consistent with the original findings. Most of those findings which deviate from the original pattern can be questioned because of the size of the cell frequencies involved or because the magnitude of the reversal is very small. Of those five deviations which are noteworthy, the two reversals involving the independent variable of role tension are interpreted as possibly casting doubt on the validity of that measure. The other three notable deviations remain basically unexplained.

Although this result of the use of the control variables is less than ideal, it is rather impressive that their use did not have more effect on the original pattern of findings, given the strong association between the control variables and some of the independent and dependent variables reflected in the data in Table 5. In spite of the fact that white-collar and high-income status is clearly associated with higher levels of morale on all three measures and with at least

15. Note was also taken of the size of the differences between the mean scores for these control groups, but no systematic pattern of differences in size was discerned.

some of the independent variables, there is a clear tendency for the associations between the independent and dependent variables to remain as they were for the total sample, when controlled by occupation and income.

SUMMARY AND CONCLUSION

In an attempt to assess the relationship between family characteristics and morale in retirement, the associations between three measures of morale (two for husbands and one for wives) and a series of measures of conjugal and intergenerational patterns were examined. The subjects were 135 white couples in which the husband had retired. All of them were living in the Piedmont region of North Carolina and Virginia. There was a wide distribution of the couples on socioeconomic dimensions. The associations between morale and the family dimensions were examined for the sample as a whole and for subgroups defined in terms of the level of the husband's previous occupation (white-collar vs. blue-collar) and in terms of the level of the couple's retirement income.

There is only limited evidence that the variables relevant to the conjugal relationship are meaningfully associated with morale. The only variable which was consistently associated with morale for both husbands and wives (both for the sample as a whole and for the subgroups formed by the control variables) was the level of the husband's participation in household tasks. In households where husbands participated, both husbands' and wives' morale was considerably higher than that of couples in households where husbands did not participate.

With respect to intergenerational relationships, the findings are somewhat surprising in light of much of the literature's emphasis on the importance of family relationships for the older person. Rather consistently, those couples (both husbands and wives) who had the lower levels of mutual support activities with their children had higher morale. Also, those couples (both husbands and wives) who espoused norms which made few demands on their children with respect to either propinquity or mutual aid and affection had higher morale. Finally, although this did not hold for husbands, it is noteworthy that wives whose children on the average lived farther away had higher morale than wives whose children lived closer.

The general picture one can extract from these findings is one of a relatively nucleated family system in which high morale is associated with relative independence of the two generations and with a functional home-based pattern of activities on the part of the older couple. In terms of disengagement theory, this can be interpreted as a pattern in which the older couple is withdrawing from outside relationships into a relatively encapsulated conjugal unit. However, it is not possible in the present study to demonstrate that "withdrawal" has occurred from intergenerational relationships, although it obviously has occurred with respect to work-based relationships. Whether or not a process of withdrawal has occurred with respect to parent-child relationships, the data seem to indicate that a more nucleated form of intergenerational pattern is most favorable for the maintenance of high levels of morale in retirement.

A very basic question may be raised in this regard, however: Is it a nucleated family pattern that leads to high morale, or is it high morale that leads to a nucleated family pattern? It seems reasonable to argue that the older person (or couple) who has a satisfying life (and thus high morale) is less in need of close intergenerational ties and is less likely to make normative demands on his relationship with his children. However, it also seems reasonable to argue that a person (or couple) who is dependent or demanding in his relationship with his children will have low morale either because his dependency violates the rather general norm of independence in our society or because his normative demands in relation to his children will not be satisfied in his relationship with them.

It appears to be neither possible nor necessary at this juncture to choose between these two interpretations of the findings. The more important point to be made is that the present study lends support to the general thesis that a nucleated rather than an extended family system is associated with high levels of morale in retirement. Given the limitations of the present study, this thesis cannot be considered firmly established, but there is sufficient support for it here to warrant its serious investigation in later research.

Section Three

COMMUNITY AND RETIREMENT

Joel Smith

Herman Turk

12. CONSIDERATIONS BEARING ON A STUDY OF THE ROLE OF THE AGED IN COMMUNITY INTEGRATION

This is a report of a study of the integrative functions of the aged in a local community which has been their regular home rather than a retirement community.[1] An increasing awareness of contradictions in an assortment of observations and findings on the social role of the aged that have emerged from social science research and social action positions provided its impetus.

One common image depicts the aged as a rather helpless, needy, and dependent lot, withdrawn (or disengaged) from the normal adult activities both of their own earlier lives and of those of middle-aged adults, requiring at best only a semi-segregated, ameliorative action program to see them through to the grave. While no elaborate documentation of this generalization is provided, there is considerable literature that supports this contention. Observations of lesser voting by the aged,[2] more conservatism on their part,[3] lesser mainte-

1. Emphasis on an integrative function is in direct contrast to the radical and divisive function of the aged about which there has been speculation. See H. L. Wilensky, "Life Cycle and Formal Participation," in Robert W. Kleemeier (ed.), *Aging and Leisure* (New York: Oxford University Press, 1961), pp. 237-239.

2. Seymour Martin Lipset, Paul Lazarsfeld, Allen Barton, and Juan Linz, "The Psychology of Voting: An Analysis of Political Behavior," in Gardner Lindzey (ed.), *Handbook of Social Psychology* (Cambridge, Mass.: Addison-Wesley, 1954), pp. 1126-1134; Angus Campbell, P. E. Converse, W. E. Miller, and D. E. Stokes, *The American Voter* (New York: John Wiley & Sons, 1960), pp. 359-389; R. E. Lane, *Political Life* (Glencoe, Ill.: The Free Press, 1959), p. 168; B. R. Berelson, P. F. Lazarsfeld, and W. N. McPhee. *Voting* (Chicago: University of Chicago Press, 1954), pp. 331-347. Many of these analyses as well as others to be cited later indicate conditions under which such broad generalizations disappear or are reversed. However, here we are inter-

nance of organizational memberships,[4] and general drawing in of both the quality and quantity of contact with the social environment[5] are all to the point. Moreover, it is consistent with such easily observed trends in contemporary American society as the formalization and lowering of retirement ages, the growth of Golden Age clubs, and the proliferation of retirement communities, segregated housing projects for the aged, geriatrics programs, old age homes, nursing homes, and other such institutions. All these imply that aged populations have special needs and/or are inadequate to care for themselves. While male separation from work implies a special segregation for the aged segment of the adult population, the additional evidence of growing age-related residential segregation in cities[6] reinforces this picture of the aged as a disadvantaged minority.

While there is no other model of the aged that is so clearly formulated, a number of discrete observations converge to call its adequacy into question.[7] Although none of them may be valid or of general import, their sheer number and convergence suggest the desirability of fresh research.

---

ested only in gross observations of the sort that help to generate and maintain a stereotype. The entire orientation of this study is that such gross regularities have to be observed under more specified conditions.

3. H. J. Eysenck, *The Psychology of Politics* (London: Routledge and Kegan Paul, 1954), p. 21; Berelson *et al.*, *Voting*, p. 331; S. A. Stouffer, *Communism, Conformity and Civil Liberties* (Garden City, N.Y.: Doubleday, 1955), p. 89; P. F. Lazarsfeld, B. R. Berelson, and Hazel Gaudet, *The People's Choice* (New York: Duell, Sloan & Pearce, 1944), pp. 23-24; Fred Cottrell, "Governmental Functions and the Politics of Age," in Clark Tibbitts (ed.), *Handbook of Social Gerontology: Societal Aspects of Aging* (Chicago: University of Chicago Press, 1960), p. 661; Campbell *et al.*, *American Voter*, pp. 210-211.

4. Lane, *Political Life*, p. 78; Wilensky, "Life Cycle and Formal Participation"; T. Cauter and J. S. Downham, *The Communication of Ideas* (London: Chatto & Windus, 1954), pp. 64, 71. Ronald Freedman and Morris Axelrod, "Who Belongs to What in a Great Metropolis?" *Adult Leadership*, **1** (November, 1952), 9.

5. Elihu Katz and Paul Lazarsfeld, *Personal Influence* (Glencoe, Ill.: The Free Press, 1955), pp. 290-293; R. H. Williams, "Changing Status, Roles, and Relationships," in Tibbitts (ed.), *Handbook of Social Gerontology*, p. 290; Cauter and Downham, *Communication of Ideas*, pp. 79, 85, 216; Elaine Cumming and W. E. Henry, *Growing Old* (New York: Basic Books, 1961), *passim*.

6. Wilensky, "Life Cycle and Formal Participation," p. 238; Frank A. Pinner, Paul Jacobs, and Philip Selznick, *Old Age and Political Behavior* (Berkeley: University of California Press, 1959), pp. 61-62.

7. We could also, for example, note some failures to observe age as a factor in differential participation rates. See Morris Axelrod, "Urban Structure and Social Participation," *American Sociological Review*, **21** (February, 1956), 3; I. L. Webber, "The Organized Social Life of the Retired: Two Florida Communities," *American Journal of Sociology*, **59** (January, 1954), 342; C. A. Anderson and Bryce Ryan, "Social Participation Differences among Tenure Classes in a Prosperous Commercialized Farming Area," *Rural Sociology*, **8** (September, 1943), 285; Wendell Bell and Maryanne Force, "Urban Neighborhood Types and Participation in Formal Association," *American Sociological Review*, **21** (February, 1956), 32-33; Howard Beers, "Current Bulletin Reviews: Social Participation Studies," *Rural Sociology*, **8** (September, 1943), 294-295.

1. Studies of the family, particularly of the English slum family, indicate that older persons of grandparental status, grandmothers especially, play crucial roles in sustaining general family organization by taking over a wide variety of household tasks and chores, even including child rearing. This permits younger married couples, who from any other point of view constitute independent households, to engage in the economic activities necessary to establish themselves. Presumably, without the help provided by such elders, these families could not establish themselves in any socially acceptable and desirable fashion and would be unable to play their designated roles in the life of the local community.[8]

2. Before concern with aging had grown to major proportions, social scientists' views of the aged had a much different cast. The difference can be indicated dramatically by recalling that communities such as Middletown evoked the image of "gerontocracy" because of the predominant influence of the older members of an upper-class family.[9] Many instances in the Newburyport studies suggest the same type of situation. From the point of view of these data, the aged, rather than being a helpless disadvantaged lot, are seen as the leading, most powerful, most advantaged, most exploitative members of the community.[10] Such observations are clearly class-related, but they do suggest the need to avoid overgeneralization and to refocus concern on variability as well as on the norm.[11]

8. Raymond Firth and Judith Djamour, "Kinship in South Borough," in Raymond Firth (ed.), *Two Studies of Kinship in London* ("London School of Economics Monographs on Social Anthropology," 15 [London: University of London, Athlone Press, 1956]), pp. 50, 63; Michael Young and Peter Willmott, *Family and Kinship in East London* (London: Routledge & Kegan Paul, 1957), pp. 52-54; Peter Townsend, *The Family Life of Old People* (London: Routledge & Kegan Paul, 1957), pp. 53-55, 148-150; Elizabeth Bott, "Urban Families: Conjugal Roles and Social Networks," *Human Relations,* **8** (1955), 357-358; J. M. Mogey, *Family and Neighbourhood: Two Studies in Oxford* (Oxford: Oxford University Press, 1956), pp. 54-55. There is evidence that similar roles are played in the United States. See Harry Sharp and Morris Axelrod, "Mutual Aid among Relatives in an Urban Population," in Ronald Freedman *et al.* (eds.), *Principles of Sociology* (rev. ed.; New York: Henry Holt & Co. 1956), pp. 433-39; Detroit Area Study, Survey Research Center, *A Social Profile of Detroit: 1955* (Ann Arbor: Institute of Social Research, University of Michigan Press, 1956), p. 18.

9. Recent literature continues to offer commentary on the matter of gerontocracy. J. R. Schmidhauser's study of judges reflects deep concern over the matter; "Age and Judicial Behavior: American Higher Appellate Judges," in Wilma Donahue and Clark Tibbitts (eds.), *Politics of Age* (Ann Arbor: Division of Gerontology, University of Michigan, 1962), pp. 101-116. In contrast, A. M. Rose considers the possibility and concludes that there is presently no basis for such concerns; "Organizations for the Elderly: Political Implications," in *ibid.,* pp. 144-145.

10. W. L. Warner and P. S. Lunt, *The Social Life of a Modern Community* (New Haven: Yale University Press, 1941), pp. 205-207, 422-423; R. S. Lynd and H. M. Lynd, *Middletown in Transition* (New York: Harcourt, Brace & Co., 1937), pp. 74-101.

11. For a description of a general organization dominated by the aged, see Arthur J. Vidich and Joseph Bensman, *Small Town in Mass Society* (Princeton: Princeton

3. Some surveys of aged populations, conducted by sympathetic persons interested in rational bases for special ameliorative programs for the aged, disclose a recurrent, rather forlorn plea by subjects that they not be removed from the ongoing life they once knew. Rather than desiring special residences, special recreational facilities, and special isolated services, these subjects would prefer the kind of assistance that would permit them, as they are able, to lead a normal life amidst other adults in the community.[12]

4. If one were not aware of or completely convinced by the research evidence and simply tried to think about this situation from a fresh perspective, common sense might dictate a very different view of the aged. In any population available for involvement in community-relevant activities, the aged, more than members of any other age group, have the greatest experience, the largest supply of leisure time, and the greatest tenure. These attributes in other situations usually make persons quite desirable and enhance their access to situations they might wish to enter.[13]

5. In all the studies reviewed in preparing this research,

University Press, 1958), pp. 24-25. In France it is observed that political activity concentrates in the population over age sixty-five; see Jean Stoetzel, "Voting Behavior in France," *British Journal of Sociology*, **6** (1955), 116. For another, less direct aspect of the political effects and effectiveness of the aged, see Sebastian De Grazia, "The Uses of Time," in Kleemeier (ed.), *Aging and Leisure*, pp. 141-142. An argument for the need of the aged to become manipulators is given by L. W. Simmons, "Social Participation of the Aged in Different Cultures," *The Annals of the American Academy of Political and Social Science*, **279** (January, 1952), 45-46. See also Jean Ogden and Jess Ogden, "Sharing Community Responsibility," *ibid.*, p. 99; and H. E. Jensen, "Some Sociological Aspects of the Problem of Aging," *Proceedings of Seminars, 1955-57* (Durham: Duke University Council on Gerontology, 1957), pp. 78-102.

12. See Jensen, *ibid.*; C. L. Stone and W. L. Slocum, *A Look at Thurston County's Older People* (Washington Agricultural Experiment Station Bulletin 573 [May, 1957]), p. 40. A cogent argument for policy to the contrary, irrespective of expressed sentiment, is offered by Irving Rosow in "Retirement Housing and Social Integration," *The Gerontologist*, **1** (June, 1961), 90; and in the mimeographed paper, "Neighborhood Friendships of the Aged: Demographic Factors" ([Cleveland]: Housing the Aged, Western Reserve University, Technical Research Memorandum 5 [1963]).

13. For a discussion of the participation of the aged in voluntary associations which begins by pointing to this as a rational possibility, see Pinner *et al., Old Age and Political Behavior*, p. 67. The tenure advantages of old age for leadership "in the non-political affairs of city and state" are mentioned by R. J. Havighurst, "Life Beyond Family and Work," in E. W. Burgess (ed.), *Aging in Western Societies* (Chicago: University of Chicago Press, 1960), pp. 344-346. It is also claimed that Goldhamer finds "concentration of membership in formal organizations to be positively correlated with . . . older age groups"; Mhyra Minnis, "The Patterns of Women's Organizations: Significance, Types, Social Prestige Rank, and Activities," in Marvin Sussman (ed.), *Community Structure and Analysis* (New York: Thomas Y. Crowell Co., 1959), p. 273. In this regard, old age as an indicator of increased opportunity with respect to leisure is reported by D. C. Miller and W. H. Form, *Industrial Sociology* (New York: Harper & Bros., 1951), p. 774. An exposition of this theme that questions whether research data will support it is offered by Clark Tibbitts, "Politics of Aging: Pressure for Change," in Donahue and Tibbitts (eds.), *Politics of Age*, p. 23.

investigators seldom report the exclusion of physically and/or mentally handicapped aged persons in either sampling or analysis.[14] If popular concern with ameliorative programs for the aged is rationally based, any randomly sampled aged population is quite likely to yield substantial minorities of such persons. It is clear that one cannot disentangle the social elements of old age from the physical without some sort of correction or adjustment for this fact. Ordinarily in research, universes are defined or samples constructed so that cases not relevant to the topic under study are excluded. It is appropriate to require that a study which seeks to assess the impact of the social aspects of old age on behavior by comparing the activities of the aged with the normal activities of younger adults be restricted to those aged who are at least potentially capable of engaging in these activities. This implies that comparative sample studies should either exclude the physically or mentally handicapped in the selection process or remove them from the total during analysis.[15]

We have, then, in our legacy of thought and research, two bodies of observations about the aged that are at least partially contradictory in their import.[16] Whenever such situations develop, fresh research, conceived with such apparent antinomies in mind, usually serves to clarify the conditions under which the competing sets of observations may be valid. The research to be reported here is intended to serve such a function.[17]

We are ultimately interested in assessing and explaining the impact of old age as a *social* phenomenon on a set of interrelated social

14. An effort to remove all such persons from a sample of aged is reported by Cumming and Henry, *Growing Old*, pp. 229-240. However, nineteen (17.8 per cent) impaired persons did gain admittance to their quasi-sample of persons seventy years of age and older.

15. Skepticism about the real limitations imposed on the aged by claimed physical inabilities is expressed by Pinner et al., *Old Age and Political Behavior*, p. 68; also by R. J. Havighurst and Ruth Albrecht, *Older People* (New York: Longmans, Green & Co., 1953), p. 198. Examples of the way in which debility and illness are invoked to explain observed declines in participation may be found in H. F. Kaufman, *Participation in Organized Activities in Selected Kentucky Localities* (Kentucky Agricultural Experiment Station Bulletin 528 [February, 1949]), p. 29; W. C. McKain and E. D. Baldwin, *Old Age and Retirement in Rural Connecticut* (Connecticut Agricultural Experiment Station Bulletin 278 [June, 1951]), pp. 42-43.

16. An almost classic example of discordant conclusions about what the role of the aged in the political process ought to be is offered in papers based on independent sets of observations by Frank A. Pinner, "Theories of Political Participation and Age," pp. 70-71, and David Gold, "Participation in Party Organizations," p. 81, both in Donahue and Tibbitts (eds.), *Politics of Age*.

17. A cogent exposition of the different policy and action implications of the different perceptions of the aged is offered by C. E. O'Dell, "Attitudes toward Political Activities among the Aging," in *ibid.*, pp. 26-35, esp. pp. 26-27.

Table 1. Degree of Institutionalization of White Population, Sixty-five and Over, in United States, South, and Sample Frame, 1960.

Population 65 and over	White population		Institutionalized white population		Percentage of group in institutions
	N	Percentage	*N*	Percentage	
United States					
65–69	5,739,224	3.6	102,334	6.4	1.8
70–74	4,391,042	2.8	118,447	7.4	2.7
75–79	2,835,318	1.8	127,822	8.0	4.5
80–84	1,480,689	0.9	119,818	7.5	8.1
85+	857,615	0.5	115,476	7.3	13.5
Total 65+	15,303,888	9.6	583,897	36.6	3.8
South 65+	3,792,595		100,064		2.6
Sample frame 65+	221		5		2.3

Source: U.S. Bureau of the Census, *U.S. Census of Population: 1960 General Population Characteristics, United States Summary*, Final Report PC (1)-1B, and *Subject Reports*, "Inmates of Institutions," Final Report PC (2)-8A (Washington, D.C.: U.S. Government Printing Office, 1961 and 1963).

attributes and behavior relevant to the ongoing life of a city. It is our contention that an inquiry devoted to the non-institutionalized, physically active aged in a non-retirement urban community is important in that it focuses on what is by far the largest segment of the aged population in the United States. While institutionalization rates are related to old age (see Table 1), if we define the older population as those sixty-five and over, then only 3.82 per cent of the aged were inmates of institutions in 1960. Moreover, while it is true that there has been an increase in the number and population of retirement communities, persons over sixty-five still have the lowest rate of geographic mobility of any age group in the adult population.[18] This implies, of course, that the majority of the aged population continues to reside in the places where some significant share of adult life prior to age sixty-five has been spent. Finally, the condition that the study be restricted to the physically active aged, or more properly those aged whose potentiality for activity is not immediately restricted by physical or mental incapacities, is dictated by our concern with focusing on the importance of old age as a social phenomenon. The manner in which this restriction was implemented and its consequences for generalizing the findings to be reported will be discussed later in this chapter.

18. H. S. Shryock, Jr., *Population Mobility within the United States* (Chicago: Community and Family Study Center, University of Chicago, 1964), pp. 350-356.

Our concerns in undertaking this investigation require a research design that will (a) permit comparison of non-handicapped aged with other adults, (b) take into account the coalescence of community norms regarding the aged and the impact of these norms on the opportunities for the aged, and (c) contrast socially equivalent aged and other adults.[19] If these conditions are to be fully satisfied, they imply both the execution of a series of community studies and the identification of appropriate intervening variables for use in analyses.

Integrative activities were chosen as a focus of the investigation both because there are few, if any, formal restraints that would deny the aged the opportunity to fare well in comparisons with younger adults (e.g., in contrast to work where they are formally barred) and because there are new policy potentialities in this area that may complement existing and proposed ameliorative programs for the aged. While we shall specify the nature of the phenomena referred to more fully in later chapters, we may briefly and partially explain our notion of things that may be integrative for an urban community.

To be integrated, communities need a structure which permits them (a) to perform functions in the larger society in a way that facilitates maintenance of a local population, (b) to maintain a corporate and collective identity, (c) to maintain an order which enables the local population to do what is necessary so that the community's functions for the larger group may be served, and (d) to have a local population so motivated that residents are constrained to behave in a manner adequate for maintaining the above three conditions. Obviously a full theoretical exposition would be necessary to elaborate all these connecting links, but even this sketchy outline of community integration is adequate to indicate that such diverse attributes of individuals as voting in local elections, being highly identified with the local community, using the community's services and retail establishments, and baby sitting

19. Social class is particularly relevant in this regard. Its role appears to be so drastic that there have been reports of instances of increasing participation with increasing age. See Bell and Force, "Urban Neighborhood Types and Participation in Formal Association." They also cited other studies yielding comparable results. See also Anderson and Ryan, "Social Participation Differences among Tenure Classes"; Floyd Dotson, "Patterns of Voluntary Associations among Urban Working Class Families," *American Sociological Review*, **16** (October, 1951), 693; Mirra Komarovsky, "The Voluntary Associations of Urban Dwellers," in Logan Wilson and William Kolb (eds.), *Sociological Analysis* (New York: Harcourt, Brace & Co., 1949), p. 384.

(so that others may hold jobs, attend meetings, etc.) can all be considered integrative for the local community. As an example of the sense in which these and other commonplace activities and events are integrative, if enough of a city's population buys locally, a maximum market is maintained for the goods and services ordinarily provided by local retail establishments—hence, a maximum variety of such establishments will be available. This latter condition, in turn, maximizes the chances that all segments of the local population will not become disidentified with their community of residence, to the extent that it minimizes the chances of their coming to look upon it as a place that frustrates their efforts to satisfy their consumptive wants and needs.

In raising a question as to the integrative role of the aged in the community, we can have two types of interests. First, we may ask if older persons have more than, less than, or the same amount of some integrative attribute as other population segments. For example, how do their voting rates compare with those of other adults? Or are they more or less likely than others to join and participate in voluntary associations? Second, we may inquire whether the aged, simply by virtue of having become old, are able to make a distinctive contribution to the integration of the community. For example, it has been observed that in some cities a specific individual is widely accepted as a symbol of all the activities that go to make the community distinctive and important. Champ Pickens in Birmingham and Al Lang in St. Petersburg are two such cases. Every such instance that we have been able to discover has been one in which the person involved has clearly been old. The earlier reference to Middletown illustrates another distinctive sort of integrative situation for the community. There, the total fabric of social life is dominated by one leading family. In such cases, the sheer amount of time required in the process of rising to leadership within the family results in the leading members of the leading family being old.

For answers to the kinds of questions raised, studies ought to be conducted in communities whose social structures are distinctive in ways that can be expected to lead to different degrees of specification and connotations of age status groups. To this end an urban typology to be reported at a later time has been undertaken.

In anticipation of the need for comparative community studies, a study was undertaken in one city, and all of the materials that will be reported derive from it. However, because the typology is not yet complete, the representativeness of the city cannot be established.

Dunholme is a Southern city in the 50,000 to 100,000 population class, with low growth for its area. Historically, it is essentially a post-Civil War city. Physically, ecological segregation on racial and class lines is far advanced. The population is largely lower-middle and lower class, depending heavily on tobacco and textile factories for employment. Racially, it is approximately two-thirds white and one-third Negro. The stratification system not only reflects the typical caste-like racial situation of the South but is also marked by a relatively sharp status cleavage that stems from a local economy which has generated only a relatively small middle class to fill the gap between the large pool of semi-skilled blue-collar workers, on the one hand, and remnants of the old local aristocracy and a fairly substantial contingent of academics employed by a local university, on the other. This situation reflects the fact that a very large share of the jobs available locally come from five large employers whose needs call for either professionals or semi- and unskilled workers. While wages are low and seasonal unemployment chronic for the labor forces of some large plants, general chronic unemployment has not been a problem. These assertions are not documented in order to preserve the anonymity of the community and our respondents.

Observations of social process in Dunholme suggest that the city does not have special problems which indicate a serious lack of integration. It is true that Dunholme exhibits quite high rates of crime, delinquency, and social disease (e.g., in one recent year it had the highest rate of newly reported cases of gonorrhea among cities of 50,000 or more in the United States);[20] but as a Southern city with over one-third of its population Negro, these conditions probably do not carry the same connotations as they may elsewhere. In contrast to these conditions, evidence suggests effective organization for meeting modern community norms. In recent years, with one minor exception, all United Fund quotas have been met. All referendums

20. A. L. Porterfield and R. H. Talbert, "Crime in Southern Cities," in R. B. Vance and N. J. Demerath (eds.), *The Urban South* (Chapel Hill: University of North Carolina Press, 1954), pp. 180-200.

to approve the issuance of bonds during at least the past eight years have carried easily. This has permitted such programs as school construction, urban renewal, construction of an East-West expressway, extension of downtown parking, construction of recreational facilities, and erection of a totally new complex of municipal buildings to be undertaken. A recent referendum that was interpreted, in essence, as approval of proposed annexation plans, carried by a three-to-one majority, a result which exhibited a great many of the patterns commonly observed by political sociologists (e.g., increasing opposition to lower status, decreasing turn-out with lower status).

Race relations are relatively harmonious in Dunholme. Aside from some mild boycotting of selected stores and lunch counter sit-ins, racial problems seem largely to be resolved at the conference table and in the back rooms. There have been few arrests for racial incidents. Negro voter registration has not been a problem for more than ten years, and registered Negro voters constitute a proportion of the total registered voters that approximates the proportion of Negroes in the total population. Lest a false impression be given, Dunholme is no paradise. There is a Citizen's Council, the Ku Klux Klan has paraded in its streets, voter turn-out is usually low, political campaigns are sometimes waged in ungentlemanly fashion, and Dunholme lags behind the growth rates of other cities in the area. However, the community is unusual neither in its merits nor shortcomings, and accomplishments suggest that the shortcomings do not create any acute problems with respect to community integration.

The study population was restricted to those people residing within the city limits, inasmuch as so many of the integrative problems of modern urban centers stem from central city-suburban differences both in structure and in residents' commitments, interests, and identification. Negroes are also excluded from the universe of study because, to a great extent, features of their community life cannot be analyzed in the same terms as those of whites. Finally, all residents of those homogenous and adjacent census tracts containing the lowest socioeconomic strata of the city's white population were also excluded. This last decision was based on two considerations. Most of the evidence indicates that locally relevant participation rates are at their lowest in these population strata at almost any age, so that chances of observing age-related changes in such behavior in this population segment were minimal.[21] Since we were faced with the universal problem of collecting a maximum amount of usable information on restricted funds, this decision was economic. However, the same decision would have been made even if resources had been greater, since members of the lowest strata of the white population, in their own fashion, live their lives as separately as do the Negroes.[22]

A randomly selected sample of adults between the ages of twenty-one and sixty-four residing at a randomly selected set of addresses was interviewed. They constituted a cross-section of all but the lowest socioeconomic segments of the city's white population. This sampling produced a group of 221 respondents, which shall hereafter be called the General Sample (GS). Since the population over sixty-five was quite small, very few aged persons would have been interviewed if they had also been selected in this sampling. It had been estimated that the sampling rate would have had to have been six times its size if we were to have reasonable assurance of securing 150 interviews with older persons. Therefore, no persons over sixty-four were interviewed in this sampling, and a separate sampling process was devised to secure data from the population aged sixty-five or more.

The unit chosen for sampling the aged population was a segment of a city street running from corner to corner and including both sides. All residences on a randomly selected street segment were enumerated in order to locate persons whose ages qualified them for the sample. In households containing a qualified member, the enumerator ascertained whether the person was usually physically and mentally capable of getting around on his own. Whenever one or more aged persons meeting these qualifications was found in a household, an interview was conducted. If a household contained more than one such resident, one was selected as a respondent by the same random process used for selecting General Sample respondents. This procedure yielded what we shall call the Old Sample (OS) of 140 persons.

Because of the lack of any standardized or consensually validated

21. Dotson, "Patterns of Voluntary Associations among Urban Working Class Families." In reviewing the later literature, the same conclusion is reached by Irving Rosow, "Adjustments of the Normal Aged," in R. H. Williams, Clark Tibbitts, and Wilma Donahue (eds.), *Processes of Aging: Social and Psychological Perspectives* (New York: Atherton Press, 1963), II, 200-201.
22. Infrequent and different types of participation by the lower social classes in Prairie City are reported by Havighurst and Albrecht, *Older People*, p. 193, and Table 21 on p. 194.

criteria for identifying an aged person who is no longer physically or mentally qualified to participate in the range of activities normal for other adults, an *ad hoc* procedure based upon individual definitions was adopted. Whenever a person sixty-five or over was reported as living in a residence, we asked if that person was "kept from getting around freely most of the time by physical handicaps, severe illnesses, or some other restriction?" If the answer was affirmative, the person giving the census information was asked for the cause of the restriction and whether a medical doctor had actually given orders to restrict the aged person to the house.[23]

These procedures led to the exclusion of forty-two persons who would otherwise have contributed thirty-five interviews to the sample. Some 12 per cent of these handicapped aged were in institutions. These institutionalized persons comprised 2.26 per cent of all the persons over sixty-five disclosed by our census, a figure that compares well with the regional rate of 2.64 per cent for whites over sixty-five. While these data suggest that 19 per cent of the city's population aged sixty-five or over is so severely handicapped physically and/or mentally that their feebleness in and of itself denies them the opportunity even to attempt to engage in the activities we were investigating, the significance of this datum for interpreting our findings is completely ambiguous. For one thing, there is no way to determine whether in this city an unusually high or low proportion of people were being excluded on this basis. The National Health Survey, which would be the most appropriate source for a standard of comparison, does not tabulate data in any fashion that permits an assessment. Whatever can be said about the consequences of our exclusion procedures must be derived from our own data.

The handicaps of the excluded persons were quite severe. Almost all such individuals could hardly move around even within their homes, since they suffered from extreme coronary or arthritic conditions or loss of sight. A number suffered from severe mental ailments that would have prevented communication. These cases would have turned into refusals of one sort or other if we had not had our exclusion principle and had tried to complete interviews

23. Cumming and Henry, *Growing Old*, p. 231, report that their experiences in establishing health impairments led them to place as much confidence in the reports of others as to potential respondents' health impairments as they would place in the reports of such potential respondents themselves.

with them. This realization helped us to account for an extreme discrepancy observed between our two samples in the rate of potential interviews not completed for such reasons as refusals and repeated failures to find anyone at home. In the General Sample, this rate ran to 18 per cent, whereas in the Old Sample it was around 1 per cent. In other words, the rates of non-obtainable interviews would have been approximately equal had we not specified physical and mental ability in defining our aged universe.

Having made the decision to exclude, however, we cannot overlook the fact that our specification of the aged universe may result in an overestimation of the presence of certain attributes, particularly behavioral ones, in the aged population as a whole. At most, this means that estimates may be inflated or deflated by as much as 20 per cent of their true magnitude, *if all of the uninterviewed handicapped aged had responded in exactly the same way on a given factor.* This fact, in turn, might affect the decision on a test of the significance of a difference observed to exist between the two samples—if one wanted to generalize that difference as one between all older and all younger adults. However, the chance of this error occurring would be great only if the uncompleted interviews with GS members did not change the estimates for that sample or moved those estimates even further from those for the aged. For what it is worth, we may report that a reconsideration of the uncompleted interviews with potential GS members suggests for various reasons that many of these people, had they been interviewed, would have reported little activity in the local community. Hence, much of the potential increased difference between the two samples would not have materialized. Rather, it is more likely that differences to be reported between the two samples are also accurate estimates of the true difference between the non-institutionalized populations of the two age segments. In any event, we are not concerned with such generalizations; our exclusion procedures are relevant and pose no special problems for our interest in the attributes of two equally able population segments.

Every member of both samples participated in a lengthy and elaborate personal interview. Interviewers reported that these interviews required from two and one-half to four and one-half hours to complete. As might be expected, interviewing time tended to be much longer for OS than for GS members. The interviews were designed to obtain information concerning the personal and social status attributes of the respondent, his attitudes toward and degree of identification with the city, his knowledge of local affairs, and reports on a wide variety of behavior which might be considered either directly or indirectly to have integrative value for the community. While it must be admitted that the length of the interview poses many difficulties with regard to respondent interest and continued participation, the results of the analyses so far undertaken indicate that the data obtained are substantially valid.

The materials to be reported in succeeding chapters vary in their purpose. Since the results of our final analyses may offer a new perspective for considering the real position of the aged in a community's integrative processes, and since we lack direct evidence as to the typicality of the research site, the following three chapters are intended to introduce as much evidence as possible to indicate what we can about how generally applicable these findings may be and the sorts of social contexts to which they may apply. In Chapter 13 we are interested in the community context in which this aged sample resides. Hopefully, by demonstrating that the aged are in no sense an organized and active status group in Dunholme, we shall justify our heavy reliance on survey-type data in these analyses. Finally, we consider whether, irrespective of the nature of group status, there are any widely held norms or attitudes in the community that may affect the opportunities of the aged for equal participation in the integrative mechanisms of Dunholme.

In contrast to this focus on the community context, Chapter 14 addresses many of the characteristics of the OS itself. Here the concern is to review evidence which bears on the question of whether our universe definition has produced an aged sample of very unusual qualities or one that bears many similarities to such samples studied by others. This same evidence will introduce attributes that bear on the formulation and interpretation of the analyses reported in the succeeding three chapters.

Chapter 15 reports very briefly an attempt at a gross morphological mapping of variations in the roles of the different age segments of a population in the integrative mechanisms of a community. Here, consideration is given as to whether differential participation in such mechanisms can be observed for undifferentiated, aggregated age-segments when a few of the more obvious attributes of old age are used as a basis for predictions.

The final two chapters report the results of detailed analyses of observed differences in the extent to which two different integrative attributes are present in the samples. Since differences have been observed or would be expected on the basis of previous research, the burden of the analysis is to discover whether these differences are direct functions of old age as such or of some other factors not physically intrinsic to age and differentially present in the two groups. The two integrative attributes involved are local political behavior (Chapter 16) and knowledge of community events (Chapter 17).

Joel Smith

13. THE GROUP STATUS OF THE AGED IN AN URBAN SOCIAL STRUCTURE

While it is commonplace to think of aged people as a group, it does not necessarily follow that they constitute a real group in a social sense.[1] When a sociologist speaks of a group, he may have in mind one or more of a variety of meanings. Running through these various meanings is a basic distinction that can be drawn between groups which are real in a social sense, and groups which are simply analytic categories. Among their many distinctive features, real groups are usually characterized by wide public recognition and the existence of some consensus as to personnel and/or attributes. In most cases, real groups also have: an identity symbolized by some term of common reference; memberships which are recognized as such by others and/or by the members themselves; and an identifiable position in the larger social structure that is associated with sets of rights, privileges, obligations, and behavioral and attitudinal patterns. Real groups that exist largely as formal organizations are unions, political parties, religions and their denominations, etc. Examples of socially recognized real groups lacking in formal organization to the same degree are Negroes, businessmen, women, and children.

In contrast, analytic categories are constructed by analysts who, by developing such categories as tools, intend to summarize popularly unrecognized attributes of social units in ways that will be useful

1. The problematic character of the reality of age groups has been noted by S. N. Eisenstadt, *From Generation to Generation* (Glencoe, Ill.: The Free Press, 1956), p. 277.

for arriving at scientific generalizations. Such terms as primary groups, reference groups, and localites exemplify analytic categories. While a formal distinction between real and analytic categories can be drawn, the distinction is difficult to maintain in reality. Two of the reasons for this, either or both of which may operate in a given case, are that: (1) the analyst never works in complete isolation, and therefore useful, important, or (apparently) successful analytic categories are likely to be diffused and popularized; and (2) the scientist often demarcates analytic groups in such a way that designations and definitions are closely akin but not exactly equivalent to popular usage.

For reasons such as these, real and analytic social categories are not fixed and finite, and in the real world socially meaningful categories and their conventional designations come and go. Not only are group categories constantly changing and somewhat amorphous as a result of the dialogue between real and analytic categories, they also change in response to the dynamic emergence of newly constituted and designated groups in social structures which change as societies adapt to constantly altering environments. Recognition of this dynamic leads us to suggest that in addition to both the real and analytic groups which may be seen in a relatively static snapshot of any social situation, there are also emerging groups —groups in becoming. (These groups, to be sure, may be real and/or analytic, in turn.)

Since the attributes of a group are investigated differently according to its nature, our first concern is with judging what type of group the old people of Dunholme constitute; the answer to this question determines the appropriate method of ascertaining their position in the social structure. Our conclusions in this regard in no way indicate the group status of the aged in any other social system, whether it be the larger society, other communities, voluntary associations, or families.[2]

In this investigation, the community's physically able aged, of course, constitute an analytic category. The universe specification and sampling procedures delineate them as such. However, do the aged also constitute a real and meaningful group to themselves and to others in the ongoing life of the community? It is our contention that the aged of Dunholme are not a real group, and, therefore, that

2. *Ibid.*, pp. 272-273. A discussion of conditions under which various analytic age groups may also become real groups can also be found in this book.

the survey data alone are largely adequate for establishing their community status. All of our observations suggest that at best Dunholme's aged constitute a group in becoming, and in many respects just an empty designation.[3] Our initial observations in orienting ourselves to Dunholme first inclined us to this position. They yielded no evidence that the community's aged are identified in the public mind as are Negroes, poor whites, employees of the local university, etc. The aged have no special organizations of conse- quence in the community, nor is there any attempt to see that they are represented as an informal group in any authoritative body. People of importance who happen to be old are important for rea- sons other than their age.

The possibility that there is no compelling evidence that the aged are a real group, in the sense of being a social fact, is not surprising. Until a few years ago, older persons constituted only an extremely small proportion of the total population, and recent increases have not been substantial enough to call special attention to the group.[4] Furthermore, the city's economic organization, its location in the South, and its substantial Negro population combine to create a large lower class. Thus, deprivations are common on the everyday scene, and the deprivations of age by themselves are not unusual enough to call the group to public attention.[5] At the other extreme, if there is an informal power system in Dun- holme, it is not totally, substantially, or significantly comprised of the elderly.[6] Nor do they possess effective organizations that might

3. For a discussion of the aged as an emerging real group, see L. Z. Breen, "The Aging Individual," in Clark Tibbitts (ed.), *Handbook of Social Gerontology: Societal Aspects of Aging* (Chicago: University of Chicago Press, 1960), p. 157. They are also characterized this way for another reason by Leo W. Simmons, "Social Participation of the Aged in Different Cultures," *The Annals of the American Academy of Political and Social Science*, **279** (January, 1952), 46. In view of the recent proliferation of voluntary associations of and for the aged, Herbert Goldhamer's argument as to the conditions under which such associations arise also suggests that Dunholme's aged have not as yet become a real group; see "Voluntary Associations in the United States," *Third Year Course in the Study of Contemporary Society*, **1** (Chicago: University of Chicago Bookstore, 1942), 3. The aged are characterized as not even an emerging group by H. E. Jensen, "Some Sociological Aspects of the Problem of Aging," *Proceedings of Seminars, 1955-57* (Durham: Duke University Council on Gerontology, 1957), pp. 78-102.

4. Detailed data on this point are presented in Table 2.

5. H. L. Sheppard offers data which indicate that "old age problems" are of very low salience for the entire state in which Dunholme is located; "Implications of an Aging Population for Political Sociology," in Wilma Donahue and Clark Tibbitts (eds.), *The Politics of Age* (Ann Arbor: Division of Gerontology, University of Michi- gan, 1962), pp. 51-53.

6. Joel Smith and Thomas C. Hood, "Community Power Structures as Delineated by a Reputational Approach," *Sociological Inquiry*, **36** (Winter, 1966), 3-14.

draw attention to them. In short, other than the fact that they may look old, the aged possess no significant or distinctive attributes that might lead to special recognition.

In addition to the evidence already mentioned, salient aspects of the survey data reinforce the conclusion that the aged are not a real group in the community. On the level of formal organization, the voluntary associations of the aged are of little consequence in the community. Only two Golden Age groups are regularly active, and these receive less than two-thirds of 1 per cent of the local United Fund budget. Seven (5 per cent) of the OS members report belonging to organizations for the aged, but only one of these persons reports that this is a significant activity for him. Nor is there any evidence of leadership for the aged as an important unorganized group in the community. While respondents do categorize as old (much more than might be expected on a chance basis) both persons and occupants of positions thought to be of special importance to the community, they never justify their selections in terms of either the nominee's age or any special role that a nominee may play for the community's aged.

Another somewhat related indication of the reality of an analytic group is the existence of a pattern of informal association that emphasizes within-group contacts largely to the exclusion of between-group contacts. It is true that in describing their three best friends OS members characterize 43 per cent of the persons so thought of as old. However, in view of the facts that (a) only women, young children, and other aged persons are available to associate with during the daytime free periods of the retired aged, (b) the label of "best friend" is most likely to be applied to an intimate with whom one has interacted for a long period of time, and (c) many best friends are recruited from persons who live nearby and are easily accessible for frequent informal association,[7] this figure does not seem to imply any exceptional exclusiveness of association within the aged group.[8] Moreover, questions asked of both samples

7. In Dunholme, as in many other cities, spatial segregation of the aged has developed. Thus, 50 per cent of the OS members resided in three census tracts which provided only 27 per cent of the GS members. See Frank A. Pinner, Paul Jacobs, and Philip Selznick, Old Age and Political Behavior (Berkeley: University of California Press, 1959), p. 62.

8. Irving Rosow reports higher rates of concentrated association for Cleveland and interprets them as showing unusually high exclusiveness of interaction; "Local Concentrations of Aged and Inter-generational Friendships," in P. F. Hansen (ed.), Age with a Future (Copenhagen: Munksgaard, 1964), pp. 478-483; also the mimeo-

concerning associations with other friends, neighbors, co-workers, and relatives all reveal extensive cross-age contacts that are important and meaningful.[9] With respect to the reality of their status as a group, then, these data reflect no organization, leadership, or associational exclusiveness among the aged.[10]

One final set of observations derived from questions intended to reveal perceptions of the power of the aged as a group in the community may be offered to corroborate this conclusion. While non-response rates run 20 to 25 per cent in the GS and around 33 per cent in the OS, among those with opinions on these items, large majorities in both samples indicate the impotence of the aged (See Table 1). An interesting aspect of these data, showing how far the aged themselves are from any consensus about common needs or goals, is that, when asked whether they would approve of efforts by the aged to act as a bloc in the resolution of community issues, only 40 per cent of the total OS (60 per cent of those with a position) favored the possibility.[11] Not only do the aged lack the power that might accrue to any real group by virtue of its very being, they also lack the power implicit in the possibility of being the object of the consideration of others. Almost all respondents had an opinion on a question concerning whether the aged were considered by others in the general process of resolving issues in the community, and approximately three-

---

graphed paper, "Neighborhood Friendships of the Aged: Demographic Factors" ([Cleveland]: Housing the Aged, Western Reserve University, Technical Research Memorandum 5 [1963]). It should be borne in mind in our interpretation, at least, that given the general tendency of peer groups to show relatively high exclusiveness in intimate relationships and the general climate of negative affect for the elderly in Western societies, the evidence of cross-generational association seemed quite high. Perhaps a more legitimate contrasting standard for interpreting such data might be the rates of intergroup association for race or sex groups. In interpreting the policy significance of these rates for the elderly, some observers suggest the desirability of restricted housing projects for the elderly. What would the reaction of most social scientists be to the argument that Negro residents should be concentrated because they are viewed with prejudice by others and maintain a high proportion of their solidary relationships among themselves?

9. Similar observations are reported by G. H. Beyer, "Living Arrangements, Attitudes, and Preferences of Older Persons," in Clark Tibbitts and Wilma Donahue (eds.), *Social and Psychological Aspects of Aging* (New York: Columbia University Press, 1962), pp. 359-364; and Peter Townsend, "The Place of Older People in Different Societies," in Hansen (ed.), *Age with a Future*, pp. 38-39.

10. Nathan Kogan's argument as to the ambivalence of the aged about their status would account for such observations as these; see "Attitudes toward Old People in an Older Sample," *Journal of Abnormal and Social Psychology*, **62** (May, 1961), 619.

11. A. T. Welford summarizes psychological evidence that would make disapproval of efforts at effective group action on the part of the aged reasonable on grounds of inadequate potential psychic resources for success; see "Ageing and Personality: Age Changes in Basic Psychological Capacities," in Hansen (ed.), *Age with a Future*, pp. 64-65.

Table 1. Attitudes Toward the Power of the Aged by Those Holding
Opinions on Three Different Aspects of the Matter.

Aspect of power	GS		OS	
	Percentage agreeing	N with opinion	Percentage agreeing	N with opinion
The old don't have much power	69.1	181	70.3	101
The old don't try to exercise power as a group	81.4	172	79.3	92
It would be good if the old tried to act as a group	73.3	172	60.4	91

fourths were clearly convinced that this was not the case.[12] Finally,
a question concerning response to the possibility that the aged might
attempt to act as a group in the future revealed no objections to the
implied premise that they did not presently constitute such a
group.[13] While these survey data are not crucial for our contention
that Dunholme's aged do not constitute a real status group in the
community, they enlarge and reinforce the evidence already introduced.

Having thus rejected the possibility that Dunholme's aged constitute a real status group in the community, we are concerned with
establishing whether they are at least an emergent group. The pattern of a wide variety of our survey findings left no doubts on this
matter. Since these data are too numerous and varied to be
treated in a complete and thoroughgoing review, we shall present
only some of the more compelling observations that emerge from
a synthesis of the materials.[14]

In order to establish the possibility that the aggregate to which
an analytic group refers may at least be an emergent group (where
there is no evidence that it has any real group status in a system), it
should be demonstrated that there exist semi-exclusive designations
which can be used by members of the larger group for referring to

12. Given observations as to the imminent possibility of mobilizing the aged for
effective action, this suggests the extent to which Dunholme's aged are only an
emerging group; see H. L. Wilensky, "Life Cycle and Formal Participation," in R. W.
Kleemeier (ed.), *Aging and Leisure* (New York: Oxford University Press, 1961), p. 239.

13. A controversy over the future political role of the aged proceeds on the premise that they do not currently constitute an organized special interest group; Frank
A. Pinner, "Theories of Political Participation and Age," in Donahue and Tibbitts
(eds.), *Politics of Age*, pp. 63-74; David Gold, "Participation in Party Organizations,"
in *ibid.*, pp. 78-83.

14. Copies of a much more thorough analysis and discussion of the data
cited here, prepared as a preliminary to this chapter, are available on request from
the author.

members of the analytic subgroup. This does not imply that
everyone means exactly the same thing or refers to the same
persons in using the term; it does not even imply that individuals whose status as members or non-members is fixed by the
investigator's definitions would accept the designation. It means only
that terms used to designate that sector of the larger group can be
used by almost any of the total group's members as though they
were meaningful and understood. In fact, if the subgroup is in a
phase of emergence rather than reality, it is very likely that close
examination of the meanings held by individuals would suggest
wide variety and ambiguity rather than a consensus.

Some data that cogently demonstrate the existence of this set of
conditions may be reviewed rather briefly. A good many of the
items in the interview referred to the aged and designated them
variously as "Dunholme's aged," "the old people of Dunholme,"
"old people," "the aged," etc. If these terms had no meaning for
many respondents, one would expect that they would be unable to
answer the questions involved.[15] Since for some items the proportion
unable to answer ran as low as 1.4 per cent, it seems reasonable to
infer that most people see such terms as having a meaningful designation. While it is true that non-responses also ran as high as 20 or
30 per cent for some of the items, this suggests that high non-response
rates on certain items resulted either from lack of knowledge about
the topic or the absence of an opinion, and not from lack of a group
referent.

The second aspect of emergence, ambiguity and variety in the
meaning of a usable and apparently useful designation, can also be
documented. Responses to a pair of questions concerning the relative size and absolute proportion of Dunholme's aged population

15. It is not uncommon in opinion and attitude studies for respondents to speak
about items concerning invented concepts with no known referent as if the respondents
thought them to be real. As a classic example, see E. L. Hartley, *Problems in Prejudice*
(New York: Kings Crown Press, 1946), *passim*. This possibility is not of concern here
for three reasons: (1) The questions deal with behavior as well as opinions and
attitudes. (2) There is meaningful consistency among responses across items irrespective of whether they refer to opinion, attitude, or behavior. (3) Observed responses
for those answering can be interpreted neither as random nor as clustered, as they
might be if the terms used, though meaningless, carried a connotation quite similar
to terms for which set responses might be expected. Finally, it might well be argued
that one of the situations that faces an emergent group as it moves toward
becoming a social reality is that it must contend with an already well-developed
stereotype set that developed during its process of emergence, particularly if a pre-
existing reference term were in common use. For the possibility of such pre-reality
stereotyping, see M. N. Richter, Jr., "The Conceptual Mechanism of Stereotyping,"
American Sociological Review, 21 (October, 1956), 568-571.

Table 2. Proportion of Urban Population 65 Years of Age or Older for Different Areas and Different Population Bases.

Area	Percentage 65 or over without regard to race		Percentage of whites 65 or over	
	All ages	21 or over	All ages	21 or over
U.S. urban	9.2	14.9	9.7	15.5
Southern urban	8.1	13.3	8.5	13.6
State urban	6.8	11.4	7.1	11.5
Central cities	6.6	11.1	7.1	11.5
Urbanized areas	6.6	11.0	7.0	11.3
SMSA's	6.6	11.2	7.0	11.4
Dunholme				
City	7.1	11.8	8.0	12.7
Urbanized area	6.9	11.4	7.7	12.2
SMSA	6.7	11.3	7.3	11.8

Source: *U.S. Census of Population, 1960.* Particular volumes and pages are not disclosed in order to preserve the anonymity of the community.

reflect this situation. As the data in Table 2 indicate, depending on one's reference for comparison, Dunholme has either the same or a lower proportion of aged than other cities. Again, depending on reference, the two most accurate choices from a list of six proportions presented to the respondents were either 5 or 10 per cent. Even though no other choices offered came close to these, only 30 per cent of the GS and 20 per cent of the OS members both chose the "same" or "less" as responses to the comparative part of the question and selected 5 or 10 per cent as the best estimate of the true proportion. The observed distributions of difficulties with this subject are summarized in Table 3.

Table 3. Distribution of Responses of GS and OS with Regard to Relative and Absolute Size of Dunholme's Aged Population (in percentages).

Response pattern	GS (N=221)	OS (N=140)
Unable to make a comparison	18.6	32.9
Selects incorrect alternative in comparing	4.5	10.7
Compares correctly, but:		
Doesn't know proportion	14.5	17.9
Selects incorrect proportion	29.4	18.6
Total of completely or partially ignorant responses	67.0	80.0
Compares correctly and estimates proper proportion	33.0	20.0

The main point here is not whether these proportions of correct choices are high or low.[16] Rather, it is that while approximately eight out of ten and two out of three of the GS and OS, respectively, report a concrete perception of the matter, there is major variation within both these groups with regard to what they think the situation is. Well over one-half of the members of each sample who claim some idea of the situation report it inaccurately. If anything may be gleaned from the scant literature on public information and knowledge, it is that interest is a factor in information possession. These data, then, would suggest that Dunholme's residents have little interest in the city's aged.[17] Implicit in these interpreta-

16. The data used as a standard here are those provided by Greer and Kube, "Urbanism and Social Structure"; Bouma, *Why Kalamazoo Voted No*; and Dahl, *Who Governs?*

17. Available information on levels of community knowledge is scant; it varies with regard to such matters as the equation of knowledge, perception, and opinion, the character of the instrument used, and the sample frame on which estimates are based. This leaves the choice of a standard for interpreting a datum like that reported here an ambiguous matter at best. While scores vary with the topic under questioning, data reported by G. M. Sykes indicate that in Plainfield, New Jersey, approximately one-half of his sample was able to answer one-half or more of forty questions asked, with performance being best in the area of local government; "The Differential Distribution of Community Knowledge," in P. K. Hatt and A. J. Reiss, Jr. (eds.), *Cities and Society* (Glencoe, Ill.: The Free Press, 1957), pp. 712-713. On a two-item information test (only one of which referred to a local matter) applied to women in Decatur, Illinois, Elihu Katz and Paul F. Lazarsfeld report that 49.2 per cent of the respondents could answer both questions correctly; *Personal Influence* (Glencoe, Ill.: The Free Press, 1955), p. 274. Donald Bouma reports the proportion of a sample of Kalamazoo residents reporting knowledge of the stand of a local association on a referendum as approximately 45 per cent; *Why Kalamazoo Voted No* (Kalamazoo: W. E. Upjohn Institute for Employment Research, 1962), pp. 30-31. In comparison with these standards, the proportions of correct responses may seem low.

In contrast, Robert Dahl reports data on a referendum for a new charter in New Haven, Connecticut, which in comparison with our data reported in chapter 17 suggest that Dunholmers are relatively more informed as to the facts on local issues; *Who Governs?* (New Haven: Yale University Press, 1961), p. 266. Nonetheless, Dahl's sample was highly informed as regards high government officials but much less so with respect to more minor political functionaries; *ibid.*, p. 264. Similarly, Scott Greer and Ella Kube report data for four areas of Los Angeles concerning the respondents' ability to name one or more local leaders which also seems considerably below the capabilities of Dunholmers; "Urbanism and Social Structure: A Los Angeles Study," in Marvin Sussman (ed.), *Community Structure and Analysis* (New York: Thomas Y. Crowell Co., 1959), p. 104. No data could be found that reports results on items analogous to those used with the Dunholme sample.

R. C. Angell, in studying the moral integration of cities, reports many statements from respondents in Syracuse, Rochester, Louisville, and Columbus indicating great facility in providing factual material in response to open-ended questions about the community. What is more germane to the interpretation of our data, however, is that he carefully gears his analysis to the assumption that people will usually be ignorant of other places. Hence, they will tend to project attributes of their own cities to all others; "The Moral Integration of American Cities," *American Journal of Sociology,* **57** (July, 1951), 27. For this reason it is a questionable procedure to use the joint chance probabilities for the comparative question (two out of three) and the actual proportion question (two out of six) to estimate a standard for uninformed but correct guessing by chance. By those standards the proportions in each sample getting both questions correct by chance, if everyone were forced to guess, would be 22.2 per cent. If those who would not venture a comparison were permitted

tions, aside from those matters already alluded to, is the assumption that this rate of correct answers is low for Dunholme.[18]

One major circumstance that could account for such scatter among various forms of error is that respondents might have no consensus on whether old age can be defined in chronological terms. Responses to a question concerning the age at which a person is considered old in Dunholme suggest that this is not the case. Only 4.5

that leeway, but all others were forced to make both guesses, it would be 18.1 per cent for the GS and 14.9 for the OS; and if only those who would venture an answer to both are considered, it would be 14.9 per cent for the GS and 10.9 per cent for the OS. The observed proportions of 33 and 20 per cent, respectively, do not seem strikingly high if we assume that the group giving correct answers included knowledgeable persons as well as guessers. This would particularly be the case if Angell's notion of a projective mechanism legitimately applies, as we firmly suspect it does.

It seems worth taking this occasion to add a parenthetical comment concerning the state of empirical data bearing on the question of public information and knowledge concerning the social system. In view of the central place that knowledge is presumed to have in sociological theories built on the notion of discrepancy (e.g., analyses of the genesis of anomie; Marxist analyses of false class consciousness, class systems, and their change; the latent-manifest distinction in functional analysis), and frequent commenting on the inadequacies of levels of knowledge and information for the operation of non-authoritarian social systems, one would expect a plentiful research literature. It is, however, woefully scant. While this could conceivably result from the different status of "social facts," social scientists concerned with levels of knowledge seem to be uninterested in even analyzing the sources of difficulty, apparently choosing instead to try to organize data treated as interchangeable regardless of whether collected under the rubric of information, opinion, perception, attitude, etc. While there is no shortage of commentary on the ignorance of the American people—Bernard Barber, *Social Stratification* (New York: Harcourt, Brace & Co., 1957), p. 197; G. A. Almond, *The American People and Foreign Policy* (New York: Harcourt, Brace & Co., 1950), p. 80; B. R. Berelson, P. F. Lazarsfeld, and W. N. McPhee, *Voting* (Chicago: University of Chicago Press, 1954), p. 308—no attempt is made to reconcile the data used with such other observations as those of Angus Campbell, P. E. Converse, W. E. Miller, and D. E. Stokes. These researchers have shown that one-third of a national sample claimed familiarity with fourteen or more of the sixteen issues in the 1956 presidential campaign on which they were questioned; that over three-fourths made such claims for half or more of the issues; that for nine of the sixteen issues 60 per cent or more of the respondents provided evidence that their claims of familiarity were authentic; and that for all sixteen an average of 62 per cent were able to provide such evidence of authenticity; see *The American Voter* (New York: John Wiley & Sons, 1960), pp. 172-175. Neither is there an attempt to reconcile public opinion poll data indicating 60 per cent or more of a sample that could give authenticated correct answers about such matters as a presidential veto, the FBI, wire-tapping, monopoly, the Marshall Plan, universal military training, and tariffs; H. G. Erskine, "The Polls: The Informed Public," *Public Opinion Quarterly*, **26** (Winter, 1962), 669-677. The point about our knowledge of the level of public information (particularly as it may concern interpretation of the data in Table 3) is, as Barber says of the evidence of knowledge of Americans concerning social class, that "the evidence itself . . . is neither abundant nor very precise. . ." (*Social Stratification*, p. 197).

18. Without being pedantic about the matter, all the data would suggest that it is legitimate to generalize L. W. Milbrath's conclusion that there is "a significant positive correlation between interest in and knowledge about politics"; *Political Participation* (Chicago: Rand McNally & Co., 1965), p. 65. For examples of such data in widely variant contexts, cf. J. N. Young and S. C. Mayo, "Manifest and Latent Participators in a Rural Community Action Program," *Social Forces*, **38** (December, 1959), 143-144; and Daniel Lerner, *The Passing of Traditional Society* (New York: The Free Press of Glencoe, 1964), pp. 139, 315-316.

Table 4. Ages at Which GS and OS Members Would Consider a Dunholmer Old (in percentages).

Age estimates	GS ($N=221$)	OS ($N=140$)
Under 60	4.1	2.9
60	14.5	12.1
61-64	1.8	.7
65	27.1	18.6
66-69	2.3	2.1
70	26.2	19.3
71-74	1.4	2.1
75	13.1	14.3
76-80	3.2	15.0
81 or more	1.8	7.1
No answer	4.5	5.8

per cent of the GS and 5.8 per cent of the OS members were unable to respond with an estimate of age. Those who did respond, however, demonstrated great variability in the age estimates given[19] (see Table 4). This might, of course, account for that part of the variability in the previously mentioned items created by respondents who either said that Dunholme had more aged or estimated an incorrect proportion, but it certainly could not account for all the ignorance and mistakes expressed.

A more important aspect of these distributions is that they demonstrate how much latent disagreement exists as to the meaning of terms used without difficulty in common discourse. In addition, inasmuch as these distributions show a clear tendency for OS members to make higher estimates than do GS members, they also suggest that variations in meaning result from comprehensible forces rather than from random disagreements. In fact, although it is aside from the point here, other analyses of these responses reveal some of the factors that might reasonably bear on such systematic differences among the estimates. In any event, the data clearly indicate that Dunholme's aged are not only an analytic but also an emerging group; they can be an object of apparently meaningful discourse even though attempts to establish a consensus meaning reveal extreme disagreement and ambiguity in local use of common labels.

If we accept the position that Dunholme's aged are neither a

19. Similar variability among Minnesotans, although based on a question which assumed that respondents already considered themselves old, is reported by M. J. Taves and G. D. Hansen, "Seventeen Hundred Elderly Citizens," in A. M. Rose (ed.), *Aging in Minnesota* (Minneapolis: University of Minnesota Press, 1963), pp. 162-163.

real nor an analytic group but are an emergent group, it is possible that there exists in Dunholme a climate of opinion that affects the chances of older persons to possess the integrative attributes that are our chief concern.[20] The existence of such a climate is possible despite the fact that the aged may not be a real group; for the existence of any category, even though it is personal rather than shared, provides a point around which attitudes and evaluations may cluster.[21] Our survey materials indicate that this is the case with Dunholme's aged. The materials already reported suggest a climate of opinion that is to some degree negative. Reports of the powerlessness of the aged and the failure of respondents to consider the aged a real group suggest as much. However, the data indicate that the situation is not this simple.

As is so often the case, the survey materials suggest that there are two levels of evaluation of the aged in Dunholme. On the level of vague, unfocused generalities, it is favorable. When particular situations and possibilities are introduced to respondents, repeated instances of prejudice and negative evaluation are disclosed. On the more unfocused level, most respondents report that they hold the aged in great respect; or they are most likely to select an old person as one who symbolically represents the essence of the city; or they see the aged as deserving of more power; or they feel responsible for one or more aged persons in the community and enjoy this feeling of responsibility.[22] However, repeated small differences be-

20. Such attitudes and values are potentially norms of considerably less flexibility. For a summary of such norms as may exist for Western countries, see R. J. Havighurst, "Life Beyond Family and Work," in E. W. Burgess (ed.), *Aging in Western Societies* (Chicago: University of Chicago Press, 1960), pp. 299-353. An indication of the importance of these norms for policy, even though they may be out of accord with reality, may be found in Bertram Hutchinson, *Old People in a Modern Australian Community* (Melbourne: Melbourne University Press, 1954), pp. 145-146.

21. Comparable observations and assumptions are reported by Seymour Axelrod and Carl Eisdorfer, "Attitudes toward Old People: An Empirical Analysis of the Stimulus-Group Validity of the Tuckman-Lorge Questionnaire," *Journal of Gerontology*, **16** (January, 1961), 79.

22. With respect to this last point, on the basis of comparisons of observations made in Western urban societies and non-Western non-urban societies, a very effective argument has been developed that such regularities as may be observed in Western societies are statistical rather than normative; R. W. Firth, "Introduction," in R. W. Firth (ed.), *Two Studies of Kinship in London* ("London School of Economics Monographs on Social Anthropology," 15 [London: University of London, The Athlone Press, 1956]), p. 14. In making similar observations about children's lack of resentment about the need to aid elderly parents on collective settlements in Israel, Yonina Talmon-Garber attributes this to the fact that (a) dependency on the child is not total, and (b) the elderly parent offers some reciprocal services; "Aging in Collective Settlements in Israel," in Tibbitts and Donahue (eds.), *Social and Psychological Aspects of Aging*, pp. 431-434. Both of these conditions exist for the samples in Dunholme.

tween the two samples on certain items, for which usually sanguine OS members[23] report glowing realities in a slightly less favorable light, suggest that Dunholmers may not carry out such attitudes in practice—that if there are attitudes with which their behavior is consonant, these attitudes are somewhat less favorable.

The data contain numerous examples of more negative feelings held by majorities or large minorities on many particular matters. Semantic differential items indicate that as compared to such terms as one's self, middle-aged men, working men, and retired men, the term "old man" is consistently ranked lower on such important aspects of judgment as freedom, usefulness, effectiveness, and satisfaction with life.[24] While this is as true of OS members as of GS members, it does not seem to imply any threat to self-esteem, for evidence indicates that the old do not identify with the status.[25] For example, in selecting a specific age as a defining criterion of "old age," the old show dramatic tendencies to push the point considerably ahead of their own chronological age; in outlining the dimensions of their self-concepts in response to a projective item, they rarely mention their age status.[26] Furthermore, in responding to questions concerning the aged in more specific contexts, it is reported that older persons are less desirable than others as members of organiza-

23. R. H. Williams, "Changing Status, Roles, and Relationships," in Tibbitts (ed.), *Handbook of Social Gerontology*, p. 290. Williams reports the Berkeley study as showing the aged to be "more content." Tendencies of the aged not to be overtly critical of others are interpreted as defensiveness by Pinner *et al.*, *Old Age and Political Behavior*, p. 69. That there is a general pattern of disregard, non-concern, low esteem, and disrespect for the old in American culture, for which such protective devices would be appropriate, is asserted by W. J. Mackinnon and Richard Centers, "Authoritarianism and Urban Stratification," *American Journal of Sociology*, **61** (May, 1956), 613. Data showing this same tendency, reflected in the form of not exercising the opportunity to observe the existence of invidious differences, are reported by Faina Jyrkilä, "Society and Adjustment to Old Age," *Transactions of the Westermarck Society*, **5** (1960), 45.

24. The data also reflect a more unfavorable ranking of "old man" by GS members, comparable to that reported by Nathan Kogan and M. A. Wallach, "Age Changes in Values and Attitudes," *Journal of Gerontology*, **16** (July, 1961), 272-280.

25. This phenomenon is repeatedly reported in the research literature. See L. R. Dean, "Aging and the Decline of Instrumentality," *ibid.*, **15** (October, 1960), 403-407; Jyrkilä, "Society and Adjustment to Old Age," pp. 43-47; Kogan, "Attitude toward Old People in an Older Sample," p. 621; H. Meltzer, "Age Differences in Status and Happiness of Workers," *Geriatrics*, **17** (December, 1962), 833-834; I. K. Zola, "Feelings about Age among Older People," *Journal of Gerontology*, **17** (January, 1962), 65-68.

26. This parallels the observation that members of a California pension organization "are reluctant to identify themselves as aged"; Pinner *et al.*, *Old Age and Political Behavior*, p. 89. See also Zena Smith Blau, "Changes in Status and Age Identification," *American Sociological Review*, **21** (April, 1956), 200; and a good concise summary by Irving Rosow, "Adjustment of the Normal Aged," in R. H. Williams, Clark Tibbitts, and Wilma Donahue (eds.), *Processes of Aging* (New York: Atherton Press, 1963), II, 207.

tions and that they have fewer chances of becoming officers,[27] that others are likely to feel responsibilities to the old as burdensome or merely obligatory rather than enjoyable, that if age makes a difference in community spirit it is the aged who have least, that others do not have the great respect for the aged that the respondent has, and so on. In general, when question wording did not reveal to the respondent that he was expressing his own opinion or feeling, the likelihood increased that negative affect for the community's aged would be revealed.

A rather poignant illustration of how this process operates in Dunholme can be derived from responses to a series of questions concerning the fate of a low-rent housing project for the community's aged, developed and proposed by the Dunholme Housing Authority without the participation of the old. More than 25 per cent of the GS and 15 per cent of the OS did not remember this recent community issue of considerable controversy.[28] The carefully planned proposal had eventually been abandoned after a campaign of protests by local property owners who freely expressed concern that older persons made undesirable neighbors. When those respondents who recalled the matter were questioned further, there were widespread admissions of awareness of this factor in the outcome of the issue. As for themselves, however, only a few admitted sharing these feelings, claiming instead, when asked, that they would not mind having the project located close to their own homes!

Psychological mechanisms involving projection to relieve guilt deriving from the holding of socially unacceptable prejudices may be at work here. Analogous processes may account for the willing approval of possible bloc status for the aged (see Table 1).[29] In

27. Observations in Prairie City suggest that old people have little chance to hold office; see R. J. Havighurst and Ruth Albrecht, *Older People* (New York: Longmans, Green & Co., 1953), p. 339. Similar observations by old people who feel unwanted in voluntary associations are reported by Pinner *et al.*, *Old Age and Political Behavior*, pp. 67-68.

28. Of eight such issues about which respondents were questioned, the housing proposal ranked third in the respondents' inability to recall. As noted in footnotes 9 and 11 of this chapter, in view of the sample's generally superior information as compared with data reported from other research, this is a relatively poor performance.

29. This type of projection is also reflected in the pattern of differences presented in the first section of a table by Meltzer, "Age Differences in Status and Happiness of Workers," p. 833. Consistent interpretations invoking different psychic mechanisms are offered by Jyrkilä in "Society and Adjustment to Old Age," pp. 15-17, who suggests that revealed attitudes toward the aged are a mask of passive indifference hiding a latent negativism; and P. E. Slater, who argues that the young project their guilt and hostility for the aged to the aged in "Cultural Attitudes toward the Aged," *Geriatrics*, 18 (April, 1963), 308-314. Our interpretation only adds to Slater's formulation the possibility of such projections to other adults as well.

view of repeated overt statements from all sources in the community condemning bloc activities of any sort by the three or more blocs that already operate actively in Dunholme, any other conclusion about this anomalous response would not seem to fit the facts.

This, then, seems to be the situation of the aged in Dunholme. As members of an emergent group they lack the strengths that pooled resources and shared identifications provide to members of real groups.[30] Nonetheless, in many concrete situations they may be treated by others as though they were members of such a group, one which appears to carry with it the onus of unfavorable and deleterious stereotypes.[31] The particular problem of the aged individual who is seeking to maintain as normal a life as his situation permits is to walk the tightrope between those favorable sentiments which residents express when situations are vague and general and those much more negative judgments which condition behavior and beliefs in particular situations. The difficulties inherent in succeeding at this task, as well as many indications of OS members' sensitivities in perceiving these underlying antipathies, may well account for the failure of older persons to identify themselves as part of an older group, which among other things serves to keep the aged in their emergent group status.[32]

In view of expected increases in the proportion of aged in the adult community, the tendency to think of them as a problem group bereft of many resources, the availability of potential leadership for the aged among persons to whom importance is attributed, and reports by the elderly of sensed disadvantages and prejudice, we might hazard the prediction that Dunholme's aged are likely to become a real group in the community.[33] Using the opinions expressed

30. In view of the number of studies cited that show some consensus on attitudes and opinions regarding the aged, it might be thought that these provide evidence that the aged are a real group. However, in all these studies, references are to ambiguous "elderly," "old people," "old man," etc. As good examples, see Peggy Golde and Nathan Kogan, "Sentence Completion Procedure for Assessing Attitudes toward Old People," *Journal of Gerontology*, **14** (July, 1959), 355-363; and Nathan Kogan and F. C. Shelton, "Images of 'Old People' and 'People in General' in an Older Sample," *Journal of Genetic Psychology*, **100** (March, 1962), 3-21. As pointed out earlier in this chapter, however, our concern is with the aged of Dunholme and their group status in its social system.

31. Kogan and Shelton, *ibid.*, pp. 17-20; and Golde and Kogan, "Sentence Completion Procedure for Assessing Attitudes toward Old People," pp. 359-360. Rosow, "Neighborhood Friendships of the Aged," p. 9.

32. The role of symbolic interaction in this process is suggested by A. M. Rose, "The Subculture of the Aging: A Topic for Sociological Research," *The Gerontologist*, **2** (September, 1962), 126.

33. This conclusion is little more than a guess about which others have disagreed.

as a guide, and in the absence of any significant shift in the status situation of the aged as the process of change from emergence to reality proceeds, we might expect Dunholme to provide its aged with a social environment marked increasingly by prejudice, deroga-tion, and social deprivation.[34]

These findings leave the impression that, if it were socially ac-ceptable, large numbers of people in Dunholme would express strong agreement with such statements as "it's nice to be old but I wouldn't want to be," or "old people are good people but I would just as soon have nothing to do with them."[35] The prognosis seems to be that the community's aged will not easily become transformed to a respected and effectively active real status group as they in-evitably increase in number.

Having thus charted the approximate position of the aged in the matrix of social structure and norms, we can now turn our attention to the actual details of the everyday social life of the community's aged. Such a review can permit us to assess whether the OS mem-bers constitute a group that is unusual in comparison with others that have been studied.

After reviewing extensive research on political behavior, Angus Campbell concludes that the prognosis is poor that the aged will become an effective real group in the national political scene; "Social and Psychological Determinants of Voting Behavior," in Donahue and Tibbitts (eds.), *The Politics of Age*, pp. 98-100. A. M. Rose comes to a similar conclusion on the basis of other evidence; see "Organizations for the Elderly: Political Implications," in *ibid.*, pp. 144-145.

34. This is the situation that Irving Rosow sees as currently characterizing the elderly whose residences are scattered throughout the community; "Retirement Hous-ing and Social Integration," *The Gerontologist*, 1 (June, 1961), 88-89.

35. Even stronger feelings are reflected by Meltzer's respondents who describe the years beyond sixty as the "worst" period of life; see "Age Differences in Status and Happiness of Workers," pp. 831-838.

Joel Smith

14. THE NARROWING SOCIAL WORLD OF THE AGED

This entire study is concerned with locating and accounting for differences in both the degree to which and modes in which older persons and other adults engage in behavior and hold thoughts that may have integrative significance for the urban communities in which they reside. Our approach to this question will ultimately involve the attempt to demonstrate that observable differences between selected groups of aged and other adults, often considered a product of the infirmities and incapacities of old age, may be accounted for by a variety of social factors. To this end, sampling procedures were adopted that were intended to minimize such handicaps as possible major causes of observed differences between age groups. In addition, analysis has shown that while Dunholme's aged are not yet formally recognized to the extent that their behavior is governed by near-manifest prescriptions, latent prejudicial attitudes do exist in the community. These attitudes bear potentially both on the opportunities of the aged to do whatever they might like and their conceptions of the responses they are likely to evoke in associating with other adults. This is the extent to which we have thus far argued the reasonableness of considering the significance of social factors in understanding certain differences among age strata.

As a result of our sampling design, with regard to the selection of both individual cases and a single city in which to conduct a study, there is the possibility that these findings may not apply generally. We have already considered some aspects of this problem while discussing the import of the procedures for defining a universe of able-bodied persons of sixty-five and over. In this chapter this matter is again addressed with data which demonstrate whether previously and commonly observed differences between the aged and other adults exist in the two samples despite the fact that the universe of aged has been limited in this way. If it can be argued that, because of a bias arising from our sampling procedures, we unfairly imply the aged in contrast to the young are better off than other studies have shown, in this chapter any sampling effects should have the reverse effect. That is, since we are considering a variety of things that may be thought of as handicaps, deprivations, and incapacities, any biasing effect from sampling should mean that Dunholme's aged are at least as badly off as our data may indicate.

We want to show whether certain possible differences between our two samples exist. We are not at all interested here in accounting for any such differences that may be demonstrated. For example, with regard to participation in voluntary associations (which will be discussed here), it is quite true that an observable lower participation rate for the aged could result from such a factor as class differences between the samples. This, however, we deem to be another problem, one we need not address if our purpose is only to demonstrate that the analyses in our final chapters may have wider meaning. In regard to this example, differences in the social class distribution of the aged and those of other age segments in communities have been considered as reasonable causes for differences of the sort we may succeed in demonstrating.[1] However, the reader should recall that the limitations imposed on the areas of sampling within the city have the effect of narrowing differences in class distributions that may exist.

We are specifically concerned in this chapter with whether the OS, being more physically and mentally equivalent to younger samples than such samples often are,[2] has escaped the shrinking and narrower life space that other investigators find associated with old

1. H. L. Wilensky, "Life Cycle and Formal Participation," in R. W. Kleemeier (ed.), *Aging and Leisure* (New York: Oxford University Press, 1961), p. 238; Irving Rosow, "Adjustment of the Normal Aged," in R. H. Williams, Clark Tibbitts, and Wilma Donahue (eds.), *Processes of Aging* (New York: Atherton Press, 1963), II, 200-201.

2. The one study that probably comes closest to this in its concern with excluding seriously impaired old people from its sample is that of Elaine Cumming and W. E. Henry, *Growing Old* (New York: Basic Books, 1961). However, they did admit nineteen (17.8 per cent) such individuals to their quasi-sample of persons seventy years of age and older (pp. 236-240). It is unlikely that more than one or two such persons gained entry to our OS by eluding our filter.

age. Evidence pertinent to this point is rather difficult to obtain without being specific, so our inquiries were focused on specific matters. In all cases we have selected aspects of life for which it seems most reasonable to conclude that, at least in part, differences result from the individual's having attained the status of being old. These will be considered in two groups. The first deals with those aspects of life for which OS respondents could provide claims of changes having occurred directly as a response to aging. The second is distinguished by both the absence of any such direct claims and the absence of any additional evidence suggesting that differences cannot at least partly be attributed to the fact that one has aged. The first group includes: (a) work, (b) consumption patterns, (c) use of normal urban consumer facilities, (d) memberships in voluntary associations, (e) friendships, (f) self-assessment of importance to the community, (g) health, and (h) religious practice.

Work

With the increasing impact of social security and pressure on the labor force, more and more jobs entail automatic and enforced retirement. Retirement in turn has begun to take on some negative connotations;[3] whereas it formerly indicated that a man had mastered the economic institution sufficiently to provide for his needs without working, it has also become a symbol of involuntary divorcement from the world of work—an enforced unemployment from which there is little or no hope of relief.[4] Studies of the unemployed during depressions indicate that one major effect of involuntary work loss is a shattering of the individual's self-esteem and a related decrement in performance in other statuses.[5] Hence, we have considered the absence of work as a socially constricting experience for our sample members.[6]

3. H. L. Orbach, "Normative Aspects of Retirement," in Clark Tibbitts and Wilma Donahue (eds.), *Social and Psychological Aspects of Aging* (New York: Columbia University Press, 1962), pp. 56-57.

4. Data to show that most retirements are voluntary and based on health reasons are reported in R. D. Dorfman, "The Labor Force Status of Persons Aged Sixty-Two and Over," *American Economic Review,* **44** (May, 1954), 635. However, since health status is not controlled and many more members of this sample than of our OS continue to work, the general relevance of his interpretation is not clear.

5. Philip Eisenberg and P. F. Lazarsfeld, "The Psychological Effects of Unemployment," *Psychological Bulletin,* **35** (June, 1938), 361-367; H. E. Jensen, "Some Sociological Aspects of the Problem of Aging," *Proceedings of Seminars, 1955-57* (Durham: Duke University Council of Gerontology, 1957), pp. 78-102.

6. While it is not crucial, this interpretation recognizes that the reasons for and nature of retirement are variable in many respects (Rosow, "Adjustment of the

In all GS families one or more of the responsible adults worked, and this was also true of all OS families in earlier years. The question remains as to the current work status of OS families, since the retirement of surviving males or their surviving wives signifies loss of contact with the world of work for the family unit. Among the sixty surviving married couples in the OS, ten of the husbands are still working at full-time jobs and four are in part-time jobs. The remaining eighty respondents are widows, widowers, spinsters, and bachelors, only five of whom are working full-time and one of whom is working part-time. In total, the OS contains only fifteen full-time and five part-time surviving workers. All other respondents have already experienced the trauma or relief of work loss.

Consumption Patterns

OS members were asked whether they had experienced various constrictions in level or style of life since age fifty-five. Any respondent reporting such a constriction was further asked whether it was because of decreased financial resources or other considerations. Of the OS respondents, 46.4 per cent reported one or more such constrictions, and of these respondents, 44.6 per cent attributed some or all of those constrictions to a weakened financial position.[7] For the entire OS, 53.6 per cent reported no constriction on these items, 20.7 per cent reported at least some based on a weakened financial status, and 25.7 per cent reported constrictions only for other reasons. The number of constrictions reported averaged 1.09 for the entire OS, and 2.34 for only those respondents reporting any constriction. Comparable averages for financially based and other constrictions for the total and the affected groups, respectively, were .50 as compared with .59, and 1.08 as compared with 1.26. OS members attributing at least some constrictions to financial considerations reported an average of 2.41, while those reporting constrictions only for other reasons mentioned an average of 1.78. One-third of those reporting financially based constrictions reported a total of sixteen other constrictions as well.

Normal Aged," pp. 216-218; M. S. Gordon, "Changing Patterns of Retirement," *Journal of Gerontology*, **15** [July, 1960], 300-304), and that the consequences of retirement may only be deleterious under special circumstances (W. E. Thompson, Gordon F. Streib, and John Kosa, "The Effect of Retirement on Personal Adjustment: A Panel Analysis," *Journal of Gerontology*, **15** [April, 1960], 165-169).

7. Results of a national survey report various unmet needs due to a lack of money at almost exactly the same rate; see Ethel Shanas, *Family Relationships of Older People* ("Health Information Foundation, Research Series," 20 [New York, 1961]), p. 56.

Some of these constrictive compromises with age occur more frequently than others (e.g., thirty-three persons reported giving up their houses as opposed to eight who reported giving up clubs). Moreover, some constrictions tend largely to be financially based, others are usually responses to other considerations, and still others are fairly equally divided in this respect. Constrictive acts in which financial considerations were not paramount included decisions to move to smaller residences, to give up automobiles, and to stop attending church. Decisions to give up club memberships and to buy lower quality clothing were based on financial considerations in a clear majority of cases. Constrictive acts attributed to decreased income in about half of the reported cases include the giving up of homes and the decreasing of expenditures for food, vacations, and household repairs.

Consumer Facilities

Urban residents normally depend upon a host of public commercial facilities to provide for their needs. The variety and frequency of use of such facilities is, among other things, a measure of exposure to a class of social contacts and experiences; these facilities also affect the pattern and rate of movement through the city. The percentage of old persons not using such facilities may be interpreted as a crude estimate of decline in use. However, not all of the younger urban residents use these facilities. By considering the percentage in the GS reporting that they do not use these facilities

Table 1. Differences in the Non-Use of Consumer Facilities by the Two Samples.

Facility type	Percentage of non-users in OS	GS	Absolute decline (OS-GS)	Rate of decline $\left(\dfrac{OS-GS}{100-GS}\right)$
Food stores	14.3	1.4	12.9	13.1
Drug stores	10.7	1.8	8.9	9.1
Furniture stores	69.3	21.7	47.6	60.8
Gas stations	57.1	12.2	44.9	51.1
Beauty parlors (females only)	30.1	——	30.1	30.1
Barber shops (males only)	——	——	——	——
Banks	22.1	7.2	14.9	16.1
Dry cleaning establishments	33.6	23.5	10.1	13.2
Restaurants and cafes	42.1	11.8	30.3	34.4
Hardware stores	56.4	13.6	42.8	49.5

as an estimate of non-use which is not related to age, we can treat the difference between these two proportions as a more refined estimate of the proportion of OS members restricting their use.

Application of these procedures reveals an absolute decline in use of consumer facilities. The final column of Table 1 is an estimate of the proportion of users among the OS who may have ceased to use a facility. While declines are common, the rate of decline varies considerably with the type of facility. In general, the types of facilities experiencing low declines are either the most vital and/or widely available throughout the city.[8] It would appear that a decline in the use of facilities is quite likely, except as it is mediated by either vital need and/or accessibility.

Memberships in Voluntary Associations

Various restrictions in the data make it impossible to say exactly how many OS members decreased their participation in voluntary associations or exactly how many experienced one or more such membership losses. However, a minimum of sixty-eight memberships given up is reported in the interviews. Respondents explain these membership cancellations in such a wide variety of ways that it is difficult to establish whether they are a direct result of being old, of attributes that are correlates of old age, or of other factors.[9] Nonetheless, in order to assess the possibility that this membership decrease was age-related, the ratios of cancelled memberships to retained memberships in the two samples were compared. The results indicate that OS members experience a minimum of approximately two membership losses for every three still maintained, whereas the comparable GS ratio is only one to three. While this considerable difference might reflect only the increased opportunity of a person who has lived longer to leave an organization, examination of the types of organizations (e.g., union memberships, P.T.A.'s, professional groups, civic groups) for which membership cancellations are reported in the two groups suggests that most of these reported by the OS were a result of passage through the age cycle.[10]

8. These observations and findings concerning lesser use of downtown facilities by OS members contradict the report of C. T. Jonassen, *Factors Affecting Shopping Habits and Attitudes* (Columbus: Bureau of Business Research, Ohio State University, 1955), p. 82.

9. Wilensky, "Life Cycle and Formal Participation," p. 238, offers a sociological explanation as to why this type of participation may decrease among the aged.

10. Declines are also reported by Frank A. Pinner, Paul Jacobs, and Philip Selznick,

Friendships

Only 20.4 per cent of the OS report that they see friends as much now as they did when they were fifty-five. Of those who report a shift, 83.5 per cent report a decline. This represents two-thirds of the OS members giving information on this matter.[11]

Self-Assessment of Importance to the Community

The old, significantly more than the younger adults, judge their activities as unimportant to the community (52.1 per cent vs. 38.6 per cent). When questioned concerning their reasons for feeling this way, 30 per cent volunteered their old age as the reason. Furthermore, slightly more than half of these specifically report that this feeling results from a cessation of earlier life activities that were deemed important. The only other reasons given with substantial frequency by OS members who express a sense of unimportance are statements of self-derogation involving assertions of personal insignificance or resource deprivations and simple affirmative assertions of general inactivity. These last two types of statements are also used most frequently by GS members to explain an expressed sense of unimportance. In addition, such GS members also mention with some frequency non-participation in civic groups or civic work. A slightly smaller group (12.5 per cent) tie it to their lack of any sense of identification with Dunholme, an explanation not offered by any OS members. Both groups also offer a wide scattering of other explanations. Of the OS members who report still feeling their activities to be important, none indicates an increase in such activities with aging.

Physical Condition and Health

In general, OS members report poorer health. This is not likely to be just a difference between populations whose general adult

Old Age and Political Behavior (Berkeley: University of California Press, 1959), p. 67. Also see R. J. Havighurst and Ruth Albrecht, *Older People* (New York: Longmans, Green & Co., 1953), pp. 192-193; and Faina Jyrkilä, "Society and Adjustment to Old Age," *Transactions of the Westermarck Society*, 5 (1960), 61.

11. Jyrkilä, *ibid.*, p. 61; Marc Zborowski and L. D. Eyde, "Aging and Social Participation," *Journal of Gerontology*, 17 (October, 1962), 426.

health was different, but rather a difference that developed with advancing age. A very much higher proportion of OS than GS members report decreasing energy as they have become older (72 per cent vs. 42 per cent). That this is an age-related phenomenon is suggested by the fact that a higher proportion of OS than GS members who consider their health to be changing describe it as getting worse. Moreover, this is probably not an empty introspective hypochondriasis, since OS members who report physical problems also report that these lead to many more restrictions on socially relevant activities than do GS members with physical problems.

Church Attendance

Church attendance is low in our youngest age group (twenty-one to twenty-seven); this group attends a little less than once a month on the average. Average attendance increases regularly to a maximum of almost once a week in the age group fifty-five to sixty-four; it then decreases regularly, being almost three times a month for those sixty-five to seventy-four, dropping to approximately twice a month for those seventy-five to eighty-four, and reaching a low of every other month for those over eighty-five. All persons who reported themselves as ever attending church were asked if and in what manner their attendance rates had changed. For the GS the reference was since adulthood, and for the OS since age fifty-five. The two samples did not differ in their rates of reporting change (GS = 42 per cent and OS = 41 per cent). However, 63.8 per cent of the GS members whose attendance rates had changed reported decreases, while 80.9 per cent of the OS sample members did so. That this is not merely a reflection of decreased religious interest on the part of the old, but a shift from social to more ecstatic religion is indicated by two facts. (1) OS decreasers report much more exposure to emotional and expressive revivalistic church services on radio and television than do GS decreasers. (2) Irrespective of pattern of change in church attendance, more OS than GS members report that they feel that some after-life has primacy over this life. Whereas only 31 per cent of the OS members think that this life has primacy, 55 per cent of the GS members subscribe to this view.[12]

12. Comparable church attendance rates, declining with age but associated with

In every area of life thus far considered, differences have been observed between the GS and OS that can be directly attributed to the process of aging. All these changes, in varying ways, have the effect of narrowing the meaningful life space of aging persons. They tend to decrease both the range of meaningful interaction and the scope of opportunities toward which the older person's resources may be applied. To the extent that inferences may be based on these findings, they suggest a reorientation from the world of men and affairs to the world of the self and to personal religion.

Other aspects of life for which differences between the two samples would be expected have also been examined. Unlike the first group, however, the conclusion that any differences which may emerge are due to a change in age status is not based on evidence as direct as that just reported. Instead, the conclusion can only be based on two considerations: (1) the absence of evidence that standards have shifted for the aspects of life being treated; and (2) the conclusions of other investigators that such differences exist and are attributable to the process of aging. In interpreting these findings it should be remembered that the data may minimize the chances of observing differences because the most handicapped, who are those most likely to show deprivations and major symptoms of withdrawal, are excluded. Hence, in general, attention should be directed more to the direction of differences between the samples than to the absolute level at which certain commonly recognized symptoms of aging occur.

Of the many interview items that bear on the total question of change in the quality and size of life space, only a selection are considered in this discussion. As shall be seen, the results are so consistent as to obviate the possibility that examination of more items would change the picture. The relevant materials can be discussed in three sections dealing with (*a*) capacities, (*b*) breadth of environmental contacts, and (*c*) self-concepts.

---

unchanging or increasing religious "interest," are reported by Pinner *et al.*, *Old Age and Political Behavior*, p. 68. Completely parallel but more elaborate findings are summarized in Michael Argyle, *Religious Behaviour* (London: Routledge & Kegan Paul, 1958), pp. 67-68. A shift in the type of religious activity that is associated with age, parallel to that reported here, is reported by N. J. Demerath, *Social Class in American Protestantism* (Chicago: Rand McNally & Co., 1965), pp. 101-103. See also H. L. Orbach, "Aging and Religion," *Geriatrics*, **16** (October, 1961), 530-540.

Capacities

Data were collected that indicate both the social and physical resources available for the individual to invest in the common social activities of daily life. In both respects the aged are handicapped in comparison with the GS members. With respect to social resources, the OS has less formal education, lower income, and a lower general social class level.[13] In other words, OS members have fewer of the public badges that elicit respect when efforts are made to enter situations which might be integrative for the community.

Despite the sampling restrictions, OS members are also more handicapped by their physical and health status. OS members to a greater degree than GS members, judge their general health to be poor,[14] and when asked to volunteer health problems that bother them, they named significantly more than did the younger group. Moreover, when asked if these problems keep them from doing things, 72 per cent of the OS members who list complaints, compared with 56 per cent of the GS, named one or more restrictions. The average number of such restrictions is significantly higher. Of those respondents reporting that they had to spend time in bed during the previous year, OS members report a higher average amount of such time.[15]

Both groups were also given check lists of complaints which are generally psychosomatic in nature but which manifest themselves as physical drains on energy in one case, and mental drains in the other. For both of these lists, OS members reported a higher average number of complaints than did GS members. In addition, as we have

13. The shifting interpretation of the meanings of different absolute amounts of formal education leaves the significance of this observed difference somewhat ambiguous. See H. D. Rawls, "Education and Social Participation: A Factor Analysis" (unpublished Ph.D. dissertation, Duke University, 1963); and Joel Smith and Horace Rawls, "Standardization of an Educational Variable: The Need and Its Consequences," *Social Forces*, **43** (September, 1965), 57-66.

14. Qualitative assessments of health are distributed almost like those observed for a Miami sample by Aaron Lipman, "Health Insecurity of the Aged," *The Gerontologist*, **2** (June, 1962), 99, and slightly better than those reported for a random sample by Ethel Shanas, *Family Relationships of Older People*, p. 41.

15. Two other studies that estimated time spent in bed by persons over sixty-five apparently did not go to the effort to exclude the chronically ill and handicapped, since they both report some sample members who are bedridden all or most of the time. Nonetheless, each also reports higher proportions reporting no days in bed than the OS does. See Shanas, *ibid.*, p. 44; Jyrkilä, "Society and Adjustment to Old Age," p. 113.

already noted, they report both significantly more energy loss than others do, and deterioration rather than improvement when a change in general physical condition is noted. It is true that all these indicators are self-reports and that there is no medical corroboration of the claims of any respondent. However, in the light of evidence that symptom reports and general self-assessments are medically reliable indicators of health status, it seems reasonable to accept these data at face value.[16]

Breadth of Environmental Contacts

The life mobility patterns of OS members indicate little breadth of experience. This does not mean that they are lifetime residents, however, because the city has had so much of its growth since 1900 that the probability of lifetime residence for aged current residents is very low. In fact, only 4 per cent of the OS have spent their entire lives in the city, in contrast to 24 per cent of the GS members. Still, the residential experiences of OS members are extremely limited in other respects. For example, only ten have ever resided in cities larger than Dunholme, and only five of these have lived in metropolises with populations of one million or more. In contrast, 87 per cent have never resided outside the South, and almost all of these have resided only in the state. Some 64 per cent have resided on farms, most of them during childhood. Hence, for almost everyone in the OS, semi-segregated residence in this moderate-sized insular Southern city is the cosmopolitan capstone of their residential histories.

Irrespective of place of residence or station in life, anyone today can maintain contact with the larger society through mass media. The mass media, however, are quite diverse in their contents, and one could exercise choices that would produce extreme diets of either very local and/or personally relevant materials on the one hand, or societal and/or cosmopolitan materials on the other. In general, previous research indicates that persons whose tastes in

16. C. R. Hoffer and E. A. Schuler, "Measurement of Health Care," *American Sociological Review,* **8** (December, 1948), 719-721; E. A. Schuler, S. C. Mayo, and H. B. Makover, "Measuring Needs for Medical Care: An Experiment in Method," *Rural Sociology,* **11** (June, 1946), 152-158; C. R. Hoffer and E. A. Schuler, in cooperation with Rosalie Neligh and Thomas Robinson, "Determination of Unmet Need for Medical Attention among Michigan Farm Families," *The Journal of the Michigan State Medical Society,* **46** (April, 1947), 443-446.

mass media materials run to the informational and cosmopolitan are also among the heavier consumers of such materials. Hence, we shall assume that lower rates of such consumption indicate a more restricted range and variety of contact with the larger society. In comparing our OS and GS on magazine reading, attendance at movies, television viewing, and radio listening, we find OS members reporting significantly less consumption in every instance.

The fact of the matter is that OS members are not tied to Dunholme by material necessities any more than are GS members. In fact, in an objective sense, they are somewhat freer to move. Despite the realities, when asked about their expectations of remaining in the community, only 2.1 per cent of the OS report that they expect to move elsewhere. This compares with 14.0 per cent of the GS members. If the group of those who are able to imagine the possibility of physically disconnecting with the community and attaching elsewhere is increased by including those uncertain about their prospects of remaining, the percentages are even further apart, rising to 7.1 per cent and 34.4 per cent, respectively. For all practical purposes, almost all of the OS members see themselves as incapable of moving from the local environment.

Furthermore, to the extent that the neighborhood is the most meaningful primary life space in the community, OS members, despite the fact that they have had more opportunity to develop a larger meaningful areal sphere of existence, report conceptions of neighborhoods no larger in size than those reported by GS members. In fact, OS members are considerably underrepresented among those respondents who conceive of neighborhoods as very large segments of the city. Hence, in all respects, OS members' areal reference for meaningful environments is locally restricted and confined to small segments of the community.[17]

It has also been observed that as people grow old both the quantity and range of social contacts diminish.[18] Consistent with other factors so far discussed, the numbers of average daily contacts

17. If Stuart Queen and David Carpenter's observations of a negative correlation between age and neighboring in St. Louis are more widely valid, this would suggest that the more narrowly conceived neighborhoods of our OS do not carry more intensive significance as a setting for interaction; see *The American City* (New York: McGraw-Hill, 1953), pp. 156-157.

18. Pinner *et al., Old Age and Political Behavior,* p. 272; Cumming and Henry, *Growing Old, passim.* Peter Townsend interprets this as a change in type rather than an atrophying; "The Place of Older People in Different Societies," in P. F. Hansen (ed.), *Age with a Future* (Copenhagen: Munksgaard, 1964), p. 40.

reported by OS members are significantly fewer than those reported by the GS. While the range of other types of persons with whom contacts were experienced is too diverse to process quantitatively, systematic examination of the reports by both samples indicates that OS members' contacts, in addition to being fewer, are also restricted to a narrower variety of situations and other persons.

Finally, aspects of leisure were examined with respect to their implications for the breadth of a meaningful social environment. As one would expect, given that there are substantially more retirees and non-working women in the OS, its members report having significantly larger amounts of leisure time than do GS members. Since considerable ambiguity still attaches to the meaning of leisure, this time estimate was checked and if necessary revised by asking a sequence of further questions concerning time spent in nineteen specific categories generally considered normal leisure activities. Not only did this procedure raise confidence in the estimates of amounts of leisure time, but it also provided information necessary for assessing the scope of leisure activities. In general, the greater the number of different activities reported as being pursued during leisure, the wider the horizon of personal interests.

When the average numbers of such activities reported by each group are compared, the OS shows a significantly lower variety of activities than does the GS (6.60 as compared with 7.87). In view of the fact that the average for the aged still seemed substantially large, the categories were examined to see if there were substantial differences between the samples in the way that they allocated their leisure time. The results of this analysis clearly demonstrate the narrower range of interests reflected in the leisure activities of the aged. Five of the activities in our list are very socially restricted in their implications, involving either no contact or primary contacts likely to minimize the flow of new information in intercourse. None of them necessarily imply acquisition and/or application of special information or any significant physical activity. The five include: (*1*) napping or resting, (*2*) just sitting and thinking, (*3*) sitting at home and talking with other household members, (*4*) visits to or from relatives, and (*5*) visits to or from friends. For the OS, these five activities accounted for 46.2 per cent of all activities reported, whereas for the GS they comprised only 37.3 per cent of those reported. The averages of the five that sample members report were

2.95 for the GS and 3.05 for the OS. The two most solitary and inactive of the five, napping and just sitting, were also the most heavily over-reported by the old.[19]

In contrast, the difference observed in the means of total leisure activities was found to stem solely from the difference in the average number of all other leisure activities—4.94 for the GS and 3.55 for the OS. All these activities involve such things as physical activity, secondary contacts with wide varieties of persons, and acquisition and/or application of information.[20] Hence, for our OS, increased leisure is more likely to be put to the service of shrinking horizons rather than expanding ones.[21]

Nature of Self-Concept

Using a method that has been applied in a variety of ways by other investigators, an effort was made to establish the characteristics of each respondent's conception of himself. The device used called for a verbatim recording of responses to the question, "What would you say about yourself in three sentences in answer to the question, 'Who am I?'" OS members report a significantly lower average number of individual details about themselves in fashioning an identity than do GS members.

Answers were so distinctively phrased that it was also possible

19. A similar distinction in leisure activities showing differential rates of decline is reported by a number of observers. Cf. Saxon Graham, "Social Correlates of Adult Leisure-Time Behavior," in Marvin Sussman (ed.), *Community Structure and Analysis* (New York: Thomas Y. Crowell Co., 1959), p. 343; Sebastian De Grazia, "The Uses of Time," in Kleemeier (ed.), *Aging and Leisure*, pp. 120-125; D. O. Cowgill and Norma Baulch, "The Use of Leisure Time by Old People," *The Gerontologist*, 2 (March, 1962), 48; Marc Zborowski, "Aging and Recreation," *Journal of Gerontology*, 17 (July, 1962), 302-309; and M. J. Taves and G. D. Hansen, "Seventeen Hundred Elderly Citizens," in A. M. Rose (ed.), *Aging in Minnesota* (Minneapolis: University of Minnesota Press, 1963), pp. 81, 149.

20. One case of differentiation in leisure activity patterns of two subgroups of aged has come to the author's attention. In this case, members of a "senior activity center" show much more diverse and active patterns of leisure time use than do non-members. Inasmuch as the description sounds very much like a community situation in which the aged are a real group (members), but with many of their number being marginal (non-members), it tends to lend credence to the observation that in Dunholme (as depicted in chapter 13) even the healthy elderly would manifest the constrictions and deprivations observed elsewhere (chapter 14). See R. T. Storey, "Who Attends a Senior Activity Center?" *The Gerontologist*, 2 (December, 1962), 216-222.

21. All of these figures on leisure activities seem to compare well with those reported by Pinner *et al., Old Age and Political Behavior*, p. 292. Also see C. L. Stone and W. L. Slocum, *A Look at Thurston County's Older People* (Washington Agricultural Experiment Station Bulletin 573 [May, 1957]), p. 3.

to interpret the context of the situation that respondents structured in formulating a response. As might be expected, most respondents seemed to construct a situation in which they were identifying themselves to others. In contrast to this majority, a fairly substantial number of respondents seemed to interpret the question as an instruction to assess themselves for themselves alone. In this sense they appeared to place the problem of representing themselves to others as secondary.[22] In comparing the two samples in this respect, significantly more OS than GS members showed such an introspective orientation to their identities (30 per cent vs. 20 per cent).[23] Thus, as compared with the younger adults, OS members reveal not only a more constricted conception of self but one that is less likely to be formulated with others in mind.

Another aspect of relation to reality that is socially based but that may also reveal itself in the individual is anomie. Stated perhaps oversimply, anomie is manifested in the individual in a disconnectedness with groups which results in decrements in one's confidence in his ability to guide his actions so that they are in accord with the expectations of others. This condition usually reflects the lack of either a meaningful or a rational connectedness with the larger social world, and it can be sensed and conveyed by persons who are not so affected by it as to develop extreme mental disturbances. Hence, at strategic points in the interview we looked for statements indicating such things as: (*1*) an inability to understand situations, or (*2*) an inability to understand one's self, or (*3*) an inability to act effectively, or (*4*) a claim of being unable to act effectively because of non-comprehension of social reality. Persons making such statements were classified as anomic. Since older persons are supposed to suffer from loss of the significant work, family, and friendship statuses that help to facilitate orientation to and comprehension of the social world, we should expect a higher proportion of OS than GS members to show symptoms of anomie.[24] While the proportions of anomic per-

22. While these data may also be interpreted as indicating only a shift from instrumental concepts to qualities of being in self-image, the important thing for our purpose is that the latter type of orientation is a less functional one for what is currently the world of community affairs. A parallel conclusion about this change in orientation to self is reported by L. R. Dean, "Aging and the Decline of Instrumentality," *Journal of Gerontology*, 15 (October, 1960), 403-407.

23. This phenomenon of change in orientation to self seems exactly like that described in a statement by Elaine Cumming and Isabel McCaffrey, cited by R. J. Havighurst, "Successful Aging," in Williams *et al.* (eds.), *Processes of Aging*, I, 309.

24. The aged are described as alienated and disoriented by Pinner *et al.*, *Old Age and Political Behavior*, pp. 268, 272.

sons in both samples can be expected to be relatively low in an integrated social system,[25] it is still higher in the OS by a significant amount.

Finally, all sample members were asked to judge the importance of their actions to the community. The question was phrased in the most positive extreme: respondents were asked whether they felt that anything they did was of any importance to the community. Inasmuch as anyone can rationally and legitimately give a positive response to this question—and not everyone does—responses can be interpreted as a self-assessment of relatedness of self to the community and/or an evaluation of the worth of that relationship. For most of the reasons already cited, we should expect OS members to report feelings of unimportance at a higher rate than GS members. In fact, a majority (52.2 per cent) report that nothing they do is important to the community, whereas only 38.6 per cent of GS members make such reports. The poignancy of this sense of unimportance and ineffectiveness in the community is heightened when we recall that more of the OS members also feel that they have no prospects of living elsewhere.

This review of contrasts between the two samples, in which the possible effects of aging on the social world of the aged can only be inferred indirectly, conforms to and enlarges upon the picture yielded by the data which provide more direct evidence that changes have resulted from aging. Despite the fact that OS members tend to disidentify with and not to accept the status of older persons, the passage of time has done its damage. Our OS members live in a narrower social world than others do. Their conceptions of their social selves have shrunk apace, and their interests have more and more turned inward. As these processes have operated, they have also suffered a related loss in their public and physical resources for claiming access to and acceptance in community affairs. Our methods of sampling may have yielded a more advantaged group than samples dealt with in other studies of the aged, but even it has not escaped the erosions and conversions of social aging. Lest it be forgotten, aside from whatever value the replication of earlier findings may have, these findings are particularly important to our purpose.

25. The Dunholme rate, as indicated in Table 1 of chapter 16, as well as the relation of that rate to age, compares well with that reported for San Francisco by Dorothy Meier and Wendell Bell, "Anomia and Differential Access to the Achievement of Life Goals," *American Sociological Review*, **24** (April, 1959), 199, and is in line with their general position on such rates (p. 201).

They indicate that these old people are not at all unusual; hence, that the results of subsequent analyses may also apply to the older populations of like communities.

Finally, one more point may be made. Our previous review of the situation with respect to norms, attitudes, and values in the community concerning age yielded a picture on the sanguine side, at least regarding overt expressions when respondents were aware of what they were revealing. No sizable fund of overt resentment was found; the sentiment seemed to suggest that one could either not see the aged as a real social group, or if they were so recognized, that it was a group that was entitled to and could command a position of respect in the community. The materials reviewed in this chapter suggest that the attributes of the aged decrease the likelihood that they will try to assert an interest in ongoing community affairs, or that they would be acceptable to others if they did make such claims. These findings give a mocking and hollow ring to those potentialities.

Joel Smith

Herman Turk

15. AGE AND SOME BEHAVIORAL AND ATTITUDINAL ASPECTS OF URBAN COMMUNITY INTEGRATION

We are now in a position to ask how the actual participation of the aged in the integrative activities, structures, and mechanisms of the city compares with that of others. We know that different perspectives suggest two potential opposing outcomes to this review. One suggests that the tenure, experience, knowledge, and availability of the aged will lead to equal or favorable comparisons. The other suggests that the shock of divorcement from work and loss of some nuclear family roles, together with a larger context of prejudicial attitudes toward old age (i.e., associating it with senility, rigidity, conservatism, etc.) will lead to lower levels of activity in these areas.

How are the integrative mechanisms of the city to be observed on the level of the individual? Since some of these mechanisms are institutional, they simply require the individual's participation in institutionalized activity segments that keep the daily life of the community functioning on an even keel. Among others, these institutional areas include the family, work, and religion. Other mechanisms are less institutionalized. They involve processes or activities that are assumed in the normative picture of a well-functioning community. Some examples of these are civic work, using commercial facilities, voting, and participating in voluntary associations. Finally, there is the matter of maintaining a normative consensus among the residents about the reality, importance, and positive value of the community.

All of these are considered integrative in the sense that smoothly functioning and effectively organized communities depend on reliable performances of their members in these areas. Adequate identification generally results in sufficient motivation and rationale for the member to continue necessary behavior because he feels that it is right and that he wants to do so, rather than because he is externally coerced. The activities involved permit local mechanisms of control, decision making, and responsibility to operate. Working, marrying and raising children, shopping, reading the local papers—in short, full participation in all the institutionalized segments of life—permits the community as a unit to fill its functional role in the larger social system and supports the entire local institutional structure that helps to maintain this functional role. It is in this sense of the analytic meaning of these patterns of activity and attitude that all factors of the classes mentioned above are considered integrative. The individual resident need not and often does not see his actions and attitudes in these terms. Nonetheless, lack of recognition does not alter the fact that when behavior is reliably and voluntarily organized to achieve commonly accepted goals, the community is likely to function more smoothly.

Data pertinent to some seventy-two behavioral and attitudinal facets of integration were collected in the interview and examined and tested for direction of differences and significance of magnitude. In every case, before examining the data, a prediction was made as to whether a difference would be expected, and if so, which sample would be expected to show more or less of the integrative attribute. Our discussion of these findings is organized on a principle emerging from this process—that is, results will be discussed in three categories: (*a*) those in which the aged are expected to show more of an integrative attribute, (*b*) those in which no difference is expected, and (*c*) those in which the General Sample is expected to show more of an integrative attribute. The meaning of our findings will be clarified as we explicate the bases of our predictions and the patterns found.

The seventy-two hypotheses were sorted into these three groups on the basis of considerations clarified by the outcomes of the earlier analyses, which serve as a context for considering the present materials. By and large, the principles involved can be summarized as follows. If we grant the possibility that there may be some validity in each of the opposing observations about the community role of the aged (i.e., that it will be as great as or greater than that of others because of tenure, knowledge, experience, etc.; and that it will be less than that of others because of incapacities, disengagement, prejudicial disbarments, etc.), then our question basically concerns the different ways in which the various age segments serve integrative functions for the community. It is not a question of how much more or less.

Various observations from previous research, repeated and enlarged by our previously discussed findings, were considered in assigning hypotheses to one of the three predictions.[1] For example, since the aged generally seem satisfied with their lot in life and tend to make more favorable judgments whenever opinions are requested, there is every reason to believe that they will be more positive and generally accepting in their judgments about the community.[2] Hence, twenty of the twenty-four items dealing in various ways with community identification were expected to go in favor of the Old Sample (see the top segment of Table 1). Contrarily, the other items, whether institutional or not, are largely behavioral and require various combinations of energy, entree, status acceptability, etc. In view of the constriction in the breadth of life space and resource deprivation reported for the aged and observed in the OS, our initial hypothesis categorization led us to expect General Sample superiority for the behavior items. Indeed, thirty-two of the remaining forty-eight hypotheses were so formulated after final consideration (see the bottom segment of Table 2).

We can best explicate the further considerations involved by reviewing the considerations bearing on the twenty deviant hypo-

1. A few of these hypotheses might have been classified differently if the preceding analyses had not been completed first. However, since we have no formal record for each of the seventy-two, we cannot say whether the number would be two, three, four, etc. We are confident, however, that it is on that order. While the areas covered by the tests sometimes overlap with those considered in chapters 13 and 14, each particular measure used here is different from any that has been previously reported and is not necessarily fixed by the previous observation. The aim in using all these measures here, whether they seem to overlap previously discussed matters or not, is heuristic. We desire to draw together in one place a fairly full profile of age-related differences in patterns of integrative attributes.

2. A much more general statement about interactive relationships and community identification may be found in S. N. Eisenstadt, *From Generation to Generation* (Glencoe, Ill.: The Free Press, 1956), pp. 272-274. Nathan Kogan's discussion of an "acquiescent" personality trait in the elderly fits well with this line of reasoning; "Attitudes toward Old People in an Older Sample," *Journal of Abnormal and Social Psychology*, **62** (May, 1961), 620.

Table 1. Integrative Attributes for Which a Superiority of the Aged Is Expected.

Integrative attributes	Sample showing more of the integrative attributes		Level of significance
	Expected	Observed	
Community-directed attitudes, values, and identifications:			
1. Would miss the community	O>G	O>G	***
2. Pride of self in community	O>G	O>G	***
3. Pride of others in community	O>G	O>G	***
4. Care for community as contrasted with others	O>G	O>G	**
5. Number of positive images of community	O>G	O>G	***
6. Number of negative images of community	O>G	O>G	***
7. Sum of community comparisons favoring local community	O>G	O>G	***
8. Sum of community comparisons favoring other communities	O>G	O>G	***
9. Balance of judgments when community is seen as unique	O>G	O>G	***
10. Judgments of community in respects in which it is like other communities	O>G	O>G	***
11. General estimate of community's quality as compared to that of other communities	O>G	O>G	***
12. Recognition of a personal symbol for the community	O>G	O>G	***
13. Presence of groups seen unfavorably	O>G	O>G	***
14. Total objects of sentiment in community	O>G	O>G	***
15. Total objects of sentiment in community—expressive	O>G	O>G	**
16. Total objects of sentiment in community—instrumental	O>G	O>G	***
17. Total objects of sentiment in community—service-welfare	O>G	O>G	***
18. Friendliness of residents	O>G	O>G	***
19. Summary index of identification	O>G	O>G	***
20. Number of things that wouldn't be missed	O>G	O>G	***
Community-relevant activity and participation:			
1. Personally knows person selected as symbolically representing community	O>G	O>G	***
2. Number of important persons known personally	O>G	O>G	<.20
3. Frequency of seeing family and close relations in community	O>G	O>G	***
4. Degree of friendliness with neighbors	O>G	O>G	**
5. Home ownership	O>G	O>G	***
6. Local media exposure (newspaper and radio)	O>G	O>G	<.20

*$p < .10$.
**$p < .05$.
***$p < .01$.

Table 2. Integrative Attributes for Which a Superiority of the General Sample Is Expected.

Integrative attributes	Sample showing more of the attributes		Level of significance
	Expected	Observed	
Community-directed attitudes, values, and identification:			
1. Number of things that would be missed	G>O	G>O	*
2. Sense of efficacy in the community	G>O	G>O	***
3. Explains actions by reference to communal norms	G>O	G>O	**
Community-relevant activity and participation			
1. Number of community issues participated in	G>O	G>O	***
2. Number of important community positions selected from list	G>O	G>O	***
3. Number of important persons named	G>O	O>G	> .80
4. Number of consensus choices on important persons named	G>O	G>O	***
5. Number of activities engaged in relevant to general community affairs	G>O	G>O	***
6. Number of memberships in voluntary associations	G>O	G>O	***
7. Number of memberships in local secular voluntary associations	G>O	G>O	***
8. Total annual meeting attendance by members of voluntary associations	G>O	G>O	< .25
9. Relative use of respondent by others as a source of opinion on community issues	G>O	G>O	*
10. Number of opinion leaders known	G>O	G>O	**
11. Number of magazines read regularly	G>O	G>O	***
12. Number of general mass circulation magazines read regularly	G>O	G>O	**
13. Number of cosmopolitan magazines read regularly	G>O	G>O	***
14. Number of non-voting civic activities	G>O	G>O	***
15. Number of "pro" opinions on progressive community changes	G>O	G>O	***
16. Number of "anti" opinions on progressive community changes	G>O	G>O	< .20
17. Number of "neutral" opinions on progressive community changes	G>O	G>O	***
18. Scale of integrative activities	G>O	G>O	***
19. Degree of comprehensiveness of information about community events	G>O	G>O	***
20. Concentration of close friends in Dunholme	G>O	G>O	**
21. Number of best friends reported when three are requested	G>O	G>O	**
22. Spread of best friends throughout community	G>O	G>O	> .15
23. Frequency of seeing best friends	G>O	G>O	**
24. Frequency of going downtown	G>O	G>O	***
25. Number of functions served by downtown area	G>O	G>O	**
26. Variety of purchases conducted downtown	G>O	G>O	***
27. Number of daily newspapers read	G>O	G>O	< .20
28. Number of Sunday newspapers read	G>O	G>O	**
29. Number of non-segmental social anchorages	G>O	G>O	***
30. Number of all social anchorages	G>O	G>O	***
31. Voting in local elections	G>O	G>O	**
32. Non-voting local political activity	G>O	G>O	***

*$p < .10$. **$p < .05$. ***$p < .01$.

Table 3. Integrative Attributes for Which No Difference Between GS and OS Is Expected.

Integrative attributes	Presence of integrative attribute in sample		Level of significance
	GS	OS	
Community-directed attitudes, values, and identification:			
1. Inclusion of community in "Who am I?" response	13%	11%	< .50
Community-relevant activity and participation			
1. Number of community issues identified as heard about	5.59	5.88	< .40
2. Number of offices ever held in voluntary associations by members	1.04	.96	< .80
3. Relative use of respondent by others as source of community facts[a]	2.48	2.45	< .80
4. Estimate of quality of community knowledge relative to others[a]	2.23	2.17	< .60
5. Number of special-interest magazines read regularly	.76	.50	**
6. Number of local information sources used	2.60	2.74	< .20
7. Number of close friends in Dunholme	17.37	17.59	> .80
8. Rate of church attendance per week	.50	.48	> .80
9. Number of segmental social anchorages	4.12	4.08	< .80
10. Range of intimate personal contacts[a]	3.35	3.03	< .20

**$p < .05$ (disconfirming).
[a]Means represent dummy variables based on responses ranked on a linear continuum of degree.

theses (see bottom segment of Table 1, top segment of Table 2, and all of Table 3). In the case of three attitudinal items (top segment of Table 2), the GS members were expected to show more positive orientation to the community than the aged. The hypothesis concerning the number of specific things that would be missed was so categorized because no fixed battery of alternative choices was offered to the respondents. In view of the OS respondents' narrower communal environments and greater general difficulty in giving full and creative responses, it seemed reasonable to expect a greater paucity of detail in answers to an item phrased in this fashion. The other two items concerned (*a*) the degree of efficacy the respondent felt his actions had for the community and (*b*) the extent to which a respondent used communal standards and norms rather than other ones in explaining actions of potential relevance to the community. On these two items more than any others it was felt that OS respondents would be most likely to feel and reflect the impact of the handicaps of age that develop from the emerging negative assessments, prejudices, stereotypes, and status handicaps reported in Chapters 13 and 14. This expectation was further reinforced by the fact that the status inequalities between the two samples also made it more difficult for OS members to formulate the relatively sophisticated comments that marked responses classified positively.

The hypothesis involving community references in the self-identity reports was put in the "no difference" category as a result of uncertainty as to the importance of counterbalancing factors. At a minimum, responses to the "Who am I?" question are affected by the interaction among the actual content of the identity, the importance placed on each segment of that identity, the respondent's ideas about how far down this importance hierarchy he should go in responding, and the respondent's ability to express fully and adequately what he had in mind. The decision that no difference should be expected resulted from the suspicion that factors bearing on the result had different weights and ran in different directions in the two samples. For example, if we could get every detail of the self-concept, we might expect GS members, being less withdrawn, to report more community references. However, since OS members have fewer references than GS members, being likely to have lost work and family statuses, those with community references are more likely than GS members to consider these references important enough to report to the interviewer. Being unable to weigh these different factors of scope and importance, it seems reasonable to assume that cancelling effects would lead to no difference.

The two hypotheses concerning personal acquaintance with an individual chosen as symbolically representing the community and personal acquaintance with important persons were judged to be ones in which the OS members would fare better than GS members. In these cases it was borne in mind that in Dunholme the term "acquaintance" implies only the loosest degree of connectedness. We were forewarned of this in pre-tests when questions concerning details of friendships could not be pursued because respondents used the term indiscriminately to refer to all other residents of the city.[3]

3. In studying friendships in even more restricted groups than the Dunholme samples, the same conclusion is reached by M. J. Arth, "American Culture and Friendship in the Aged," in Clark Tibbitts and Wilma Donahue (eds.), *Aging Around the World: Social and Psychological Aspects of Aging* (New York: Columbia University Press, 1962), p. 533.

Since acquaintanceship implies little positive action, accessibility, or acceptability, and since we already knew both that older persons are overrepresented in choices of symbolic and important persons and that OS members have lived in the community longer than GS members, we judged that OS members would fare better on these items.

The hypotheses concerning frequency of contacts with family and close relatives and friendliness in neighboring relationships were also categorized in favor of the aged. Again, the constricted life space of the aged in contrast to the much more widely diffused demands upon and opportunities for younger adults was a salient consideration. In addition, relatives and neighbors are the most easily accessible significant others in the community. Such relationships can be maintained with a minimum input of physical and mental energy, an amount that is inadequate for maintaining more secondary contacts. In fact, in considering relatives, OS members have an initial advantage in that a considerable number of them reside in multi-family households.[4] Similar classification of the home ownership hypothesis is based on the small number of transients in the OS. The local media hypothesis was treated the same way in view of the extreme non-cosmopolitanism of the OS referred to in the previous chapter.

All of the behavioral hypotheses for which no difference was expected concern arenas or objects of action in which accessibility is great and energy requirements low (see bottom segment of Table 3). For example, as measured here, knowledge of issues required that a person merely report having heard about a major issue that had been publicly discussed and reported in the community both formally and informally over a long period of time. In contrast, knowledge of the details (see line 19 of bottom segment of Table 2) requires more active searching out, sometimes to the extent of having access to inner circles. In that case differences were expected and, in fact, observed.

In addition to ease of access, many of these items for which no difference was hypothesized are characterized by an age irrelevancy. For example, the holding of an office in a voluntary association can have occurred at any age, but the respondent reports the experi-

4. Similar generalizations about this situation of old persons and family are offered by Peter Townsend, "The Place of Older People in Different Societies," in P. F. Hansen (ed.), *Age with a Future* (Copenhagen: Munksgaard, 1964), pp. 38-40.

ence currently. Similarly, anyone of any age group may have friends and relatives. Segmental anchorages are so designated because they involve a type of institutional participation which, while occurring in the community, is only irrelevantly based there. Hence, such participation may even have the non-integrative consequences of deflecting interest and energy away from the community. The institutions involved are neighborhood, family, friends, and church—all the most age-irrelevant segments of social life. Again, in contrast, a hypothesis of difference was formulated for non-segmental community anchorages, which included, for example, making use of the downtown area (see line 29 of bottom segment of Table 2). Here differential access based on the social or physical reality of old age can be expected to be and is a factor.

Some of these tests are not completely independent of one another because there are a few scales or indexes constructed in part from items which are also tested separately. Nonetheless, as the tables show, the evidence summarized in Table 4 is so consistent that it seems unnecessary to adjust our conclusions for these few partially overlapping items. Moreover, since we are interested in

Table 4. Summary of Outcomes of All Tests Involving Integrative Attributes Classified by Type of Hypothesis and Type of Attribute.

		Direction of difference observed				
			Confirms			
Type of Attitude	Con-tradicts	n.s.	.10	.05	.01	
1. Community-directed attitudes, values, and identifications Hypothesis direction						
O>G	—	—	—	2	18	
=	—	1	—	—	—	
G>O	—	—	1	1	1	
2. Community-relevant activity and participation Hypothesis direction						
O>G	—	1	—	—	1	
=	1	5	—	—	—	
G>O	1	2	1	2	13	
3. Total tests Hypothesis direction						
O>G	—	2	—	3	21	
=	1	10	—	—	—	
G>O	2	3	2	9	19	

over-all patterns, it seems strategically better to avoid detailed comment on particular items whenever possible. Detailed discussion of the testing of each hypothesis would mire us hopelessly in a welter of procedural and statistical details.[5]

A level of significance was set so that a hypothesis of difference would be accepted or one of no difference would be rejected whenever the probability of obtaining by chance a difference as great or greater than that observed was 10 per cent or less. This is somewhat higher than conventional 5 per cent and 1 per cent levels only because of uncertainty as to the effects on the results of the sampling restrictions for the aged population. Since it developed that decisions on only two test results were affected by this decision, this caution was probably unnecessary. In reading Table 4, it should also be borne in mind that confirming tests of hypotheses of no difference are recorded in the "confirms—not significant" column and disconfirmations in the "contradictory" column of the "=" row. Of the seventy-two tests, three showed patterns of difference contradicting that which was expected, one of these to a significant (5 per cent) degree. Of the sixty-nine tests in which directional expectations were realized, five involved differences not sufficiently large to reach any pre-chosen level of significance, and two reached only the 10 per cent criterion. Forty of the remaining fifty-two significant hypotheses were significant at the 1 per cent level or well beyond.

A recurrent theme runs through these commentaries on hypotheses, and it should be stated more generally. Since almost without exception the data support the judgments deriving from this theme, it can be thought of as substantiated as far as this particular analysis can go. Given a mechanism that may have integrative consequences for the urban community, the data suggest that the more accessible, the more public, the more individualistic, the less subtle and sophisticated, and the more unselectively ascriptive its organization, the greater the likelihood that an older population will compare favorably with a younger one. As the attributes of given mechanisms tend to be more like the polar opposites of these qualities, the greater the likelihood of a lesser role for the aged in the operation of that mechanism.

The range of integrative functions that the aged may have in

5. Much of this material will either be available in future publications or can be obtained by contacting the senior author.

a community, of course, is not fully depicted by the assortment of mechanisms reviewed here. Such matters as the extension of assistance, which either resolves what might otherwise become community problems or facilitates the ability of others to make direct integrative contributions (e.g., baby-sitting so that young parents can hold down jobs or attend meetings), have not been touched upon here. These other possibilities are quite unfocused and difficult to isolate. Since it is our aim only to establish some of the conditions that bear on the extent to which and the manner in which the aged make their integrative contribution, these other potential contributions of the aged are not pursued.

These findings on the type and degree of integrative activity of the aged population suggest that their re-entry to full membership in the community requires public awareness of the wide variety of factors that lead to the development of an effectively integrated community. Thus, even if these findings imply that the aged can never again be expected to contribute in the wider-ranging, more active mechanisms of integration, there remain important alternative modes of contributing that are equally worthy of respect and through which they might easily contribute.

However, our subsequent analyses even call into question the conclusion that the aged are not capable of raising and/or altering their levels and styles of participation in the community. For while we have shown that many of these mechanisms are age-related, we have not shown whether they are the products of old age per se or of some other factor(s) whose distribution in segments of a community's population is related to age. It is our intention to report two analyses that demonstrate the potentials of such an approach. The two are only a representation of a number of others that will be tried. They are presented here both to stimulate further interest and to serve as illustrations. Their selection is purely fortuitous. No others, as yet, have been attempted.

Herman Turk
Joel Smith
Howard P. Myers

16. UNDERSTANDING LOCAL POLITICAL BEHAVIOR: THE ROLE OF THE OLDER CITIZEN*

Introduction

A rather wide range of phenomena is suggested by the term "politics." Experts disagree considerably over what politics should or should not connote. Since it would not be possible to do justice to all of its aspects in a discussion of this length, it seems reasonable to restrict the following consideration of the political role of the aged to some activities which are generally accepted as political. Our decision as to how to restrict our topic is conditioned also by (*a*) our interest in evaluating two alternative classical theories about the nature of the process that leads to political arrangements; and (*b*) our own preference for enlarging the scope of phenomena with which most behavioral studies of politics deal. For these reasons, our particular concern shall be individual behavior in local community political issues.

This behavior includes voting, holding of opinions on issues about which decisions are made in the political arena, and activities, conventionally recognized as political, that are ancillary to the outcomes of political decisions. Most studies of political behavior deal with voting or opinions—often without considering the two simul-

---

* This chapter originally appeared under the authorship of Joel Smith, Herman Turk, and Howard P. Myers, with the same title, in *Law and Contemporary Problems*, **27** (Spring, 1962), 280-298. It appears here in a slightly revised version.

taneously. Studies of ancillary political activities—for example, campaigning, circulating petitions, attending meetings—are as rare as whooping cranes. In this sense, then, we hope to fill in the picture of that segment of political behavior in the United States in which all individuals have an opportunity to participate.

In addition to this restriction, our concern is with such behavior as it occurs in the local community and as it is concerned with local communal issues. Most of what we know about political behavior has to do with issues of state, regional, national, or international scope. While it may be true, for example, that the same factors are associated with voting in both presidential and mayoralty elections, this is still a question to be assessed. Of course, there are reasons for suspecting that the dynamics of the local political situation and the behavior of the community's citizens in this context may be different. Mention need be made of only a few rather obvious differences in the two situations.

First of all, almost without exception voting rates in strictly local elections are notoriously lower than they are in national elections. Secondly, citizens are much more directly accountable to their peers for their behavior with respect to strictly local political issues —in the local community it is easier to know who each person is, where he stands, and how he acted. Thirdly, the individual has a wider variety of political decisions to cope with in local political affairs. On the national level it is easy to see one's choices as resting between persons, parties, and/or slogans. In the local arena, while these same decisions have to be made, often choices also have to be made among non-partisan candidates and among alternative courses of action on issues subjected to referendums.

Aside from these rather elementary observations that may be made by anyone who contrasts community and national politics, there is evidence from systematic research that strongly suggests discontinuity between the two processes. For example, in national elections the votes of the disaffected have been in favor of changes from ongoing trends,[1] whereas at the local level votes for the status quo have been attributed to disaffection.[2] Furthermore, two types

1. For an extensive review of such findings, see S. M. Lipset, P. F. Lazarsfeld, A. H. Barton, and Juan Linz, "The Psychology of Voting: An Analysis of Political Behavior," in Gardner Lindzey (ed.), *Handbook of Social Psychology* (Cambridge, Mass.: Addison-Wesley, 1954), pp. 1126, 1134-1150.
2. Summarized in J. E. Horton and W. E. Thompson, "Powerlessness and Political Negativism: A Study of Defeated Local Referendums," *American Journal of Sociology*,

of influence systems that coexist in local communities have been distinguished. One is local and the other cosmopolitan, and a different kind of person is instrumental in each.[3] All in all, the weight of these observations favors the desirability of a fresh examination of local political processes in their own terms. Projections of generalizations based on the study of extra-community politics may not be justified.

The position of the aged in any political process is of special interest, particularly at a time when increasing portions of the American population fall into this category. The aged present a disquieting paradox in a society that subscribes to democratic ideology—a philosophy that rests on the faith that wise and proper political decisions are appropriately made only by the aggregate choices of a fully participating, fully informed electorate. Critics decry the fact that in a social system based on such a political philosophy the structure operates in such fashion that large numbers of citizens do not participate, and even larger numbers are not adequately enough informed to participate effectively.[4] The disquieting paradox of the aged stems from the fact that while they are the one group in society most likely to have the time and experience to participate in politics effectively, they seem to be largely inactive, incompetent, and disengaged from political concerns.[5] This situation warrants special examination of the political behavior of the aged, not only because of its pragmatic significance, but also because it should yield strategic evidence as to the relative applicability of the two major alternative models of political process that have attracted the major thinkers throughout the intellectual history of Western civilization.

---

67 (March, 1962), 485; also Kurt Lang and Gladys E. Lang, *Collective Dynamics* (New York: Thomas Y. Crowell Co., 1961), pp. 413-422.

3. See R. K. Merton, *Social Theory and Social Structure* (Glencoe, Ill.: The Free Press, 1957), pp. 387-420.

4. See H. H. Hyman and P. B. Sheatsley, "The Current Status of American Public Opinion," in Daniel Katz, Dorwin Cartwright, Samuel Eldersveld, and Alfred Lee (eds.), *Public Opinion and Propaganda* (New York: Dryden Press, 1954), pp. 33-48; P. F. Lazarsfeld and R. K. Merton, "Mass Communication, Popular Taste, and Organized Social Action," in E. G. Swanson, Theodore Newcomb, and Eugene Hartley (eds.), *Readings in Social Psychology* (New York: Henry Holt & Co., 1952), pp. 74-85; David Riesman and Reuel Denny, "Do the Mass Media Escape from Politics?" in Bernard Berelson and Morris Janowitz (eds.), *Reader in Public Opinion and Communication* (Glencoe, Ill.: The Free Press, 1953), pp. 327-333.

5. See Lipset *et al.*, "Psychology of Voting," pp. 1126-1134; Elaine Cumming and W. E. Henry, *Growing Old* (New York: Basic Books, 1961), pp. 75-105; also Samuel Stouffer, *Communism, Conformity, and Civil Liberties* (Garden City, N.Y.: Doubleday, 1955), p. 93.

Two Alternative Models of Political Process

The first of these models views the electoral scene as a market place characterized by the rational adjustment of competing interests held by various individuals and subgroups. Here the resolution of issues is a function *either* of the preponderance of certain self-oriented interests over other interests in any anonymous social situation, *or* of the relative ability of various subgroups to command the political conformity of their members, *or* of the relative strengths of certain coalitions compared to those of other coalitions. This can be called a *segmental* or *self-interest model*[6] of issue participation, and it has predominated in empirical studies of political behavior. Its main strength is in explaining—though not perfectly—why participation is on one side of an issue rather than on another. However, it is inadequate for explaining why there should be participation *at all.*

The second model, which can be called a *civic responsibility model*,[7] views political participation as an obligation dictated by the standards of a social whole that is divided on how best to achieve the common interests of its members. It has received little attention in empirical research. While such a model may be a good predictor of participation rates, it has appeared to be an insensitive predictor of the direction of such participation. Both conceptual models seem necessary if the concrete democratic process is to be understood fully. Concern with the second of these models is occasioned by its relative neglect in other studies, rather than by any conviction that it is the more salient of the two under all circumstances.

Related Views of Society, the Individual, and the Urban Community

The political process occurs within the framework of a society or a community, and therefore it must be understood in terms of organized social life and the behavior of the individuals who comprise society. When the political process is viewed in these terms, it may be seen that the two alternative models of political participa-

6. For example, see W. E. Binkley and M. C. Moos, *A Grammar of Politics: The National, State, and Local Governments* (New York: Alfred A. Knopf, 1949), pp. 3-8.
7. E.g., see A. L. Lowell, *Public Opinion and Popular Government* (New York: Longmans, Green & Co., 1926), pp. 8-15.

tion are likely to have had their genesis in two classic issues, the first of which pertains to the nature of the bonds that hold the body social together, and the second of which addresses itself to the motivation of the individual.

Society has been seen as having either or both of two principal mechanisms of integration. The first follows a quasi-economic argument and is best exemplified by such early social contract philosophers as Hobbes and Rousseau. Social order is viewed as the outgrowth of the competition for power, the adjustment of selfish ends, and a division of labor in which contracts are entered into for purposes of mutual protection and mutual gain. Certain positions in psychology which consider man as biologically determined can most readily be linked to this conception of social reality. Both the behavioral psychology of Pavlov and Watson and the psychoanalytic orientations of Freud consider human behavior to be self-gratifying and self-protective. Society is seen either as reducible to the total of such strivings by its individual members or as a constraint which is placed upon them so that humanity will not revert to the jungle.

The second major perspective views social life as organized by what Comte has called universal consensus and what Durkheim labeled the collective conscience. This position implies that for the greater part societies or communities are held together through unity of outlook, identification with the whole, and a common morality. Linked to such a concept of society are psychologies which suggest that society is an inextricable part of the individual's self. Such psychologies appear in the works of Cooley and Mead, who suggest that if the self is shaped by the society, then commitment to the standards of that society is a means of self-realization. Freud's concept of the superego tends a little toward such a psychology, but its definition as a coercive force brings it only halfway between the two extreme positions we are considering. Few contemporary scholars would support the one position to the exclusion of the other, but in terms of the relative emphasis to be placed on each, the conceptual polarity is still very much alive.

Traditionally, the urban community has been examined to a large extent in terms of the quasi-economic model. Park's and Burgess's[8] classic studies depicted the city as a product of competition

8. See R. E. Park, "The Urban Community as a Spatial Pattern and a Moral Order," in R. E. Park, *Human Communities* (Glencoe, Ill.: The Free Press, 1952), pp. 165-177; also E. W. Burgess, "The Growth of the City: An Introduction to a Re-

for the use of land, giving rise to processes of ethnic and occupational invasion or succession. Accompanying this picture of urban social structure there has emerged a picture of the isolated, rootless, amoral city dweller,[9] who resolves his condition either by self-service or by self-destruction. Recently, however, this picture of a utilitarian city with its overindividualized citizen has been said to apply fairly closely only to certain cities and less well to others.[10] Different cities are said to have different bases of integration; some rest on a base of competition, individualism, and economic interdependence, but others rest on tradition, pride, and an altruistic or dedicated citizenry. In short, it is likely that studies of participation in various aspects of urban life must consider both models.

Local Election Studies

The few studies which have been concerned with behavior on local issues seem to view the city either as a collection of competing interest coalitions or as composed of a politically apathetic mass that can sometimes be activated in a protest vote. Formulas have been developed for predicting the resolution of an issue on the basis of the number of economic or political groups for and against a proposal and the amount of co-operation in each camp.[11] Voter turnout, then, is seen as an indication of the effectiveness of such coalitions. Studies of school bond elections and fluoridation votes, on the other hand, suggest that by and large urban dwellers are politically disinterested. However, every so often they see themselves as the "outs" in a fit of near-Marxist class consciousness and rise against measures viewed as the property of the "ins."[12] In short,

search Project," in Robert Park, Ernest Burgess, and R. D. McKenzie (eds.), *The City* (Chicago: University of Chicago Press, 1925), pp. 47-62.

9. See Mirra Komarovsky, "The Voluntary Associations of Urban Dwellers," *American Sociological Review*, 11 (December, 1946), 686; Lillian Cohen, "Los Angeles Rooming-House Kaleidoscope," *ibid.*, 16 (June, 1951), 316; H. W. Zorbaugh, *The Gold Coast and the Slum: A Sociological Study of Chicago's Near North Side* (Chicago: University of Chicago Press, 1929), pp. 69-86.

10. E.g., see R. C. Angell, "The Moral Integration of American Cities," *American Journal of Sociology*, 57 (July, 1951), Part 2, *passim*; W. I. Firey, *Land Use in Central Boston* (Cambridge, Mass.: Harvard University Press, 1947), *passim*.

11. Examples of this approach may be found in R. C. Hanson, "Predicting a Community Decision," *American Sociological Review*, 24 (October, 1959), 662; and D. C. Miller, "The Prediction of Issue Outcomes in Community Decision Making," *Proceedings of the Pacific Sociological Society*, 25 (June, 1957), 137-147.

12. Horton and Thompson, "Powerlessness and Political Negativism," *passim*; Lang and Lang, *Collective Dynamics*, pp. 418-421; H. L. Wilensky, "Life Cycle and Formal Participation," in Robert Kleemeier (ed.), *Aging and Leisure* (New York: Oxford University Press, 1961), p. 239.

such studies employ a utilitarian, individualist model of the city and
a self-interest model of political process that shows promise of being
able to predict the turnout for and the resolution of certain kinds
of issues.

However, the self-interest model does not explain a major finding in a study of *habitual* voting patterns in St. Louis.[13] Here it was
suggested that persons who voted in more local elections than did
others also tended to vote in a greater number of less local and
national elections, and that persons who did not vote in national
elections tended not to vote in *any* election. Since the *more local*
the election, the more likely it is to involve citizen self-interest
directly, self-interest seems to be an inadequate explanation of such
voting patterns. Moreover, if the apathy arising out of social isolation can account fully for non-participation in voting, then by the
same reasoning one would expect city dwellers to be even more
apathetic about national elections than about local ones.

What is missing in these local election studies is any hint that
people might vote because they feel they *should* vote and that differential political participation might be explained at least partially
in terms of differential access to norms of civic responsibility. The
nature of many local issues also bears mention. Voting for school
bond issues, hospital financing, fluoridation, urban renewal, and
other such projects may be viewed as a vote for community "progress." What is important to note is that a vote for progress is an
identification of one's own interests with those of the *city as a whole*,
not any of its interest factions. Since sacrifices are required, it may
be considered a vote against *immediate* self-interest. Hence, the civic
responsibility model may help to explain the *direction* as well as the
fact of voting in local elections.

Voting Models and the Aged Voter

Studies of the political behavior of the aged suggest that old
people are radical,[14] conservative,[15] or unresponsive in their political

13. J. C. Bollens (ed.), *Exploring the Metropolitan Community* (Berkeley: University of California Press, 1961), pp. 184-185, 430-431.
14. Lipset *et al.*, "Psychology of Voting," pp. 1149-1150.
15. H. J. Eysenck, *The Psychology of Politics* (London: Routledge and Kegan
Paul, 1954), p. 21; B. R. Berelson, P. E. Lazarsfeld, and W. N. McPhee, *Voting* (Chicago: University of Chicago Press, 1954), p. 331; Stouffer, *Communism, Conformity,
and Civil Liberties*, p. 89; P. F. Lazarsfeld, B. R. Berelson, and Hazel Gaudet, *The*

behavior. Their conservatism has been attributed to their vested interests in the status quo, their radicalism to their opposition to a society which rejects them, and their unresponsiveness to their senility or their normlessness. Only the latter observation suggests that political participation may have a moral base, a point to which we shall return.

Studies of national elections have depicted the self- or subgroup-oriented voter as largely apathetic. He votes if "opinion leaders" point out to him that his interests are best served by doing so. He refrains from voting while under cross-pressures. His feelings of responsibility to vote are largely irrelevant. Explanations of the low rate of voting by old persons are of the same order. It has been uncritically attributed to the absence of interest groups for the aged, the inconsistent status positions that create cross-pressures (e.g., the habitual Republican with a sharply reduced socioeconomic status), and the separation from both job and disabled contemporaries that removes the aged from the opinion leaders. Such explanations have been assumed but have not been tested.

The notion that the normless person does not vote, however, involves use of the concept of *anomie* (normlessness). This provides the first clue that people may sometimes vote simply because they feel they should. Since it has, indeed, been established that persons high in anomie vote less than non-anomic persons,[16] a moral base for voting is implied. Insofar as morality must constantly be renewed through social interaction, the aged, with their attenuated social contacts, become a somewhat more anomic group. Thus, not only their non-voting but also their non-support for "progressive" proposals might be explained in terms of disengagement from the total social system, rather than in terms of subgroup pressures that cause votes one way or another, or place the aged in conflict. Besides being a paradoxical problem group for the polity, old persons become strategic research subjects in the application of the civic responsibility model of voting behavior.

People's Choice (New York: Duell, Sloan & Pearce, 1944), pp. 23-24; Fred Cottrell, "Governmental Functions and the Politics of Age," in Clark Tibbitts (ed.), *Handbook of Social Gerontology: Societal Aspects of Aging* (Chicago: University of Chicago Press, 1960), p. 661; Angus Campbell, P. E. Converse, W. E. Miller, and E. D. Stokes, *The American Voter* (New York: John Wiley & Sons, 1960), pp. 210-211.

16. See R. E. Lane, *Political Life* (Glencoe, Ill.: The Free Press, 1959), p. 168; and A. W. Kornhauser, H. L. Sheppard, and A. J. Mayer, *When Labor Votes* (New York: University Books, 1956), pp. 189-200.

*Local Political Behavior From the Standpoint of a Civic
Responsibility Model*

The discussion to follow will assess the value of the civic responsibility model in understanding local political behavior. If it can be shown to apply to one urban community, its relevance to other communities must then receive careful consideration. This model suggests that the more fully the individual is tied in with various aspects of the life of the community, the more likely he is to vote and to participate in other political actions. The corollary to this is that the aged person who remains highly implicated in the social life of his community will participate as much as other such persons and that the aged who are not so implicated will participate no less than their younger counterparts. These twin predictions are predicated on the notion that rather thorough implication in the community creates and supports a sense of civic responsibility. If so, the relationship between age and political participation must be seen in these terms.

The holding of opinions is the more passive side of the political process. If the above argument is correct, analogously, one might expect that holding any opinion on an issue is associated with community implication as defined above. Similarly, the tendency to support "community progress" should increase with increases in such community implication. Therefore, age may be related to holding an opinion per se, and to holding a "progressive" opinion, only insofar as age affects the chances for being implicated in the total social life of the community.

The Community and the Sample

As a Southern city, Dunholme has a predominantly one-party political system, a shifting set of social standards that tends to define which elements of the population should not participate politically (e.g., women and Negroes), and a generally low level of political participation.[17] These considerations suggest that different social segments of the community live in different social worlds vis-à-vis politics; hence, that analysis be restricted to individuals who share a relatively homogeneous social environment. For this reason, wom-

17. See V. O. Key, Jr., *Southern Politics in State and Nation* (New York: Alfred A. Knopf, 1949), *passim*.

en were excluded from the analysis. (Negroes and members of the
lowest socioeconomic strata of the white population would also have
been excluded had they been sampled.) Additionally, those who
had not lived in Dunholme long enough to have participated
in all of the issues considered in the study were excluded from both
samples. This exclusion left the GS and the OS with seventy-six
and forty-four men, respectively.

Some Verification of Previous Findings

Certain variables have been found to be relatively consistent
predictors of voting rates. In the present research, it proved possible
to check whether Dunholme is unusual in any of these respects.
Table 1 shows voting rates for selected subgroupings of the combined samples before the sample deletions.[18]

Voting rates were determined from respondents' replies to questions about whether they had ever voted in a local election or in
a local primary, and whether they had voted on a specific proposal
to unify city and county governments, or on a specific school bond
proposal. With very few exceptions, persons who voted on the last
issue also voted on the other three; those who voted on unification
also voted in primaries *and* local elections; and those who voted
in primaries also voted in local elections. As in the St. Louis study,
this meant that voting versus non-voting is a generalized tendency,
and not just "issue-specific."[19] The table presents the extent to which
each subgroup voted in these four instances, counting one for each
affirmative response to the questions on voting.

Part A of the table shows that voting increases with age up to
advanced middle age and then decreases.[20] For our purposes, the
fact that age is associated with voting behavior in Dunholme, much
as it has been found to be elsewhere, is strategic. It suggests that the
explanation for this phenomenon in Dunholme may also apply to
other cities.

Parts B and C of Table 1 also suggest that the local voting
patterns are not unusual. Here, as elsewhere, men vote more than

18. Old persons are disproportionately represented in such a combined sample,
but a more complex sample-by-sample analysis does not alter the relationships reported in Table 1.
19. Bollens, *Exploring the Metropolitan Community*, pp. 184-185, 430-431.
20. See Lipset *et al.*, "Psychology of Voting," p. 1127; Campbell *et al.*, *American
Voter*, pp. 210-211.

Table 1. Mean Extent of Voting in Selected Subgroups of the Combined Samples.

Subgroup characteristics	N	Mean extent of voting
A. Age		
22-27	20	1.65
28-34	27	2.08
35-44	54	2.50
45-54	59	2.51
55-64	33	2.24
65-74	94	1.86
75-84	35	1.54
85 and over	7	0.71
B. Sex		
Male	120	2.54
Female	209	1.79
C. Socioeconomic status		
I (Working class)	26	0.92
II	85	1.71
III	96	1.79
IV	57	2.53
V (Upper-middle class)	65	3.00
D. Information score		
0	12	0.25
1	10	0.60
2	11	0.09
3	13	1.00
4	19	1.21
5	46	1.54
6	53	2.15
7	81	2.48
8	84	2.95
E. Number of information sources		
0	11	0.36
1	60	1.10
2	113	1.99
3	115	2.55
4	30	3.07
F. Anomie		
Present	60	1.70
Absent	269	2.15
Total sample	329	2.07

women, and voter turnout increases with socioeconomic status (i.e., income and occupational prestige).[21] Part D refers to a community information score given to the respondents. They were asked whether they had heard of such events as possible disbandment of the local baseball team, an old-age housing plan, fluoridation of the city water supply, and the like, and were scored one for each such event they knew. This relationship between information and voting has been established in the literature and also appears here.[22] Part E of the

21. *Ibid.*
22. See G. M. Sykes, "The Differential Distribution of Community Knowledge," in Paul Hatt and Albert Reiss (eds.), *Cities and Society: The Revised Reader in Urban Sociology* (Glencoe, Ill.: The Free Press, 1957), pp. 715-716.

Table 2. Voting Rates of Males in Three Age Groups (in percentages).

Extent of voting	Age		
	22–39	40–64	65 and over
3-4	62	77	52
1-2	22	8	23
0	16	15	25
Total per cent	100	100	100
(*N*)	(37)	(39)	(44)

table confirms other findings that the greater the number of sources of information used by the respondent, the more likely is the person to vote.[23] Information sources enumerated in this section are personal acquaintance with at least one community power figure, personally knowing an individual of symbolic significance in the city, reading of the local newspaper, and listening to radio. The higher this index, the higher the voting rate.

Finally, respondents were classified as anomic if: (*a*) they indicated they were subjectively disengaged from society in answer to a question about the importance to the community of what they do; and/or (*b*) they gave no social value or social status references in responding to the question, "How would you answer the question 'Who am I' in three sentences?" Fairly graphic examples of the former include statements such as:

"I'm just a small cog in a big machine."
"Sometimes I feel like I don't mean anything to anybody."
"I'm not important to anyone. . . ."

The latter is illustrated by:

"Someone in the way. Nothing else."
"I don't know. I'm me. I'm just an ordinary person."
"I can't think of anything to describe me."
"I can't answer that. I'm an average person."

All other respondents were called non-anomic in the absence of evidence to the contrary. Part F of Table 1 shows that anomic persons voted less on the average than those who were non-anomic. Despite the crudeness of the measurement of anomie, a rather general observation is confirmed.[24]

23. Lipset *et al.*, "Psychology of Voting," p. 1140.
24. Lane, *Political Life*, p. 168; Kornhauser *et al.*, *When Labor Votes*, pp. 189-195.

In Dunholme, then, age, sex, socioeconomic status, information, information sources, and anomie are associated with the voting rate, much as they are elsewhere. Aside from the support for these some-what routine contentions that the data offer, they do take us part of the way toward an answer to the theoretical question of concern; both the observed general nature of voting versus non-voting and the relationship between anomie and voting suggest the applicability of the civic responsibility model.

Political Participation by Males of Different Ages

The men in our study were divided into three groups: those under forty, those between forty and sixty-four, and those of the Old Sample. Hereafter, these groups will be referred to as "young," "middle-aged," and "old." This division was necessary to provide sufficient numbers of cases for analysis in each category. Table 2 shows a rising and descending trend of voting by age similar to that reported for the total sample, and aged men voting least of all.

Table 3. Political Activities (Other Than Voting) of Males in Three Age Groups (in percentages).

Number of political activities (other than voting)	Age		
	22–39	40–64	65 and over
2-4	32	33	16
1	46	23	27
0	22	44	57
Total per cent	100	100	100
(*N*)	(37)	(39)	(44)

We might assume that other kinds of political participation would display a similar ordering of age groups. Therefore, respondents were evaluated in terms of a number of other political activities in which they may have engaged.[25] Table 3 shows the distribution of the number of such activities engaged in by members of each age group. Here the youngest men are the most active, while the oldest men again display the lowest level of political activity.

25. These activities included working for their side in a local vote, having given an opinion on an issue when asked, having signed a petition, belonging to a political group, having taken sides on a local issue.

Another generalization that has been made about the older citizen is that in the absence of anything specifically relevant to his interests (e.g., old-age assistance, specific demagogic appeals) he will be less likely than others to have formed an opinion on a political issue.[26] If he does form an opinion, that opinion is usually characterized as conservative.[27] Four recent political issues in Dunholme were proposals for social change: fluoridation of the water supply, city-county government unification, urban renewal, and downtown shopping center redevelopment. A count of the number of opinions for, the number of opinions against, and the number of "no-opinions" within each age group yielded the information contained in Table 4. It may be seen that the two younger age groupings display higher rates of opinion formation and greater indorsement of change. However, the rate of opinion formation *opposing* change does not vary with age, contrary to the usual generalizations. This suggests the inadequacy of a rationalistic "conflict of interests" model in explaining age differences in opinion; if there were such conflict, not only should affirmations of change decrease with age, but opposition should also increase.

Table 4. Progressivism of Opinions on Political Issues Held by Males in Three Age Groups (in percentages) .

| | Age | | |
Opinion	22–39	40–64	65 and over
For change	48	49	35
No opinion	26	26	40
Against change	26	25	25
Total per cent	100	100	100
(*N* of responses)	(148)	(156)	(176)

Finally, the adequacy of the civic responsibility model in explaining age differences in political behavior can be assessed by predicting that old men would be more anomic than young or middle-aged men.[28] Table 5 tests this assertion and shows that the older men are indeed the most anomic. In summary, in Dunholme

26. Wilensky, "Life Cycle and Formal Participation," pp. 237-239.
27. *Ibid*; Stouffer, *Communism, Conformity, and Civil Liberties*, pp. 89-102.
28. Wilensky, "Life Cycle and Formal Participation," p. 239; Lane, *Political Life*, pp. 168-169.

Table 5. Incidence of Anomie Among Males in Three Age Ranges (in percentages).

Anomie	Age		
	22–39	40–64	65 and over
Present	16	10	25
Absent	84	90	75
Total per cent	100	100	100
(*N*)	(37)	(39)	(44)

advancing age is associated with increased anomie, decreased political activity of all kinds, and an increased tendency to have no opinion or not to support proposed changes.

Community Implication and Political Participation

The frame of reference of the present analysis requires that voting and other political behavior be examined as a potential function of the extent to which a resident is thoroughly implicated in the ongoing social life of his community. Three ways in which community residents may be so implicated to a greater or lesser degree were selected for analysis.

Some persons have greater *commitment* to remain residents in the community than others. At the extreme, some persons find they must stay irrespective of whether they desire to leave. A vivid example of this condition is provided by a fifty-seven-year-old widow who lacks income and lives with a son whose work keeps him here. Such a person, though free, is tied to the community almost as thoroughly as a prison inmate is tied to his place of incarceration. Conversely, others have to leave regardless of how much they may wish to stay. This phenomenon receives an almost classic illustration in the case of a forty-eight-year-old spinster whose only retirement resource is a home for retirees maintained in another city by an association to which she belongs.

The respondents were scored according to the degree of their individual commitment to remain. The extreme scores referred to respondents whose choices as to place of residence were determined in one direction or the other by situational factors no longer under their own control—those forced to leave and those constrained to stay, respectively. Others received one point on the commitment score for each of the following attributes: owning a home, having long tenure with his current employer, having children in high school, feeling directly responsible for the care of another Dunholmer (not in one's own household), and having all or most of one's friends in Dunholme. The commitment score, therefore, could range from zero to seven.

Another way in which persons demonstrate the extent of their implication in the ongoing social life of the community is in terms of the intensity and extent of their participation in the various matrices of social contact available in the community. A *social anchorage* score was constructed by scoring one for each of ten behavior patterns actually manifested.[29] The total score could range from zero (no anchorages) to ten (high anchorages).

The first two measures of community implication refer largely to objective aspects of social structure and behavior. The third refers more to subjective dispositions. An index of *community orientation* separated persons who said they thought, felt, and acted in terms of the entire community from those who responded only in terms of segments of the community or in terms of the advantages and disadvantages the community had for them personally.[30]

These three aspects of the way in which individuals are related to the community were found to be associated with one another in an interesting pattern—one which made it possible to combine them into a single index. Almost all persons who were community-oriented had a social anchorage score greater than six and a commitment score greater than three. Almost all persons with a social anchorage score greater than six also had a commitment score greater than three. In other words, the majority of the respondents (86 per cent) displayed one of the following patterns of implication: high in all

29. These included the following broad categories of social activity: using mass media; leisure and recreation; participation in voluntary associations; work; the community; school; family; religion; friendships; and neighborhood. It may be seen that the last four refer most clearly to *segments* of the community only; however, scores based on these were so closely associated with those based on the remaining attributes that all were combined into a single score.

30. A person was defined as community-oriented if he indicated participation in non-political civic activities such as volunteer welfare work, community planning, or charity drives, and who expressed positive (or negative) evaluations of Dunholme's over-all attributes (e.g., progressive—non-progressive, friendly—non-friendly people) or because they said people *should* act and feel in these ways. All other persons were classified as non-community-oriented.

Table 6. Extent of Anomie Manifested in Groups with Different Degrees of Community Implication (in percentages).

Anomie	Community implication type			
	4	3	2	1
Present	9	15	10	38
Absent	91	85	90	62
Total per cent	100	100	100	100
(N)	(23)	(40)	(31)	(26)

Table 7. Voting by Members of Groups with Different Degrees of Community Implication (in percentages).

Extent of voting	Community implication type			
	4	3	2	1
3-4	96	73	50	29
1-2	0	16	21	34
0	4	11	29	37
Total per cent	100	100	100	100
(N)	(24)	(44)	(28)	(24)

three, high anchorages and high commitment only, high commitment only, low in all three. Although it does not prove it, such patterning supports the possibility that social anchorages are formed on the basis of commitment and that such anchorages lead to community orientation. The four types of patterns were scored four, three, two, and one, respectively, in an index of community implication, with deviant patterns being assigned one of these scores by standard procedures.

If community implication is a positive and anomie a negative correlate of civic responsibility, it is to be expected that implication is negatively associated with anomie. This is borne out by the information in Table 6. Small numbers of cases are probably responsible for the absence of a perfect linear relationship between the two variables, but in general the results suggest that implication and anomie are closely associated and that henceforth the community implication index can—among other things—safely substitute for the relatively insensitive measure of anomie that was available.

The first prediction that can be made on the basis of this

Table 8. Political Activity (Other Than Voting) of Groups with Different Degrees of Community Implication (in percentages) .

Number of political activities (other than voting)	Community implication type			
	4	3	2	1
2-4	62	32	7	8
1	21	43	32	29
0	17	25	61	63
Total per cent	100	100	100	100
(*N*)	(24)	(44)	(28)	(24)

index is that the greater the community implication, the higher the rate of voting. Table 7 shows strong confirmation of this prediction for the combined samples. Almost all of the most highly implicated persons voted regularly, whereas less than one-third of the least implicated persons did so. Moreover, the rate of non-voting decreased with greater community implication.

Turning to other forms of political participation, a similar prediction was made: the greater the community implication, the greater the participation in non-voting aspects of the political process. Table 8 strongly supports this prediction. As community implication lessens, the rate of non-participation rises from one out of six to almost two out of three.

Finally, if an opinion for change means a pro-community opinion, the rate of having an opinion should be higher with higher community implication, and such opinion should be more in favor of change. Table 9 demonstrates this to be the case. The rate of no opinion increases with lower community implication, while the rate

Table 9. Extent of Progressivism Manifested by Groups with Differing Degrees of Community Implication (in percentages) .

Opinion	Community implication type			
	4	3	2	1
For change	59	45	37	31
No opinion	14	29	39	44
Against change	27	26	24	25
Total per cent	100	100	100	100
(*N* of responses)	(100)	(171)	(109)	(100)

favoring change decreases. The rate of opposition to change remains the same for all degrees of community implication. This suggests that the unimplicated person does not oppose change, he simply does not support it. Perhaps, then, the word "change" could be replaced by the phrase "welfare of the community."

The intimate relationships between community implication and the extent and nature of political participation speak strongly for the predictive value of a civic responsibility model in local political processes. This would be the case if the community is one which has norms supporting political participation for the sake of community welfare. In such a case, the implicated person would not only be more likely to learn and internalize these norms but also have greater access to the channels available for implementing them. We feel that such norms are more and more prevalent in contemporary American communities—Dunholme included. Such a situation comports well with the community responsibility model.

COMMUNITY IMPLICATION AND THE POLITICAL PARTICIPATION OF OLDER MEN

Our findings support a picture of politically inactive older men, who are less likely than others to support community change but who are no more likely than others to oppose it. They also suggest that political activity, as well as the support given to community change (but not its rejection), are closely linked to the individual's degree of objective and subjective immersion in the *total* life of the community. However, our argument leads us to expect that

Table 10. Community Implication Among Males in Three Age Ranges (in percentages).

Community implication type	Age		
	22–39	40–64	65 and over
4	16	28	16
3	62	46	7
2	8	16	43
1	14	10	34
Total per cent	100	100	100
(*N*)	(37)	(39)	(44)

older men are the political men they are only to the degree that they are generally less implicated in the community than are others.

Table 10 demonstrates that the OS members are indeed less community-implicated than are the other two age groupings. Three-quarters of the young and middle-aged samples are in the two highest implication types, whereas three-quarters of the old sample are in the two lowest ones. If the older persons are to be compared to others with like degrees of community implication, might not their political behavior be quite like that of the others?

Table 11. Voting by Age and Community Implication (in percentages).

| Extent of voting | Community implication type | | | | | |
| | 3-4 | | | 1-2 | | |
	22-39	40-64	65 and over	22-39	40-64	65 and over
3-4	69	90	90	38	40	42
1-2	17	7	0	37	10	29
0	14	3	10	25	50	29
Total per cent	100	100	100	100	100	100
(N)	(29)	(29)	(10)	(8)	(10)	(34)

Table 12. Political Activities (Other Than Voting) by Age and Community Implication (in percentages).

| Number of political activities (other than voting) | Community implication type | | | | | |
| | 3-4 | | | 1-2 | | |
	22-39	40-64	65 and over	22-39	40-64	65 and over
2-4	38	44	50	38	0	9
1	48	28	20	12	30	29
0	14	28	30	50	70	62
Total per cent	100	100	100	100	100	100
(N)	(29)	(29)	(10)	(8)	(10)	(34)

Table 11 shows that among persons similarly implicated old persons are as likely as others to be regular voters. Table 12 concerns other political activities and leads to similar conclusions. Older persons are equal to middle-aged persons in their rates of non-voting participation.

The opinions expressed with respect to the four proposed changes

Table 13. Progressivism by Age and Community Implication (in per-
    centages).

Opinion	Community implication type					
	3–4			1–2		
	22–39	40–64	65 and over	22–39	40–64	65 and over
For change	47	55	58	53	33	29
No opinion	25	22	20	38	37	45
Against change	28	23	22	9	30	26
Total per cent	100	100	100	100	100	100
(*N* of response)	(116)	(116)	(40)	(32)	(40)	(136)

show a comparable pattern (see Table 13). The community-implicated old men differ little from other community-implicated men
in their responses. Congruently, older men who are not implicated
are like similar middle-aged men.

While it has been argued that all these observations are consistent with and even predictable from the community responsibility
model, it might be contended that the data are also consistent with
still another interpretation. It could be said that two syndromes have
been depicted, "caring" and "not caring" about one's home community, and that action in the local political arena is but a segment
of the syndrome. In contrast, we account for political activity and
opinion in terms of degree of access to those community structures
which lead first to acceptance of norms and then to expression of
this acceptance in appropriate action. In this view, access need not
depend upon caring.

We can choose between these alternatives. It should follow from
the "caring" interpretation that groups with little implication in
the community would show less identification with it than groups
which are more implicated. The community responsibility model
leads to no such prediction; from this point of view political participation is a function of access to the social structure, and the development of identification may be independent of whether one has access.

Fortunately, a ready, though approximate, indicator of identification with the community was available in answers to a question
about whether the respondent took pride in being a Dunholmer.
Since old people and women have been characterized as having
relatively less access than their counterparts to most of the resources

Table 14. Distribution of Community Pride Among Men and Women in the GS and OS (in percentages) .

Community pride	Men		Women	
	GS	OS	GS	OS
Present	70	89	79	90
Absent	30	11	21	10
Total per cent	100	100	100	100
(N)	(76)	(44)	(117)	(92)

of the society, we examined the distributions of positive claims to pride among homogeneous age and sex groupings. The findings reported in Table 14 clearly contradict the "care syndrome" interpretation, without negating the community responsibility model. There is no difference in pride between the two sexes, while older persons report feelings of pride *significantly more* than do the GS members. Hence, it appears that people who "really care" nonetheless may be non-participants because their status attributes deprive them of access to forms of social participation that lead to such behavior.[31] All this suggests that old persons behave and think differently from younger ones on the local political scene only insofar as they are *less a part of the total community.* Given equal membership, the findings suggest that the paradoxical political role of the aged might disappear.

CONCLUSION

The citizen's implication in the total life of the community has predicted with relative precision not only rates of political activity and opinion formation but also the direction of positions taken on issues. Through the use of old age as a critical case, the implication approach has pointed a way toward understanding disproportionate rates of political deviance in specific segments of the community. These results indicate the necessity of considering the civic responsibility model in understanding the political process. They also clarify another point recently made in political theory.

31. Both implication and voting were unrelated to identification with the community.

In his synthesis of empirical voting studies, Talcott Parsons[32] attempted to account for the relative harmony that is rapidly established after a partisan campaign. He attributes such equilibration (*1*) to shared belief in the democratic process (generalized norms of civic responsibility in our terms), (*2*) to general disinterest in political issues, and (*3*) to the cross-pressures that arise from the fact that the individual belongs to numerous subgroups and consequently interacts with members of all (usually two) major factions. The findings of the present study extend his theory by suggesting that the range of the individual's participation in such subgroups not only may make for uncertainty and tolerance but may also increase his exposure to the norms of civic responsibility. This, in turn, indicates the desirability of ascertaining the circumstances under which a heightened range of exposure leads to political inactivity and apathy, and those under which the same experiences result in heightened activity and interest.

Finally, the use of the extent of implication as a predictor of local political activity and opinion in this community suggests that political activity was only a special case of *community activity in general.* By this we mean that the greater the number of ways the individual is tied to the community, the greater will be his access to *any* of its norms, political *or* other. The more parts of a total structure to which the individual is exposed, the more he will be oriented to the norms of the whole. The handicap of the elderly may not lie so much in anything intrinsic to old age as such as it may lie in the lack of access to the total structure of the community.

32. " 'Voting' and the Equilibrium of the American Political System," in Eugene Burdick and Arthur J. Brodbeck (eds.), *American Voting Behavior* (Glencoe, Ill.: The Free Press, 1959), pp. 180-220.

Joel Smith
Howard P. Myers
Herman Turk

17. URBAN COMMUNITY KNOWLEDGE FROM A NORMATIVE PERSPECTIVE[*]

Sociological theories of individual behavior largely reflect one or the other of two major emphases: (*1*) action based on special interests of individuals or subgroups or (*2*) action based on conformity with the shared norms of a broader social system.[1] Theories of the first type characteristically emphasize the role of coercive mechanisms of social control in producing conformity and predictability in the face of potential conflict and disorder; theories of the latter type emphasize solidarity, cohesion, and consensus. The appeal of interest theories has grown with the concomitant trends toward large-scale society and urbanization. However, inasmuch as such theories inadequately account for the behavioral predictability and conformity that still characterize the large and complex urbanized society, theories of the latter type continue to hold considerable appeal.

Irrespective of the detailed accuracy of this broad characterization of behavioral theory, it is clear that these two alternative positions pose different tasks for the sociology of human behavior. Because theories which view behavior as a response to group norms have somewhat less currency than interest theories, it seems appropriate to ascertain whether this point of view can parsimoniously

[*] This is a revision of a paper presented at the August, 1963, meetings of the American Sociological Association.

1. A fuller development of the discussion contained in this paragraph, together with appropriate citations, may be found in Joel Smith, Herman Turk, and Howard P. Myers, "Understanding Local Political Behavior: The Role of the Older Citizen," *Law and Contemporary Problems*, **27** (Spring, 1962), 282-286.

account for some behavioral data. With this interest in mind, data that report particular activities of urban residents in which self-interests can obviously be a relevant factor provide a severe test of the adequacy of the normative model.

Since individuals vary in behavior of the same general category, any normative theory must also accept the possibility of concomitant variation in the impact of the norms. The allocative mechanisms of complex social systems can account for this variation in the impact of norms, for as we have seen in the preceding analysis of age differences in voting, they set the different degrees, modes, and styles of participation of the nominal members of such systems.

Norms that govern behavior in a structure are both learned and reinforced by the members' participation in activities which are conducted within the framework of the structure. Such activities of nominal members may vary in form, amount, and intensity of personal relevance. It follows that the extent to which a nominal member of the structure behaves in accordance with its norms is a function of the way in which he actually participates in the structure.

Specifically, Dunholme is the structure to be considered and its residents are the nominal participants. The previous argument implies that behavior relevant to the community will be guided by community norms to the extent that residents' modes of participation in the community provide opportunities for learning and reinforcing the relevant norms. While there is, of course, a considerable variety of ways in which a city resident's mode of participation in the ongoing social life of that community may vary, the index of implication used in Chapter 16 effectively summarizes most of those that are germane. It is our central thesis that the greater the implication with the community (or any comparable structure), the greater the access to and internalization of community (or other relevant) norms, and consequently the greater the chances of behavior conforming to these norms.

It was found in the preceding chapter that two normatively supported positions—that of high political participation and that of favoring community progress—were positively associated with the degree of community implication. Moreover, typically observed age differences in such political variables were removed when the implication variable was introduced into the analysis. Both the political inactivity of the aged and their apparent conservatism proved to be no different from that of younger persons, once the generally lower access of old persons to the norms of the community—their lower community implication—was taken into account. Thus, a finding which is typical of many studies could be explained at least as parsimoniously in terms of the normative model as it could be in terms of a theory of self-interest.

In view of these findings, it is desirable to test the normative theory of community behavior further by using data of another sort—knowledge of significant public events in the community.[2] This also gives us a second opportunity to examine apparent GS-OS differences under conditions of comparable access to the social structure of the community and its norms. Community knowledge has been studied previously,[3] although not as much as we might expect in view of the significance of shared knowledge in promoting group solidarity and cohesion. The data reported from these studies do not indicate the superiority of either of the viewpoints mentioned here. They seem consistent with either.[4]

We begin with the major premise that variations in the degree of implication in the social structure of a group are directly related to variations in the degree of knowledge of and conformity to the norms of the group. We observe that American norms for any structure in which participation is democratic prescribe that members inform themselves fully on all matters at issue within it. On this basis, the following general hypothesis was formulated: the greater the implication in the structure of the community, the greater the degree of knowledge about issues arising within it; and differences in the implication of younger and older adults account for differences in the amount of their community knowledge. While it is quite possible that the implication index described earlier may be highly correlated with self-interest (the need for information) or with op-

2. The data reported here, together with all related procedures, derive from Howard P. Myers, "Community Implication and Ignorance, Possession, and Veridicality of Community Information" (unpublished M.A. thesis, Duke University, 1963).

3. R. K. Merton, "Patterns of Influence: A Study of Interpersonal Influence and of Communications Behavior in a Local Community," in P. F. Lazarsfeld and F. W. Stanton (eds.), *Communications Research, 1948-49* (New York: Harper & Bros., 1949), pp. 180-219; G. M. Sykes, "The Differential Distribution of Community Knowledge," *Social Forces*, **29** (May, 1951), 376-382; A. A. Fanelli, "Extensiveness of Communication Contacts and Perception of the Community," *American Sociological Review*, **21** (August, 1956), 439-445. Some comments relevant to the current status of sociological studies of knowledge and information may be found in footnote 17 of chapter 13 of this volume, pp 218-219.

4. Myers, "Community Implication and Ignorance, Possession, and Veridicality of Community Information," pp. 4-10.

portunities to obtain information, these possibilities do not provide a basis for predicting higher degrees of knowledge on the first level than on the second level of the index. In this particular case only the presence of a community orientation in the former distinguishes the two levels, and this is not an attribute included in any utilitarian theory.

The data used to test this hypothesis derive from the 180 GS and 133 OS members who had lived in Dunholme during the time these matters were at issue. The actual items in the implication index and the procedures used in combining them are described elsewhere.[5] The distribution of sample members among the four implication levels appears in Table 1.

Table 1. Distribution of Sample Members Among Implication Levels.

Implication level	GS	OS	Composite weighted sample
1 (highest)	34	12	36.50
2	94	18	97.75
3	29	59	41.31
4 (lowest)	23	44	32.18
Total	180	133	207.74

Respondents were also questioned about their knowledge of eight major issues that had arisen in the city during the four or five years preceding the interview. The issues included: (*a*) unification of the city and county governments; (*b*) loss of the local minor league baseball team; (*c*) fluoridation of the city water supply; (*d*) undertaking of an urban renewal program; (*e*) undertaking of a redevelopment program for the downtown shopping area; (*f*) building of a low-rent housing project for elderly people; (*g*) cancellation of all local passenger train service; and (*h*) a school bond election. A general filter question determined which of these issues the respondent was familiar with, and details of each such issue were then probed in follow-up questions.[6]

The detail score was computed as follows. Bits of information

5. *Ibid.*, pp. 23-28; and Smith *et al.*, "Understanding Local Political Behavior," pp. 292-293.

6. The exact formats of these questions may be found in Myers, "Community Implication and Ignorance, Possession, and Veridicality of Community Information," pp. 28-33.

were tabulated for those five issues on which follow-up questions provided respondents with extensive opportunities to go into detail. Since we were concerned with the amount of detailed information possessed by people having general awareness, we dropped from the analysis five sample members who were not aware of any of the five issues. A check of the correctness of the responses provided to the follow-up questions showed no drastic differences in accuracy among the samples or implication groups. Therefore, no effort was made to screen the bits on their correctness. In order to equate the different issues, which varied considerably in the numbers of bits that could have been reported, and because the true upper limit of bits was indeterminate, each respondent's bit-count on an issue he had heard of was summed and divided by the sum of maximum bit-counts for those issues. The maximum bit-count for an issue was the largest number of bits reported by a single respondent on that issue. The average for a sample and/or implication group was computed as the average of these averages.[7]

Considerations involved in formulating hypotheses concerning the differences between samples on the various items reflecting integrative mechanisms (see Chapter 15) have already sensitized us to certain differences between our two measures of community knowledge. The count of issues that respondents report having heard about involves something so public and so effortlessly achieved that no differences were expected and none were observed. On the other hand, the measure involving the reporting of details deals with relatively less public data requiring more effort to obtain. Hence, we predicted and in face found that, on the average, GS members would possess a greater quantity of detailed information than OS members $(\bar{\chi}_G = 24.22; \bar{\chi}_0 = 17.37; t = 4.18; p < .01)$.

In line with the theory being expounded, we would hypothesize that when opportunity for access to the structure is equalized, age differences in number of details reported will disappear. Implication was used as a control to test this hypothesis. The expectation is that the average number of details reported by members of each sample implicated in the community to the same degree will not differ significantly. As Table 2 reveals, this expectation was not realized. While implication is clearly related to differences in the number of details reported in both samples, differences between the two be-

7. Detailed procedures for computing these averages are reported in *ibid.*, pp. 29-30.

Table 2. Mean Amount of Detail Reported on Five Community Issues by Sample and Implication Levels.

Implication level	GS		OS	
	Mean	N	Mean	N
1 (highest)	32.47	(34)	23.92	(12)
2	24.90	(94)	15.78	(18)
3	15.24	(29)	17.02	(59)
4 (lowest)	20.52	(23)	16.70	(44)

	Analysis of Variance			
	Degrees of freedom	Sums of squares	Mean squares	F
Implication	3	162.95	54.32	7.67**
Sample	1	48.62	48.62	6.87**
Implication × sample	3	38.47	12.82	
Individuals	305	2158.11	7.08	

**$p < .01$.

come minimal at the lower levels of implication. However, both main effects remain highly significant.

Reflection on this finding led us to consider whether there were any other differences between members of the samples that also needed to be equated before our expectations could be realized. We have already noted the fact that OS members are not nearly as verbal as GS members in responding to unstructured questions, and that they give answers notable for their paucity of detail. One possible control, then, would involve equalization of the groups on some factor likely to affect the general richness of response in the entire interview.

One factor that immediately suggests itself as affecting ability to formulate ideas and express them is formal education. The utility of education as an additional control was further recommended by the fact that OS members had been found to have significantly less formal education than GS members (see Chapter 14). Therefore, it was decided to retest the observed sample differences in amount of detail, simultaneously holding constant both level of education and degree of implication. The size of the two samples prevented the use of more than two educational levels, so a decision had to be made as to an appropriate point at which to divide high and low levels of education. Analysis of the relation of education to amount of detail showed that detail increased regularly as education did, so that any cutting point would serve our purpose. Hence, completion of eight years of school was decided upon since it was the only possible cutting point that provided a sufficient number of cases for the eight cells required by our test.

Table 3. Mean Amount of Detail Reported on Five Community Issues by Sample, Education, and Implication Levels.

	High education				Low education			
	GS		OS		GS		OS	
Implication level	Mean	N	Mean	N	Mean	N	Mean	N
1 (highest)	32.30	(33)	31.67	(6)	38.00	(1)	19.00	(5)
2	26.09	(79)	17.17	(12)	18.67	(15)	12.60	(5)
3	18.63	(19)	16.51	(37)	7.78	(9)	18.00	(20)
4 (lowest)	25.00	(16)	18.95	(19)	10.29	(7)	15.41	(22)

	Analysis of Variance			
	Degrees of freedom	Sums of squares	Mean squares	F
Implication	3	542.65	180.88	6.67**
Sample	1	47.09	47.09	1.74
Education	1	135.60	135.60	5.00*
Iample × implication	3	122.10	40.70	
Sample × education	1	4.01	4.01	
Smplication × education	3	17.71	5.90	
Sample × implication × education	3	151.63	50.54	
Individuals	289	7831.88	27.10	

*$p < .05$.
**$p < .01$.

The revised hypothesis now stipulated that when both degree of implication (an access factor) and level of education (a personal skill factor) are controlled, there will be no significant difference in amount of detail on community knowledge reported by the two samples. Table 3 shows the results of this analysis. Both implication and level of education produce significant differences among the mean amounts of detail reported, but sample age does not. Means at lower levels of education (holding implication constant) tend to be lower than those at higher levels. And most significantly they tend to decrease with implication, the largest differences being between the first and second implication levels.[8]

In a general way, these findings for both hypotheses confirm the utility of the normative model of the community in explaining the community-relevant behavior of its residents. It seems reasonable to assert that a sizable majority of the residents of this city are of the type to which this model applies. Moreover, with respect to the theoretical issue raised here, the strategic datum is the difference in information possessed by the groups displaying the two highest degrees of implication. In all comparisons, differences are consistently in the predicted direction, with or without the insertion of education as a control. Since the index distinguishes among these two types only in terms of the generality of their orientations to the particular local community, and since access to information at these two implication levels is not differentiated by the fact of social position, the normative approach offers a far more parsimonious interpretation than the utilitarian individual interest approach.

To summarize, although we lack longitudinal data, the analyses suggest that the securing of public community information results from a process in which an individual is first "captured" in the community structure (commitment), and then proceeds to locate and diffuse his activities more and more within that structure (social anchorages), and finally develops a positive identification with the particular community as a whole (orientation). In any community in which knowledge of local issues is normatively prescribed, each degree of implication implies greater learning and acceptance of this norm (as well as any other such communal norms). Its internalization implies that more and more positive effort is put into norm-conforming activity. In addition, however, as greater implication demonstrates greater acceptance of the community and its norms, the individual will also be in a position to receive information without active effort—information which others deem important to his role in community affairs.

As regards the aged, we again see an expected and previously observed difference manifesting itself not so much as a consequence

8. Although our thinking did not lead us to test any hypotheses concerning the number of issues for which awareness was reported, a parallel analysis was conducted on these data. The results of that analysis added substantial support to the reasoning followed here. Whereas age differences on that factor were originally minimal, they become significant with *OS members reporting more awareness of issues than GS members on the same implication-education level.*

of an intrinsic quality of old age but as a reflection of the status position of the aged in the community's structure. Any change in the normative system that would permit a more equitable reassignment of the aged in this structure might well result in a significant increment in their integrative contributions. As Chapter 13 indicates, the currently uncrystallized group status of the aged may offer the time for such changes to transpire, although the latent attitudes, stereotypes, and opinions concerning the aged do not make such a prognosis very favorable.

Section Four

AGING AND SELF ORIENTATION

Kurt W. Back

Kenneth J. Gergen

18. COGNITIVE AND MOTIVATIONAL FACTORS IN AGING AND DISENGAGEMENT

Many personal characteristics conventionally used in research, such as age, sex, race, and occupational status, may be looked at in two ways: as intrinsic features of the person and as social traits derived from societal prescription. In the case of aging, many physiological and psychological changes have been documented (e.g., cellular deficiencies, diminished reactions, slower reaction time). Many of these changes would seem to cause the aged person to lose contact with the social environment.[1] However, such loss in contact is not an ironclad necessity. More complex tests show a possibility of compensation among older people that may more than counteract many of the primary losses. Older people may make use of their accumulated learning experiences and frequently perform as well as or better than younger persons, if they are willing to engage themselves in the task at hand.[2] On the other hand, looking at aging on a societal level, we know that different societies have different social prescriptions for older persons and varying norms for the various age groupings.[3] In Western society such norm prescriptions fre-

1. Frigyes Verzár, *Lectures on Experimental Gerontology* (Springfield, Ill.: Charles C. Thomas, 1963); Jack Botwinick, "Research Problems and Concepts of the History of Aging," *The Gerontologist*, **4** (September, 1964), 121-129; Alfred Weiss, "Sensory Functions," in J. C. Birren (ed.), *Handbook of Aging and the Individual* (Chicago: University of Chicago Press, 1959), pp. 503-542.

2. David Wechsler, *The Measurement of Adult Intelligence* (Baltimore: Williams & Wilkins Co., 1949); A. I. Welford, *Ageing and Human Skills* (London: Oxford University Press, 1958).

3. Leo H. Simmons, *The Role of the Aged in Primitive Society* (New Haven: Yale University Press, 1945).

quently include the relinquishing of various functions, especially in work, family relations, and control functions in social institutions. Again, in other instances it is possible that accumulative power during a lifetime may give the aged person an increasing amount of power and involvement within the society. This is true, even in our society, in fields such as politics and finance. Thus, changes due to aging can be seen as the result of natural and socially determined factors mediated by the self-evaluations of the person himself.

Both kinds of theory represent a more or less closed system, deriving behavior as necessary functions of one set of variables—social or individual. Taken to the extreme, each of these theories is vulnerable to attack, especially on empirical grounds, although they may be logically consistent. We shall try to avoid this difficulty by proceeding from an intermediate concept, that of personal orientation. A person does orient himself within the limits given by individual capacities and the social situation, but we accept the possibility of choice at some point, and this may lead to a definite commitment of further orientations.

The present approach stems in part from a current theory which has attempted to develop a personal base for the aging process— namely, disengagement theory.[4] This theory suggests that the aged person recedes socially and psychologically from his environment and that these processes are intrinsically determined. It is not the norms which force the aging person out of the society; the emphasis of the theory is in opposition to the position of aging as a function of societal prescriptions. The personal acceptance of this withdrawal by the aged person would be a correlate of successful aging. However, as far as they are established by younger people, the norms assign productivity a supreme value. Thus, it is difficult for a young person to accept the idea that anyone would want to withdraw from society and lead a more detached, contemplative life.

Disengagement theory has drawn deserved attention to the fact that the so-called losses during the aging process are not necessarily losses from the point of view of the aged person. Elaine Cumming and William E. Henry have succeeded in showing that disengagement is not detrimental and can be accepted as a normal concomi-

4. Elaine Cumming and William E. Henry, *Growing Old* (New York: Basic Books, 1961).

tant of aging. They have some difficulties, however, in showing that disengagement is actually beneficial—for instance, that people who withdraw more are more satisfied with aging.[5] The theory has also been criticized from several other points of view. For example, the theory may be too dependent upon intrinsic conditions, while aging and disengagement may be quite dependent on environmental conditions.[6] Nor has it been demonstrated that intrinsic psychological disengagement is a basic necessity. There is great individual variability in the amount of withdrawal observed in aging. Therefore, withdrawal cannot be said to be a necessary way of acting. These criticisms suggest that disengagement theory has tended, in contrast to the focus on social norms and rejection of the aged, to overemphasize physiological and psychological factors.

However, it is possible to consider social disengagement from the point of view of personal orientations. This would correspond with an early formulation of David Riesman, based on the same study from which disengagement theory later developed. Basing his ideas on an intensive study of aging in Kansas City, Riesman[7] argued against a single, intrinsic process of aging, but he differentiated among three different types of aging which he calls autonomous, conformist, and anomic. The first of these may be held to be roughly parallel to an adjustment gain in old age, the second to maintenance in old age, and the third to a loss in adjustment in old age. From Riesman's point of view, conformity thus facilitates continued adjustment. Conformity to social norms might be seen as corresponding to disengagement. The anomic's adjustment can be viewed as the struggle against accepting the norms of aging, while the autonomous would be the type who does not want to withdraw or detach and succeeds in not doing so.

Implicit in Riesman's formulation is the notion that the person is highly aware of the physical and social world in which he exists. Both the deterioration of bodily capacities and social reinforcement register significantly in the experience of the person. To return to the distinction made in the initial paragraph of this chapter, from the more phenomenal point of view social withdrawal is not a neces-

5. Sheldon S. Tobin and Bernice L. Neugarten, "Life Satisfaction and Social Interaction in the Aging," *Journal of Gerontology*, **16** (1961), 344-346.

6. George L. Maddox, "Disengagement Theory: A Critical Evaluation," *The Gerontologist*, **4** (June, 1964), 80-82.

7. "Some Clinical and Cultural Aspects of the Aging Process," in his *Individualism Reconsidered* (Garden City, N.Y.: Doubleday Anchor Books, 1955).

sary result of changes in either the person or his social environment. Rather, withdrawal would seem to depend on the manner in which the person processes the information he receives. It is at this point that the person's orientation to the world comes to play a crucial role, for differences in personal orientation will have a great impact on the processing of information. The person who feels that his days are numbered, for example, will react to information about long-term investments in a much different way than one who feels that all of his life is ahead of him. Based on this emphasis, it is now possible to introduce two important parameters of personal orientation.

A major distinction in the present theoretical orientation corresponds to the long-standing dichotomy between cognitive and motivational factors. In the cognitive domain we can begin with the general notion of *effective life space*. Effective life space can be defined by the extent of the world the person is willing to accept as relevant to his conduct (including any facts about the world—past, present, and future). In general, it can be postulated that effective life space is highly related to age. The world of the child is highly constricted. His attention is largely focused on orienting himself to his immediate environment and familiarizing himself with the continuity of time. Both tasks must be successfully accomplished before the larger world of adolescence and adulthood can be encountered. It is during adolescence that psychological development and social conditions act together to further expand the life space. During early adulthood, a person probably reaches his maximum effective life space. The amount of time which he considers important to his life and the degree of involvement with the world at large become excessive and comparatively fixed. However, different persons vary in size of life space, depending partly on social position, education, and past experiences, and partly on physiological and psychological factors such as attention span, intelligence, and preferred personality dispositions.[8] Gradually, in late middle age, the life space tends to constrict. Physiological changes which limit the person's effective engagement with the world tend to diminish the life space. Accumulated experience may counteract this process to a great degree. Thus, rather than a gradual constriction of the life space, intrinsic physical

8. Kurt W. Back and Kenneth J. Gergen, "Apocalyptic and Serial Time Perspectives and the Structure of Opinions," *Public Opinion Quarterly*, **27** (Fall, 1963), 427-442.

decline may force a sudden onset. This constriction may often occur quite late in life, after, say, sixty or seventy.

The modification of the life space seems to parallel other theories of development for the later ages. For instance, E. H. Erickson's[9] fundamental choices of different stages of life seem to depend on the type of life space under consideration at that time. The profound psycho-social crises which he postulates for the early stages of life relate to self-identity. However, the principal stages of adulthood deal primarily with the person's relationship to society: solidarity vs. isolation in young adulthood, and generativity vs. self-absorption in middle age. The contraction of life space in old age would be paralleled by the choice of integrity vs. despair in old age. Here again it is the emphasis on the person himself which is decisive. The positively valued choice leading to integrity and wisdom merges the boundaries of self and society.

Erickson's dichotomies will also serve as introduction to a second major aspect of development: the emotional investment of the person in his environment. This investment, which corresponds to the energy the person is capable of expending, is perhaps maximal during adolescence and young adulthood, but it would seem to decline gradually and evenly throughout the remainder of life. Emotional decline in aging has been a general assumption of gerontologists, although little direct evidence has been obtained. Empirical evidence is complicated by the fact that changes as measured could be due to restriction of life space as well as to decline of the energy level. Thus, measures of intellectual decline as shown in experiments could be due to lack of involvement of the aged person in the situation as well as to actual intellectual decline.[10] Similarly, the greater neutral response of the older respondents in interviews may be due to lack of interest in the interview or to less feeling about issues.[11] However, some evidence points to emotional withdrawal as such. Studies of verbal behavior have shown less affect in older samples than in younger ones, and projective tests have pointed in the same direction.[12] Even animal experiments have shown less emotion-

9. E. H. Erickson, "Growth and Crises of the Healthy Personality," *Psychological Issues*, 1 (1959), 50-100.
10. Maddox, "Disengagement Theory."
11. Kenneth J. Gergen and Kurt W. Back, "The Disengaged Respondent," *Public Opinion Quarterly* (in preparation).
12. M. J. Lakin and Carl Eisdorfer, "A Study of Affective Expression among the Aged," in Clark Tibbitts and Wilma Donahue (eds.), *Social and Psychological Aspects of Aging* (New York: Columbia University Press, 1962), pp. 650-654.

al behavior in older organisms.[13] A similar distinction to the one made here is formulated by psychiatrists in the field of aging; it is a distinction between recession and regression. At least at one stage the former is purely emotional withdrawal, while the latter includes a host of changes in the adaptive system. Although psychiatrists express doubt about a complete reduction of the drive system, leaving it an open question, they too can conceive of differences in cognitive and emotional changes in the life cycle.[14] In their interdisciplinary study of forty-seven aged men, James C. Birren *et al.* find the slowing down of response to be a general function of aging, as opposed to life space changes which depend on specific deprivations.[15]

We consider restriction of the life space and emotional decline as two basically independent processes occurring roughly over the same span of time. These two curves may coincide at certain points. Equilibrium or disequilibrium may occur if the effective life space exceeds energy level or vise versa. Further, different conditions in adulthood might affect both the time and kind of decline of the life space and the energy level, and therefore they might not necessarily allow disengagement to be a possible condition of aging. Thus, we view successful disengagement as not being something that is intrinsically necessary, but rather as an equilibrium condition which a great part of the population may reach. It would seem that the process of disengagement, seen as the interaction of two variables, is least efficiently studied in case studies with small numbers. A more appropriate approach would seem to be the use of a large number of subjects representing a variety of population groups. We shall show that some changes due to aging are more easily comprehended if they are related to one condition or the other and that some depend on the relationship between the two.

In the following pages, we shall use a method which seems to us particularly adaptable to exploring the processes of aging. This is the method of secondary analysis of survey data. Here it is possible to analyze the responses of a great number of people from all population groups and ages on a great variety of topics. The use of

13. Jack Werboff and Joan Havlena, "Effects of Aging on Open Field Behavior," *Psychological Reports,* **10** (1962), 395-398.

14. M. E. Linden, "Regression and Recession in the Psychology of the Aging," in N. E. Zinberg and Irving Kaufman (eds.), *Normal Psychology of the Aging Process* (New York: International Universities Press, 1963), pp. 125-142.

15. James C. Birren, Robert W. Butler, Samuel W. Greenhouse, Louis Sokoloff, and Marion R. Yarrow (eds.), *Human Aging* (Public Health Service Publication No. 986 [Bethesda, Md.: 1963]).

large (1,600 or larger) samples and the possibility of using several independent surveys help in applying a general theory such as the one proposed in these pages. The variety of questions used and different historical contexts give us confidence that no trick of question design or immediate circumstances account for differences between the different age groups. The data have been collected over a twenty-year span and thus cannot be interpreted in terms of intergenerational differences. On the other hand, the data have the drawback of having been collected for different purposes, where the variables we are investigating were of secondary interest or even possible sources of error to the original investigator. In many instances the kind of interpretation which we are giving to a question was only tangentially intended in the questionnaire, and thus the actual relationships may be quite small. Here again the replication in several different studies under different conditions can compensate for indirect evidence obtained in each case. For the same reason, the total pattern of relationships will be the main point of interest, and significance tests will be omitted.

The three chapters which follow represent an attempt to expand on the foregoing and to demonstrate the utility of considering cognitive and motivational factors in aging for several highly disparate topics. Chapter 19 further develops the notion of equilibrium and includes data on morale and psychological well-being. In Chapter 20, both cognitive and motivational factors are considered together and related to bodily care and concern. Chapter 21 dwells more intensively on the concept of life space and shows its relation to attitudes toward international conflict. The data presented in the following chapters can hardly be said to validate the present theoretical notions to the exclusion of all others. However, the major strength of the arguments would seem to be their capacity to unify and interrelate highly diverse areas of study.

Our whole procedure will be as follows. The implications of the theory sketched here will be applied to the topics under consideration—morale, somatic concern, and attitude toward international concerns—and compared with approaches which others have used to study these topics. Then a number of surveys will be scanned for relevant items, and the answers to them will be analyzed by age (mainly in three age groups: under forty, forty to fifty-nine, sixty and over). Consistent trends in these diverse questions will then be discussed.

Kurt W. Back

Kenneth J. Gergen

19. PERSONAL ORIENTATION AND MORALE OF THE AGED

Discussions of successful aging must confront the question of the relationship between aging and happiness or morale. Clearly this question is put too generally, assuming some pan-human pattern. But even if it is reduced to the context of present-day American society, one still finds an almost polar opposition of views. One side stresses the possible achievement of serenity and happiness in old age; the other stresses the gradual decline of many functions and positions within the society and an almost necessary lack of morale for these reasons. The second point of view is frequently accepted by people discussing aging and often reflects the values of the young and middle-aged in the society. If activity, power, and effectiveness in interpersonal relations, to take only a few conditions, are necessary for morale, clearly the decline of many functions and of possibilities for effectiveness in society would lead to decline of morale. Even such harsh and simple realities as decline of health and financial worries could be assumed to lead to lowered morale among the aged. Thus, it is the fact of physiological decline and the attempt of the younger group to exclude the older from effective participation which give support to the theory of declining morale. Further, as the helping professions usually have the greatest contact with those older people who really have problems and complaints, they are likely to act as spokesmen for this point of view, even berating the younger groups as being responsible for their elders' condition. It frequently comes as a surprise when studies find that some signs of maladjustment decline in old age and that the theory of serenity can be confirmed even in our society.

These large variations in morale of the aged and in attitude toward it cannot be treated as a purely individual matter. We shall attempt to show in this chapter that it is possible to account for even wide discrepancies in morale and adjustment of the aged by a few simple principles, especially by the distinction of cognitive and motivational changes and their relative levels—that is, by the theory we have discussed in the preceding chapter. As we have done there, we can use disengagement theory as our starting point.

In their book, *Growing Old*,[1] Elaine Cumming and William E. Henry have explained disengagement theory as hypothesizing that because of psychological and physiological changes the aged person wants to be less involved in the society and has less ability to maintain contact with other people and to engage in a variety of roles. Hence, the separation of the aged from the rest of society is not necessarily a burden on the aged and may be a positive factor. As we have said before,[2] the theory explains either too little or too much. If disengagement is a biologically necessary development in aging, it would be much more constant and less influenced by social condition than it appears to be. On the other hand, if it is just one of many conditions which can happen during aging, it would need to be more specific to be a viable concept.

We have tried to specify and limit the concept of disengagement further by postulating two processes, one cognitive and one motivational. The progressive decline of these two processes is slightly different during the life cycle. The emotional and motivational trend, the product of energy, reaches a peak in early adulthood and declines rather steadily thereafter. The cognitive aspect, or what we have called the effective life space, expands during early adulthood but does not contract as quickly as the energy level, partly because the accumulated experience by itself can counteract a biologically determined decline. Thus, effective life space stays relatively constant during much of adulthood and then declines rather suddenly as the balance between accumulated experience and biological decline shifts toward the declining side. The conjunction of these two curves will then lead to some equilibrium conditions when we can assume morale to be high and to some conditions of disequilibrium when discomfort ensues. This may happen when either the

1. (New York: Basic Books, 1961).
2. See above, chapter 18, for a full discussion.

energy can no longer invest the complete life space or alternately when it is too large for the real effective life space. The rapid and not quite parallel increases in both life space and energy level in youth can easily bring about some of the classic crisis situations of adolescence, such as frustration when energy exceeds the available scope. An equilibrium level can then be reached in early adulthood, corresponding to the maximum effective life space and energy level. At least in our culture, this condition is considered to be the dominant or normal condition and the model of high morale. This equilibrium then tends to be disturbed when the energy level declines faster than the life space and the person becomes anxious about performing in the arena he has set for himself. It would suggest the anxiety and low morale encountered in late middle age, perhaps in a person's fifties. If the effective life space declines, too, a new equilibrium can be reached. However, this is on a lower level of energy sufficient for a small effective life space. At least in our culture, this is a surprising adjustment which is encompassed by the positive value of disengagement. Different outcomes are, of course, possible; one such would be a longer duration of the ability to keep an effective interest in a wide variety of things—that is, in maintaining a large life space along with a wise manipulation of existing energies. On the other hand, the two developments may never reach a point of equilibrium and then lead to the picture of the unhappy aged who are most likely to seek help. In his theorizing about the Kansas City study, David Riesman[3] distinguishes the adjustive type of person, whom we would suppose to have an equilibrium, from the autonomous type, of whom we expect very high morale and high functioning, and the anomic type, who has exceptionally low morale. In light of our two variables, the anomic type of person has a disequilibrium between energy and life space, while the autonomous type maintains the life space on a much higher level and is able to use his energy to invest it. We can see here a certain regularity of the type of equilibrium possible; the way the curve fell during earlier life would be predictive of the kind of adjustment reached. It would also be reasonable that certain population groups are more likely to fall into one or the other categories. For instance, education, which helps to increase the life space, will also

3. "Some Clinical and Cultural Aspects of the Aging Process," in his *Individualism Reconsidered* (Garden City, N.Y.: Doubleday Anchor Books, 1955).

lead to either great frustration or greater likelihood of keeping up the life space in an adjustive way.

The type of person whom Riesman has called autonomous, which is the one we describe as maintaining both curves on a relatively high level, is clearly the type of older person preferred by the culture. Most descriptions of happy aging as a matter of course accept this as the only way for a person to age happily. For instance, Natalie H. Cabot[4] describes the active and creative member of the New England Aging Center as being equipped with large life space. We have here exceptionally well-balanced people who are put up as a model of successful aging. On the other hand, some descriptions of the problem of the aging will lay great stress on a special sample of people with disequilibrium as those with whom psychiatrists and social workers are most likely to come into contact.[5] Because of their prominence, these two groups are likely to be noticed out of proportion to their representation within society. If we talk about a society at large, it is likely we shall have to consider primarily the adjustive type of person who finds equilibrium at a lower level and who also comprises the dominant form in the population.

Studies with representative population samples have shown, in general, that morale is related to aging. One of the most thorough studies of mental health among Americans finds an improvement of adjustment measures with age.[6] Of the several measures, however, one of them (which the authors term immobilization, meaning a tendency not to act at all) becomes stronger with age. This contrast could be a paradox. However, it does fit into our model showing a decrease in action and the possibility of having a decrease with inadequate adjustment to it. Of course, in a population survey, this is again the modal trend. If the extremes become stronger in either way, this provides a choice—in Erickson's terms—between integrity and despair.

Through the use of population studies, which will again capture mainly the modal trend, we shall show the distinction between the two kinds of decline and their relation to morale. As evidence of decreasing life space, we shall take facts about the change of opinion

4. *You Can't Count on Dying* (Boston: Houghton Mifflin Co., 1961).
5. Ethel Shanas, "The Unmarried Old Person in the United States: Living Arrangements and Care in Illness, Myth and Fact," a paper prepared for the International Gerontological Research Seminar, Markaryd, Sweden, August, 1963.
6. Gerald Gurin, Joseph Veroff, and Sheila Field, *Americans View Their Mental Health* (New York: Basic Books, 1960), pp. 212-214.

Table 1. Age and Optimism.

	Under 40	40–59	60 and over
Percentage believing in another world war in next five years	33.9 (313)	48.7 (228)	74.5 (102)
Percentage believing United States losing cold war	47.7 (414)	61.3 (310)	64.8 (122)
Percentage believing cancer not curable	33.5 (475)	37.7 (358)	51.7 (143)
Percentage afraid of atomic plant in neighborhood	20.4 (348)	23.6 (267)	38.9 (90)

Source: AIPO #558, January 4, 1956.

of the aged toward public issues or their lack of interest in such issues. We can compare this finding with evidence taken from similar surveys about interests and energy level, and finally with the question of morale throughout the life cycle.

The opinion of the aged on public questions is frequently characterized by pessimism. Table 1 shows the examples taken from one survey on several such questions. The pessimistic response increases uniformly on questions as to whether there will be a war in the next five years, whether the United States is losing the cold war, and whether cancer is curable. In line with our previous discussion, however, we might well ask whether this is pessimism in the usual sense of the word—that is, a depressive emotion about future events —or whether it is merely a matter-of-fact statement of a likely but unfavorable outcome. We have noted in other papers[7] that pessimism is also an indication of a shortened time perspective, of the feeling that one has only one other chance to settle an issue (what we have called apocalyptic time perspective). In fact, the fourth question in the series, the response to the possibility of having an atomic plant in the neighborhood, may be seen either as an indication of pessimism or as an indication of the apocalyptic perspective of not being willing to take any chances.

Another example may show more clearly older people's lack of interest in the environment. In 1950 postal service was severely curtailed as an economy measure. In a subsequent Gallup poll, two questions were asked: "Have you yourself noticed any slowing down in the time it takes mail to reach you since the new postal

7. Kurt W. Back and Kenneth J. Gergen, "Apocalyptic and Serial Time Perspectives and the Structure of Public Opinion," *Public Opinion Quarterly*, **27** (Fall, 1963), 429-442. Also, see below, chapter 21.

Table 2. Knowledge and Concern About Postal Cut (in percentages).

	Under 40	40–59	60 and over
Have you yourself noticed any slowing down in the time it takes mail to reach you since the new postal service cut went into effect?			
Yes	34.9	45.7	46.6
If yes, does this make any difference to you?			
No	54.7	49.0	59.5
Total N	444	326	148

Source: AIPO #457, June 27, 1950.

service cut went into effect?" The people who said "yes" to the first question were asked, "Does this delay make any difference to you or not?" Positive response to the first question—knowledge of the reduced service—does increase with age; the aged notice events which go on around them. However, this knowledge is not translated into concern, and the delay makes little difference to the aged. With news events which are a little further from the immediate concern of the person, even knowledge decreases and indifference becomes more pronounced. In fact, the style of response changes in a corresponding direction with age. In another paper[8] we have shown that "don't know" and "don't care" answers increase with age, and that in any scale where shades of opinion would be possible, the aged are more likely to avoid the shadings and stick to "no difference" answers or to the extremes. This difference in style of response at times makes evaluation of the actual answers more difficult. However, this difference in style can also be interpreted as merely the end of the continuum of diminishing concern with many issues. In Chapter 21 we shall show how this diminishing concern of the aged leads them to prefer a radical solution in international affairs, and how this is related to a decreased life space.

In contrast to this general pessimism, let us consider older people's evaluation of their own condition. We have here data from one study which asks the respondent to evaluate his job or housework, whatever the main duty of the person was at the present time. In addition, the question was asked whether he enjoyed his work, whether he enjoyed his time in activity more than other time, or

8. Kenneth J. Gergen and Kurt W. Back, "The Disengaged Respondent," *Public Opinion Quarterly* (in preparation).

Table 3. Age and Preference for Activities (in percentages).

	Under 40	40–59	60 and over
Do you enjoy your job (or housework)?			
Yes	43.0 (726)	52.4 (616)	69.4 (317)
What time do you enjoy more, on the job (or housework) or others?			
On job	45.9 (653)	54.5 (543)	63.8 (279)
Would you be happier on a different job?			
No	70.8 (719)	71.3 (600)	78.9 (313)
Would you be happier if you had more money?			
No	23.4 (726)	27.4 (614)	37.6 (338)
Would you like to live to be 150 years old?			
No	60.6 (622)	60.8 (533)	67.7 (285)

Source: AIPO #549, June 22, 1956.
Note: Numbers differ because percentages are taken only from definite answers.

whether he would be happier with a different job; the aged person showed a definite preference for his present condition. The next few questions in this series, however, cast some doubt on whether this means positive enjoyment or an adjustment at a restricted level and an unwillingness to change. These questions relate to a possibility of change in a direction which would generally be seen as favorable. One question was whether the person would be happier if he had more money and the other concerned whether he would like to live to be 150 years old. In both cases the aged person was more likely to reject the question. This shows mainly the picture of indifferent acceptance and even an unwillingness to prolong the present state, which would be paradoxical if he assumed a deep satisfaction with it.

Table 4. Age and Worry (in percentages).

Do you worry about:	Under 40		40–59		60 and over	
	A lot	No worry	A lot	No worry	A lot	No worry
Making ends meet	31.1	17.2	30.1	26.0	20.6	42.1
Another war	22.8	25.0	27.5	26.0	20.3	41.3
Keeping job	15.0	53.3	12.0	58.3	4.7	78.9
Money in old age	15.8	41.5	23.2	35.9	21.6	51.1
Your health	14.7	44.1	17.3	38.5	14.9	49.8
A good place to live	23.1	38.2	16.9	50.0	7.8	69.5
N	621		488		223	

Source: AIPO #456, June 2, 1950.

We now come to direct questions of morale. The most explicit of the several questions on this topic are those concerning worries. The questions range from general topics to some very specific personal worries. In light of our previous discussion, it is not surprising to see that fewer older people than younger people worry about war. However, personal concerns, too, seem to be less important to them. Again, we might understand that the topics which are typically concerned with the life of younger people, such things as keeping a job or a good place to live, become less important to the aging. But those problems which seem to be more connected with the life of the older person, such as making ends meet, money in old age, or health, also seem to have become less important. The trend of these questions is important in the light of our previous discussion. Many people reach a peak of worry in middle age, and a reduction in worry only occurs at the age of about fifty. This seems to be the age where the life space and the extent of possible worries are still great enough to permit the person to be concerned about his ability to take care of them. There is a great stress at this point between a person's problems and his ability to take care of them, and here worry reaches a peak. After this age, a new balance at a lower level of worry seems to set in; it is shown by the preponderance of "no worry" opinions among older persons. This is not merely an idiosyncrasy of this particular survey and time but seems to be a regular finding of similar tests described in other surveys. However, the more general the questions, the less specific the concerns they evoke and the less we find a curvilinear relationship. The freedom from worry of the aged seems to be a constant fact.

DISCUSSION

Our discussion of aging based on data we have taken from public opinion surveys has stressed two points. The first is that aging and morale in aging are of one piece with the style and life orientation of a person. Thus, morale becomes more meaningful in the context of the way the person spent his earlier life and his other adaptations than in terms of aging as such. Earlier, in Chapters 2-6, it was shown how important adaptation to retirement is in relation to the previous work role of a person. Similarly, the person's world view in retirement, such as his opinions on general issues, will depend very much on the general life style and other factors during retirement or aging. The second point is related to the first, namely, that morale cannot be understood as a uni-dimensional trait of a person, but that there are several types of high and low morale. From the point of view of the majority of younger people, successful aging includes participation within society as far as possible. This kind of aging may be good for some people, but aging may be just as successful if it includes adaptation to a different level of activity in concordance with a smaller life space. If all cognitive and motivational procedures of a person are adjusted to a different lower level, a person may also be satisfied and find little difficulty in aging. Thus, different types of morale of the aged may be described as the different patterns of aging which may occur among several people.[9]

Our data have shown that if a population sample is taken, the detached way of aging seems to predominate generally. By and large, the aged have few complaints and would want few things changed. However, this is not due to a particularly high level of achievement but to a general kind of indifference. We have thus tried to distinguish the effects that changes in cognitive structure and energy level have on the general orientation of the aged. We have found some evidence that the typical age of highest discrepancy is during a person's fifties—before old age begins. Among samples of the general population, we principally described the most prevalent process of aging; this process may be very different in special groups studied by different investigators. In Chapter 7 we have shown that morale looks somewhat different in self-ratings. Although their morale might still be absolutely quite high, people who have retired, especially those who were in upper-white-collar positions, are likely to rate themselves lower than they should—as if they were looking at themselves from the standard of a peak of activity. However, if asked about his own feelings in more objective questions, the same person will not show decrement of morale.

In general, we may conclude that the question of morale of the

9. Thus, Marion Yarrow has noted that compulsive and schizoid personalities are more effective in coping with life in old age than paranoids; "Relationships with Social-Psychological Data," in J. C. Birren, R. W. Butler, S. W. Greenhouse, Louis Sokoloff, and Marion Yarrow (eds.), *Human Aging* (Public Health Service Publication No. 986 [Bethesda, Md.: 1963]), p. 302.

aged is meaningless, because morale and aging are both complex phenomena. We have translated the question of morale into that of patterns of equilibrium during the course of different lives and have indicated a method of detecting some degree of regularity and understanding in the emotional quality of life orientation occurring in a person's later years.

Kenneth J. Gergen
Kurt W. Back

20. AGING AND THE PARADOX OF SOMATIC CONCERN

That an individual's conduct is highly dependent on the way in which he perceives the world around him is quite apparent. Behind this truism, however, lies a host of subtle and important psychological problems. To what aspects of his environment does the individual attend, and why? How are various perceptions organized and integrated? How do such perceptions become articulated with behavioral dispositions? The present chapter derives from a concern with a number of these issues as they relate to the person's position in the life cycle. More specifically, the present focus is on the ways in which two major aspects of a person's perceptual world combine to determine his behavioral dispositions as he grows older.

The physical changes which take place during a person's life span have received much close attention. In addition to the more obvious changes in skin tissue, hair, and teeth, investigations have also demonstrated a decrement in muscle strength,[1] a decrease in cardiac output,[2] a decrease in active body mass,[3] and a deterioration of sensory functions.[4] It is also apparent that a person's body makes up an important component of his perceptual world.[5] Given the bodily changes described above, it would follow that a person's

1. M. B. Fisher and J. E. Birren, "Age and Strength," *Journal of Applied Psychology*, **31** (October, 1947), 490-497.

2. François Bourlière, *Genescence et Sénilité* (Paris: Doin, 1958).

3. E. C. Anderson and W. H. Langham, "Average Potassium Concentration of the Human Body as a Function of Age," *Science*, **130** (September, 1959), 713-714.

4. A. D. Weiss, "Sensory Functions," *Handbook of Aging and the Individual: Psychological and Biological Aspects* (Chicago: University of Chicago Press, 1959).

5. Paul Schilder, *The Image and Appearance of the Human Body* (New York: International Universities Press, 1950).

view of himself would likewise undergo modification as he grows older.

If the person's perception of his body reflects in a roughly accurate fashion the changes actually occurring, what changes in the behavior of the person might be expected as a result of his perception? With his health on the wane and his life more dependent on the daily attention given to the body, one might well anticipate that the aged person would become increasingly concerned with his physical functioning. It might be expected, for example, that he would give greater attention to his diet and to medical advice. In the same vein, it might be expected that due to the deterioration of his outward appearance, the aged person would make increasing attempts to improve this appearance and offset the process. For example, he might compensate for signs of aging by attending more closely to clothing, jewelry, cosmetics, etc.

Such a view seems eminently reasonable until one takes into account an additional aspect of a person's perceptual world. As the authors have speculated in Chapter 18, a second relevant aspect of a person's orientation to the world is his spatio-temporal life space. Each person sees himself as being capable of action within a certain time segment and within a certain spatial area. The process of aging might be characterized as a gradual constriction along both the spatial and temporal dimensions. As the person passes into later years, he feels that the amount of time left to him is less and that less of the world is relevant to his behavior.[6]

What behavioral dispositions might result from the individual's consideration of his body within the context of a delimited spatio-temporal existence? With his body becoming less capable of action within any extended period of time or area, the individual is rendered less capable of making major investments in his environment. He is less able to invest himself in a promising career, in intense interpersonal relationships,[7] or in any courses of action which require extended amounts of time.[8] Also relevant is the reported general decline in participation in voluntary organizations and less

6. Kurt W. Back and Kenneth J. Gergen, "Apocalyptic and Serial Time Orientation and the Structure of Opinions," *Public Opinion Quarterly*, **27** (Fall, 1963), 427-442; Kenneth J. Gergen and Kurt W. Back, "The Disengaged Respondent," *Public Opinion Quarterly* (in preparation).

7. Elaine Cumming and W. E. Henry, *Growing Old* (New York: Basic Books, 1961).

8. Back and Gergen, "Apocalyptic and Serial Time Orientation and Structure of Opinions"; Gergen and Back, "Disengaged Respondent."

voting on the part of persons over fifty-five.[9] In short, the likelihood
of a successful return resulting from a major investment of the self
is less promising for the aged person.[10]

Having accounted for both the person's perception of his body
and the spatio-temporal context in which his body is seen to function, we are now in a position to reassess the matter of bodily concern. As a result of the feeling that his potential is curtailed and
that self-investments are less promising, it would seem that the aged
person might react in just the opposite fashion from that indicated
by common sense. Paradoxically, it would seem that rather than
compensating for his physical deterioration, the aged person might
well manifest *less* concern for his body. In other words, a prevalent
feeling among the aged might be that there is little to be gained
by constant care for the internal processes and external features of
one's body. Concern with neither of these bodily aspects has a high
probability of successful return. In a sense the present study is foreshadowed by a summary of aged consumer habits appearing in a
1957 issue of *Nation's Business*.[11] In this article, F. D. Lindsey points
out: "Older persons spend . . . a smaller proportion of [their income]
for . . . toilet articles, barbers, beauty parlors, and other personal
care items and services."

The major findings related to the above arguments were obtained through a secondary analysis of public opinion data. Questions appearing on a number of Gallup and Roper surveys were
examined, and all those containing relevant items were chosen for
analysis. For each item the relationship between age and dispositions or attitudes toward the body was assessed. In each instance
percentages were computed only for those respondents expressing
an opinion on the individual item. Earlier work[12] indicated a nega-

9. A. M. Rose, "The Impact of Aging on Voluntary Associations," in Clark Tibbitts
(ed.), *Handbook of Social Gerontology: Societal Aspects of Aging* (Chicago: University
of Chicago Press, 1960).

10. J. W. Atkinson, *An Introduction to Motivation* (Princeton: D. Van Nostrand
Co., 1964), has outlined a theory of achievement-oriented performance. In this theory,
one important component influencing the magnitude of motivation is felt to be the
person's probability of success. Constriction of the life space might be considered
roughly analogous to decreasing the probability of success. By limiting the time and
space in which achievements can be attained, the range of events which might yield
success is reduced and therefore the probability of success is also reduced.

11. For a more thorough discussion of "meaningful activity" for the aged person
in his environment, see J. E. Anderson, "Environment and Meaningful Activity," in
Richard Williams, Clark Tibbitts, and Wilma Donahue (eds.), *Processes of Aging*
(New York: Atherton Press, 1963).

12. Gergen and Back, "Disengaged Respondent."

tive relationship between age and opinions. Aged persons were less prone to give a response on a variety of issues. The present method thus avoids differential opinions as a source of bias. In addition, for a number of the items (particularly those dealing with attitudes toward clothing), it was apparent that the person's socioeconomic level might be an important confounding variable. Since it is generally known that a negative relationship exists between age and socioeconomic level, a breakdown of the data by both age and socioeconomic level was appropriate.

In several instances it was also possible to expand the data base for the present study by examining additional sources. For example, the Bureau of Labor Statistics, the Public Health Service, *Life* magazine, and the Chicago *Sun-Times* had all made extensive studies of certain behavior related to our present concerns.

RESULTS

Internal Care

Diet. Following the above rationale, it would be predicted that the aged person will manifest less concern with his internal bodily processes than will his younger counterpart. Thus, when considering gastro-intestinal functioning and bodily metabolism, it would be expected that the aged person would be less restrictive and cautious about his dietary intake. Data relevant to this question were found in a commercial study undertaken by Roper in 1941. This

Table 1. Age and Dietary Care (in percentages) .

	Under 40	40–59	60 and over
Not important to think of proteins, vitamins, or minerals	3.4 (1,130)	4.8 (820)	7.8 (154)
Do nothing to get proper amount of vitamins	67.1 (2,511)	70.6 (2,029)	84.2 (550)
Pay attention to appetite rather than science	41.3 (2,268)	46.2 (1,773)	60.9 (468)
Would not like any additional information about meat	59.8 (1,287)	69.3 (1,009)	83.1 (243)
Don't approve of family overeating for reasons other than health	6.6 (498)	5.4 (373)	11.8 (93)

Source: Roper Comm. 1-A, January, 1941.

study dealt primarily with eating habits, and more specifically with attitudes toward meat. Five items used in this survey were related to bodily care, and the results for these items are featured in Table 1.

The first of these items dealt with the respondents' rankings of the importance of proteins, vitamins, and minerals in planning meals. It was felt that lack of concern with one's bodily welfare would be reflected by the response that it was not important to consider any of these dietary elements. Although not dramatic, the results indicated that aged respondents did tend to feel that it was less important to consider these elements. More dramatic confirmation was obtained when respondents were asked whether they did anything to get the proper amount of vitamins. In this instance, over 84 per cent of the eldest group indicated they did nothing, while only 67 per cent of the younger and 70 per cent of the middle age groups answered in a similar fashion. An additional item rounded out this picture of general disregard for sound diets among the aged. Respondents were asked whether it was more important, in trying to keep healthy, to pay attention to what their appetites told them to eat or what modern science prescribed. As indicated in Table 1, there is a marked increase after age sixty in preference for the first alternative.

In this same study, which clearly made salient considerations of health in eating, the query was raised as to whether there was any knowledge or information about meat which respondents did not have and would like to have. Although certainly not a direct test of the theoretical notions, it was felt that the lack of interest in additional information about the foods one ingested would indicate a lack of bodily concern. As shown in Table 1, the aged respondents were much less anxious to have such additional information.

Those respondents who disliked allowing themselves or members of their families to eat as much as they wanted were asked their reasons for feeling this way. A wide variety of responses was obtained, but a cluster of these pertained directly to the issue of health (e.g., "it's bad for blood pressure" or "bad for the kidneys"). As can be seen in Table 1, as age increases there is a trend toward responding with non-health- as opposed to health-associated reasons.

The pattern of results is thus quite consistent in revealing what appears to be a general lack of concern on the part of the aged person for his dietary intake and resulting health. Not only does the aged person seem to be less sensitive to issues of health in his diet; he does not seem to desire any additional information bearing on this issue, scientific or otherwise.

Medical concern. Items from two further surveys dealt with the respondents' dispositions toward preventive medical practices. The first item appeared on a Gallup survey of August, 1957, during which time an Asian flu epidemic was at its peak. Respondents were first asked whether they had read or heard anything about the epidemic. Aged respondents proved no less likely to have known about the epidemic than the younger groups. However, respondents were also asked whether they planned to take shots to protect themselves if a vaccine became available. Whereas 81.9 per cent of those below the age of thirty-nine $(N = 439)$ and 78.3 per cent of those between the ages of forty and fifty-nine $(N = 451)$ planned to take the shots to protect themselves, only 67.8 per cent of those sixty and over $(N = 258)$ planned to do so.

The value of bodily exercise for the aged has been well-documented in medical circles.[13] It also seems a safe assumption that medical advice to the aged has reflected the need for such exercise. It thus becomes a valid question as to whether the aged person actually engages in this health-saving activity. An item on a Gallup survey of January, 1956, asked all respondents whether they had engaged in any form of bodily exercise during the preceding day. While 69.6 per cent of those respondents thirty-nine and below $(N = 660)$ and 62.8 per cent of those between the ages of forty and fifty-nine $(N = 500)$ had exercised the day before, only 59.6 per cent of the sixty and over group $(N = 558)$ had done so.

Further data on medical care and aging were found in the ancillary sources noted above. It seems obvious that the aged person requires a greater amount of medical attention than his younger counterpart. Data gathered by the Public Health Service[14] from approximately 235,000 persons clearly document the increased medical requirement for the elderly. For example, the rate of per-

13. J. L. Whittenberger, "The Nature of the Response to Stress with Aging," *Bulletin of the New York Academy of Medicine,* **32** (May, 1956), 329-336; W. S. Priest, "Anticipation and Management of Cardiac Decompensation," *Geriatrics,* **12** (May, 1957), 290-296; and also E. L. Bortz, "The Vitality of the Vascular System," *Geriatrics,* **12** (May, 1957), 275-283.

14. *Health Statistics from the U.S. National Health Survey: Older Persons Selected Health Characteristics* (Public Health Service Publication No. 584-C4 [Washington, 1960]).

sons afflicted with a heart condition rises from 71.5 per 1,000 in a sample of persons between the ages of fifty-five and sixty-four to 120.9 in a sample of persons sixty-five years and older. Arthritis and rheumatism double in rate over the same age intervals, and visual impairments show a similar increase. On the other hand, if one examines the average number of physician visits per person per year, the Public Health data[15] show only a minimal increase in number of visits with advancing age. Whereas the fifty-five to sixty-four group sees a physician on the average of 5.8 times a year, the sixty-five and over group consults a physician on the average of 6.8 times a year. It is also the case that the number of general checkups increases little with advancing age. Of those who made visits to a physician, 8 per cent of the twenty-five to forty-five group, 10 per cent of the forty-five to sixty-five group, and 11 per cent of the sixty-five and over group receive a general checkup. Immunizations actually show a slight decrease after sixty-five years of age. As in the case of the Asian flu shots, this may be a consequence of shortened time perspective.

Through data compiled by the Bureau of Labor Statistics[16] it was also possible to assess the average family expenditure for medical services (excluding insurance payments) as related to aging. The data were broken down into nine income groups. In order to exclude maternity expenses, comparisons were made for those age groups, in tens of years, after age forty-five. The data reveal that in only one of the nine income groups ($4-5,000) do medical expenditures show a consistent increase with advancing age. In every other group the amount spent on medical services with advancing age is almost as likely to decrease as it is to increase. In summary, these results seem to provide a general indication that the marked increase in disability associated with advancing age is not at all counterbalanced by an increased investment in medical care.

External Care

Clothing and appearance. The data thus far described have consistently indicated a general lack of concern on the part of the aged

15. *Health Statistics for the U. S. National Health Survey: Preliminary Report on Volume of Physician Visits* (Public Health Service Publication No. 584-B1 [Washington, 1958]).

16. *Survey of Family Incomes, Expenditures and Savings, All Urban Areas Combined* ("*Study of Consumer Expenditures, Incomes and Savings,*" Vol. XVIII [Philadelphia: Wharton School of Finance and Commerce, University of Pennsylvania, 1957]).

for the internal welfare of the body. However, it was ventured above that this lack of concern was general and should thus pertain to external aspects as well. One major way an aged person may compensate for deficiencies in physical appearance is through clothing. If sensitized to the aesthetic value of clothing, the aged person may markedly offset the manifest signs of aging. On the other hand, if one takes into account the person's view of himself in a spatio-temporal context, such compensation would not be predicted. Instead the limited life space, as represented by a diminishing capacity for action, should lead to a decreased interest in the aesthetic aspects of clothing.

A number of items appearing on a Roper commercial survey were relevant to this issue. Two of these items asked directly about the criteria respondents held important when choosing clothing. The first dealt with women's suits, and the second with men's summer suits. The response alternatives to these questions could be divided into two major categories: a number of the alternatives were distinctly *aesthetic* in nature (e.g., liking for the color or pattern, flattering style, good fit), while the remainder emphasized the *utility* of the garment (e.g., the suit would stand hard wear, it would be useful on many different kinds of occasions, or it should be a good bargain). As can be discerned from Table 2, for both of these items there is a general increase with age in the percentage of persons endorsing the utility criteria, as opposed to the aesthetic. In addition, this relationship seems to be generally independent of socioeconomic class.

Two additional items were less direct, but equally revealing. If the aged person pays less heed to the aesthetic aspects of his own dress, it also seems plausible that he would be less likely to see clothing as a criterion for judging others; however, if clothing were used in such judgments, the aged person would be more likely to use the criterion of utility than that of aesthetics. In other words, it would psychologically justify one's emphasis on utility if he did not use clothing as a criterion to judge others, and if forced to do so, he did not use the criterion of aesthetics.

The first item relevant to this issue asked to what extent a person's impression of others of his own age was influenced by the clothing they wore. The second was concerned with the aspects of their own clothing which respondents felt members of the opposite sex

Table 2. Age, Socioeconomic Class, and Attitudes Toward Clothing (in percentages).

	Low socioeconomic class			High socioeconomic class		
	Under 40	40–59	60 and over	Under 40	40–59	60 and over
1. Utility criterion in choosing women's suits	51.8 (2,630)	52.8 (1,086)	58.8 (665)	43.3 (383)	44.3 (377)	47.2 (182)
2. Clothes do not influence impressions	6.5 (885)	8.7 (725)	16.1 (535)	1.9 (103)	5.6 (149)	11.1 (81)
3. Utility criterion in choosing summer suits	52.8 (1,866)	55.7 (1,349)	60.0 (857)	48.1 (261)	47.6 (344)	48.4 (159)
4. Utility criterion in judging others	3.5 (1,933)	7.9 (1,412)	8.4 (1,165)	4.6 (257)	10.4 (345)	11.0 (200)

Source: Roper Comm. #42, May, 1950.

considered important when they met for the first time. Again, the alternatives to this latter question fit the categories of aesthetics (e.g., color and style) versus utility (e.g., material and durability). As can be seen in Table 2, for both of these items the aged person seems less concerned with the aesthetic aspects of clothing. Not only does he see clothing to be of less relevance in judging others; he is also generally less inclined to use the aesthetic criterion when he does judge on basis of clothing.

In a survey of consumer behavior made for *Life* magazine,[17] some 34,000 persons were asked about their various monthly expenditures. In this survey, five age groups were used: under thirty, thirty to thirty-nine, forty to forty-nine, fifty to sixty-four, and sixty-five and over. It was found that the eldest group applied a smaller percentage of their income than any of the other groups in each of the following categories: hair preparations, toilet and facial tissues, shaving supplies and equipment, general personal care items (including toilet soap, deodorants, and mouth wash), jewelry and watches, clothing accessories and care, and household waxes, polishes, and cleaners. While it is difficult to assess the total meaning of these results due to their lack of control by socioeconomic level, data from the Bureau of Labor Statistics[18] provide more conclusive results. As will be recalled, on this survey there were nine different income groups for each of the seven age groupings.[19] When examining the average annual expenditures for personal care items (including toilet articles, preparations, and personal care services), it is found that, across all but two income groups, the thirty-five to forty-five group expended the greatest portion of their income on personal care. After age forty-five there is a highly consistent decrease in the average personal care expenditure across all income groups with advancing age. For all but two economic groups, the lowest investment in personal care items is found in the seventy-five and over group; in the two odd cases, the sixty-five to seventy-five group spent the least amount on personal care of all remaining age groups. These data, then, seem quite consistent with the hypotheses developed above.

17. *Life Study of Consumer Expenditures*, Vol. I (New York: Time, Inc., 1957).
18. *Ibid.*
19. Age groupings were in tens of years with the exception that all those under twenty-five were collapsed into a single group and all those seventy-five and over into a second group.

Table 3. Age, Income, and Purchase of Personal Care Items (in percentages).[a]

	Low income			Medium income			High income		
	Under 45	45–64	65 and over	Under 45	45–64	65 and over	Under 45	45–64	65 and over
1. Deodorant on hand	91.4	72.2	63.0	96.7	93.7	74.0	96.2	96.6	82.0
2. Mouth wash on hand	58.4	64.7	57.2	67.1	75.2	66.1	72.4	79.0	78.0
(N)	(904)	(529)	(602)	(4,353)	(1,769)	(339)	(1,624)	(1,040)	(100)
3. Hair tint on hand	11.5	12.4	2.9	13.2	16.4	4.2	16.0	18.6	13.9
4. Home permanent on hand	6.7	8.6	4.5	9.1	9.1	3.0	8.9	8.8	8.3
(Female N)	(564)	(362)	(377)	(2,350)	(823)	(165)	(880)	(479)	(36)
5. Indigestion remedy on hand	59.3	64.5	54.5	69.1	69.6	53.1	69.2	68.0	65.0
(N)	(904)	(529)	(602)	(4,353)	(1,769)	(339)	(1,624)	(1,040)	(100)

[a]These data were made available through the courtesy of Dr. Scott Cunningham of the Harvard Graduate School of Business Administration and through the Chicago *Sun-Times*.

A more detailed account of the relationship between aging and purchase of personal care items was obtained from a survey conducted for the Chicago *Sun-Times*. The survey included over 11,000 persons in the Chicago metropolitan area and was aimed primarily at obtaining information on home purchases. Among other things, respondents were asked whether they had the following products on hand: deodorant, mouth wash, hair tint, and a home permanent. Table 3 presents the percentages of persons having each of these products on hand. In each case, the data are broken down by age and income (low = under $4,999; medium = $5-9,999; high = $10,000 and over). Data from this survey concerning the purchase of indigestion remedies are also included in the table, as they relate to the above discussion of internal care. As indicated in Table 3, for almost all of the personal care items there is a pervasive decrease in purchase with increments in age. It is interesting to note, however, that where reversals of trend occur, they are largely confined to the young—middle comparison. Apparently for at least some personal care items, it is the middle-aged person who tends to be more conscientious about his appearance, corresponding to his greater worry in general which we have discussed in Chapters 18 and 19, Table 4.

Desire for Somatic Change

Thus far it has been reasoned that the aged do not manifest care for their bodies because with a delimited life space there is little "payoff" for doing so. It would also follow that there would be little desire on the part of the aged to alter certain superficial aspects of their bodies. A change in facial appearance, for example, would be less needed or wanted by the elderly person because there is little advantage to which such an alteration could be turned. Of course, this is not to suggest that the aged person would not be appreciative of a rejuvenation of basic bodily processes. If this were possible, one might also expect to find a change in life space concomitant to the renewed health and vigor. Data to support the notion that the aged are less likely to prefer changes in bodily features were found on two separate surveys. On both of these surveys respondents were asked whether they would prefer to weigh more, less, or remain at their present weight. It was also possible to obtain a height—weight ratio for the same respondents and as a result of

Table 4. Age, Sex, Somatic Size, and Percentage Desiring Change as Opposed to Remaining the Same in Body Weight.

	Males		
	Under 40	40–59	60 and over
Lightweight	52.1 (217)	46.3 (177)	35.0 (117)
Average	26.0 (154)	18.0 (145)	16.7 (78)
Heavyweight	40.2 (224)	48.8 (275)	39.7 (151)
	Females		
	Under 40	40–59	60 and over
Lightweight	44.9 (428)	39.5 (190)	32.9 (82)
Average	58.6 (133)	50.0 (116)	42.3 (52)
Heavyweight	86.0 (172)	68.7 (252)	18.8 (64)

Source: AIPO #457, 1950; #568, 1956.

these data to classify each respondent into one of three categories: lightweight, average, and heavyweight. This information could thus be used to provide statistical control for any marked shifts in weight resulting from age. The data from both surveys were collapsed; Table 4 contains a breakdown by age, height–weight ratio, and sex for those who preferred to change their weight (either to become lighter or heavier). As can be seen, regardless of the actual weight of the respondent, with advancing age there is a pervasive downward trend for both male and female respondents in the percentage of persons preferring to change their weight as opposed to remaining the same.

On the second of these surveys, respondents were also queried as to whether they would like to be taller, shorter, or remain the same height. The results indicate that whereas 27.1 per cent ($N = 584$) of the sample aged thirty-nine and below desired to change, and 24.0 per cent ($N = 479$) of the forty to fifty-nine group desired to change, only 18.6 per cent ($N = 225$) of the group over sixty preferred to alter their height. These results would thus seem to be quite consistent with the other indicators of somatic concern.

DISCUSSION

The above results seem to indicate that passage through the life cycle is highly associated with a lessened concern with one's body.

This lack of bodily concern seems to manifest itself not only in dispositions toward diet and preventive medicine, but also toward the clothing chosen to be worn. While no single result in the above analysis can be considered conclusive, the consistent pattern of results is highly provocative.

The most intriguing and perhaps the most important aspect of the above findings is the implicit contradiction of common-sense expectations. Compensation for bodily deficiencies is a widespread phenomenon. The existence of entire business enterprises devoted to such activities as creating garments which emphasize or conceal parts of the body, producing cosmetics which conceal skin blemishes or modify the quality of the hair, or manufacturing pills which provide sufficient vitamin intake is ample evidence of this fact. And yet, why should persons who are most in need of such compensatory measures tend to be the ones who adopt them least?

To be sure, there are some instances in which the above findings might be reversed. Given that there is physical deterioration, it would certainly be expected that the aged spend proportionally greater amounts of money on prescribed drugs, visual and auditory aids, and energy-saving conveniences. Empirical evidence supports this contention.[20] However, the above results suggest that where such activities are not necessary for maintaining a minimal subsistence level, the aged will be less prone to invest themselves.

The notions of body image and life space offer a convenient rationale for understanding this lessening of somatic concern. In a sense this approach parallels one developed in the area of social perception. Studies in this area[21] have clearly shown that a person's perception of another is not only dependent on the behavior of this other person, but also on the context in which the observed behavior occurs. The present rationale suggests that the image of one's body is not sufficient to explain one's behavior toward the body. Rather it is fruitful, if not necessary, to consider the spatio-temporal context in which the body is perceived.

It is, of course, true that a plausible explanation is only a be-

20. Selma Mushkin, "Age Differentials in Medical Spending," *Public Health Report*, **72** (February, 1957), 115-120.

21. E. E. Jones, R. G. Jones, and K. J. Gergen, "Some Conditions Affecting the Evaluation of a Conformist," *Journal of Personality*, **31** (June, 1963), 270-288; E. E. Jones, K. E. Davis, and K. J. Gergen, "Role Playing Variations and Their Informational Value for Person Perception," *Journal of Abnormal and Social Psychology*, **63** (September, 1961), 302-310.

ginning. For example, there are certainly competing explanations which might just as satisfactorily account for certain of the findings. Aged persons raised in a given period may simply be more skeptical of science and feel that nutrition and preventive medicine are meaningless issues. They may also be reflecting generational differences in attitudes toward clothing. The consistency of the present findings over a sixteen-year span would tend to vie against such explanations, and the present rationale is more parsimonious. However, it is also clear that more definitive research is necessary. In the present instance, independent indicators of body image and life space would be highly desirable.

Using the above rationale, one may also fruitfully view certain pressing problems in social gerontology. For example, there have been a number of instances in which health protection clinics have been established to provide inexpensive medical treatment for the aged. In one such case[22] the clinic was finally forced to close because of the lack of clientele. Similar disinterest on the part of the aged has been experienced in other such clinics.[23] It has also been noted that the aged tend to adopt very poor nutritional habits.[24] While a number of independent reasons have been advanced to explain these various phenomena, the present notion of body image and life space offers a possible explanation of widespread applicability.

From this latter point of view, it is also possible to speculate about possible courses of action which might be taken to alleviate such problems. While it may be exceedingly difficult to alter the body image, the modification of the life space would seem to be a less formidable possibility. As intimated above, apathy among the aged may result from the feeling that there is neither sufficient time nor space for fruitful investment of one's limited capacities. However, there is no absolute criterion for establishing exactly what constitutes a "fruitful investment," and it may well be that the aged person carries with him a definition or standard developed in younger years. Such a standard may well be inapplicable and mal-

22. K. F. MacLeod, "Well Oldster Health Conferences," *Nursing Outlook*, **6** (April, 1958), 206-208.

23. Bernard Kutner, David Fanshel, Alice Togo, and T. S. Langner, *Five Hundred over Sixty: A Community Survey on Aging* (New York: Russell Sage Foundation, 1956); R. T. Monroe, "The Mechanisms of the Geriatric Clinic and its Place in the Community," *New England Journal of Medicine*, **258** (May, 1958), 882-885.

24. R. T. Monroe, *Diseases and Old Age* (Cambridge, Mass.: Harvard University Press, 1951); Bortz, "Vitality of Vascular System."

adaptive during the later years. Thus, if significant relearning could take place, one might modify the definition of what a useful and fruitful investment is in light of limited capacities. Whereas the aged person may not be able to start a new business or develop into a political leader, there are many useful pursuits which would take advantage of the remaining bodily capacities. In this sense, the aged population represents an untapped labor force, and a program to develop suitable jobs for such persons would seem to have great promise. In a sense, the Protestant ethic may still pervade the aged population, along with the feeling that only the useful body is worth caring for. Provided he had a way of making use of his body within a delimited life space, the aged person could develop a continuing concern for his bodily welfare.

Kenneth J. Gergen
Kurt W. Back

21. COGNITIVE CONSTRICTION IN AGING AND ATTITUDES TOWARD INTERNATIONAL ISSUES*

The notion of effective life space has thus far been treated with a broad brush. The definition of life space as the extent of the world that a person is willing to accept as relevant to his conduct is explicitly vague and imprecise. Although the term bears an obvious similarity to early formulations of Kurt Lewin,[1] caution has been exercised in endowing it with various field theoretical properties. Indeed, at this stage of theorizing there are several reasons for purposely allowing this nodal construct to remain in its ambiguous state.[2] For one, in its general form the term has many implications which would not be as apparent with a more concrete definition. It encourages an extension of initial thinking with such diverse areas as social perception, phenomenology, decision-making theory, phenomenal time, existentialism, and others. In addition, the general form of the construct is advantageous in that it does not commit one to a single set of operational procedures nor to a single source of data.

* Based on "Aging, Time Perspective, and Preferred Solutions to International Conflicts," by the same authors, which appeared in *Journal of Conflict Resolution*, **9** (June, 1965), 177-186.
    1. *Principles of Topological Psychology* (New York: McGraw-Hill, 1936).
    2. For a more detailed account of the functions and advantages of theoretical terms of this type, see Rudolph Carnap, "The Methodological Character of Theoretical Concepts," in Herbert Feigl and Michael Scriven (eds.), *Minnesota Studies in the Philosophy of Science* (Minneapolis: University of Minnesota Press, 1956), I, 38-76; or Kurt W. Back's notion of "myth language," in "The Game and the Myth as Two Languages of Social Science," *Behavioral Science*, **8** (1963), 66-71.

If anything, the foregoing chapters would attest to the wide diversity of data which can be seen as relevant.

The present chapter represents an attempt to deal with a single aspect of the life space in greater detail and to demonstrate the relevancy of this derivation to attitudes toward international relations. More specifically, the interest is in the ramifications of the above discussion (see Chapters 18 and 19) concerning the effects of aging on the constriction of the life space, in general, and the constriction of time perspective, in particular. The relationship between constriction of time perspective and preferences for certain types of solutions to problems in international relations constitutes the major focus.

Although there are certainly a number of environmental conditions which can influence a person's solutions to international problems, it might be said that each person possesses a particular orientation to life which will predispose him toward making certain kinds of choices regardless of environmental circumstances. A person who consistently regards others with suspicion, for example, should react in a fairly predictable fashion to peace overtures by other nations. Among such personal dimensions a person's orientation in time would seem to have considerable importance for the types of solutions he prefers. More specifically, when little future time is taken into account, more immediate or total solutions should be preferred. If the future is not relevant for an individual, then solving a problem in the present should be more appealing. In addition, looking into the future also implies a consideration of additional aspects of a problem. The more aspects of a problem that are considered, the less extreme or complete can any solution be. These notions have been supported by evidence presented in an earlier paper.[3]

Time perspective may be affected by several factors. Immediate changes in the environment can often cause shifts in mood; empirical evidence seems to indicate, for example, that reminding one of his personal death can restrict his time perspective.[4] A lack of time perspective can also result from a lack of education. On the other hand, there may be some intrinsic factors which render individuals

3. Kurt W. Back and Kenneth J. Gergen, "Individual Orientations, Public Opinion and the Study of International Relations," *Social Problems*, 2 (1963), 77-87.

4. Paul Wohlford, "An Investigation into some Determinants of Extension of Personal Time" (unpublished Ph.D. dissertation, Duke University, 1964).

more or less susceptible to whatever environmental conditions prevail. One such factor would seem to be the position of a person in his life span. Does the person who has many fruitful and absorbing years ahead of him perceive events with the same perspective as one who has passed the peak of his productivity and faces the end of life? The answer would seem to be "no." Earlier work has shown a direct relationship between aging and indices of time perspective. The young adult population tends to take into account more of the future than does the aged population. Similarly, in a study of planning in three-generation families, Reuben Hill[5] found that members of the older generation planned least, had proportionately more indefinite and short-run plans, and executed fewer plans than the two younger generations.

The rationale for this link between one's temporal orientation and aging may be complex. It would seem that the aged person does not consider far distant events primarily because he does not project his existence far into the future. Fewer future contingencies may thus be considered by the elderly person in his attempts to come to grips with present problems. With few contingencies to consider, solutions may tend to be more absolute or extreme. In addition, total solutions to problems may be more appealing because they promise an immediate end to the problem rather than continued ambiguity. It is not necessary to wait months or years to see the problem resolved. As Shaw's character, Captain Shotover, remarks, "Take care: I am in my dotage. Old men are dangerous: it doesn't matter to them what is going to happen to the world."

To summarize thus far, it can be reasoned that the aged person may prefer resolving international problems in a more immediate or extremist fashion. Because of a restricted temporal orientation, he may avoid solutions which extend into the distant future, and his solutions will often reflect a lack of attention to future contingencies. The focus of this paper, first of all, will be on the relationship between age and preferred solutions to problems of international scope. Secondly, in order to test the generality of these findings, the relationship between age and a number of national and local problems will be examined. Since temporal orientations should tend to permeate all choices, there should conceivably be a con-

5. "Decision Making and the Family Life Cycle," in Ethel Shanas and Gordon Strieb (eds.), *Social Structure and the Family: Generational Relations* (Englewood Cliffs, N.J.: Prentice-Hall, 1965).

tinuity in types of solutions preferred over a variety of problems. Finally, an additional implication growing out of the relationship between aging and time perspective will be examined. Specifically, time perspective may be highly related to the range and type of causal agents considered. If this is so, then aging would lead to modifications in the perception of the causation of events.

RESULTS

Attitudes Toward International Problems

Problems which most directly bear on the hypothesis that aging leads to preference for short-range solutions are those which offer the following alternative solutions: (*1*) *annihilation,* or the aggressive stamping out of the person or persons creating the problem; (*2*) *denial* of the problem, which may take the form of withdrawal from the area of difficulty; and (*3*) *compromise,* or the finding of a solution which lies in an intermediate position in comparison to the other alternatives. Following the above discussion, the first two of these alternatives would fit into the category of short-range solutions; either course of action would lead to an immediate end to the problem (though perhaps not a lasting one). The third, more moderate, alternative would follow from a more long-range view of world events. If future repercussions of present action are taken into account, then such a solution should be preferred.

From the data available for examination, four questions offering these alternatives were found. Two of these questions dealt with the Korean crisis and two with cold war situations. For three of these questions, three age groups could be formed (under forty, forty to fifty-nine, and sixty years and over), and preferences for extreme solutions could be examined as they related to age. The results for these three questions appear in Table 1. As can be seen, for two of these questions there is a positive, monotonic relationship between age and preference for both of the short-range solutions. For the third item, concerning U. S. action in the Korean War, there is a clear increase in preference for short-range solutions between the under forty and forty to fifty-nine groups; however, such preferences tend to drop slightly after age sixty. In general, these results would seem to support expectations.

Table 1. Aging and Preferences for Short-Range Solutions to International Problems (in percentages).

		Under 40	40–59	60 and over
1. Under what circumstances do you think the United States should go to war with Russia?	Slight provocation	10.8	13.9	16.9
	Never fight	7.1	8.6	10.8
	Total short-range	17.9	22.5	27.7
	Moderate	82.1	77.5	72.3
	(N)	(619)	(533)	(213)
2. What should the United States do about fighting in Korea?	Greater aggression	6.3	6.5	15.4
	Pacifism	9.9	11.8	21.4
	Total short-range	16.2	18.3	36.8
	Moderate	83.8	81.7	63.2
	(N)	(335)	(279)	(117)
3. What should the United States do next in war with Korea?	Extreme war	26.2	31.1	30.3
	Extreme peace	14.0	19.7	16.5
	Total short-range	40.2	50.8	46.8
	Moderate	59.8	49.2	53.2
	(N)	(343)	(264)	(109)

Source: AIPO #415, March, 1948; #457, June, 1950; #474, April, 1951.

The fourth item, from a Roper survey taken in 1950, was given to two groups of respondents of different ages (one eighteen to twenty-five years and the other forty to fifty-five years). They were asked which of the following statements they came closest to agreeing with:

    a. Russia has to be stopped and the best way is to fight before they get any stronger.

    b. While Russia must be stopped, we have a good chance of avoiding war by keeping prepared and showing them we mean business.

    c. The most important thing is for this country not to get into another war—regardless of what happens in the rest of the world.

Following the above line of thought, for this question both the first and third answers were considered short-range alternatives. The results indicate that the more elderly group preferred both of the short-range solutions more than the younger group did. The younger group, on the other hand, preferred the moderate solution. Although these differences were only slight (younger group preference for

Table 2. Aging and Preferences for Short-Range Solutions to International Problems (in percentages).

	Under 40	40–59	60 and over
1. Advocate U. N. bombing of Communist China	52.4 (433)	56.8 (315)	60.2 (128)
2. Advocate sending fewer foods and supplies to Europe	34.6 (627)	38.1 (517)	40.2 (251)
3. Against foreign aid	32.9 (547)	42.6 (507)	46.7 (261)

Source: AIPO #474, April, 1951; #399, June, 1947; #596, March, 1958.

extremes = 22.4 per cent, older group = 26.4 per cent), a χ^2 test between the two groups was significant at beyond the .01 level.

A second group of questions offered additional support. For these questions only two alternative answers were offered, and in each case it was felt that one of the alternatives represented a greater consideration of the future than the other. The first, which appeared on a survey during the Korean War, asked whether the respondent advocated the United Nations carrying the war into Communist China. As this would ultimately mean a total annihilation of the source of the Korean conflict, it was felt that this was a short-range solution. As can be seen in Table 2, again it is found that the aged preferred the short-range solution to a greater extent. Additional support for the present interpretations was found by subdividing each age group into those who felt that provoking Red China would bring all-out war versus those who did not feel so. When responses to the question of whether the United Nations forces should attack Communist China or not are considered as a result of age *and* predictions of an all-out war, it is found that the result shown in Table 2 is accounted for almost entirely by those in each age group who felt that there *would* be a resultant world war. In other words, when no world war was expected there was virtually no difference among the age groups in advocating the bombing of Red China. When world war was anticipated as a result of this bombing, the aged preferred the bombing to a significantly greater extent than the younger group.

Two additional questions dealt with foreign aid. Foreign aid in any form was felt to be an example of a long-range method for insuring the spread of democracy around the world and the ultimate defeat of communism. Short-range alternatives to such a problem would include a direct assault on Russia (annihilation) or the adoption of a complete isolationist position (denial). As can be seen in Table 2, for both questions regarding foreign aid the results were as anticipated: the elderly were more opposed to foreign aid than the younger groups.

Attitudes Toward National and Local Problems

As mentioned above, a second aim of this paper was to explore the continuity of preferences for short-range solutions among the aged from problems of international scope to those of national as well as local importance. In the first of the relevant surveys, the following problem was raised:

> During the next 13 years some 41,000 miles of new highways will be built by the U. S. Government. Do you think that the Government should or should not do something about the billboards, advertising signs, and the like along these new highways?

The short-range solution to the problem of billboards, of course, would be to have the government step in and *do* something. As Table 3 indicates, this was indeed the choice of the elderly population to a greater extent than the younger. It was further asked *what* the government should do: forbid, regulate, or do nothing. Looking at only those who on the first question advocated the government's stepping in, the percentage of persons feeling that the government should "forbid all advertising" versus "regulate" was analyzed. It was felt that the former alternative to a greater extent than the latter would represent a way of handling the entire problem on an immediate basis. Here too the aged advocated "forbidding" to a greater extent than the younger groups. A problem which was somewhat similar in nature dealt with professional boxing. When this was raised, we again find that the elderly preferred to handle the problem by banning boxing altogether.

The Roper survey, in which only the two age groups participated, again included a question which offered alternatives that seemed to fit the triadic pattern discussed above. The issue concerned whether the present system of private ownership of business should remain, change gradually so that the government takes over basic industries, or shift completely to governmental control. Whereas the first alternative seemed to represent a denial of the fact that there is a problem, and the third an annihilation of the problem, the second alternative seemed to represent a more long-range approach. For this problem the elderly group preferred both the first and third alternatives to a greater extent than the younger group did. Again the total differences were not large (younger group preference for extremes = 83.2 per cent, older group = 88.3 per cent); but this difference also proved to be statistically reliable ($\chi^2 = 18.91$; $p < .001$).

A second group of questions dealt with attitudes toward various aspects of child rearing and training. In bearing the responsibility for a child's adjustment to society, at least one dimension along which parental tactics may vary is that of discipline. Extreme punishment or coercion would be one way of achieving at least the overt behavior desired from a child on an *immediate* basis (though future repercussions are almost sure to result). On the other hand, denial of the problem would be represented by simply turning one's back on the child's behavior. Some intermediate level of discipline, it would seem, would treat the future of the child with more reasonableness. Although there was no evidence concerning denial, three questions did offer punitive alternatives which were rather extreme versus rather moderate. As can be seen in Table 3, for each of these questions preferences for alternatives of greater reliance on punishment increased with age. The elderly preferred to a greater extent to publish the names of teen-age first offenders and advocated stricter discipline in both the home and school.

Table 3. Aging and Preferences for Short-Range Solutions to National and Local Problems (in percentages).

	Under 40	40–59	60 and over
1. Advocate doing something about billboards	62.6 (546)	78.5 (530)	81.0 (226)
2. Advocate "forbidding" rather than regulating billboards	15.8 (467)	28.5 (474)	27.7 (188)
3. Adovcate banning of boxing	40.9 (562)	50.0 (416)	53.1 (236)
4. Advocate publishing names of teen-agers in trouble for first time	29.5 (525)	33.0 (522)	41.0 (307)
5. Believe discipline in homes not strict enough	70.4 (115)	75.0 (204)	77.7 (166)
6. Believe discipline in schools not strict enough	85.2 (122)	89.1 (211)	92.8 (167)

Source: AIPO #580, March, 1957 (1,2); #549, June, 1955 (3); #588, August, 1957 (4); #538, October, 1954 (5,6).

Aging and the Perception of Causality

These latter findings, indicating that the aged tend to prefer stricter measures in dealing with the young, appear to have additional implications. These findings would also seem to indicate that the aged person may be much less concerned with the notion that the environmental influences to which a person is subjected may influence him profoundly in later years. In a sense, this means that individuals are treated as if their personalities are constant. From this point of view, environmental influences may control behavior in a situation, but basic personality does not change. If behavior of an opponent depends mainly on unchanging personality, it is reasonable to come quickly to a settlement, either giving in or seeking quick victory. If environmental conditions are thought to be paramount, a slower procedure for changing these conditions is indicated.

Phrasing this argument in a slightly different way, it would seem that the elderly person may tend to restrict the scope of causal sequence. Rather than perceiving a person's behavior as the result of his history or other factors impinging on him, his behavior may be viewed more as resulting from the internal characteristics of the person alone. In Fritz Heider's[6] terms, the locus of causality for behavioral events may be viewed as more intrinsic than extrinsic to the person. Such a view of causality would also seem to follow directly from the consideration of the aged person's orientation in the world. If his orientation in time and space indeed is more restricted—as earlier evidence has indicated—such a restriction should directly affect his perception of causality. In other words, the concept of extrinsic causation is based almost entirely on a consideration of the temporal and spatial context in which an event occurs. For example, it is often too easy to judge a person's behavior negatively when we are not aware of the early events which might have affected him. Similarly, governmental actions, especially the actions of foreign governments, may be judged harshly when one is not aware of all the factors in the environment which influenced these actions. If temporal and spatial orientations are not extended, the view of the causal locus of a person's actions will seem to reside

6. "Social Perception and Phenomenal Causality," *Psychological Review*, **51** (1944), 358-374.

more in the person than in the environment in which he has lived or is living.

Some additional support for this view was found in a Roper survey on mental health taken in Louisville, Kentucky, in 1950. In this survey a number of hypothetical case histories were presented, and the respondent was asked what he would do about the person involved. These questions were of the open-ended variety, and responses were naturally quite varied. However, for three of these case histories several of the response categories cohered and it was possible to delineate two types of preferences: *punitive* (incarceration, direct punishment, social isolation, etc.) and *environmental change* (changing the living or working environment, increasing understanding of others, psychiatry, etc.). The following items were responded to with either one or both of these types of responses:

1. Now I'd like to ask you a question about a fifteen-year-old boy who has been in trouble repeatedly for staying away from school and has recently stolen an automobile.
2. Now here's a woman who became suspicious of her neighbors and falsely accused them of saying things about her.
3. Here's a middle-aged man who lost interest in his work, worried about everything and thought life was not worth living.

If the above speculations are correct, it might be expected that the aged person, because of his restricted view of time and thus of causality, would tend to recommend that punitive measures be

Table 4. Aging and Preferences for Punitivity vs. Environmental Change (in percentages).

		Age		
		Under 40	40–59	60 and over
1. Juvenile delinquent	Punish	34.0%	39.4%	47.4%
	Change environment	18.5	12.5	11.3
	(N)	(1256)	(829)	(310)
2. Suspicious woman	Punish	36.8	43.3	43.0
	Change environment	32.6	26.8	22.3
	(N)	(842)	(522)	(184)
3. Worried man	(No punish alternative)			
	Change environment	31.2	21.5	16.0
	(N)	(1269)	(781)	(257)

Source: Roper Poll, Com. 43.

taken. On the other hand, the aged person should be less inclined to choose the type of alternative which would view the person's personality as the result of extrinsic determining factors, i.e., the environmental change alternative. As can be seen in Table 4, the expectations are fully supported. In each case, indorsement of the punitive alternatives increases with age, and indorsement of the environmental change alternative decreases. Although these results are at least suggestive, it goes without saying that the possibility of modifications in the perception of causality as a result of aging needs much more direct empirical verification.

DISCUSSION

Personality of the Aging

The above findings would seem to indicate that, in regard to a wide variety of problems, the aged population in the United States tends to prefer more short-range or extreme solutions. This appears to be the case, not only with problems of international scope, but also with national as well as interpersonal problems. It has also been reasoned that such preferences are the result of a limited time perspective, and that the constriction of time perspective is a normal result of the aging process. It was further suggested that one result of a constriction in temporal orientation was a modified perception of causality. For the aged individual, a person's actions may be viewed as resulting more likely from internal or intrinsic factors rather than as having been environmentally produced.

Although the present results were generally consistent with the time perspective rationale, there are several additional considerations. Although earlier work indicated that the aged person has a more restricted time perspective, this is certainly not the only characteristic of the personality make-up of the aged person. There is some evidence that he may also be limited in space perspective. Rather than taking into account aspects of the world at large when dealing with pressing problems, the aged person may tend to consider only those factors which are in close proximity to him. It has also been argued that when only a few factors are considered relevant to the solving of a problem, the resolution of such a problem will tend to be extreme. When many factors are considered, resolutions will ordinarily represent some *compromise* among the various factors. Thus, in many of the instances cited above, a prediction on the basis of delimited space perspective would have been quite relevant.

There is also abundant evidence that age tends to be related to education; more elderly citizens are generally less well educated than younger adults. Earlier research[7] has also shown that those with little education tend to have a more constricted time perspective. The question arises as to whether education could account for the above results. To check on this possibility, a random selection of the items used above were analyzed, using both age and education as predicting variables. The results of these analyses indicated that age, independent of educational level, was generally related to preferences for short-term solutions. However, it should be noted that although respondents with either a grammar or high school education (grades zero through eight, or nine through twelve) confirmed the hypothesis, for college-educated respondents (above the twelfth grade) the relationship was much less marked and in some cases absent.

Additional factors may also enter the picture. It has been noted that the aged respondent reacts differently in the interviewing situation.[8] For example, it may be that the elderly person in the interviewing situation may attempt to avoid role expectations; he may attempt to shock a young interviewer by responding in a very extreme fashion. Such an interpretation could also account for some of the present findings. Elaine Cumming and William E. Henry[9] have also theorized that the process of aging is one of progressive social disengagement, which may manifest itself and lead to the expression of more idiosyncratic or extremist views (defined as deviations from the norms) in the interviewing situation.

Thus, although the present results are certainly consistent with the time perspective rationale, they are not necessarily inexplicable from other points of view. Although such is the case in almost all studies which use age as an independent variable, there is an important point to be made here. Freud often pointed out that be-

7. Kurt W. Back and Kenneth J. Gergen, "Apocalyptic and Serial Time Orientations and the structure of Public Opinion," *Public Opinion Quarterly,* **27** (1963), 427-442.
8. Kenneth J. Gergen and Kurt W. Back, "The Disengaged Respondent," *Public Opinion Quarterly* (in preparation).
9. *Growing Old* (New York: Basic Books, 1961).

havior is not simply determined; it is "over-determined." By this he meant that any behavior is the final common path for a multitude of processes. To explain any behavioral event in only one way did not exhaust the meaning of the behavior; rather, each explanation only dealt with a different aspect of the same behavior. In essence, this is the problem faced by any researcher in dealing with the behavior of the aged individual. Any behavior of the aged person is the final common path of many different processes—processes which have been modified to some extent by the fact of his growing old.

SUMMARY

The present study seems to suggest very strongly that a person's preferences for solutions to problems of international, national, and local import are related to his age. More specifically, the aged person tends to prefer those solutions which would terminate such problems as rapidly as possible. Evidence was presented indicating that such preferences were a function of the aged person's restricted time perspective and his tendency to attribute causality to the act or to a situation rather than to environmental circumstances.

INDEX

INDEX

Achievement, 82-83, 88-89; and job deprivation, 87; and retirement orientation, 75-77, 81
Activities, *see* Retirement activities
Activity rates, *see* Labor force participation rates
Activity styles: and aged, 302; and self-evaluation, 115-118
Adjustive aging, 291, 298
Age structure: and fertility rate, 6-9; and mortality rate, 6-8; and older worker, 8-10
Aged: attitudes toward, 221-224; capacities, 235-236; and church attendance, 233; and community integration, 195-209, 243-253; and consumer facilities, 230-231; and consumption patterns, 229-230; defined, 219-220, 222; and education, 333; as emergent group, 215-217; and family organization, 197; formal organization of, 213; and group norms, 285; group status of, 210-225; health of, 232-233, 235-236; informal associations of, 213-214; institutionalized, 200; and leisure, 238-239; and mobility, 200; and morale, 296-305; norms for, 289-290; personal orientation and morale, 296-305; personality of, 332-334; and political behavior (local), 254-276; political characteristics of, 260-261, 267; and power, 214-215; proportion of population, 217; and public events, 300-301; sample studies of, 199, 205-208, 226-227; and self-concepts, 239-240; and self-ratings, 232; social world of, 226-242; special needs, 195-196, 198; and voluntary associations, 227, 231-232; and voting model, 260-261; and voting rates, 263, 266; and work, 228-229
Aging: cognitive and motivational factors in, 289-295; emotional and intellectual decline in, 293-294; and morale, 305; and perception of causality, 330-332; and personal orientation, 290; physical, 306; and somatic concern, 306-321; types of, *see* Autonomous aging; Conformist aging; Anomic aging
American Bar Association, 50, 136
American Medical Association, 50, 136
Analytic groups and aged, 210-225 *passim*
Anomic aging, 291, 298

Anomie, 240-241, 261, 265-266, 267, 270
Appearance, 312-317
Association, voluntary, *see* Voluntary association
Autonomous aging, 291, 298-299
Autonomy, 123-129
Autonomy measure, 122

Back, Kurt, 53
Birren, James C., 294
Blau, Zena Smith, 60, 91
Blue-collar worker, 14, 25, 49; and morale, 186-190; and social involvement, 62; and unemployment, 22; work week hours, 28; *see also* Semi-skilled worker
Bodily concern: desire for somatic change, 317-318; external care, 312-317; internal care, 309-312; *see also* Appearance; Clothing; Diet; Medical concern; Somatic concern
Bott, Elizabeth, 141
Bureau of Labor Statistics, 309-312, 315
Burgess, Ernest W., 76, 258

Cabot, Natalie H., 299
Capacities of aged, 235-236
Caplow, Theodore, 124
Causality, perception of, 330-332, 334
Change, acceptance of, 142, 144-145, 147, 149, 151, 153
Chicago *Sun-Times*, 309, 317
Child-rearing, attitude of aged toward, 329-332
Children, *see* Intergenerational relationships
Church attendance, 233
Civic responsibility model, *see* Political process
Clothing, 312-317, 319, 320
Cognitive constriction, and attitude toward international issues, 322-334
Collective conscience, 258
Community, views of, 257-259
Community implication, 276; and commitment, 268; commitment score, 268-270, 284; and community orientation score, 269-270, 284; and education, 282-284; and group norms, 278, 279-285 *passim*; and political participation, 268-275; and social anchorage score, 269-

270, 284; and voting rates, 271; *see also* Community integration
Community integration: and aged, 195-209, 243-253; defined, 201-202; measuring, 243-253
Community pride, 274-275
Comte, Auguste, 258
Conflict, perceived, 142, 144, 147, 149, 151, 153
Conformist aging, 291, 298
Conjugal dyad: consistency within, 147-152; reaction to retirement, 160-172
Conjugal relationship, 176-180
Conjugal role, 134, 136, 139, 141, 156, 159; joint, 140, 141-144, 157-158; segregated, 140, 141-144
Conjugal role tension, 169, 176-179, 186, 188-189
Conjugal value consensus, 176-177, 179, 186-187
Consumer facilities, and aged, 230-231
Consumption patterns of aged, 229-230
Cooley, Charles H., 258
Cumming, Elaine, 290, 297, 333

Demand and employment, 21-25
Demographic trends, 5-10
Dictionary of Occupational Titles, 109
Diet, 309-311, 319, 320
Disengagement, 174, 192, 290, 297-298, 333; cognitive and motivational factors in, 289-295; and voting models, 261
Dissaving, *see* Savings
Dunholme, 203-285 *passim*; described, 203-205
Durkheim, Emile, 258

Eckaus, R. S., 15
Education: and aged, 333; and community implication, 282-284; and employment, 11; and obsolescence, 13; and older worker, 16, 40; requirements, 14-15; and time perspective, 333; and worker levels, 15
Effective life space, 292-295, 301, 303-304, 307, 313; and energy level, 297-299; and international issues, 323; and relearning, 321
Elections, 259-260
Emergent groups and aged, 215-225 *passim*
Emotional decline, 293-294
Employment, 40; and demand, 9; demand for, 41; and education, 11; and equity, 34-39; and income, 39; and industrialization, 10-13; and supply and demand, 21-25
Energy level, 304; and effective life space, 297-299
Environmental change, preference for, 331-332
Environmental contacts of aged, 236-239; *see also* Social involvement
Equity and employment, 34-39

Erickson, E. H., 293, 299
Europe: output per capita, 26; work hours per week, 27
Extended family type, 141-143, 145, 153-159, 181-183, 192

Familial involvement, 173-175; and socioeconomic level, 174-175
Family patterns: and retirement, 135-136; and retirement morale, 173-192; and socioeconomic level, 185-191; *see also* Extended family type; Individuated family type; Modified extended family type; Nucleated family type
Farber, Bernard, 176-177
Female worker, 7-9 *passim*; and industrialization, 12; labor force participation rate, 25
Fertility rate, 40; and age structure, 6-9
Foreign aid, attitude of aged toward, 327-328
Freud, Sigmund, 258, 333
Fried, Edrita G., 76
Friedman, Milton, 34
Friedmann, Eugene A., 75, 76, 77, 81
Friendships of aged, 232
"Fruits of technical progress," distribution of, 36-39

George, Henry, 37
General sample, defined, 205
Gergen, Kenneth, 53
Gerontocracy, 197
Gross national product, 16
GRR, *see* Reproduction rate, gross
Group norms, 277-285; and aged, 285; and community implication, 278, 279-285 *passim; see also* Normative behavior
Group status, of aged, 210-225; *see also* Analytic groups; Emergent groups; Real groups
Growing Old, 297

Havighurst, Robert J., 75, 76, 77, 81
Health: and aged, 232-233, 235-236; and autonomy, 126-127; and involvement, 125-127; and optimism, 126-127
Heider, Fritz, 330
Henry, William E., 290, 297, 333
Hill, Reuben, 134, 324
Hobbes, Thomas, 258
Husband-wife relationship, *see* Conjugal role
Husband's participation, 176-179, 184-187, 191

Income: and consumption levels, 38-39; and demand for leisure, 29-34 *passim*; and leisure, 40-41; median, 32; per capita, 26-27; and retirement, 32-33, 38; and retirement orientation, 81
Income deprivation, 83; defined, 70; and

job deprivation, 87-88; and middle-status worker, 89
Individual, views of, 257-259
Individuated family type, 181-183
Industrialization, 4; and employment rates, 10-13; and older worker, 39-40; and work life, 27
Inflation, 35-37, 41
Inkeles, Alex, 29
Integrative attributes, 244-253 passim
Integration, community, see Community integration
Integration mechanisms, 243-253 passim, 258, 259
Intellectual decline, 293-294
Interest and involvement, 127-129
Intergenerational relationships, 134, 137, 139, 141, 152-153, 156-159, 174, 187, 191-192; and morale, 180-183
International issues: annihilation, 325, 328; attitude of aged toward, 322-334; compromise, 325; denial of, 325, 328; and effective life space, 323; short-range solutions, 325-328
Involvement, 123-129; and aging, 125; and health, 125-127; and interests, 127-129; and work role, 127; see also Social involvement
Involvement measure, 121

Job deprivation, 53, 73, 86-87, 89, 116-117, 123; and occupational status, 68-74; scale of, 52-54, 122; and self-evaluation, 85; and social involvement, 68-74
Job orderliness, 56-57, 59, 61-62, 74; and self-evaluation, 60, 67, 68-72; and social involvement, 61, 63-67, 73-74
Job satisfaction, 79, 80, 83, 86-87, 88, 89

Kutner, Bernard, 52, 175

Labor and recruitment, 10
Labor demand, 40; and older worker, 17; in post-war Soviet Union, 9; wartime, 9
Labor force: female in, 7-9 passim; and leisure, 28-29
Labor force participation rates, 5, 11; and females, 5, 8-9, 25; and males, 5; and older worker, 15, 16, 25
Labor mobility: curbs on, 17-21; and older worker, 4
Labor supply and demand, 4
Lang, Al, 202
Larson, Olaf F., 58, 65
Leisure, 25-34; and aged, 238-239; defined, 29; demand for, 29-30; and income, 27, 40-41; relation to work, 29-34
Lewin, Kurt, 322
Life, 309, 315
Life expectancy, 27, 28; and industrialization, 6; and older worker, 5-8
Life space, see Effective life space
Lindsey, F. D., 308

Lipman, Aaron, 135
Litwak, Eugene, 142, 146
Local election studies, 259-260
Local problems, see National and local problems
Long, C. D., 15
Lorge, Irving, 77
Lower occupations and retirement, 167-169; see also Semi-skilled worker
Lower-white-collar worker, 46

McGee, Reece J., 124
Mass media, 236-237; and voting rates, 265-266
Mead, George H., 258
Medical concern, 311-312, 319, 320
Middle occupations and retirement, 167-168; see also Middle-status worker
Middle-status worker, 47, 51, 52-53; and job satisfaction, 79; and object manipulation, 109-114; and retirement counseling, 91-92; and retirement orientation, 78-89; and self-evaluation, 67, 68-74; and self-ratings, 122-129; and social involvement, 55-74, 93; see also Middle occupations
Mobility and aged, 200
Modified extended family type, 142-143, 145, 153-157, 181-183
Morale, 71-72, 73, 116, 123; and aging, 305; and intergenerational relationships, 180-183; measures of, 175-176; in retirement, 173-192; scale of, 52-54, 122; and self-ratings, 304; and socioeconomic level, 185-191
Mortality rate, 10; and age structure, 6-8
Mutual support norms, 180-181, 183-187, 189-191

National and local problems, short-range solutions of, 328-329
Nation's Business, 308
New England Aging Center, 299
Norm orientation, see Norm-value clusters
Norm-value clusters, 138-159; distribution of, 152-156; findings, 145-147; and industrialization, 157; measures, 142-145; and socioeconomic status, 152-157
Normative behavior, 284; and knowledge of public events, 279-284
Normative family type, 142-143, 145, 147-153
Nucleated family type, 133-134, 135, 140-143, 145, 153-159, 181-183, 187, 192; and industrialization, 140, 142; and morale, 182-183

Object manipulation, 107-108
Obsolescence: and older worker, 4; and re-education, 13
Occupational status, 46, 50-56, 74; and achievement, 82, 87; and activity style, 117; and exposure to information, 99-

102; and income deprivation, 88; and job satisfaction, 80, 86; and object manipulation, 109-114; and reactions to retirement, 165-166; and retirement income, 171; and retirement orientation, 76, 77, 85, 94-98; and self-evaluation, 59, 67, 68-72; and social involvement, 55-74; and work commitment, 86; see also Blue-collar worker; Lower occupations; Middle-status worker; Semi-skilled worker; Upper occupations; White-collar worker

Old sample, defined, 205

Older worker: and accelerated obsolescence, 4; and age structure, 8-10; and automation, 21; and demographic trends, 4-10; and employment costs, 19-20; and industrialization, 4-5, 10-13; and labor mobility and pricing, 4; and life expectancy, 5-8; and obsolescence, 13-16; and supply and demand, 4

Optimism, 123-129

Optimism measure, 122

Osgood, Charles E., 121, 122

Output, see Productivity

Parent-child relationship, see Intergenerational relationships

Parents, see Intergenerational relationships

Park, R. E., 258

Parsons, Talcott, 133, 140, 141, 146, 157, 276

Pavlov, 258

Personal orientation, of aged, 290, 296-305; see also Self-concepts

Personality, 332-334

Pessimism, 300-301

Phillips, Bernard S., 134

Pickens, Champ, 202

Political behavior, local: of aged, 254-276; characteristics of, 255-256; community and sample, 262-263; defined, 254-255

Political participation: by age, 266-268; and community implication, 268-275, 278; and progressivism, 278; see also Political behavior, local

Political process: civic responsibility model, 257, 260-262, 266-267, 272, 274-275; self-interest model, 257, 260

Populations, age structure of, 6-10

Pre-retirement, see Retirement orientation

Pricing: curbs on, 17-21; and money value, 35; and older worker, 4; and unemployment rate, 23

Private ownership, attitude of aged toward, 328-329

Productivity: age-specific, 17-18; and health, 8; and older worker, 17-18; per capita, 28; and retirement, 18-20; as value, 290

Progressivism, 278; by age, 274

Propinquity norms, 143, 180-183, 186-188, 190-191

Public events: and aged, 300-301; awareness of, 279-284

Public Health Service, 309, 311-312

Punitivity, preferences for, 331-332

Quasi-economic model, 258

Real groups: and aged, 210-225 passim; defined, 210-211

Recession, 294

Re-education, see Education

Regression, 294

Reproduction rate: and age structure, 7; gross, 6-7, 10

Retirement: compulsory, 32; as constraint, 228; early, 23; and family patterns, 135-136; and income, 32-33, 38; information on, 90-105; length of, 27; morale in, 173-192; orientation toward, 75-89; preparation for, 90-105, 169; and productivity, 18-20; reactions to, 160-172; roles, 90; and self-evaluation, 67, 75-89, 90-105; self-ratings, 120-129; significance of, 120-121; and social involvement, 63-67; and status, 106-107; study of, 50-56; and work role, 46-54

Retirement activities: and object manipulation, 109-114; and work commitment, 113-115; and work continuity, 106-119; see also Activity styles

Retirement counseling, 91-93; see also Retirement, information on

Retirement orientation, 84-89; and achievement, 81; and income, 81; information on, 91, 94-98

Retirement planning and information, 98-102

Riesman, David, 53, 291, 298

Rossi, Peter H., 29

Rousseau, 258

St. Louis voting patterns, 260, 263

Savings, 34-35, 38, 41

Segmental model, 257

Self-concepts, of aged, 239-240; see also Self-evaluation

Self-evaluation, 67, 68-74, 75-89, 90-105; and activity styles, 115-118; and exposure to information, 102-105; and job orderliness, 60; in retirement, 52-54, 59-74 passim; and social involvement, 60, 61; and work continuity, 108-109; see also Self-ratings

Self-interest, 277-285

Self-interest model, see Political process

Self-ratings: method, 121-122; results, 122-129; and retirement, 120-129

Semi-skilled worker, 14, 46, 48-54; and income deprivation, 89; and job satisfaction, 79; and object manipulation, 109-

114; and retirement counseling, 91-92; and retirement orientation, 78-89; and self-evaluation, 67, 68-74; and self-ratings, 122-129; and social involvement, 55-74, 92-93; *see also* Lower occupations
Service workers, 14
Shanas, Ethel, 121
Shaw, George Bernard, 324
Simpson, Ida Harper, 91
Simpson, Richard L., 90, 91
Skills, types of, 107
Social credit for aged, 37, 41
Social involvement, 173; and age groups, 58; changes in, 68-74; index of, 62-63; and job orderliness, 63-67; and occupational status, 63-67; and pre-retirement, 55, 64-65; in retirement, 55-74; and self-evaluation, 60, 61; *see also* Community integration
Society, views of, 257-259
Socioeconomic levels, 185-191
Socioeconomic status: and norm-value clusters, 152-156; and voting rates, 264-266
Somatic concern, 306-321
Soviet Union, postwar labor demand in, 9
Space perspective, 332-333
Status, occupational, *see* Occupational status
"Strain toward consistency," 138-159 *passim*
Streib, Gordon F., 45, 70, 73, 76, 82, 135
Suci, G. J., 121
Supply and employment, 21-25

Taietz, Philip, 58, 65
Tannenbaum, P. H., 121
Task sharing, 142, 143, 147-149, 151, 153, 170; *see also* Husband's participation
Technology, *see* Industrialization
Temporal orientation, *see* Time perspective
Thompson, Wayne E., 52, 70, 73, 75, 76, 85, 89, 93, 101
Time perspective, 323-324; and aging, 324-325; and education, 333; *see also* Cognitive constriction
Tuckman, Jacob, 77

Unemployment: causes of, 20-23; and government, 20-21; kinds of, 21-22; rate of, 23-25; remedies for, 24
Universal consensus, 258
Upper occupations, and retirement, 167-168; *see also* White-collar worker

Urban behavior patterns: and group norms, 277-285 *passim*; and self-interest, 277-285 *passim*

Utilitarian model, 259-260
Value orientation, *see* Norm-value clusters
Voluntary associations, aged in, 227, 231-232
Voting models: and aged, 260-261; and disengagement, 261
Voting patterns, 260
Voting rates: and age, 263, 266, 273; and anomie, 265-266; and community implication, 271; determination of, 263; and mass media, 265-266; and socioeconomic status, 264-266

War, attitude of aged toward, 325-327
Watson, John B., 258
White-collar worker, 14, 25, 49, 51, 52-53, 73-74; and job satisfaction, 79; and morale, 186-190; and object manipulation, 109-114; and retirement counseling, 91-92; and retirement orientation, 78-89; and self-evaluation, 67, 68-74; and self-ratings, 122-129; and social involvement, 55-74, 93; and work week, 28; *see also* Upper occupations
Wilensky, H. L., 28, 56, 57, 58, 60, 61, 62
Williams, Robin M., Jr., 139-140, 147
Withdrawal, *see* Disengagement
Work: and adaptation to retirement, 31; and aged, 228-229; orientation toward, 75-89; relation to leisure, 29-34; and retirement, 45-54; social value of, 45; *see also* Job satisfaction
Work commitment, 80, 83, 86, 87, 88, 89, 116-117; scale of, 78
Work continuity: and retirement activities, 106-119; and self-evaluation, 108-109; and work commitment, 113-115
Work hours, 27
Work-life expectancy, 27
Work orientation, 84-89
Work role, 90, 106-107, 120; and retirement, 46-54
Work time, distribution of, 33-34
Worker, *see* Blue-collar worker; Female worker; Older worker; Semi-skilled worker; Service worker; White-collar worker
Worry, 302-303

Young Men's Christian Association, 50, 136